BAHAMA ISLANDS
A Boatman's Guide to the Land and the Water

FOURTH EDITION

BAHAMA ISLANDS

◆◇◆◇◆◇◆◇◆◇◆◇◆◇◆◇◆◇◆◇◆◇◆◇◆◇◆◇

A Boatman's Guide to the Land and the Water

By J. Linton Rigg

REVISED BY HARRY KLINE

CHARLES SCRIBNER'S SONS   New York

To Nancy Ann

Contents

Nassau, New Providence, and Adjacent Cays / 97 C H A P T E R 7

Eleuthera / 117 C H A P T E R 8

CHAPTER 9   Andros / 135

CHAPTER 10   The Exuma Cays: The Pièce de Résistance
of West Indies Cruising / 151

The Pilot's Pleasures / 286   CHAPTER 15

Illustrations

Charts

Preface to the Fourth Edition

In the thirteen years since J. Linton Rigg updated this twenty-two-year-old volume for its third edition, almost everything in the Bahamas has changed, including some of the geography. The country's government, which was then very "quaintly British," has reflected the world's nationalistic surge resulting in a predominantly black government which has moved to complete independence from the United Kingdom. Technical advancements in the boating and private aircraft industries and their subsequent "booms" have shortened the course lines to the islands and made the Bahamas a foreign/nearby, year 'round playground for the moderately affluent yachtsman-pilot with a "time-table" yen for adventure.

While Nassau itself has become a bustling center of tourist activity, banking aggregates and foreign business headquarters, the Out Islands have, for the cruising visitor, remained for the most part unspoiled and unchanged. Their clear waters, fresh salt air, and attractive climate can only be enhanced by the introduction of modern facilities. It is in an effort to record these changes that this fourth edition is written.

All sketch charts in this volume were prepared by the author, as were some of the photographs. The remainder of the photographs were furnished through the courtesy of the Bahamas Tourist News Bureau.

H.K.

Preface

It must be understood that this book is in no way an official document; it is the sum of the writer's knowledge collected over the years. While all information in the text and on the charts is reliable as of the time we obtained it, the Bahamas are noted for being "subject to change." Hurricanes, storms, and developers are no respecters of soundings or charted shore lines. Thus it is recommended that for up-to-date cruising directions, the *Yachtsman's Guide to the Bahamas* be used in conjunction with this volume.

The publishers have requested that in making this book available to the public, it be understood that neither they nor the author be held responsible for any inaccuracies.

From Blunt's *The American Coast Pilot*, edition of 1812, the following note is quoted:

Navigators should be cautious, while crossing the Bahamas Bank, never to follow vessels, if they alter course often, as the New Providence Wreckers have frequently decoyed them for the purpose of plunder; a crime which the most barbarous nation would punish with the greatest severity. This is not published to give offense to anyone, but it applies to some of the Providence Navigators, and it is our duty to point out danger to Mariners, from which the Editor will never deviate, or hide from investigation.

This is the spirit in which this book is written. We are happy to say that the present day Providence Navigators are most reliable and we count several of them amongst our closest friends.

H.K.

Introduction

From the Coast of California to the South Sea Islands of the Pacific is a matter of about 4,000 sea miles. From the Coast of Florida to the South Sea Islands of the Atlantic is a mere forty-five miles, a matter of four and one-half hours in a ten-knot boat.

Were it not for the merciful intervention of the Gulf Stream these South Sea Islands, better known as the Bahamas, would be as crowded as Florida. However, and very fortunately, the Gulf Stream has a fearful reputation which serves the very good purpose of separating the sheep from the goats, the former staying on the mainland, while the hardy and independent old goats push on to new pastures. It is not to be presumed from this that the Bahamas are full of goats (quite the contrary). But at least they are not full of sheep and there is plenty of room to breathe.

This fantastic archipelago, stretching from off the Coast of Florida almost to Haiti, contains 690 islands and 2,387 rocky cays. It stretches approximately 700 miles from east to west, and has an aggregate land surface of 5,468 square miles.

The inhabitants of these islands are a proud, simple, and God-loving people. They are friendly and, with the exception of a few opportunists, they are honest. Until recently, when the islands gained their independence, they were British subjects and inordinately proud of it. Now however, with the much discussed Nationalization movement of its government, the quaint Colonial charm of the near past is fast disappearing. The soft accent of the Colonial British has remained, however, and is pleasantly unmistakable.

As a year 'round cruising ground for yachtsmen we would be hard put to find the equal of the Bahamas Island waters anywhere else in the world. Good cruising grounds should be easily accessible if they are to be enjoyed by others, except the fortunate few to whom time means nothing. Nassau, the capital of the Bahama Islands, and the logical center for all cruising operations, is only 160 miles from Miami, Florida, or an easy one or two days' run in any kind of decent weather. Andros, the Exuma Cays, or Eleuthera are only a short day's run from Nassau. If a man cannot spare that much time he can fly over from Miami to Cat Cay in 20 minutes, from Miami to Nassau in 35 minutes and from Nassau to Harbour Island in 25 minutes.

Having gotten across the Gulf Stream, the yachtsman will find a cruising paradise of unbelievable charm and beauty; crystal-clear water tinted by coral-pink sands; peaceful harbours abounding in maritime life; good sailing breezes at all times, and probably the most perfect climate in the world. Here it is never very hot, nor very cold. Even during the summer months there is usually a fresh breeze and the humidity never soars, which cannot always be said of south Florida. Here the temperature ranges in the seventies and eighties year 'round. Almost everything is different in the Islands, the food, the manners and customs, and of course, the English language as it is spoken here. So you see, even with recent developments, both political and material, you can still get away from it all in the Bahamas—and what more could anyone ask for a holiday?

Cruising to the Islands involves a certain amount of offshore work. Therefore the success of such a cruise depends rather more than ordinarily on the type of boat, the fitting out and the handling of her. It is possible to go from Florida over to the Bahamas in almost any kind of boat. It is also possible to go over Niagara Falls in a barrel. However, if you intend to enjoy yourself rather than make yourself and your friends miserable, it might be just as well to consider what is the most desirable type of boat for your purpose and get her if you can.

BAHAMA ISLANDS
A Boatman's Guide to
the Land and the Water

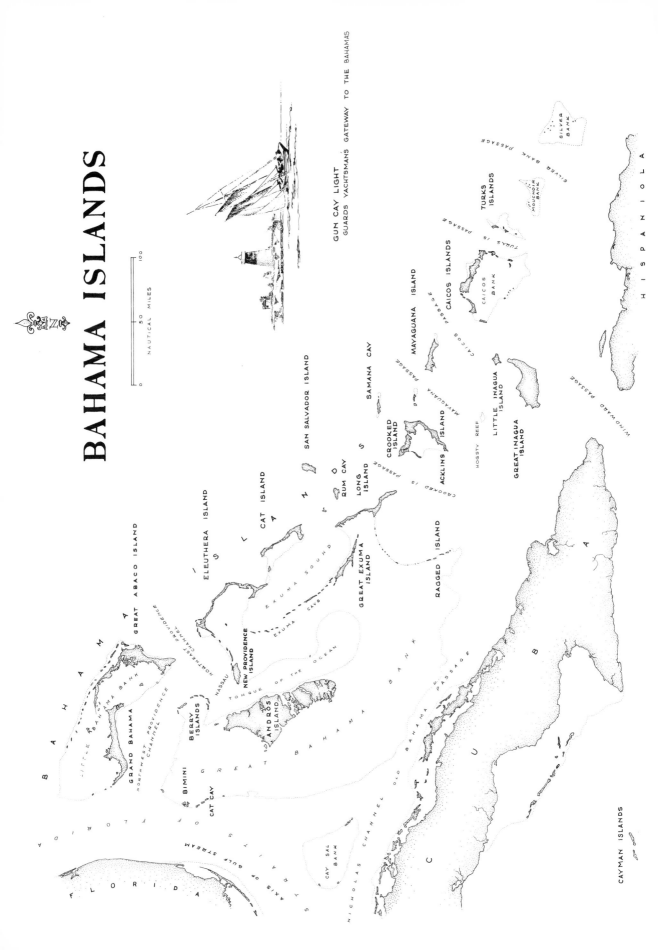

BAHAMA ISLANDS

NAUTICAL MILES
0   50   100

GUN CAY LIGHT
GUARDS YACHTSMANS GATEWAY TO THE BAHAMAS

FLORIDA

STRAITS OF FLORIDA

AXIS OF GULF STREAM

B A H A M A

GRAND BAHAMA

LITTLE BAHAMA BANK

GREAT ABACO ISLAND

NORTHWEST PROVIDENCE CHANNEL

PROVIDENCE CHANNEL

BIMINI

CAT CAY

BERRY ISLANDS

NASSAU

NEW PROVIDENCE ISLAND

ELEUTHERA ISLAND

ANDROS ISLAND

TONGUE OF THE OCEAN

G R E A T   B A H A M A   B A N K

CAT ISLAND

SAN SALVADOR ISLAND

RUM CAY

SAMANA CAY

EXUMA SOUND

EXUMA CAYS

GREAT EXUMA ISLAND

LONG ISLAND

MAYAGUANA ISLAND

CROOKED ISLAND

ACKLINS ISLAND

CROOKED IS PASSAGE

MAYAGUANA PASSAGE

CAICOS PASSAGE

CAICOS ISLANDS

CAICOS BANK

TURKS IS PASSAGE

TURKS ISLANDS

MOUCHOIR BANK

SILVER BANK PASSAGE

SILVER BANK

HOGSTY REEF

LITTLE INAGUA ISLAND

GREAT INAGUA ISLAND

WINDWARD PASSAGE

H I S P A N I O L A

RAGGED ISLAND

OLD BAHAMA PASSAGE

CAY SAL BANK

NICHOLAS CHANNEL

C U B A

CAYMAN ISLANDS

Bahamas History: A Sea Story

As certainly as the history of the Islands, like its climate, has been for the most part gently variable and tranquil, it must follow that the story of the Bahamas, situated as they are, is a sea story. From the first voyage of Columbus through the succession that followed, seafaring and fishing played the predominant role in the Islands' livelihood. Following Columbus' discovery and the subsequent raids of the Spanish fleet, pirates, wreckers, rum-and-blockade-runners gathered to write the basic sailing directions yachts and tourist-filled cruise liners use today.

It was not until 150 years had passed that any consideration was given to settling the Islands and for that period Bahama history is dark indeed.

Then in 1649 William Sayle, a former Governor of Bermuda, led a group of seventy settlers to "Segatoo Buhama." The group was seeking the establishment of a community where they could enjoy "liberty of conscience," thus Sayle later renamed Segatoo "Eleuthera" from the Greek word "freedom." It was hard going for the small band, there being considerable disatisfaction and dissention. The group eventually split, the original staying on Eleuthera while the splinter group resettled on nearby St. Charles Island where they founded Spanish Wells. Surprisingly, this rivalry is still evident in North Eleuthera today. By 1657 Sayle, disappointed in the lack of success of his venture returned with most of his followers to the homeland, leaving a number of families to be recorded in history as the Bahamas' earliest settlers. Today their names are found in every corner of the Islands: Bethell, Bullard, Carey, Culmer, Dorsett, Evans, Ingraham, Knowles, Kemp, Lowe, Nubold, Pinder, Sands, Sawyer, and Watkins.

The period that followed was that of the Lords Proprietors when weak and inefficient government laid open the Islands to a multitude of pirates whose constant forays on Spain's heavily laden transports provoked some of the bloodiest reprisals imaginable. Most of the attacks were made on Nassau, as by now it had become established as the "pirates' nest" of the West Indies, as well as the seat of government, such as it was. It is generally believed that in this period the slave trade began in these Islands.

A British seafarer, Captain Woodes Rogers (already famous for his rescue of Alexander Selkirk which inspired Defoe's story *Robinson Crusoe* in 1717), convinced the Lord Commissioners of Trade that with proper authority he could expell the pirates and restore order there. The proprietors were induced to forfeit the rights to their holdings in payment for their gross inefficiency and Rogers, armed with a Royal Proclamation of pardon for pirates who would surrender, descended upon Nassau, as the new Governor, to "clean house." Within a year he had restored Fort Nassau, formulated a land grant plan to attract new settlers, and brought a thousand pirates to their knees. Despite this herculean effort, his job had only begun.

Lack of funds and moral backing along with ill health forced Rogers back to England, where he watched his successor undo all that he had accomplished until that Governor was recalled and Rogers, still ill, was forced to return to start over. This time, with the help of cotton and sugar, he was able to encourage further development and also bring more of the pirates to the gallows. However, sick and discouraged at his seemingly slow progress, he died in 1732 and was buried in Nassau.

As much of a loss as this must have seemed for the colony, Rogers had accomplished his task. The pirate ranks had been thinned, the country was being settled, and the Spanish, while not completely out of the picture, had lessened their attacks—all of which gave the country a brighter outlook. Captain Woodes Rogers is the hero of Colonial Bahamian history, for without his special efforts, there is no telling what course the future of Atlantic commerce might have taken and how it might have affected the entire western hemisphere.

What might have seemed the end of the days of piracy, marked the beginning of the wrecking "industry," the same wanton intent by the same people, only this time, working within instead of outside the law. Deliberate wrecking grew and prospered along with advancing commerce.

The Bahamas depended on the American Colonies for their provisions and during the American Revolution, mostly due to the Naval blockade, were impoverished to a near starving condition. Further, in 1782 Spain, already at war with England, seized Nassau. The occupation was brief however, only one year, Nassau being restored to England by the Treaty of Versailles in 1783.

The greatest impact the American War of Independence had on the Colony was the great influx of Loyalist sympathizers who began moving to the Bahamas that same year. Skeptical of the future of the newly formed "United States" and attracted by the generous land grants, 6,000 to 7,000 persons, both black and white, migrated here to be "nearer the Crown." When it is considered that the Islands' population numbered no more than 4,000, this migration introduced social problems heretofore unknown. Not only did the newcomers double the white population and triple the black, but they made the original whites a definite minority. The new whites were more experienced and progressive in applying their knowledge, whether in commerce, agriculture, or government; so it is understandable that the native-born Bahamians were resentful. By the time of the Napoleonic Wars and the War of 1812, however, the fusion of the two peoples had begun, strengthening the Bahamian character considerably—at the time little removed from a life of piracy. No doubt, too, the constant apprehension from fear of attack by foreign ships fostered an even closer bond between the two peoples.

The brief success and decline of the post-war plantation system resulting mainly from misuse of the lean soil of the Islands, prefaced the Emancipation by several decades. So, many of the planters, while not in the least sympathetic with the home government's abolitionist sentiments, were in fact, for economic reasons, ready to throw in the sponge if they had not already done so. Naturally those who had been successful did not give up without a fight, but it is believed that the Emancipation proceeded here easier than elsewhere in the Americas. Similarly it is conceded that the lot of the Bahamian slave was never as severe as in the sugar islands to the south or the cotton plantations of the Carolinas.

In the years that followed, pineapples, tomatoes, and citrus were exported to England and America and the sponge industry began. Wrecking had by now reached the point where it was controlled by licenses issued by the Governor and the relocation of navigational lights to lure ships onto the reefs was common practice. These practices led to the erection of a number of lighthouses by the British Imperial Board of Trade, for the protection of navigators, thus reducing the national income and the Government's revenue along with it. A further blow to the Colony's income came in 1848 when the Turks and Caicos Islands and their lucrative salt industry were placed under the protective wing of Jamaica. Turks and Caicos Islands are today an independent Crown Colony in their own right.

The greatest prosperity of all came to the Islands as a result of Lincoln's blockade of the Confederacy. England needed the South's cotton and the South needed ammunition, so Nassau was the obvious place to make the exchange. Best of all, it involved intrigue, a natural incentive for sons of pirates, and it all took place on the high seas where the Bahamian was at his best. The war years were exciting indeed, money was plentiful—easily made and freely spent. But as most wars have a way of being resolved, when it was over the country was worse off than before.

Until prohibition gave the economy its next opportunity, the Islands experienced another of those long, slow periods of development, during which the seeds of tourism were sown; and the sisal industry flourished briefly during World War II.

Surprisingly it was not the Bahamians but the Americans who did the bootlegging during the twenties. Bahamian merchants merely supplied Nassau, Bimini, and West End with the commodity, leaving the Americas to run the risks posed by the federal agents stationed off New York Harbor and the Florida and Carolina coasts. The revenue derived from the import of spirits did much to bolster the economy as the money was used chiefly to develop tourism, which began to show promise during the 1930's with airlines and steam ships bringing in annual numbers almost equal to the Colony's population. World War II further bolstered the economy by building a Royal Air Force training station and a busy ferry command base on New Providence.

Following the war the tourist program was renewed with vigor and with the curtailing of Cuba's established tourist industry, the flow was diverted to the Bahamas and success surpassed all expectations. The Bahamian preoccupation with ships and the sea had turned to pleasure craft, and the Bahamas became the scene of some some of the world's leading boating events. In 1967 alone two world sailing championships were held in the waters off Nassau.

However, in addition to prosperity the tourist industry brought with it a certain amount of discontent and subsequent social reform. The Bahamas' ruling class (white), numbering only 15 per cent of the total population, were greatly out-numbered by the blacks and in the 1966 national election lost their already narrow margin in the government. Under the strong leadership of Prime Minister Lynden O. Pindling, the Bahamas gained their independence from Great Britain on July 10, 1973.

From before the days of the earliest settlers to the present the history of the Bahamas has been predominantly a sea story. So was it not fitting that in 1964 the first Olympic Gold Medal ever awarded to a Bahamian should have been to a star sailing champion, a seafaring descendant of one of the earliest settlers: Durward Knowles of Nassau.

IMPORTANT HISTORICAL DATES

1492	Landing of Christopher Columbus at San Salvador.
1629	Charles I granted Bahamas to Sir Robert Heath, Attorney General of England.
1649	Eleutherian Adventurers made first organized attempt to settle Bahamas.
1670	Charles II granted Bahamas to six Proprietors of South Carolina.
1671	Hugh Wentworth appointed by Lords Proprietors as first Governor of Bahamas (Wentworth died before he assumed office, was succeeded by his brother John).
1695	Lords Proprietors authorized construction of fort and city to bear name of Nassau, honoring William III, former Prince of Orange Nassau. Until this date the settlement was known as Charles Towne.
1697	Fort Nassau completed on site now occupied by British Colonial Hotel.
1717	Lords Proprietors surrendered civil and military government.

1718	Woodes Rogers became first Royal Governor of the Bahamas. Captain Rogers restored order to the Bahamas by pardoning nearly 1,000 pirates who surrendered, hanging others, forcing others to flee.
1728	King granted rights of parliamentary government to Bahamas.
1728	Arms of the Colony, bearing motto Expulsus Piratis Restituta Commercia, adopted. (Pirates Expelled, Commerce Restored)
1741	Erection of Fort Montagu begun.
1776	American Naval squadron, under Commodore Ezekiel Hopkins, took Forts Montagu and Nassau without resistance, held them for a day, then departed peacefully.
1782	Bahamas capitulated to Spain.
1783	Bahamas restored to Great Britain by Treaty of Versailles. Nassau brilliantly retaken by Col. Andrew Deveaux. Influx of Loyalists from America ushered in period of agricultural development.
1787	Lords Proprietors surrendered proprietary rights to King.
1787	Erection of Fort Charlotte begun.
1793	Fort Fincastle built.
1838	Slavery abolished. Freed slaves settled on lands in the several islands where they resided.
1861–1865	Nassau became one of the chief bases for supplies for Confederate blockade runners. Royal Victoria Hotel built.
1913	Wireless telegraph station established.
1919–1933	U.S. prohibition created boom in Bahamas where good liquor was legal and plentiful.
1923	British Colonial Hotel completed.
1929	First scheduled overseas flight from Miami, Florida, to Nassau. Pan American World Airways Sikorsky-38.
1964	New Bahamas Constitution gave the Islands internal self-government modeled on the British Constitutional pattern with a Premier, cabinet of ministers, appointed Senate and House of Assembly elected by the people. The Governor, appointed by Queen Elizabeth II, held responsibility for foreign affairs, defense and security.
1966	First black government voted into power. Bahamas currency changed from the pounds system to a decimal currency system. (New Bahamian dollar = 7 shillings)
1971	Royal Victoria Hotel closed. Bahamas new motto adopted, "Forward, Upward, Onward Together."
1973	July 10th; Full independence from Great Britain; the Bahamas are now an independent country.

The Boat

Some people dream of owning an island. When you own a boat—in a sense—you own all the islands.

In choosing the right sort of boat for a cruise to the Bahamas, here are some of the factors which should be taken into consideration.

Someone with a weak stomach has said that the waters of the Bahamas are either too deep, too shallow, or too rough in between. Obviously he had the wrong sort of boat. Many of the best harbours in the Bahamas are pretty shallow at the entrance. Some of the best sailing routes are also over comparatively shallow banks. A draft of four to five feet is ideal. A draft of over six feet becomes burdensome and anything over that is very difficult. According to the old rules, boats drawing less than four feet were usually too flat in hull form to be good sea boats. However with the development of the new deep "V" hulls, an entire new philosophy has emerged to introduce a new range of cruising "buffs" to the joys of Bahamas cruising.

One's particular taste and personal needs, the extent of his resources and the time he can devote to a cruise pretty much dictate the kind of boat he will use. Time was, due to the scarcity of fuel stations in the Bahamas, that an auxiliary or motor sailer provided the only answer. For many blessed with the extra leisure time these are still the answer. However with the growth of dependable yachting services here over the last twenty years, the small boatman on a time-table vacation who can make do with a sandwich lunch underway instead of a full course meal at a gimbaled table, can enjoy the same good cruising. His boat should not be less than 26 feet in length. For him the same protected harbours and idyllic anchorages await the end of his daily runs, even though he doesn't loll on deck all the way. Of course, he will have to be selective in the weather he is faced with each day lest he jar his crew into a hatred for all boats. But once he is underway, owing to his power and speed, the passages are comparatively short, allowing more time at each end for sight-seeing, skin diving and all of the good things in which the Bahamas abound.

It used to be that any vessel cruising these waters had to have a two hundred and fifty mile cruising radius and that drums of fuel had to be shipped ahead via island freighter. Now any seaworthy twin engined boat with a 150-mile range can enjoy cruising the best of the Bahamas. These days your longest passages between fuel supplies are the seventy-six mile run across the Great Bahama Bank between Cat Cay and the Berry Islands, the eighty-five mile run across the Little Bahama Bank between West End and Great Abaco and the fifty-one mile run from North Eleuthera to Great Abaco. It is even possible now to take a boat with this range clear to Haiti or the Dominican Republic via the fuel stations at Long Island, Crooked Island, Mayaguana and Caicos without carrying it in drums on deck. But what is possible and what might be more practical from the standpoint of comfort and security is something else again; like going over Niagara Falls in a barrel, there is no real need to do so.

Not that we are particularly affluent or are of the privileged few with heaps of time on our hands; but our choice of the "ideal" boat for these Islands is still the auxiliary or motor sailer, which can readily sail if she has to. In either case, a boat which has both power and sail. It is a wonderfully comfortable feeling to know that if your engine quits you can still carry on under sail alone. Also it is nice to have power enough to push you to a position from which you can lift your sheets and sail away.

Her size should be not less than forty feet overall for comfort, nor over sixty feet overall for handiness in small places. Her draft should be four and a half or five feet. The sail plan should be divided up for ease of handling in open sea conditions, preferably a ketch, or if that is not available, then a schooner, cutter, or yawl in order of suitability. Our friend Herbert McKinney of Nassau says that he made a very successful cruise down to Andros in an old Cape Cod Cat, but we do not advise that. If your cruiser does not have a dog house, put on a deck shelter of some kind if you can. The wind blows almost continually and it is mighty nice to sit out of it without having to go below.

(Fitting Out

Much has been written to assist yachtsmen in fitting out. This many-cornered subject cannot be completely covered in one chapter, so we will try to give only some general advice.

It goes without saying that your boat should be sound and seaworthy (but we will say it again as we have seen so many arrive in the Islands that are not). If she is not, then make her so. Most East Coast yachtsmen who embark on West Indies and 'round the world cruises every year come to grief somewhere along the Atlantic Coast, usually before they have actually gotten off to sea. In almost every case they were found to be creeping along the coast ready to duck in to the nearest port if it came on to blow, because they were not sure of their ship and their gear. It is a well known fact to every seaman that a ship is safer offshore than along the coast and that no boat, ship, or vessel should venture outside unless she is fitted to go offshore and stay there in dirty weather.

The thing to remember is that where you are going there is no United States Coast Guard to nurse you. The average yachtsman is so accustomed to having somebody come along to help him out when he is in trouble that he finds it almost impossible to visualize a world in which he will be virtually on his own. At home and all along the United States Coast line, he is watched over, surrounded by shipyards, ship chandlers, service stations, yacht clubs, insurance agents, dry stores, water policemen, and what not.

However, to a degree, take heart; you are not completely alone, thanks to the efforts of a volunteer organization in the Bahamas known as Bahamas Air Sea Rescue Association or BASRA. This small nucleus of dedicated citizens headed by former New Yorker, Ben Astarita, and Captain Durward Knowles, stand by 'round the clock with their own boats and airplanes ready to assist where there is a possibility of loss of life. But over the 5,468 square miles of the Bahamas it's a bit like looking for the proverbial needle in the haystack to find a distressed yacht, much less get assistance to it on a howling, dirty night. So you see, while cruising these Islands the yachtsman must be prepared to stand on his own feet, make his own repairs, and solve his own problems. BASRA stands by on 2738 KHz.

A good sailorman should sit down and try to visualize every possible contingency and make the necessary provisions and preparations to handle it all by himself. This means primarily learning your ship, her gear and machinery, how to run it, and how to make it run when it stops. Even though the prospective cruise may be a short one in matter of time and distance, your ship should be as well fitted out as if she were off on a long voyage. With the possible exception of celestial navigation, the same problems confront the captain, and the same sea conditions may try the ship, as if she were going on a trans-Pacific voyage. Dirty weather at sea is dirty weather at sea, anywhere and in any ocean. It isn't pleasant, so to be prepared for anything is to enjoy everything.

There are a few facilities in the Bahamas for hauling out or repairing yachts, even though they might be widely spaced. There is a marine railway at Marsh Harbour on Abaco; yacht-sized travel lifts at West End and Lucaya, Grand Bahama; and small railways at Green Turtle Cay and Man of War, Abaco; Spanish Wells, Eleuthera, and Salt Pond, Long Island. There are, of course, complete hauling facilities at Nassau. At any one of these one can find competent mechanics to make engine repairs, but replacement parts might be scarce. (It's always a good idea to carry at least one spare part for every "vital" part of your engine.) There are reliable service stations with ample fuel supplies, both gasoline and diesel oil, at the following places:

Bimini
Cat Cay

Berry Islands: Great Harbour Cay, Chub Cay.
New Providence: Nassau, Lyford Cay.
Grand Bahama: West End, Lucaya, Deep Water Cay.
Abaco: Walker Cay, Green Turtle Cay, Crown Haven, Cooper's Town, Treasure
  Cay, Great Guana Cay, Man of War Cay, Marsh Harbour, Hope Town.
Andros: Nichol's Town, Fresh Creek, Mangrove Cay.*
Eleuthera: Spanish Wells, Harbour Island, The Current, Hatchet Bay, Governor's
  Harbour, Rock Sound,* Davis Harbour, Cape Eleuthera.
Exuma: Highborne Cay, Norman's Cay, Sampson Cay, Staniel Cay, George
  Town.
Long Island: Stella Maris, Salt Pond, Clarence Town,* Diamond Roads.*
Cat Island: Bennett's Harbour,* Smith Town,* Hawk's Nest.
Crooked Island: Landrail Point.*
Acklins Island: Chester's.*
Inagua: Mathew Town.*
Caicos: Providenciales,* South Caicos.

   *Fuel by truck or drum, sometimes unreliable.

NOTE: Oil Company Credit Cards
Inasmuch as it is up to the individual service facility, oil company credit cards are
not universally accepted in the Islands.

Food supplies, both canned and frozen, can be obtained in many of the
Islands, and, of course, fish and conch everywhere; but the cost of "store"
food is often double what it is in Florida, where most of it comes from. So
the sensible thing to do is to fit the boat out fully in Florida and only depend
on getting fish, conch, vegetables, and fresh fruits in the Islands. Take along
a good supply of canned butter. It lasts indefinitely and is really good.

Nassau is the place to replenish your liquor locker. There are proabably
more liquor stores there, per square mile, than any other place on earth. Bay
Street is lined with them and prices are quite low compared with those in
the United States. Good rum which sells for around $6 per bottle in the
United States costs less than $4 there.

Charts should be purchased in the U.S.A. Our U.S. Naval Oceanographic charts are the best and the cheapest of any in the world. The average
is a little over $2.50 each, and for $20 you can buy every chart necessary to
cover the Bahamas. As a matter of fact, until as recently as the early sixties,
the most accurate Bahamas charts available were the touched-up results of
British surveys performed between 1836 and 1885 by sailing ships and long
boats. These were the old 26 series published by the U.S. Naval Hydrographic office and they contained a number of inaccuracies. When you think
of it, it's amazing how well the old sailors navigated through the Islands with
both their crude charts and the awkward and inefficient rigs of their sailing
ships. Of course, in those days there was not the emphasis on time and
schedule that there is today and with caution the watchword, they could
heave-to or anchor to await favourable winds to continue their passage.

The newer Naval Oceanographic series was lofted from photographic aerial surveys and are as accurate as charts can be. They are graphically listed in the U.S. Ocean Survey office's catalog of nautical charts and publications for Region #2. Write: Distribution Division (C-44) Riverdale, Maryland 20840. Don't expect to find British Admiralty charts in Nassau; they are hard to find and having stemmed from the same original surveys as the U.S. 26 series, contain many of the same shortcomings.

Don't try to save money on the purchase of charts. Some dark howling night when you are running the entrance into some crooked little harbour with outlying reefs, you would gladly trade your boat for that seemingly extravagant chart you elected to eliminate. You cannot have too many charts and if your boat is a small one where chart storage is either at a premium or non-existent, we recommend filing these large, awkward sheets, folded in half, under your bunk mattress. Then, by posting a "ready reference" on the bunk board, you will be insured dry, flat storage and instant availability when they are needed.

The *Yachtsman's Guide to the Bahamas* is a popular priced, official publication sponsored by the Bahamas Ministry of Tourism that is re-edited and illustrated by Harry Kline each summer prior to the cruising season. In it can be found finite sailing directions for all areas of the Bahamas, plus up-to-date tide tables, light list, harbour charts, list of airstrips, and a cruising facilities index. The detailed sketch charts in the *Guide* are also updated each year and Tropic Isle Publishers makes them available in an enlarged, easily-read set that is handy for making your own notes right on the chart itself. Incidentally, as in the *Guide*, all soundings indicated on the sketch charts in this book are low water soundings.

Last, but definitely not least, equip your boat with a good radio telephone of at least 60 watts. This will enable you to converse with the U.S. Coast Guard, the Miami and Nassau marine operators, and other boats anywhere in the Bahamas. A radio phone is probably your best investment toward safety afloat, plus being a most handy way of checking the weather while underway and notifying friends and relations of your whereabouts and well being.

Other special equipment which adds greatly to the pleasure of cruising in the Bahamas is a plastic water glass and a grain. A water glass is nothing more than a plastic bucket with a transparent bottom, but with it you can see the shackle on your anchor in forty feet of water or spot articles lost overboard. Through it you can watch the movements of fish and other marine life—a fascinating pastime. A grains is a three-pronged and barbed fork on the end of a long pole. With it you can pick up conch, sponges, etc. from the bottom. We have always marked ours with graduations every foot and stored it vertically in a ring and socket in the shrouds, readily available as a sounding device when the water gets thin. However, used in conjunction with the water glass you can have good sport with it. No native Bahama boat sails without one.

U.S. NAVAL OCEANOGRAPHIC OFFICE CHARTS OF THE BAHAMAS

* Navigational Charts Covering all of Bahamas.

New No.	Old No.		Description of Area Covered
11013	1002		Florida, Cuba, Bahamas.
11160	1112	*	Florida, Gulf Stream, Bimini.
11161	5989		Straights of Florida, Southern Part.
26240	5993	*	Crooked Island Passage to Windward Passage.
26251	0422		Great Inagua: Alfred Sound, Mathew Sound Road.
26252	2805		Islands and Anchorages (Southeastern Bahamas) Hogsty Reef, Crooked Island, Port Nelson, Mayaguana.
26253	2806		Harbours and Anchorages: Mira Por Vos Pass, Wide Opening, Clarence Harbour.
26254	2498		Jumentos Cays: Stony Cay to Wet Rock.
26255	0341		Ragged Island Anchorage, Raccoon Cut.
26256	0340		Jumentos Cays: Nurse Channel.
26257	1612		Highborn Cut (Exuma), Wax Cay Cut (Exuma), Ragged Island Harbour, Golding Cay Entrance (Andros).
26258	1158		Berry Islands: Great Stirrup Cay.
26260	5995	*	Caicos Islands and Adjacent Passages.
26261	1000		South Caicos: Cockburn Harbour.
26262	0885		Grand Turk Island: Western Approaches, Southwest Anchorage.
26263	5726		Mayaguana Island: Abraham Bay.
26280	5994	*	San Salvador to Mayaguana and Crooked Island Passage.
26281	2807		San Salvador: Approaches, Cockburn Town.
26300	5991	*	Andros Island to San Salvador.
26301	5955		Cat Island and Southern Part of Exuma Sound.
26302	5724		Great Exuma Island: Elizabeth Harbour.
26303	5956		Tongue of the Ocean, Southern Part.
26305	5954		Eleuthera Island and Northern Part of Exuma Sound.
26306	1611		Cays to Eleuthera: Douglas and Fleeming Channels.
26307	1241		Eleuthera Island: Northwestern Part, Central Part.
26308	5953		Tongue of the Ocean: North Part, Andros to Exuma Cays.
26309	1377		New Providence Island.
26310	0949		Nassau Harbour
26311	2497		Berry Islands: Southern Part.
26320	5990	*	Little Bahama Bank.
26321	2499		Abaco: Pelican Harbour, Great Abaco Island (Southern Part)
26322	0998		Abaco: Whale Cay Channel, Green Turtle Cay Anchorage.
26323	2471		Grand Bahama: Freeport Harbour and Approaches.
26324	1854		Anchorages and Harbours Great Bahama Bank: Great Isaac Anchorage.
27040	5992		Old Bahama Channel to Ragged Island.

A sailing dinghy will save many a long row and, equipped with a light-weight outboard motor, is ideal for exploring and fishing in shallow waters. It should be equipped with a waterproof compartment containing emergency rations, water, a first aid kit, and flashlight.

Paint the spinner of your taffrail log black, and barracuda and shark won't be snapping it off as quickly. Better still, install one of the newer retractable, non-fouling speed and knot recording meters; then you will never be in doubt as to your course on short passages.

([Study the Art of Anchoring

No phase of boat handling shows a man's seamanship as quickly or as publicly as the act of anchoring. In a matter of minutes the master of the little ship must weigh and decide definitely his strategy with regard to size and type of anchors, type and length of chain or cable, draft of vessel, kind of holding ground on the bottom, distance to be rowed in dinghy, position of other vessels, position of lee and weather shores, tide, wind, sea, future weather, and a few other things. If he comes up with the right answer instinctively he is a seaman. If not, he is an unhappy and anxious man for the duration of his visit.

All important books on seamanship have chapters on the problems of anchoring. Read them if you have time. If not, we suggest that you study and practice the use of two anchors as the Bahamians use them. Bahama anchorages are usually in the lee of an island with a cross swell working in, or in a small hole between islands where there is considerable tide but no room in which to swing. In either case it is desirable to hold the boat in one position and not allow her to swing all over the place. For this purpose two anchors are set in line with the tide and the bow is winched in tight between them. This will hold the bow in the exact position desired and allow the stern to tether to the wind and tide.

When lying in an anchorage where there is a cross swell running, causing a roll, simply box your boat around with the anchor cables, one forward, one aft, until she lies either head to or stern to the swell, and "requiescat in pace."

([Planning the Cruise

Having found your ship and fitted her out, it is now wise to plan your cruise intelligently. It is all very well for marine vagabonds and dreamers to go knocking about from port to port with great nonchalance. Time means nothing to them. However, the average man who must get back to his responsibilities will seldom have more than a month or six weeks to spare for his holiday. By planning a cruise carefully he can cover a great deal more territory and see twice as much as the man who has no plan at all.

If you have only one week in which to make the cruise, you can do no better than to go from Florida to Nassau and back, which should be easy in that time. In two weeks you can cruise from Florida to the beautiful Exuma Cays and back. In three weeks you can add Eleuthera to the Exuma Cays. In one month you can start off from Miami, see a good bit of the Berry Islands, Nassau, the Exumas, Eleuthera, Abaco, Grand Bahama, and get back to Palm Beach.

The best cruising months in the Bahamas are April, May, June, and July, though some of the nicest cruising weather we have experienced has been in December, what the Bahamians call "Christmas weather." In January, February, and March "northers" are most prevalent. The summer months are hurricane season, and West Indians go by the rhyme (with reference to hurricanes):

> "June—too soon—
> July—standby—
> August—the worst—
> September—remember—
> October—all over."

However, there have been hurricanes as late as January.

What with the latest technical advances in tracking hurricanes these storms no longer pose any real threat to yachtsmen cruising in Bahamian waters. Fortunately the Bahamas lie in the lee of Hispaniola, which often seems to govern the track of the storms as they progress northwestward. Those which pass to the south of Hispaniola usually continue on a westerly course across Cuba and into the Gulf of Mexico. Those which move northward across the eastern tip of Hispaniola seem to parallel the Bahamas, keeping well out on the Atlantic, eventually hitting Bermuda or entering the United States on the east coast at the Carolinas. Even in light of the good record the Bahamas have enjoyed in recent years (only three major hurricanes since World World II), Bahamian boatmen usually take all necessary precautions. There are excellent "hurricane holes" all through the Abaco Cays and in a few of the creeks of Andros, New Providence, North Eleuthera, southern Cat Island, and the Exuma Cays.

(Clearing

There once was a time when the business of clearing a yacht out of the U.S.A., then back in again, was enough to drive the yachtsman all the way to the funny farm. This was mainly due to the fact that for lack of a category for pleasure boats the United States Treasury Department required the same paperwork for all seagoing vessels. So for all intents and purposes your knock-about or cruiser might just as well have been the "Queen Elizabeth." However, with the mid-fifties boom in pleasure boating and so many boatmen in the Florida area desirous of "going foreign," the Customs Department, in an effort to relieve its overburdened staff, eliminated all requirements for clearing by privately owned pleasure vessels.

So now it is not necessary for the yachtsman or private flyer to concern himself with anything but getting safely across the Gulf Stream and into the sanctuary of Bahamian waters.

United States citizens do not need passports to visit the Bahama Islands but foreigners on board should contact immigration officials for special departure instructions.

Try to arrange the arrival to your first Bahama port of entry during weekday business hours, as overtime charges for off hours, Sundays, and holidays can be expensive. You will be "cleared in" by a customs agent who will issue you a "transire." This is a small piece of paper which authorizes you to cruise or fly over the Bahamas without further ado. It is customary, but not necessary, to show the transire at the various ports you visit; however it should be turned in at your last port of call before departing the Bahamas.

On entering you will be asked the value of your boat and contents. If your stay in the Islands should exceed six months, 10 per cent of the boat's declared value will be due.

The procedure for getting back into the United States, like that for departing, has also been streamlined and, unlike the past the process is now quite pleasant. In fact the boarding officer now processes the master's papers himself and individuals on board are furnished a short form on which they must declare purchases made outside the U.S. Current rules are that adults returning from a foreign visit of over 72 hours may bring in, duty free, $50 in value in retail purchases once a month, which may include one U.S. quart of alcoholic beverage and 200 cigarettes. Boarding rules now read: "All passengers and crew must remain aboard the vessel until cleared by the boarding officer, and no persons from the shore should be permitted to come aboard. The only person who may leave the vessel prior to clearance is the master and he *only for the purpose of reporting his arrival*. It should be remembered that no baggage or other article may be removed from the vessel prior to inspection and that all items acquired in foreign ports must be declared."

The Gulf Stream

The Gulf Stream, as has been written before, is the mightiest river in the world, its current more rapid than that of the Mississippi or the Amazon, its volume more than a thousand times greater. Rising out of the bowels of the earth in the tropics, it flows all the way to the Arctic. Its influence is so tremendous that were it diverted from its course the whole of Western Europe would only be fit for habitation by Eskimos.

The entire volume of this enormous stream comes boiling through the Straits of Florida where, at the narrowest part, it is about 43 miles wide and 500 fathoms deep. It is deep indigo blue in color and in the winter its waters have an average temperature of about 76°. The velocity in its axis is 4½ knots, and the current flows in a northerly direction. Both velocity and direction of the surface water, in which a small boat sails, are affected to some extent by the prevailing winds. The velocity is also considerably retarded by proximity to each shore. We have found that a good rule for navigating across the Stream is to allow for an average northerly current of 2 knots from shore to shore.

The Gulf Stream has a fearful reputation, but the fact is that with the average prevailing winds it is no rougher than any other bit of open water in the world. As long as the wind causes water to undulate there will always be waves, and little ships must sail up and down them if they want to get anywhere. With the prevailing winds, which are usually from ENE to SE, the Gulf Stream is just a piece of open water with a bobble on top and no ground swell. When it blows from NW through to NE, a typical norther, the current of the Stream is fighting the wind and it makes quite a rumpus on the surface. Still we doubt if it is any rougher than the English Channel and certainly not as cold. No sensible person will claim that it is anything but uncomfortable, but it is neither impassable nor nearly as dangerous as most people seem to think. And again, there are only about 43 miles of it.

The thing to do under these conditions is to take it easy. Shorten down and jog along at the speed which is easiest on your ship. The harder you drive a boat the more uncomfortable she must be. If you want to be as comfortable as possible under the circumstances, "heave 'er to" and enjoy the beauty of the scene around you. There are few sights in this world more beautiful than the sun shining through the body of a white crested wave.

❨ Seasickness

It is tragic that so many lovers of the sea and sailing avoid going to sea because they fear seasickness. Little do they realize that most sailors get seasick at some time or other. The normal human being, designed to travel on a steady surface, should have a tendency to become emotionally upset if thrown around every which way. The same human being, if normal, will inevitably adjust himself to the new conditions in due course. This period of adjustment, of course, varies with the individual. Some people get over it in a matter of minutes; some take hours; others, days. The thing to remember is that nothing in life is permanent, neither the gale, nor the motion, nor the seasick feeling.

If you are a particularly hard case to cure we suggest that you carry a stock of Dramamine tablets. These should be taken well in advance of the anticipated time of need, so here again planning is necessary. The tablets do have a tendency to make you drowsy, so try to schedule your activities accordingly. Munching dry crackers, staying out in the fresh air, and keeping your eyes fixed on a solid shoreline (if one happens to be in view) are all ways of easing "that queasy feeling."

❨ Pilotage

Because of their universally shallow depths and crystal clear waters, pilotage on the banks, or "pilotage by eye" as it is called locally, is an art unique to the Bahamas. Unless you are making one of the few deep water passages along one of the major sea lanes, you will be crossing the banks in 3 to 4 fathoms where you will have the bottom in sight at all times. For anyone cruising here for the first time this can be both startling, and if the water becomes "thinner" than predicted, it can be downright terrifying. Needless to say, until one is familiar with the routes, the thought of night passages should be eliminated.

Pilotage by eye is merely judging the depth of the water by the color of familiar marine growths on the bottom. Coral formations usually range in color from yellow to mustard to brown. Sand is usually white. Visualizing the water as a very pale blue-green filter you can see how it could, at various depths, affect the colors of these formations, thus giving the practiced eye a pretty accurate "reading" of the actual depths of the bottom. With additional depth (or filter thickness) a sand or marl bottom will tend from white in the shallows to pale green in 2 to 3 fathoms to blue in 3 to 5 to various shades of deeper blue in depths beyond. The yellowish colors of coral heads are unmistakable on the surface but under a fathom or two they take on a russet or brownish hue and the deeper they go the blacker they become. When the bottom is rocky the blue of the 10 to 15 fathom depth may become a dark green, while in shallow water where grass and stones cover the sea bed, the pale green takes on a brownish cast. Some of the smaller coral heads are ringed with white sand, these have been "eaten clean" by the fish which inhabit the head, so the Bahamians claim. Cloud shadows can sometimes be confused with rocky patches and so it goes. Obviously the more one has practiced this art the more proficient he will be. Some of the Bahamian fishermen and pilots seem to have been born with this gift.

❬ The Weather

With all the modern methods of communication available to the cruising man in this day and age, there is very little excuse for ever getting caught out in a bad blow here. A ten cent telephone call to the Weather Bureau in Miami will get you some of the most complete weather analysis available, and the U.S. Coast Guard broadcasts a 24-hour weather forecast on 2182 KHz at 0700 and 1900 daily, while the Miami marine operator announces the same information fifteen minutes later on 2031.5 KHz and 2118 KHz. Also, reliable weather forecasts are given on the radio from various Florida stations and the Nassau station, ZNS, at least three times every day.

If you have no radio, and are out of touch with telephones, you can still predict the weather with a reasonable amount of accuracy if you know the signs. The only bad weather in this area during the winter months is what is called a "norther." This is a cold frontal system, the remnants of those which advance across the United States from the Pacific Northwest each year, dumping heavy snows from coast to coast and driving Florida's winter visitors southward before them. By the time these systems have moved out to sea and been warmed by the Gulf Stream there is usually little left of them, their affects being felt no further south than Great Exuma in the Central Bahamas. There are those few exceptions, however, that penetrate the full length of the Bahama chain.

The advent of a norther is very obvious. The normal Easterly Trade Wind will die out and shift to south and southwest, usually with rain squalls and a falling barometer. The wind will work its way around to the west, the barometer will start to rise, then the wind will go northwest and start to blow. A norther may only last twenty-four hours, or it may blow for four or five days. The average one lasts about three days. Then the wind will shift to the northeast and die out, or go on around to the east and the normal trade winds will come in again. December and January are the worst months for northers. We have known two in one week and five in one month. By April they are practically over. In the Bahamas the weather is wonderful! For complete details for an average year, see the table below.

Month	Temperature				Amount Rainfall in inches	Degree Humidity in per cent
	Shade, Minimum	Shade, Maximum	Range	Mean		
Jan.	67	77	10	72	—	79
Feb.	65	74	9	69	—	79
March	69	79	10	73	.28	76
April	75	84	13	78	3.28	72
May	75	85	10	80	2.96	74
June	74	85	11	79	9.01	79
July	76	86	10	81	7.62	77
Aug.	77	88	11	82	4.25	83
Sept.	75	88	13	81	5.46	76
Oct.	73	85	12	79	6.20	78
Nov.	68	82	14	75	.52	75
Dec.	63	77	14	70	1.64	70

Cooling trade winds from the Atlantic mingle with warm air from the south to produce for the Bahamas one of the best and most refreshing climates in the world. In an average year, according to the Nassau Met Office, the thermometer shifts less than 30 degrees. From an average minimum reading in December of 63 to a high in August of 88, the temperature variation is just 25 degrees.

Sailing Routes and Instructions

Being now ready to get underway for Nassau and "other places beyond the seas," as the British Bill of Health used so prettily to put it, you will have to decide on your sailing route and lay your course. This course will be largely dictated by weather conditions, plus the characteristics and ability of your ship.

The three best sailing routes from the Florida coast to Nassau are:

1. From Miami to Gun Cay, over the Great Bahama Bank to Northwest Channel Light, and from there to Nassau. Total distance 161 miles. On this route you can go into Gun Cay, Cat Cay, or Bimini harbours, all good safe anchorages. After passing Northwest Channel Light you can stop off at Chub Cay, or Little Whale Cay in the Berry Islands, only half a day's run from Nassau. Boats drawing more than five feet of water should not take this route.

2. From Miami or Port Everglades up to and around Great Isaac Light, then to and around Great Stirrup Cay in the Berry Islands, and down to Nassau, a distance of about 181 miles, depending on where you start from. This is the deep sea route for vessels of any draft. It is the sailing route over which the annual Miami-Nassau Ocean Yacht Race is sailed.

3. From Palm Beach over to West End, which is back of Settlement Point, on Grand Bahama Island, a jump of 55 sea miles. Then a leisurely cruise eastward across the Little Bahama Bank, around Great Abaco Island, down to Eleuthera Island, and from there to Nassau. In reverse this is the best route for the voyage home from Nassau if you can afford the time. Vessels drawing more than six feet of water should not take this route.

◖ Route No. 1

Wait for good weather, and if yours is a sailboat make the crossing at night. This has two advantages. First, the breeze, and consequently the sea, are usually more moderate at night. Second, you make your landfall while it is still dark and so can identify the lights with more accuracy.

One of the difficulties about cruising among small islands is that they all

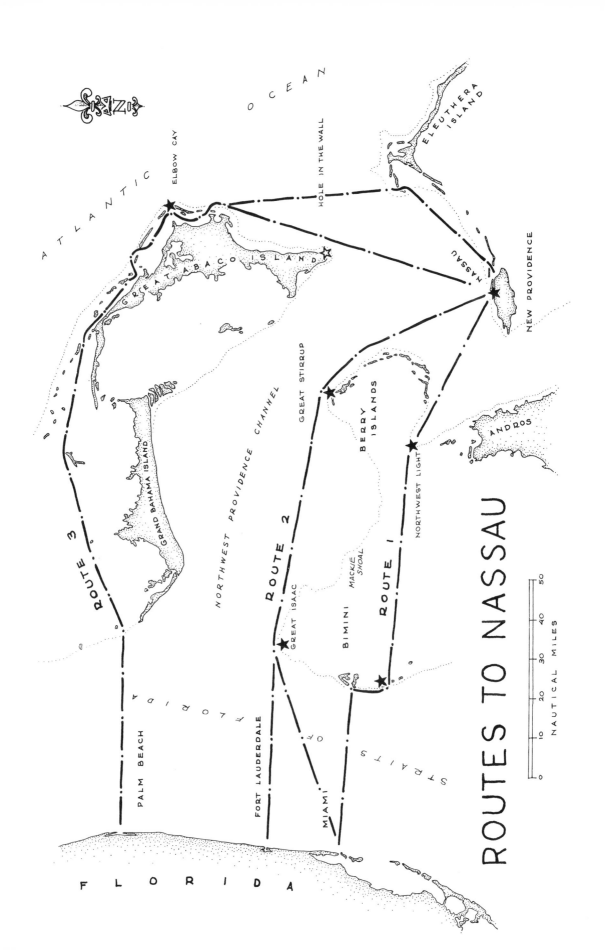

ROUTES TO NASSAU

look alike to the unpracticed eye, but a light, plainly seen in the dark, has characteristics which are exactly described on the chart, and in the Light List, and cannot easily be mistaken for any other light in that vicinity. For instance the light on Gun Cay flashes every ten seconds. If you are anywhere near your course and pick up a ten-second flashing light it is bound to be Gun Cay and no other. Lay your course, according to your speed, to compensate for a two-knot average set to the north from shore to shore. The distance to be run is 45 sea miles. If your little ship averages five knots it will take her nine hours, and she will be set two nautical miles per hour, each hour to the northward, or a total of eighteen miles. Therefore lay your course for a point eighteen miles south of Gun Cay, which is close enough for all practical purposes, and about seven hours later you will be picking up Gun Cay Light,which has a range of visibility of fourteen miles.

If you are cruising under power the principles of dead reckoning are the same, so with there being proportionately fewer sailors among us each year, let us languish behind our rose-colored glasses and proceed as though you have a sailboat.

It is important that you know the speed of your boat, whether it is power or sail, not only through the water, but over the bottom and under varying conditions of wind and sea; otherwise all calculations for dead reckoning are pure guesswork. Any kind of sea slows down a small boat tremendously, the only exception being a light displacement hull in a following sea. If you run into rough water slow down and take it easy. Unless you are racing, it is a shame to punish a boat or her passengers more than you have to. Taking unnecessary chances of damaging your ship, gear, or machinery is sometimes exciting, but never good seamanship.

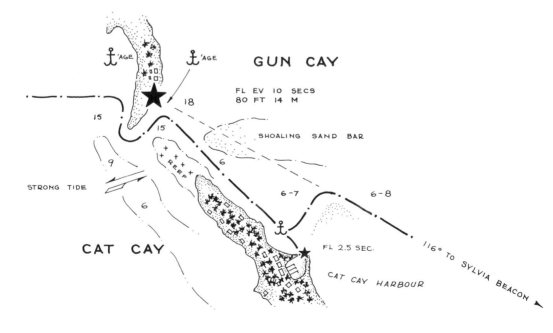

The best entrance is between Gun Cay and Cat Cay. Get the light on Gun Cay bearing 090° from you and go in on that bearing, steering straight for the light. When the south point of Gun Cay bears S x E from you, swing around to starboard and around this point close to shore, keeping about 50 yards off the cliffs. Follow the shore of Gun Cay until the light bears NW from you and you'll be in a good safe anchorage in 2½ fathoms of water, the prettiest, clearest water you ever saw. You are now on the western edge of the Great Bahama Bank.

If you make your crossing so as to pick up the land in broad daylight, you should be able to see the tower of Gun Cay Light with the naked eye when you are about ten miles away, if the visibility is good. Shortly thereafter you will pick up the trees to the south of it which are on Cat Cay. The Gun Cay Light is easy to distinguish in the daytime, being a round tower with the lower part white and the upper part pink. There are also four or five small pink houses scattered around the light.

Gun Cay anchorage, like a good many such anchorages in the Bahamas, gets its protection on one side by solid land, and on the other by shallow water. The degree of protection afforded is determined by the depth of this shallow water. If, as is the case here, the water on this shallow side is one fathom or more in depth, a short steep sea can develop when the wind blows from over the shoals. Thus Gun Cay anchorage is all right when the wind is in the west, but in a fresh norther or northeaster it is pretty rough. When the wind is in the east you can lie on the west side of the Cay.

(Cat Cay

Three-quarters of a mile southeast of Gun Cay Light will be found the entrance of Cat Cay Harbour, which is on the east side of Cat Cay. This is an artificial harbour protected by stone jetties, and it is a good shelter in any weather for boats drawing up to ten feet. There is a small, conical, white stone lighthouse at the end of the east jetty with a 2.5 second light on it. The channel into the harbour is buoyed and the small black channel buoy, which marks the eastern side of the channel, is only about ten feet from the end of the jetty on which the lighthouse stands.

Supplies and all yachting facilities are available here at somewhat better than stateside prices. Always remember, when cruising the Bahamas, *you*, as a tourist, seagoing or otherwise, are the main contributor to the Bahamian economy. All resaleable items, foodstuffs, etc., have to be shipped in at short haul rates which boost the prices on familiar items by about two-thirds. The only exception is liquor, which, due to the high state and federal taxes in the U.S., is almost twice the price of the same brand in the tax-free Bahamas. It is difficult to understand why all fuel and petroleum products should be

Cat Cay's Protected Harbour. *H. Kline*

so much higher, though (diesel fuel 35–45 cents per gallon and regular grade gasoline 50–60 cents per gallon), as these are originally obtained from the tax-free storage facilities at Freeport and Nassau, and with the low cost of bulk shipping throughout the Bahamas should reflect a better price than they do.

Originally developed as a very exclusive private fishing club by the late New York advertising executive, Louis R. Wasey, the Cat Cay Club provided a country manor atmosphere for its membership which read like "Who's Who in U.S. Finance." However, like all institutions which have depended solely upon one man's magnetism for its continued success, after Mr. Wasey's death the "manor" fell into confusion and decay. Mainly, the members who had been promised an exclusive "hideaway" for an eternity were confronted with the very practical aspects of how one can keep it going without both new blood and new money. So, after a decade of false starts on the sale of the island and several dock-damaging storms, Mr. Wasey's daughter sold the Cat Cay Club to a small group of businessmen headed by Willard F. Rockwell, Jr., Chairman of the Board of North American Rockwell Company. At a reclamation cost of $8 million the Cat Cay Club is again open and swinging! New concrete piers line the coconut-bordered harbour. There are complete fueling facilities, a 30,000 gallon per day distillation plant, and the modestly stocked commissary is back in operation. Even the famous Cat Cay International Tuna Tournament has been re-established.

Cat Cay's tariff is slightly high for the average visitor—$12,500 initiation fee plus yearly dues of $1,000 for a limited membership of 200. Keep in mind, however, that this offshore playground is an exceptionally beautiful island, a mere 25 minutes away from Miami via Chalk's Flying Service. Nevertheless, we repeat, "When you own a boat, you own all the islands." So, tie up at Cat Cay and enjoy the Club's visitor facilities—they are first rate. Jimmy, the dock attendant, will be there to welcome you with charm and dispatch. He has weathered all the storms and changes and knows the area as well as anyone we know.

Cat Cay is a Port of Entry for the Bahamas and the office of the Customs Inspector is conveniently located next to Jimmy's office at the head of the dock. We have always preferred clearing into the Bahamas at Cat Cay rather than at Bimini or Nassau because here the officer needs only to see your quarantine flag from his office window to know of your presence. At Bimini and Nassau he must be summoned from his office, which at Nassau is downtown, and his visit will cost you his round trip taxi fare.

So clear here and while you're at it, top off your fuel tanks for the long run across the banks. The price of fuel may be high compared to Florida, but it is comparable to fuel prices all over the Bahamas and you'll have the security of a full supply in preparation for one of the Bahamas' longest single passages, 76 miles to the next "gas station" (Chub Cay).

⟮ Bimini

The entrance to Bimini Harbour lies just nine miles north of Gun Cay Light and is between the southern end of North Bimini Island and the northern end of South Bimini Island. Unless you have a local pilot it should not be attempted after dark except at high tide or with a boat drawing more than six feet of water. If you are coming in from the north, south, or west you will look in vain for a light on Bimini as there is no aid to navigation, but the lights of the settlement mark it unmistakably.

As soon as you anchor off Bimini, local pilots will approach you to guide you in. They will probably ask for a $20.00 pilot fee and accept much less. We have always used Bahamian pilots when cruising in questionable or unfamiliar waters and found them to be excellent seamen, interesting companions, and a storehouse of pertinent local information. In any event, make it a rule to always agree on the price before you sign him on and pay him what you think his professional ability is worth to you. This is no time to bargain hunt and chances are that this may be his primary source of income.

It is unfortunate that Bimini, as a major gateway to the Bahamas, has never maintained a reliable deep water channel at its entrance. Being so close to the powerful movement of the Gulf Stream, the shallow sand banks around the harbour entrance are subject to frequent change and many good boats meet disaster here each year. So if you elect not to use the services of

NORTHWEST
BAHAMA BANK

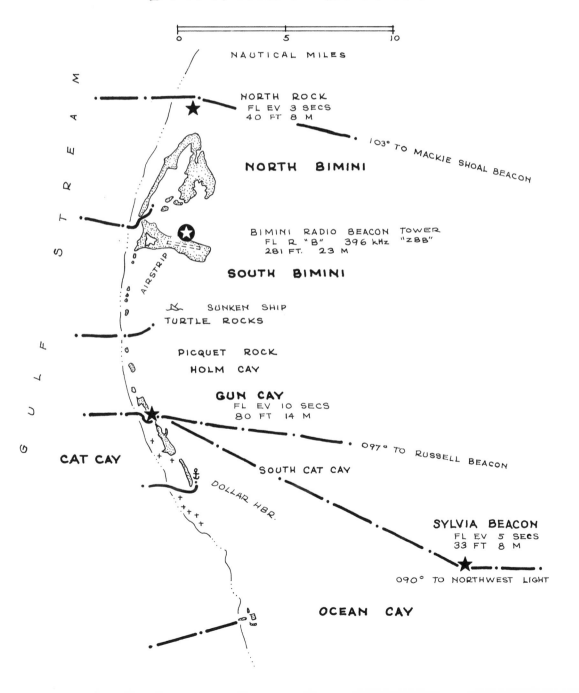

GREAT ISAAC
GP FL (2) EV 15 SEC
152 FT 18 M

HENS AND CHICKENS

0   5   10

NAUTICAL MILES

NORTH ROCK
FL EV 3 SECS
40 FT 8 M

103° TO MACKIE SHOAL BEACON

NORTH BIMINI

BIMINI RADIO BEACON TOWER
FL R "B" 396 kHz "ZBB"
281 FT. 23 M

SOUTH BIMINI

SUNKEN SHIP
TURTLE ROCKS

PICQUET ROCK
HOLM CAY

GUN CAY
FL EV 10 SECS
80 FT 14 M

097° TO RUSSELL BEACON

CAT CAY

SOUTH CAT CAY

DOLLAR HBR.

SYLVIA BEACON
FL EV 5 SECS
33 FT 8 M

090° TO NORTHWEST LIGHT

OCEAN CAY

G U L F   S T R E A M

AIRSTRIP

a pilot and decide to go it alone, proceed across the bar *during daylight hours only* on a 103° bearing on the radio tower on South Bimini, or 76° bearing on the red and white water tower farther down the island, as these are the channels which have proven to be the ones open most often over the years. Five feet can be carried across here at low tide and into the deeper water which parallels the beach. From there the obvious blue channel leads off in a northerly direction into Bimini's main harbour.

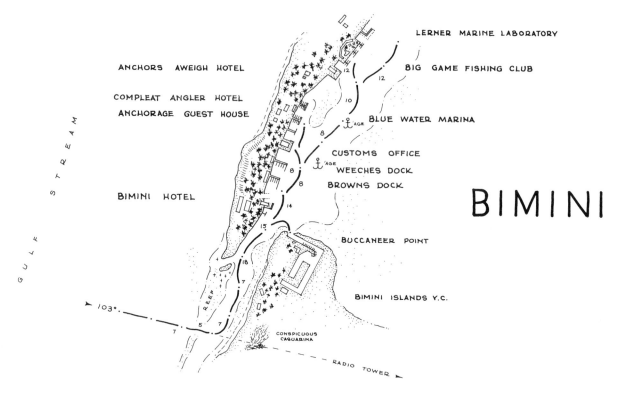

If you have not already cleared officially at Cat Cay you must fly your quarantine flag as soon as you have tied up and not venture ashore until the customs agent has paid you a visit.

Bimini is really two islands, North Bimini and South Bimini. The village on North Bimini is called Alice Town, and here sport fishermen from all over the world have congregated for the past 50 years. Everything necessary for their equipment and enjoyment has been developed here, and it is undoubtedly one of the most important fishing centers in this hemisphere. There are boats for hire, first rate fishing guides, fuel, ice, water, bait, fishing tackle, hotels, yacht marinas, night clubs, several good restaurants, airline service, telephones, post office, public library, and a Church of England.

No less than 6 hotels are now in operation here: the Bimini Hotel, Brown's, Seaview, Bimini Blue Water Hotel and Marina, and the Bimini Big Game Fishing Club owned by the famous Bacardi family of Nassau and Bermuda. One of the most charming of the Bimini hotels is Neville Stuart's

Anchor's Aweigh, located just up from the harbour in the center of the town. Neville Stuart and Harcourt Brown have been largely responsible for the development of the island as a fishing resort and like to recall memories of the exciting prohibition days and the rum-runners who thrived here. Also, Helen Duncombe's Compleat Angler Hotel was Ernest Hemingway's hangout and there are many momentos from earlier days.

The main street on North Bimini is the palm-lined Queen's Highway where, interspersed along its length, there are an assortment of shops, straw markets, restaurants, and night clubs that really swing on a Saturday night, or any night during "tournament time."

The extensive sand flats that separate North and South Bimini contain a wealth of sea life: conch, helmet, murex, and sponge are here for the picking, and when the tide is out bonefish can be cornered in the tidal pools. We learned to clean conch at Bimini on our first visit many years ago, then made a conch salad with green peppers, bird peppers, onions, and fresh lime. What a feast it was!

South Bimini is a somewhat larger island and was used in past years by farmers of North Bimini for agricultural purposes, but in recent years has been developed as a small boatman's cruising headquarters with excellent facilities. The new Bimini Marina and Hotel even specializes in dry storage for boats up to 30 feet in length, a natural package for the weekend sport fisherman who would rather fly to his "playground" than cruise there.

Bimini's Western beach borders the Gulf Stream. *Bahamas Ministry of Tourism*

The Government airstrip is on South Bimini and there are daily scheduled flights to Nassau and Florida. Colonel Mackey of Mackey Airlines dredged a small basin at the South point of the island with a marked channel leading in from the Gulf Stream. This could be a handy, easily-accessible refuge when North Bimini's bar is impassable; however, the companion facilities ashore are in a sad condition.

Ponce de Leon's famous "Fountain of Youth" was supposed to have been located here, and we have looked for it in vain. In recent years archeologists have discovered a pattern of submerged walls or faults extending east into the Gulf Stream off Bimini's north shore, reviving the old suspicion that the Great Bahama Bank might have been the original Atlantis which was supposed to have sunk into the sea more than 10,000 years ago.

One of the most interesting places to visit in Bimini is the Lerner Marine Laboratory of the American Museum of Natural History. In their pens along the waterfront of Alice Town you can study porpoises, sharks, rays, tarpon, turtles, bonefish, barracudas, and a host of smaller fry all swimming around in their native element. In the laboratory ashore scientists are busy conducting research on shark behavior and cancer.

Sad to say that busy little Bimini, with its graceful stands of coconut palms and spectacular western beach, is being changed and spoiled by an influx of foreign visitors. It all started during Prohibition days when hundreds of rum-runners made this their headquarters. Now it is a headquarters for sport fishermen, and easy money has spoiled the small population, some of whom encourage their children to beg to have their pictures taken only as an excuse for a tip. However, it remains a beautiful island and is still well worth a visit. The harbour, once you are in, is a good place to lie in any weather as the shallow water on the east side is so very shallow that no sea ever makes up there. Supplies of food, diesel oil, and gasoline can be obtained on shore. There is, however, a shortage of fresh water and if it is necessary to fill your tanks we suggest tasting it first.

(Great Isaac

Great Isaac Island is three-quarters of a mile long and lies in a NE-SW direction. There is a good 3-fathom anchorage in the lee of the island, which, in the event of a northwest gale is safe though not exactly smooth. The Great Isaac Lighthouse stands in the middle of the island. This is a group flash light, flashing twice every fifteen seconds; and its 300,000 candlepower beam is visible for eighteen miles. It is well kept and dependable. The lighthouse is of cast iron construction, 152 feet high and painted white. It stands out well on the horizon. It was locally called the "Victoria Light" after Queen Victoria.

⟪ Dollar Harbour—South Cat Cay

Round Cat Point, the southern tip of South Cat Cay, keeping a hundred yards off the beach. Anchor anywhere. The sand ridges to the east and northeast are practically bare at low water, protecting you from any sea from that quarter. Shelling on them should be excellent and there are usually enough conch for your chowder pot.

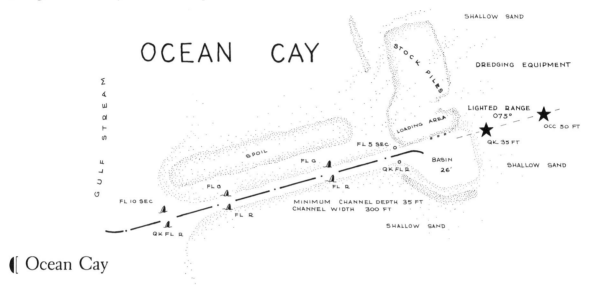

⟪ Ocean Cay

The newest Cay in the Bahamas is controversial Ocean Cay. It lies nine miles south of Cat Cay and was built as a by-product of an aragonite sea mining operation, a subsidiary of the Dillingham Corporation. Aragonite is a natural form of limestone which has precipitated to the sea bottom in the form of a calcium carbonate sand. It is essential in the manufacture of cement, chemical lime, steel, glass, paper, and agricultural fertilizers. Royalties on the operation when it reaches its peak will mean $500,000 per year to the Bahamas Government, a real shot in the arm for the economy. On the other side of the ledger, however, are the doubts that have been expressed by conservationists and ecological interests that continued subterranean fallout from the project could prove harmful to the delicate balance of sea life in its lee. In answer to these queries Dillingham has retained the services of Dr. Durbin Tabb of the University of Miami to keep a watchful eye on the surrounding sea life in the hopes that it will not be harmed. In the meantime, Ocean Cay, with its artificial harbour and conspicuous cluster of heavy mining equipment, might provide a well marked refuge to yachts on passage. Sea birds have already appointed it a man-made rookery—time will tell.

⟮ Across the Great Bahama Bank:

Route 1

In crossing the northwestern part of the Great Bahama Bank, all you have to worry about is Mackie Shoal. This shoal lies 32 miles E ½ N from Gun Cay Light. As it has only three feet of water on it you must be careful to give it a wide berth, for the currents are uncertain and hard to estimate exactly. Generally the flood tide sets on to the bank, and the ebb tide off of it. However the winds have quite an effect on the surface current also. The best courses, in our opinion, are:

For boats drawing up to five feet—steer ESE or 116° from Gun Cay Light. Having run this course for 16½ miles you will come to a big, steel, lattice-work tower which has a flashing white light on it. The characteristics of this light are one flash every five seconds, the visibility range is eight miles. From this structure the course is due east for 46 miles to Northwest Channel Light, leaving Russell Beacon, a similar steel lattice-work tower, one mile to port at the 32-mile mark.

For boats drawing up to nine feet it is better to enter the banks at South Riding Rock (21 miles south of Cat Cay) and steer 067° for 57 miles to a point one mile south of Russell Beacon, then proceed due east the remaining 14 miles to NW Channel Light.

Just inside South Riding Rock there is a deep, fair-weather anchorage with good holding ground over a sandy bottom.

An alternate course is to go around the north end of North Bimini, sail 32 miles on a 103° course to Mackie buoy, flashing every 1½ seconds, then 124° for 28 miles to NW Shoal bell buoy, flashing every 2 seconds. When approaching NW Channel Light from the northwest this buoy marks the western extremity of a sandy shoal which parallels the western approach to the light on the northern side. It is 3 miles from the buoy to the beacon.

Northwest Channel Light is a skeleton steel structure, painted white, black, and red. It is somewhat hard to find in the daytime. At night the light on it is visible for about eight miles, and is sometimes out. If you have difficulty finding it, anchor and wait for better conditions, or get a latitude sight. Passage through here at night is not to be advised if it can be avoided, for not only is the channel difficult to see, but fishing sloops anchored around this area usually carry no riding lights. In the daytime you will not have long to wait before seeing other vessels sailing through, as there is a fair amount of traffic here. When you pick up the light, pass it close aboard, leaving it on your starboard hand when bound east. We usually pass the light about 50 yards off. Then take up 106° for the remaining 14 miles to Chub Cay, or 116° for the final 50-mile leg into Nassau.

Route 2

For vessels of any draft from Miami, or Port Everglades, to Nassau:

Unless the wind is in the north or northeast, the further south you start from the better off you are. Starting from Miami insures a good set under you from the Gulf Stream. Starting from Port Everglades you will have the stream to buck.

With the average prevailing wind you will have a nice, easy reach to Great Isaac—then a beat to windward for 67 miles up the Northwest Providence Channel to Great Stirrup Cay. You can get shelter fom a norther back of Great Isaac Island, and there is a good harbour back of Great Stirrup Cay. For instructions on entering this harbour, see Chapter V on the Berry Islands. From Great Stirrup Cay to Nassau is 52 miles, also usually dead to windward.

Route 3

From Lake Worth Inlet (Palm Beach) to West End (55 sea miles):

During the lusty days of prohibition, smuggling liquor into the United States was one of the world's major industries. Quite a large percentage of this liquor was smuggled in on the Florida East Coast, and the Port of West End, Grand Bahama Island, was a beehive of activity. Thousands of cases of the best Scotch, gin, rum and champagne were piled up along the waterfront and hundreds of fast rum-runners sailed out of that port daily. We have been told that as many as 1,000 boats sailed in and out of there every week, loaded to the gunwales with liquor. This is no doubt an exaggeration. Nevertheless West End was the number one liquor-smuggling port, with Bimini a close second.

West End

There are two artificial harbours at West End, either of which offers complete protection in any weather. The approach to the Grand Bahama Yacht Marina is on an easterly course one-third north in the channel between West End and Indian Cay. When between the two cays the marked channel will be open to you to the SE, so proceed in on that heading. Five feet can be carried in here at low water.

The entrance to the commercial harbour at West End is also approached on an easterly heading. Head for the northwesternmost point of land and you will pick up the flashing red and green lights of the entrance channel when you are a fair distance off. A nine-foot draft can be taken into this harbour at low water; however there are few facilities for yachts here as compared to those next door.

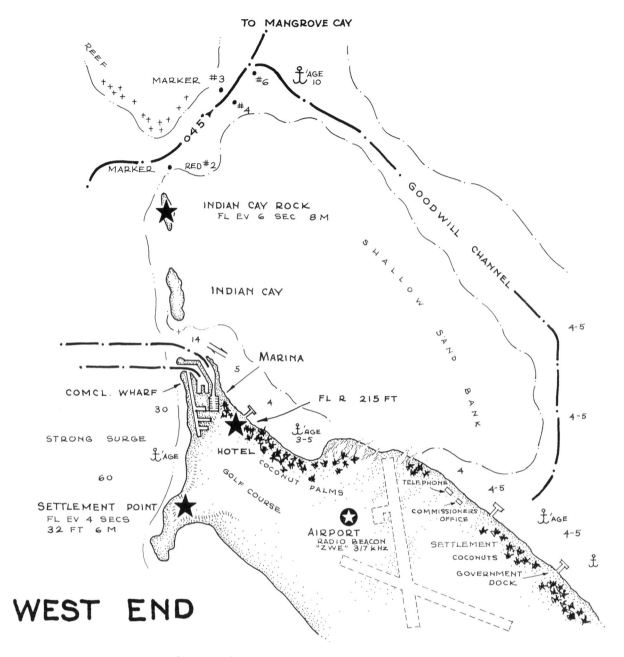

TO MANGROVE CAY

REEF

MARKER #3

#6

045°

#4

$\updownarrow$'AGE 10

MARKER

RED #2

INDIAN CAY ROCK
FL EV 6 SEC 8 M

INDIAN CAY

GOODWILL CHANNEL

SHALLOW SAND BANK

4-5

14

MARINA

5

COMCL. WHARF

30

4

FL R 215 FT

$\updownarrow$'AGE 3-5

4-5

STRONG SURGE

60

$\updownarrow$'AGE

HOTEL

COCONUT PALMS

GOLF COURSE

4

TELEPHONE

COMMISSIONERS OFFICE

4-5

SETTLEMENT POINT
FL EV 4 SECS
32 FT 6 M

AIRPORT
RADIO BEACON
"ZWE" 317 kHz

SETTLEMENT
COCONUTS

GOVERNMENT
DOCK

$\updownarrow$'AGE
4-5

$\updownarrow$

WEST END

If you prefer to anchor off West End Settlement, enter the Bank immediately north of Indian Cay Rock and follow the Goodwill Channel as indicated on the accompanying chart.

West End has everything for the yachtsman. All services are available including a small, but well equipped, boat yard with a travel lift and the small marine store next to the dockmaster's office carries most of the items you would need during your brief stay. West End is a Port of Entry for the Bahamas, so hoist your quarantine flag when entering (if you have not cleared elsewhere) and try to do so during regular business hours. In recent years we have experienced what seemed like unnecessary delays on the part of the boarding officer, who was probably hoping that if we were inspected after business hours we would not object to overtime charges. However, quickly allowing that we had tied up at four in the afternoon, we stood our ground and ours was a very pleasant, but formal, inspection.

The hotel facilities at West End, were built originally as a Billy Butlin Holiday Camp, planned to attract the less affluent vacationer who patronizes similar resorts in England. Its proximity to the Florida coast promised success, but before the place could get into full operation, the devaluation of the British pound put it into bankruptcy. At the time a very astute banker said, "The hotel will be sold several times and the third buyer will make money." As the third buyer is now the Jack Tar Hotel chain this prediction seems to have come true. The hotel is one of the largest in the Bahamas and with its 18-hole golf course, well-equipped game fishing fleet and international airport with daily jet service to Nassau and Florida, serves as an excellent site for U.S industrial conventions. It has an enormous swimming pool, several huge assembly halls and rows of guest wings laid out in parallel lines like military barracks, all covering some 68 acres of attractively landscaped property.

Like Bimini, West End's background in rum-running and its close proximity to Florida and "Americanized" Freeport has led to its own spoilage by hosting free spending vacationers. But—stick with us, neither Bimini, West End, Freeport, nor even Nassau today, represent the charm and dignity of the islands we came to love. They are merely the gateways to the boatman's Bahamas—the Out Islands—where you can cruise year 'round in protected waters and sun-drenched solitude without being encumbered with the complexities of modern civilization.

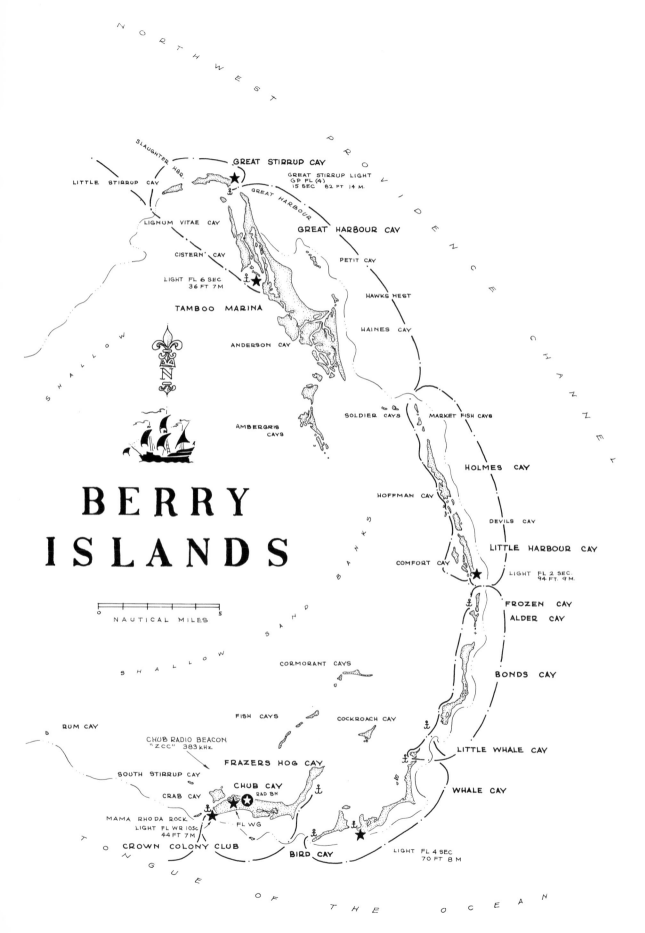

BERRY ISLANDS

The Berry Islands

The Berry Islands lie on the northeastern edge of the Great Bahama Bank. They are unapproachable from the west except at the north end, as the bank on that side shoals to an average of three feet. There are a number of good harbours and innumerable lees and anchorages where you can drop a "lunch hook."

At the south end there are good anchorages and a modern marina at Chub Cay. On the east side snug harbours will be found at Little Whale Cay, Alder Cay, Frozen Cay, and Little Habour Cay. At the north end there is the largest harbour of all which is Great Harbour, back of the lighthouse at Great Stirrup Cay. At the west end of Great Stirrup Cay is Slaughter Harbour and on the west side of Great Harbour Cay is Bullocks Harbour and the unique new Tamboo Marina.

Chub Cay Club's protected harbour. *Bahamas Ministry of Tourism*

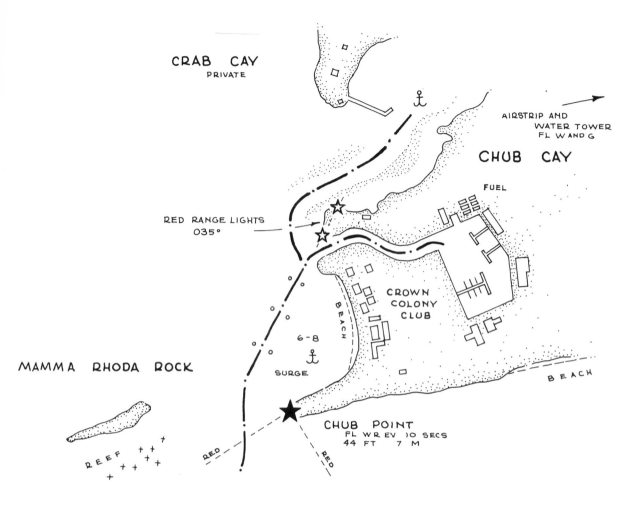

CRAB CAY
PRIVATE

CHUB CAY

AIRSTRIP AND
WATER TOWER
FL W AND G

FUEL

RED RANGE LIGHTS
035°

CROWN
COLONY
CLUB

MAMMA RHODA ROCK

BEACH

6-8

SURGE

BEACH

REEF

RED

CHUB POINT
FL WR EV 10 SECS
44 FT   7 M

RED

⟨ Chub Cay

   Sailing to the eastward across the northern edge of the Tongue of the
Ocean from NW Channel Light there is no anchorage until you get to Chub
Cay, though the fishing along this 14-mile leg is outstanding. Best to keep
over the blue water, 10 to 15 fathoms, and troll. Here you can catch king
size grouper and bothersome barracuda most of the year, while trolling with
ballyhoo during April and May will fill your fish box with dolphin. To us
there is no better eating fish, which usually makes this passage one of our
leisurely ones.

   On the west end of Chub Cay, just north of Chub Point, which has a
ten-second, flashing red, sectored light, there is an anchorage where you are
protected from the prevailing easterlies. This cove carries a persistent surge
under most conditions, so anchor as far north and as close to the beach as
you can. The anchorage serves as the entrance to the semi-private Chub Cay
Club whose man-made marina ranks as one of the most complete in the
Islands. The Club was built in the early sixties by a splinter group of the

exclusive Key Largo Club in the Florida Keys, whose interests lay in the development of the Tongue of the Ocean as a sport fisherman's mecca. The venture has been successful as the record catches noted on the Club roster would indicate. Under the management of Nassau's Billy and Penny Turtle, the Club maintains rental units for its members and guests surrounding a pool-patio overlooking the cove. There's a well-stocked commissary, able mechanics available 'round the clock, and a 5,000-foot airstrip with daily flights to Nassau and Florida. Naturally the Club has a fleet of sport fishermen and bonefish skiffs for charter. Chub Cay is also a Port of Entry for the Bahamas, so if in your haste to reach Nassau you neglected to clear, you can do so here.

Immediately north of the Chub Cay Club is Crab Cay, a privately owned island. In the narrow channel which separates the two are several pools which will carry a draft of four feet at low water. Conveniently, the bottom is good holding in deep sand for the strong tidal flow that passes through.

❴ Frazers Hog Cay

The Berry Island Yacht Club at Frazers Hog Cay is no longer in operation. Once the only fuel source in the Berry Islands, the Club's fun bar has been quieted and the premises have fallen into disrepair. Only the anchorage remains, an uneasy one at best; it was the only reason for the Club's being built there in the first place. Frazers Hog Cay is a pretty island and several Americans have built winter residences on it.

The entrance to Frazers Hog Cay is easy to find, and to get in and out of in any weather. Head for the southern end of Bird Cay, when that is about half a mile east of you, turn and run north into the anchorage, which will be plainly visible with its high stand of coconut trees lining the shore. Keep close to the Frazers Hog Cay side of the opening, as the channel runs along that shore, about 100 feet from the shore at the entrance. The shoals to the eastward are plainly visible in the daytime, having only about two feet of water on them. There is nine feet of water at the entrance at low tide and about two fathoms inside. A little over a mile up this channel and just beyond a point of land lies the old yacht club and dock. There is seven feet of water at the dock at low tide. The best anchorage is a half mile beyond, with good holding ground in about three fathoms of water. Boats of shallow draft (3–4 ft.) can continue up this channel and cruise up the Berry Islands, keeping on the lee side all the way. North of Frazers Hog Cay around the Fish Cays the bonefishing is great, while crawfishing around Cockroach Cay can be most productive.

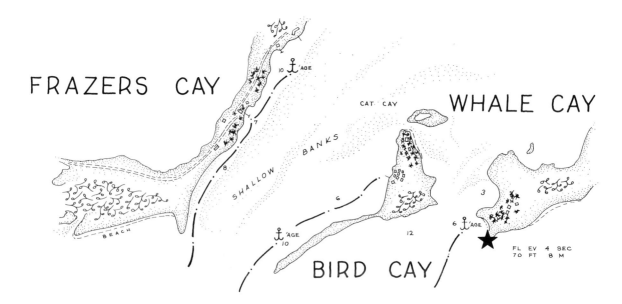

FRAZERS CAY
WHALE CAY
CAT CAY
BIRD CAY

FL EV 4 SEC
70 FT 8 M

◖ Bird Cay

Conspicuous with its prominent stand of casuarinas, this cay is the next island east of Frazers Hog Cay. There is a small anchorage with good shelter from easterly winds inside the west end of the island with ten feet of water at low tide. This is abreast of the quarry, where stone was obtained for the various buildings which were erected on the island. An Englishman, Francis Francis, owns Bird Cay and has developed it into one of the most attractive and self-sufficient private "kingdoms" in the Bahamas. The manor house, which, unlike most Bahama great houses, does not face the sea, stands on the north end of the Cay, facing the inner waters of the banks.

Mr. Francis's excellent island manager, and an inexhaustible source of information on the Southern Berry Islands and New Providence, is Gerry Leonard, who with his delightful family, has been in residence on Bird Cay for upwards of 20 years. Gerry's Bahamian work force, most of whom have been imported from Nassau, have the benefit of all modern conveniences set in a charming "old world" community which includes homes, church, community building, commissary, and an unbelievable garage-paint shop-carpentry complex. An invitation to go ashore is needed before any visiting party should be initiated.

◖ Whale Cay

This is the private island of Marion Carstairs, an Englishwoman well known for her speedboat racing and aviation interest in past years. The establishment of this island was once a model of enterprise and efficiency.

There are a number of houses, including a large manor house, church, schoolhouse, and general store. Miss Carstairs now lives in Miami, Florida, and the island, being private property, should not be visited without her permission. There is a resident caretaker.

There is a light on the southwest end of Whale Cay which, though untended, is quite reliable. It is 70 feet high, flashing white every four seconds and is visible eight miles. West and north of this light is a nice cove called Buckle Cut, where anchorage can be had in six feet of water at low tide. You are well protected from easterly winds here, but it is not a quiet anchorage as the sea swell tends to work in around Whale Point. A better anchorage will be found at the north end of the island between Whale Cay and Little Whale Cay.

The entrance to Little Whale anchorage is quite straightforward, the deepest water being on the north side of the channel. When heading north at sea you will not see this entrance until you are abreast of it, as the two islands, being close together, appear at a distance to be only one island. However, when you get closer you will see a stone monument on the southeast end of Little Whale Cay, and a pole marker on the northerly end of Whale Cay; the entrance cut is between the two. A reef extends east for about 100 yards from the northeast point of Whale Cay where good water is found. After clearing this reef, head in due west. You will see a rock almost in the middle of the channel. This can be passed on either side, but the best water is north of it. There is a minimum depth of eleven feet, at low tide, in this channel.

The anchorage inside is well protected on the north and south by the two islands and by the shallow banks to the west. The best holding ground is immediatley west of the concrete pier on Whale Cay where you will be well out of the surge that rolls in through the entrance cut.

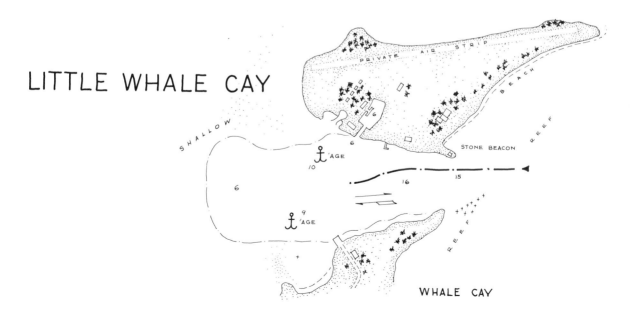

LITTLE WHALE CAY

WHALE CAY

⟪ Little Whale Cay

This lovely little island lies just north of Whale Cay. It is the vacation home of Mr. and Mrs. Wallace Groves of Freeport, Grand Bahama, and being private property should not be visited without permission of the caretaker, Captain Kenneth Lightbourne, who usually extends the hospitality of the cay to the occasional visitor if he is not too busy to show them around.

Little Whale Cay has been owned by the Groves for almost 40 years and has been developed exclusively as a winter home and hobby; no commercial activities are operated there. It is about 100 acres in area, with several attractive beaches and the highest elevation is about 50 feet. All of the land is either landscaped or occupied by buildings. A Bahamian service force lives on the Cay, having their own combination "Our Lady Star of the Sea" church and community hall. The other buildings consist of the main residence, guest house, manager's house, boat captain's houses, machine shop, warehouse, and extensive workers' quarters. A charming and perfectly protected yacht harbour has been constructed inland on the southwest side of the cay and a 1,200-foot hard-packed coral airstrip has been cleared on the north side. There is also an inland fresh water lake covering about five acres, one of the very few to be found in the Bahamas. The cay is fairly self-sufficient with greenhouse and irrigated garden, several farm animals, and a highly developed flock of fowl consisting of native domesticated teal and mallard ducks, Canada geese, turkeys, guineas, and an assortment of wild ornamental fowls.

⟪ Bonds Cay

Steep-to on the ocean side, shoal on the west side, no anchorage anywhere. There is a passage with a minimum depth of 2½ fathoms from the sea to the inside bank between the north end of Bonds Cay and the south end of Alder Cay. However, this passage is fairly narrow as rocks extend out from the shore on both sides. The passage north of Frozen Cay is much better. Bonds Cay is the property of realtor Conway Kitteridge of Orlando, Florida.

ALDER CAY ANCHORAGE

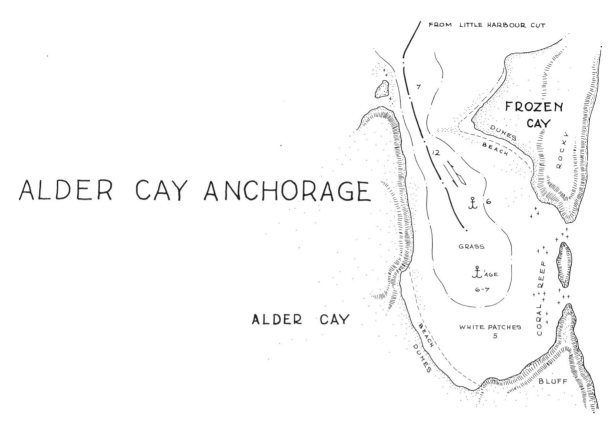

⟨ Frozen Cay and Alder Cay

There is a good wide entrance from the sea between the north end of Frozen Cay and the south end of Little Harbour Cay. The only obstruction to it is a lone rock lying a quarter of a mile southeast of the south end of Little Harbour Cay. The minimum depth over the bar is three fathoms.

A small inner harbour, called Alder Harbour, lies between Alder Cay and Frozen Cay in the bight formed by Alder Cay on its northeast side. This is at the extreme southern entrance of Frozen Cay. Steer south along the west side of Frozen Cay until you see the entrance, then southeast into it. There is five feet on the bar at low tide, and nine feet inside. On the chart this harbour appears to be wide open to the sea. Actually it is well protected by a series of reefs on the seaward side, and a good smooth anchorage in ordinary weather. We have lain here for a week at a time watching the moon rise and the Miami-bound cruiseships out of Nassau slip northward across its path. The high bluffs lining the south side of the anchorage are a rookery for brown noddys and terns while the clean beach and sand spit on the north side, which usually abounds with conch, make Alder Harbour one of the most interesting remote anchorages in the Bahamas. Both Alder and Frozen cays are the property of Willard F. Rockwell of Pittsburgh, Pa., who looks with favor on keeping the area a bird sanctuary.

LITTLE HARBOUR

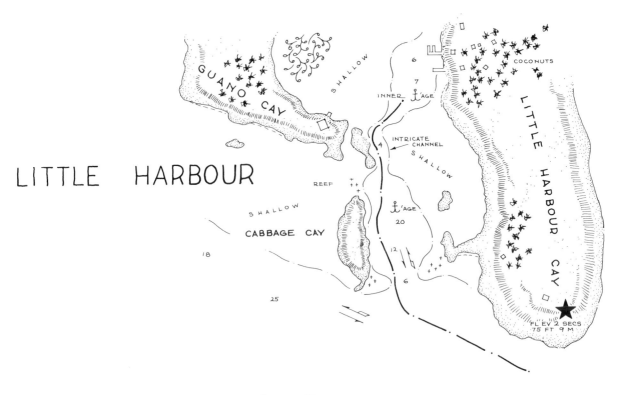

⟨ Little Harbour Cay

Here is the best natural harbour in the Berry Islands. It is well named, the inner harbour being little, snug, and a veritable hurricane hole.

Little Harbour Cay is easy to distinguish, high and bold, with a light on a pole high up on the hill at its southeast end. This light is usually not lighted and must not be depended upon. Coming in from the sea keep about 100 yards off the beach while rounding the southern end of the cay, to avoid the sunken rock which lies a quarter of a mile southeast of the point.

You will then see a small rocky cay lying about 200 yards west of the south end of Little Harbour Cay. This is called Cabbage Cay, and the entrance to the harbour lies between it and Little Harbour Cay, favoring the western side of the channel. A draft of six feet can be taken in at low tide, and depths up to 2½ fathoms will be found inside. The best anchorage is about 50 yards east of the north end of Cabbage Cay, in 2½ fathoms. Here you are well protected in winds from every direction, though it is not always glassy smooth. Sometimes if the wind is in the southeast, and there is much sea outside, a surge will come in around the point and be uncomfortable, though never dangerous.

The inner harbour, or hurricane hole, is a round basin opposite the settlement, about 200 yards north of the anchorage mentioned above. The passage in to it is both narrow and intricate, and should not be attempted except on a rising tide. We advise the use of a local pilot. If you are drawing more than four feet you will have to wait for high tide anyway, pilot or no pilot, and while you are waiting you can make a survey in your dinghy. The channel lies on the west side of the entrance, the deep water being between the grassy patches which are plainly visible. A draft of six feet can be taken in at high tide, and the rise and fall of tide here is about three feet. When once inside the basin it is advisable to anchor bow and stern, as there is not enough room to swing. There is six feet in the basin at low tide, and here it is as smooth as a millpond in any weather though the mosquitos are bad at times. The settlement is very small and friendly, fresh vegetables can be obtained, and limes from the biggest lime tree in all the Bahamas, in Mrs. Lightbourne's front yard.

Little Harbour Cay to Bullocks Harbour—the Banks passage from Little Harbour to Bullocks Harbour as outlined in the *Yachtsman's Guide*—is an intricate shoal water route over shifting sand bars for vessels of four feet draft only, and should not be attempted without the aid of a local pilot. The run north in the lee of the cays to the Market Fish Cays is good for 3½ feet in any tide and is comparatively straightforward. The cut between Market Fish and Abner cays is wide open and easy to negotiate in most weather.

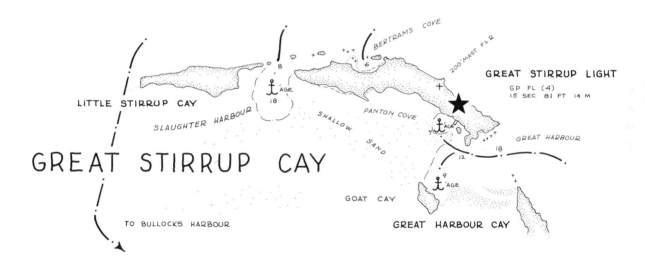

⟨ Great Harbour

The light on Great Stirrup Cay is one of the most important in the Bahama Islands, marking this critical corner of the Northwest Providence Channel. It is a group flash (four) every fifteen seconds, 81 feet high, visible 14 miles. The 200-foot U.S. tracking station tower located 150 yards northwest of the lighthouse has a flashing red light at its top which is visible 18 miles on a clear night. The entrance, between the north end of Great Harbour Cay and the east end of Great Stirrup Cay, is three-eighths of a mile wide and 3½ fathoms deep. Goat Cay, a high wooded island, lies on the southwest side of the harbour and is a good mark to steer for. You can carry a draft of seven feet at low tide to within 100 yards of Goat Cay.

Great Harbour is a poor place to lie and the devil of a place to get out of in a northeaster. With the prevailing trade winds there is nearly always an uncomfortable roll from the sea as the entrance is wide open to the northeast. For a smooth anchorage you must proceed northwest into Panton Cove, or all the way around Little Stirrup Cay into Bullocks Harbour. The passage into Panton Cove lies close along the southeast point of Great Stirrup Cay, paralleling that shore, about 50 yards off the beach, in a northwest direction, for a quarter of a mile, until past the little cay (Snake Cay) in the cove. This cay has a pole marker on it. Anchor with the lighthouse bearing about NNE. The maximum draft which can be taken in here at low tide is seven feet. The edge of the shallow bank to the West is only 200 feet from Snake Cay.

(Bullocks Harbour

This harbour lies on the bank side of Great Harbour Cay, between Bamboo Cay and Cistern Cay, about 3½ miles south of Great Harbour. Bullocks Harbour is the anchorage most favored by the fishing fleet in this area as a crawfish station is located here and the mangrove creeks north of the harbour are relied upon for hurricane protection. There is a bustling small settlement bordering the south side of the harbour which, until recently, relied almost entirely on the crawfishing industry for its existence. Now it provides much of the work force for the huge Great Harbour Cay real estate development to the South.

At Bullocks Harbour a nice person to know is Mrs. Popel, who at one time served as resident nurse and operated the only grocery store and restaurant on the island. Now, with a booming community crowding up around her and her medical responsibilities turned over to the company clinic, she smiles across an immaculate, oil cloth covered table in her sparsely patronized restaurant and warmly agrees that the current prosperity is bound to bring changes, concluding with, "most of them should be for the better," reassuring us, and herself as well.

The best route into Bullocks Harbour is to use the development's channel markers which will guide you in from the west end of Little Stirrup Cay, five miles to the northwest. Permanent pole markers point out the best water over which vessels of 6½-foot draft can be carried in at low tide.

At the northwestern extremity of Bullocks Harbour the southwest point

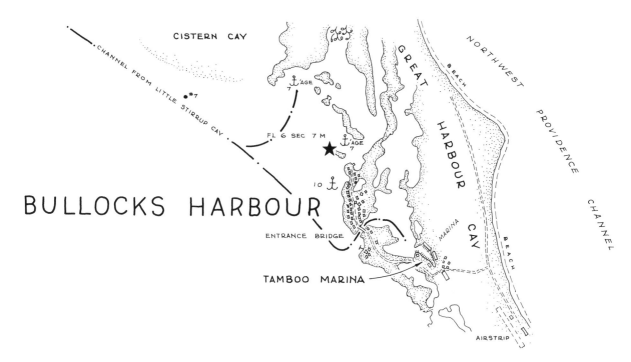

of Cistern Cay hooks around to the south and provides good protection in all winds from West to Southeast. The bight on the south end of Cistern Cay is lined with a sand beach, which is comparatively steep-to. You can literally run the bow of your boat right up to the beach and make your bowline fast to a tree. A wonderful place to lie in a mild norther.

◖ Great Harbour Cay

The luxurious new real estate venture on Great Harbour Cay is the brainchild of Freeport developer, Lou Chesler. It encompasses most of Great Harbour Cay and all of both Bamboo and Anderson Cays, all in all about 2,000 acres. Center of interest here is the $2 million dollar club house which is flanked on one side by a championship 18-hole golf course and on the other by an $8 million dollar, 90-slip marina. The development has its own 4,000-foot hard-surfaced airstrip and is a Port of Entry for the Bahamas.

Tamboo Marina is located on the inland waters between Bamboo Cay and Great Harbour Cay. This deep body of water is surrounded by high, steep elevations (70 feet is considered high in the Bahamas) and has been named "Bay of the Five Pirates." It should provide excellent cover from any conceivable weather. The entrance to the marina from the sea, described earlier, follows the long established route and a new cut was dredged across the middle of Bamboo Cay to gain access to the marina inside.

The cut inside is spanned by a swing bridge which can be opened if necessary and the marina office monitors 2182 KHz (M.V. Tamboo). Tam-

boo is a full service marina capable of accommodating boats up to 135 feet in length. Unique are the 60 or more waterfront townhouses set into the hillsides overlooking the bay. Each has it own private concrete dock with living quarters above, topped off with a garage and patio.

The entire establishment has an austerity reminiscent of Miami and Freeport, where imported service personnel working far from home reflect an almost dedicated disinterest in their jobs. Out of context here, this portion of the "brave, new world" is hard to relate to in a setting where only a few short years ago we careened "Spindrift" on the settlement waterfront with the help of the townspeople for lack of any marine repair facilities.

A half a mile south of the north point of Great Harbour Cay, overlooking a spectacular ocean beach to the east and the shallow south bight of Great Harbour to the west, Fred Pfister of New Jersey built a most attractive 20-unit hotel known as the Great Harbour Club. Constructed in large part by the hand of our talented artist/friend, Jim Watson of Buffalo, New York, it is a masterful job of combining the native stone building with the surrounding natural windswept terrain. Unfortunately, through lack of management, the club has been abandoned and nature's erosive processes have begun to take their toll.

([Slaughter Harbour

A poor harbour in a norther, but smooth in the prevailing easterlies. Numerous rocks obstruct the entrance but a draft of seven feet can be brought in without difficulty. It should not be attempted at night.

([Great Stirrup Cay

The most northerly of the Berry Islands and at one time considered the most important. During the reign of King William IV a town was laid out here, to be named Williamstown in honor of the King, and a customs house erected to collect his pocket money. The King died and so did the town. A few scattered ruins can still be found in the undergrowth ashore. The only inhabitants of the cay at present are the two lighthouse tenders, their families, and the tracking station crew. Anyone who sails the sea in his own ship cannot fail to respect the integrity of these men who tend the lights faithfully under all conditions of weather and human trial. You will find them pleasant people who will welcome your visit, and proudly insist that you climb the lighthouse staircase to see their brightly polished ward, then sign their visitors' log before you depart.

Opposite, Tamboo Marina is protected by high ground. *Bahamas Ministry of Tourism*

On visiting the U.S. tracking station a short walk away, surrounded by electronics equipment, you will find two either tremendously enthusiastic, or utterly bored, young Americans. Their comparatively short sojourn on "these rocks" has one of two affects on these men; if they are enjoying their stint their quarters will be cluttered with snorkling, diving, boating, and fishing equipment. If they are not, you are likely to find the TV on full blast and a sullen reception. In either case it is always a good place for an exchange of paperback books, the sailor's friend on many a long passage.

On the northwest side of Great Stirrup Cay there is a lovely bight called "Bertrams Cove," and adjacent to it on the east side is the tomb of Manuel Bertram, Commander of H.M.S. Tweed, whose survey work in the Bahamas is responsible in great measure for the basis of the N.O. series charts we use today. The tomb is in a remarkably good state of repair and bears the following inscription, in longhand, without any punctuation:

SACRED

To the memory of
Manuel Bertram
Late Commander of H.M.S. TWEED
Who departed this life of toil
July 20th 1834
After serving his country faithfully 33 years
Aged 44 years
O Bertram the man and the brother
Art thou gone and left forever
Hast thou crossed that unknown river
Life's dreary road
Like thee we shalt not find another
The world abroad
He was borne to the earth by the crew
That he died with he had the tears
Of the shipmates and prayers of his friends.

H.M.S. Tweed

Little Bahama Bank and Abaco Cays

⟨ Grand Bahama Island and Freeport

Grand Bahama Island itself is not a particularly pretty island, being low, flat, and heavily wooded. The pitch pine forest here is one of the largest stands of that variety of pine to be found anywhere in the world. There are a few nice coves and good sand beaches on the south side of the island. The north side is very shoal, with a maze of uncharted cays and mangrove swamps. However, having slumbered for most of its civilized existence, the island has suddenly emerged in the middle of this century as one of the most important developments in the Bahamas. This was largely due to the energy and foresight of Wallace Groves, an American financier who owns Little Whale Cay in the Berry Islands. Recognizing the potentialities of Grand Bahama's geographical position (adjacent to many of the more important shipping routes), Mr. Groves and his associates, notably the shipping magnate, Daniel K. Ludwig, and British millionaire, Charles Hayward, have built a tremendous industrial enterprise around Hawksbill Creek on the south side of Grand Bahama Island. This entire area of some 50,000 acres has been very aptly named "Freeport." The basic plan was for the bunkering of ships

Freeport's Harbour Inn Marina. *Bahamas Ministry of Tourism*

49

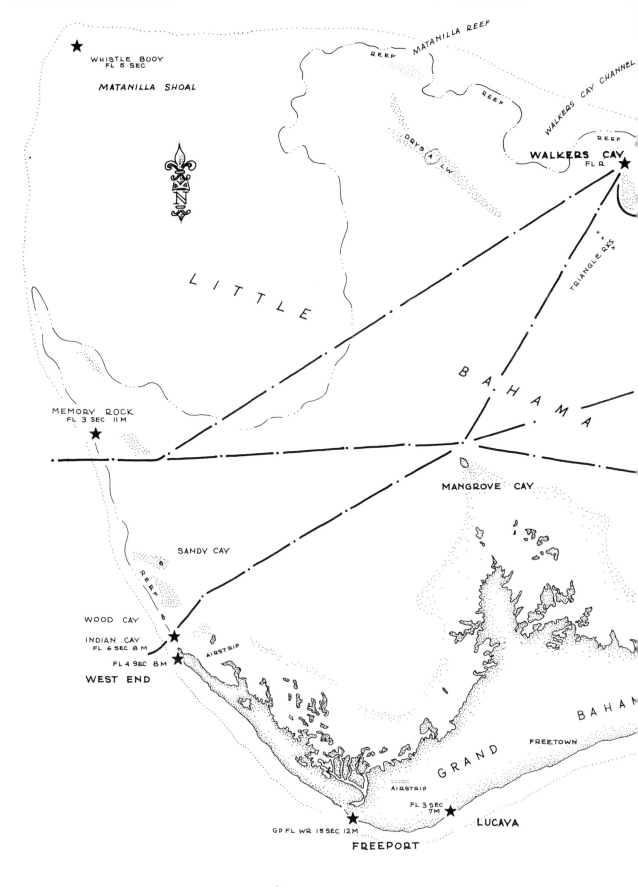

LITTLE BAHAMA BANK

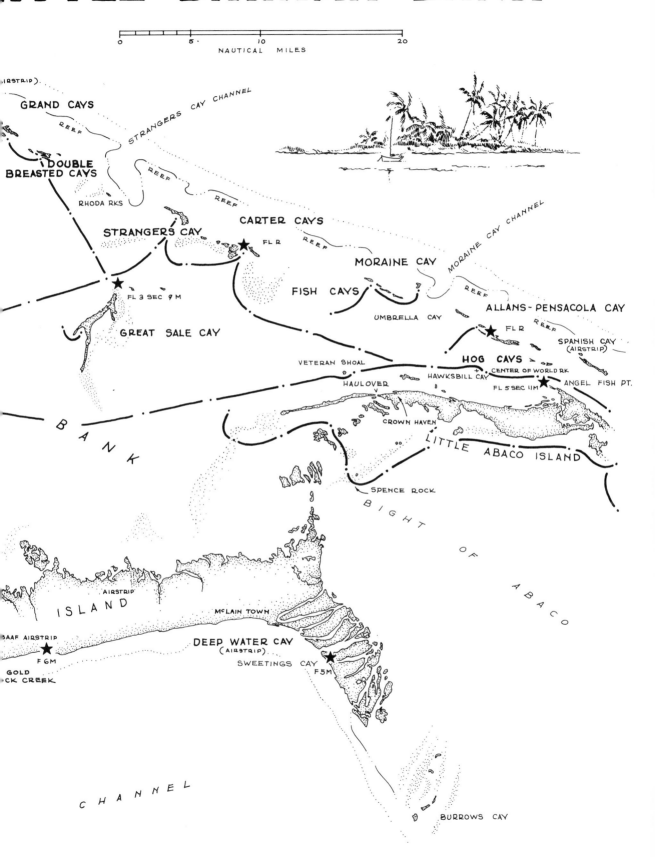

NAUTICAL MILES
0 5 10 20

(AIRSTRIP)

GRAND CAYS

REEF

STRANGERS CAY CHANNEL

DOUBLE
BREASTED CAYS

REEF

RHODA RKS

REEF

STRANGERS CAY

CARTER CAYS

FL R

REEF

MORAINE CAY CHANNEL

FL 3 SEC 9 M

MORAINE CAY

FISH CAYS

REEF

GREAT SALE CAY

UMBRELLA CAY

ALLANS-PENSACOLA CAY

FL R

REEF

SPANISH CAY
(AIRSTRIP)

VETERAN SHOAL

HOG CAYS

HAWKSBILL CAY

CENTER OF WORLD RK

FL 5 SEC 11 M

ANGEL FISH PT.

HAULOVER

B A N K

CROWN HAVEN

LITTLE ABACO ISLAND

SPENCE ROCK

B I G H T

O F

A B A C O

ISLAND

AIRSTRIP

McLAIN TOWN

BAAF AIRSTRIP

F 6 M

DEEP WATER CAY
(AIRSTRIP)

SWEETINGS CAY

F 5 M

GOLD
CK CREEK

C H A N N E L

BURROWS CAY

and required the erection of large storage tanks on shore. These are piped offshore to the moorings, where there is a minimum depth of 45 feet so that vessels can fill their tanks without having to enter a harbour, a considerable saving in both time and money. These moorings lie half a mile offshore, and are served by an 18-inch Bunker "C" pipeline, an 8-inch diesel pipeline, and a fresh water pipeline. Bunker fuel can be delivered to a ship at the rate of 5,000 barrels per hour.

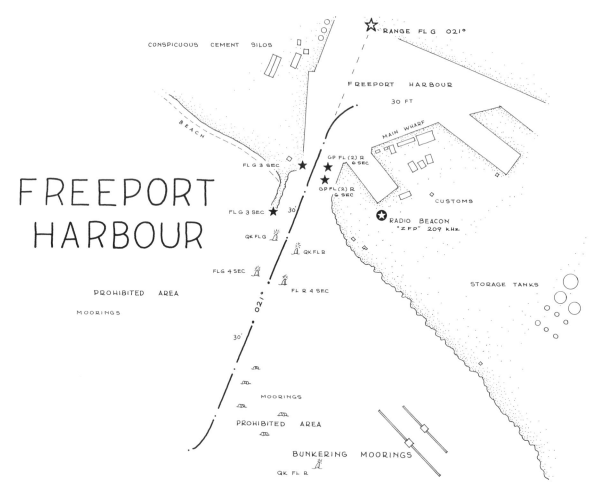

Freeport Harbour was dredged from what used to be Hawksbill Creek and carries 30 feet of water. Ocean-going cruise ships can tie up at the modern pier here to discharge their passengers intending a visit to the gala new tourist facilities and gambling casinos at Lucaya, seven miles to the east.

There is no law in the Bahamas allowing the Government to generally exempt companies from future taxes on income, capital gains, etc. There is, however, a law known as the Hawksbill Creek Grand Bahama (Deep Water Harbour and Industrial Area) Act of 1955, under which the Government of the Bahama Islands entered into an agreement with the Grand Bahama Port Authority, Ltd., under which the Port Authority acquired from the Crown 50,000 acres of land for the purpose of developing it as an industrial and commercial estate served by suitable port and harbour facilities. This area is known as Freeport. Under this Act, business firms operating in this free port will pay no income taxes, no capital gains taxes, no real estate taxes, and no personal property taxes for 30 years from 1955. In addition, for 99 years from 1955, no customs taxes, no customs duties, except on foods for personal consumption, and no taxes on bank remittances will be paid. This act was an agreement and contract between the Bahamas Government and the Grand Bahama Port Authority under which the tax exemption was granted in consideration of the Port Authority carrying out certain major harbour work on that island.

Many large industrial firms were attracted by the advantages of Freeport and the whole area has rapidly expanded into a city of commercial importance. In the short fifteen years of its existance its population has grown to 16,000; fifteen hotels have been built, offering a total of 3,380 rooms, while residential land sales have fostered the dredging of over 50 miles of navigable canals with six outlets to the sea. Freeport's skyline from offshore now has all the appearances of a miniature Miami Beach!

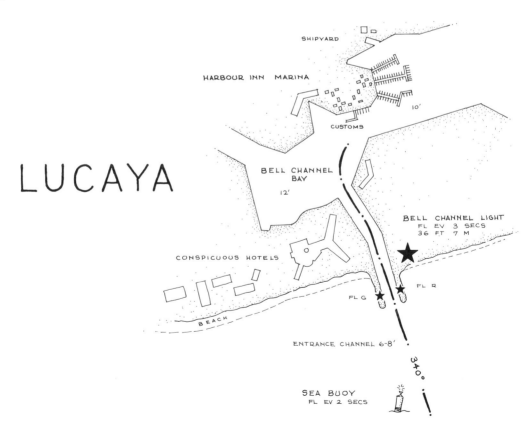

Even though Freeport and Lucaya are situated well off the protected cruising lanes and the coast along here offers little more than an uncomfortable lee shore, there are ample facilities for small boats at the well-equipped marinas inside. Harbour Inn Marina on Bell Channel Bay, serving as Lucaya's Port of Entry, offers the services of a customs officer in attendance right on the dock and an elaborate shipyard with a 30-ton travel lift lies immediately north of the marina.

It was within a mile or two of the entrance to Bell Channel Bay that the Freeport "Beach Boys" made their 2½ million dollar treasure find in 1964. The heavily encrusted wreck, which yielded 15,000 pieces of Spanish silver coin, lay almost undistinguishable a few hundred yards offshore in shallow water. As it happened, it was the remains of a ship of the Spanish fleet which Dutch Admiral Hyens had captured off Cuba in 1628. As he was escorting his spoils toward Holland a storm had forced two of the overladen vessels ashore. The Freeport "Beach Boys" had found one of them. Curses and superstition, often linked so closely with treasure, must have accompanied this find, as the "Boys," plagued with governmental red tape and salvage expenses far beyond their means, realized little for their efforts but the thrill of discovery and $100,000 in debts. The coins, suddenly flooding a collector's market, were eventually authenticated by a London dealer and are now in Bahamas' shops, so that the "Beach Boys" may retrieve some of their share.

Unique in Freeport is the International Bazaar, six acres of shops and buildings representing every major country in the world. An architectural nightmare, with its conglomeration of European, Oriental, South American, and Asian curio shops and restaurants, the Bazaar offers some genuine foreign imports at attractive prices as well as hours of fascinating browsing.

Freeport is so spread out we would advise renting a car so you can enjoy everything, such as a swim off powdery Taino Beach. Take along a quick change so you can stay on for cocktails and an excellent steak at the Stoned Crab, an unusual piece of pyramidal architecture, but a beachcomber's delight, overlooking the shore east of the city.

Probably the most important single attraction at Freeport has been its legalized gambling. The two exotic casinos there rival only Las Vegas in their elegance and have vexed Miami Beach promoters with their nightly gambling flights from the mainland. In the 1966 Bahamas general elections the casinos, along with the Hawksbill Creek Act, played an important role as prime targets for the opposition, who contended that the Bahamian people were not getting their fair share from the Freeport adventure. Unfairly the world press leaped onto the bandwagon, spotlighted the casinos in several controversial, half-fact-half-fiction exposés, and left a lasting blemish on the community as a whole.

Many have wondered how Freeport has faired since the change of Government. The Hawksbill Creek Act, as originally written, still applies; however, in the new Government's zeal to better the living standards of the people, it has unintentionally inhibited foreign interests there. The foreign investor with a business already established ashore now finds it increasingly difficult to renew work permits for his key employees and his alternate choice of local help is not always the best solution to his problem. This, we have no doubt, is the result of little more than growing pains, which only time, effort, and patience will heal.

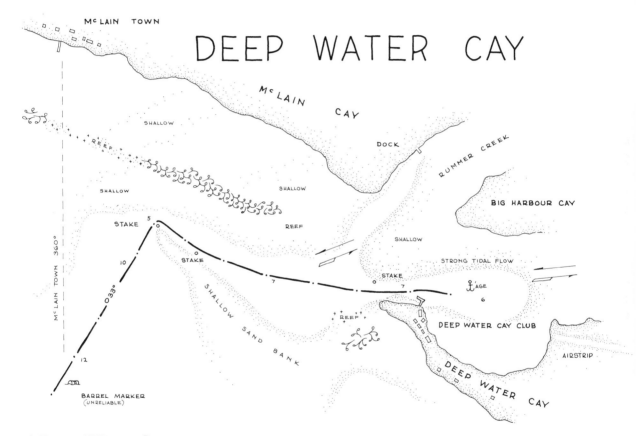

◖ Deep Water Cay

At the eastern end of Grand Bahama on what is defined on the charts as Carrion Crow Harbour, Gil Drake of Palm Beach maintains a unique fishing camp. All petroleum products are available at the camp dock which will accomodate several game fishing vessels of moderate size. The anchorage, which carries 6 to 7 feet, lies just east of the dock and is well protected by the nearby shallow conch beds. The entrance channel will carry four feet at low water with care taken for shifting sand bars.

Ashore, the Deep Water Cay Club, which is open October through July each year, offers a cozy atmosphere with its panelled lodge situated high on the cay overlooking the surrounding banks. Naturally, fishing is the main topic of conversation here, the Club specializing in every type. The nearby bonefish flats are considered some of the most productive in the Bahamas. Immediately east of the Club, Gil maintains a 2,200-foot grass airstrip which is sometimes soft after a heavy rain. Best to contact his Palm Beach office if you intend using it.

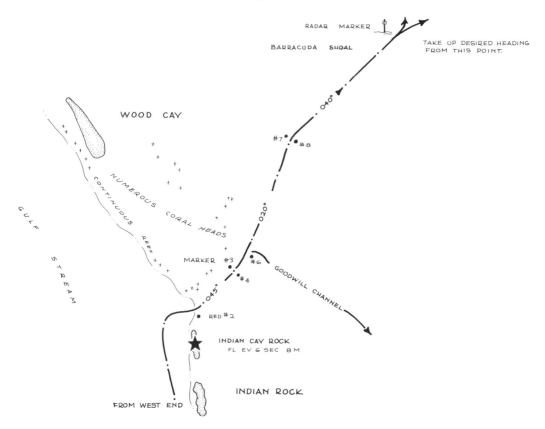

◖ Little Bahama Bank

On departing the marina at West End (as descibed in Chapter 3), cruise north past Indian Cay Rock and enter the bank via the well-marked channel there. A strong tidal rip is usually experienced in this channel and even though the markers are equipped with automatic flashers, we do not recommend negotiating this channel in the hours of darkness until one is completely familar with the prevailing conditions. Having passed the markers, the stake and the entrance to the Goodwill Channel, continue on a heading indicated on the accompanying sketch chart to Barracuda Shoal, at

which time you may take up a heading to Mangrove Cay. This passage is good for boats drawing no more than five feet. You will now be passing over the Little Bahama Bank and if it is a calm day, you will be able to see the sea gardens below you for hours on end in two fathoms of water, clear as crystal. We used to string two steering lines from the wheel at the stern to our perch on the bowsprit where we would gaze, fascinated, at our shadow gliding across the bottom, scattering schools of fish before it.

Yacht harbour at West End. *Bahamas Ministry of Tourism*

ABANDONED TOWER

⚓ 6

MANGROVE CAY

THICK MANGROVES

◖ Mangrove Cay

Mangrove Cay is identified as the northernmost cay in the myriad of islands bordering the north shore of Grand Bahama Island. It is about a mile long and has an abandoned tower on its northern end which was used in a recent survey of these islands by a U.S. geodetic survey team. The island offers no more than a comfortable lee with good holding (sand) around its perimeter, except to the southeast where there are some submerged rocks. The island can be passed to the south if your boat draws no more than 3½ feet; however, the water on the north side is generally better, carrying almost two fathoms all the way to Great Sale Cay, 21 miles farther to the east.

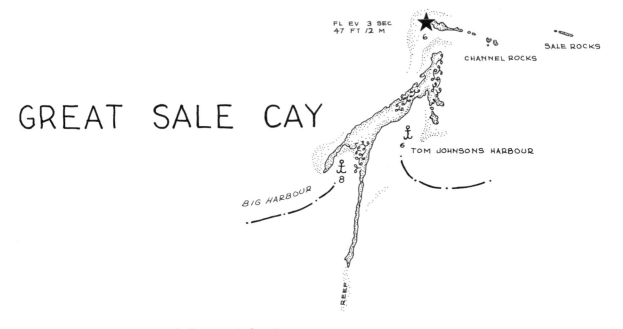

◖ Great Sale Cay

Great Sale Cay lies north and south and is 5½ miles long. Immediately to the north of it lies Little Sale Cay, on which stands a light, flashing every three seconds, and visible 9 miles. Great Sale Cay is low, rocky and, for the most part, covered by scrub. Of the two harbours there, Big Harbour, which lies under the small spit extending from the western side of the island, is the best. Big Harbour carries 7 to 9 feet over a good holding mud bottom and offers good protection from W through N through SE. The protecting western spit was once the site of a U.S. Missile Tracking Station, but was wrapped up and taken home in the early sixties, leaving the foundations still intact. The western anchorage, known locally as Tom Johnson's Harbour, is quite shallow but offers a good lee from the northwest. Great Sale Cay, like Mangrove Cay, is a good place to anchor for the night when you are bound east or west across the Little Bahama Bank.

If proceeding east from Great Sale Cay and your boat carries no more than five feet draft, give the southern point at least a four-mile berth to avoid the rocky shoal that extends southeastward as there is only 2 to 3 feet on it at low tide. From there you can continue on an easterly course to West End Rocks, Veteran Shoal, Hawksbill Cays, and Center of the World Rock before rounding the northwestern tip of Great Abaco Island bound for the Abaco Cays.

Incidentally, there is nothing on Center of the World Rock to indicate the center of the world. It is a plain, barren rock about eight feet high and serves merely as a seagull rest.

If your boat draws more than five feet, your departure from Great Sale Cay should be via Barracuda Rocks Channel. This will take you 'round the north end of Little Sale Cay, being careful to avoid the shallow sponge bar that extends over a mile westward from the north end of the island.

Fuel is available at the Crown Haven concrete wharf which lies south of the Pear Cays. Fresh fruits and vegetables can be purchased here as the season provides.

A few hundred yards west is Haulover Cut, a narrow cut through the island in which the tide flows at a spectacular rate. This small waterway through which the local smack boats sail at high slack was provided many years ago by the Bahama Government to save time for the fishing boats which worked both sides of Little Abaco Island. It's a real thrill to sluice through here in your dinghy on an incoming tide, but be careful of the winding channel at the south end as it takes a deft hand on the tiller to avoid the rocks.

◖ Bight of Abaco

The western end of Little Abaco marks the northern entrance to the Bight of Abaco (see charts of Little Bahama Bank and Great Abaco)—a remote, unpopulated area of the Bahamas that is seldom visited by cruising yachtsmen and as seldom fished, even by the far flung Spanish Wells fleet. The "Bight" comprises a cruising area of about 1,000 square miles extending down the lee of Great Abaco from Cave Cay at the north to Sandy Point at the South and is bordered on its NE perimter by a myriad of cays of every description. Here cover can be found from any conceivable wind. Cruising the Bight is an interesting experience, especially for the individual who wants to go it alone. And if you're a sailor and have the choice, we would suggest entering the Bight at Sandy Point and sailing up the lee of the cays with the prevailing wind on your quarter. It will give you a lesiurely sail in protected water all the way.

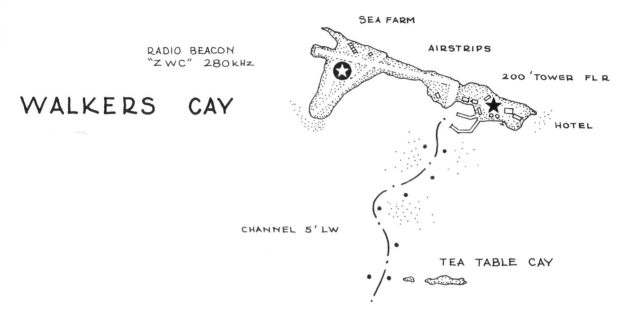

WALKERS CAY

RADIO BEACON
"ZWC" 280kHz

SEA FARM

AIRSTRIPS

200' TOWER FL R

HOTEL

CHANNEL 5' LW

TEA TABLE CAY

◖ Walker's Cay

Let us consider that you chose to sail from Mangrove Cay, the 23 miles to Walker's Cay direct. A little over midway you would sight Triangle Rocks about one mile south of course at approximately the same time you made your landfall on Walker's Cay, which is much higher, five miles beyond. Between Triangle Rocks and Walker's Cay there are a number of shallow sand bars that dry at low water and are plainly visible. They lie a short distance east of course and as you progress northward they converge onto Tea Table Cay, off the western end of which you will pick up the entrance channel stakes, which in turn will lead you into Walker's Cay Harbour.

With the exception of two small uninhabited cays lying close to it on the northwest side, Walker's Cay lies further to the west than any of the cays in the Abaco group, and is actually the most northerly of all the Bahamas. It is a charming little island about one mile long, 50 feet high and well wooded.

The harbour is on the south side near the east end of the island and it carries five feet of water at low tide, the rise and fall of the tide being about four feet. Because the southwest point of the island extends farther south than west, there is good protection here in a norther, the only bad breeze direction being from the southwest and the wind is seldom in that quarter.

Just before World War II, Walker's Cay was leased from the Bahamian Government for 99 years by a group headed by Palm Beach aviator-sportsman, "Buzz" Shonnard, whereupon it quickly obtained a reputation as one of the most popular game fishing resorts on the east coast. Several years ago Precision Valve Corporation of Yonkers, New York, bought the interests here and expanded the island's facilities considerably, including the opening of the Bahamas' only marine breeding station. The original hotel with its enormous lounge and stone fireplace served as the nucleus for a modern new 34-room addition with several outlying guest cottages situated around two swimming pools, fresh and salt water. The protective jetty was extended to completely enclose the harbour and with the new docks, snack bar, and tackle shop Walker's Cay now has a full service marina. This marina can supply all petroleum products, even aircraft fuel at the tiedown area adjacent to the two paved runways. Charter air service is available here with flying time to Palm Beach only 50 minutes.

Here, in four years' time, under conservation-minded, corporation president Robert Abplanalp, a maricultural farm has been established where studies are being made in the raising of crawfish, stone crab, turtle, shrimp, snails, and grouper. Last year (1971) 5 million conch were seeded on the banks surrounding Walker's Cay. These will have matured enough for harvesting by 1974. It is Mr. Abplanalp's noble belief that to properly run a sport fishing business one should at the same time be concerned with the propagation of the species. At Walker's Cay no fish cleaning is permitted on the docks. Instead, air conditioned cleaning rooms have been reserved for the purpose, and all scraps are ground up for fish feed and chumming. In this immaculate ecological environment bonefish have been caught as close in as the marina entrance. Walker's Cay is indeed a model fishing adventure that may in great measure point the way to a new era in world food farming.

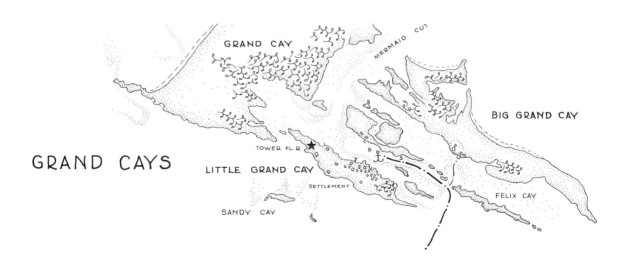

❨ Grand Cays

An archipelago of picturesque little cays with an inside harbour that will remind you of someplace in Maine. The entrance to this enchanting spot is shown in detail on the accompanying sketch chart and because it is rather intricate we suggest that you follow it closely. A five-foot draft can be taken into the settlement harbour at low tide where a yacht can lie at anchor over a white marl bottom in 6 to 9 feet. As a strong tide runs through, the usual two anchors are recommended, setting them as described earlier, off the bow "Bahama style." Grand Cays settlement is basically a fishing village where the inhabitants who are not employed at Walker's Cay, five miles way, make their living pretty much from the sea alone. When approaching the island on a calm day you will see several small boats anchored with their crews diving for crawfish, conch, and the like. After you have anchored inside they will usually follow you in, stopping alongside to see if you want any fresh seafood, and if you like it as much as we do, take them up on their offer as the price will certainly be right. The settlement is an artist's dream with its weathered and brightly trimmed slanting shanties. There are no roads, no need for cars on this small cay, only steep paths from house to house. When one passes by he feels as though he's trespassing until he sees the welcome smiles framed in the open windows. Now you are in the Bahama Out Islands, far from the bustle of Bimini and West End, your Bahama cruise has finally begun and all at once you feel warmly welcome. At the New Palms Bar you don't have change for another tad of rum, but you get one just the same as everyone laughs and introduces themselves with the most enthusiastic handshakes you'll ever get. They tell you about when Harry Etheridge used to headquarter here and anchor his dinghy right where you are as he sketched the harbour on the spot. Then in a more serious tone they confide about the newer visitor from Washington who sometimes visits the big house on yonder cay to relax a few days and let the Bahama sun temporarily wash away a few of the world's cares. You will like Grand Cays, which incidentally is a Port of Entry for the Bahamas, and you will find it hard to tear yourself away.

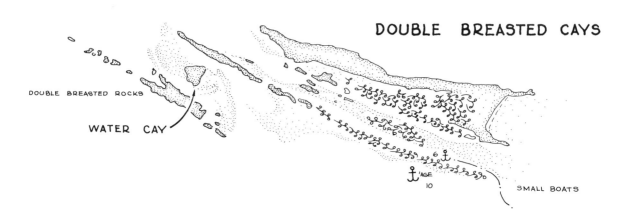

DOUBLE BREASTED CAYS

DOUBLE BREASTED ROCKS

WATER CAY

SMALL BOATS

❨ Double Breasted Cays

Much like Grand Cays, though uninhabited, Double Breasted Cays forms a miniature archipelago through which you can meander for hours finding something of interest at every turn. On our last visit we anchored midway off the south side and loaded the dinghy with "fixins" for a picnic and then meander we did, not being able to decide which of the little beaches would be the best choice until we fell upon Water Cay in the western bight. Here we discovered a tiny island surrounded by a perfect swimming beach with satiny smooth water. There was enough buttonwood in the underbrush to cook the crawfish we caught under a nearby rock and we wondered why it was named Water Cay until we dug a small hole and found fresh water there.

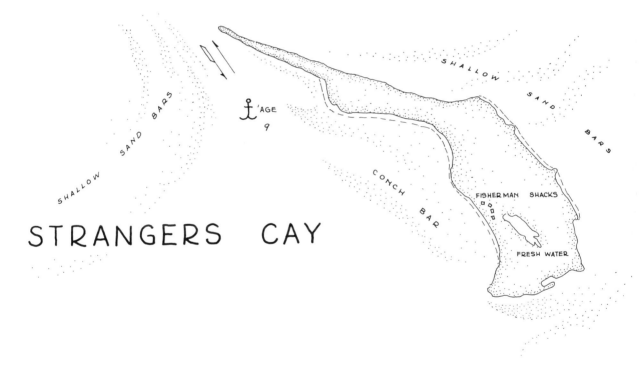

STRANGERS CAY

❨ Stranger's Cay

There is a good anchorage outside the shoal sand to the southwest of the cay which is approached on a line from Little Sale Cay. Care should be taken not to get entangled with the maze of horseshoe-shaped sand bores that extend south two miles from the east end of the island. Stranger's Cay is a pretty island, tufted at its highest point by a conspicuous stand of coconuts intermixed with citrus. Legend has it that the citrus and coconut were originally planted here along with a little sugar cane in the early 1800's, by a treasure-minded Englishman by the name of Villiers. It is said that the treasure he discovered in the caves on the hill eventually brought about his death at the hand of his brother-in-law. To this day local Bahamians are reluctant to enter the small, rocky caves here.

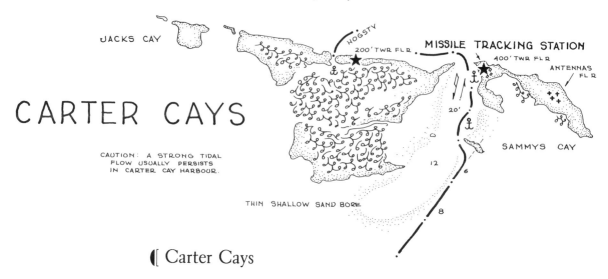

CARTER CAYS

CAUTION: A STRONG TIDAL FLOW USUALLY PERSISTS IN CARTER CAY HARBOUR.

JACKS CAY

HOGSTY 200' TWR FL R

MISSILE TRACKING STATION
400' TWR FL R
ANTENNAS FL R

SAMMYS CAY

THIN SHALLOW SAND BORE

❲ Carter Cays

An excellent landmark with its cluster of lighted, bayonet towers, the U.S. Tracking Station at Carter Cays can be seen for miles. The approach to the harbour under Little Carter Cay is an easy one following the accompanying chart. When anchoring off the settlement inside make certain that you are positioned well toward shore and out of the strong tidal flow and that your anchors are dug in. We spent a sleepless, squally night here many years ago playing "drag the anchor" with a small cruiser joining in alongside. The anchorage has a hard bottom and in our haste to get ashore upon our arrival we merely dropped the usual two anchors, backed down to snug them and went on our way. When we returned at sundown the small cruiser had anchored alongside, giving us little maneuvering room to dig ours in further. We retired, trusting to luck, only to be awakened at midnight for the gymnastics that were to continue into the wee hours. Classically the cruiser had dropped his single anchor forward of ours and he tripped us on the first gust. Had we been secure, our starboard anchor would have held us both comfortably for the night. Needless to say, the 22-mile sail to Grand Cays the next morning seemed an eternity and we've never visited Carter Cay since without going over the side to "kick in the hooks."

Ashore at Carter Cay there is a small seasonal settlement where the fishermen from Little Abaco camp during the fishing season. As there seems to be almost daily traffic between there, Crown Haven, and Fox Town, fruits and produce are sometimes available. Visitors are usually welcome at the tracking station, except when there is a shot scheduled at Cape Kennedy and all hands are on the job. The youthful crew usually welcome the sight of new faces, especially if they are feminine and unattached, whereupon all stops are pulled and an evening's entertainment of dancing is scheduled.

There is an interesting anchorage at Big Carter's Cay accessible through the northern entrance to Carter Cays Harbour. Because boats have been stored here in the mangroves for hurricanes it takes the name "Hogsty" or "safety hole." There is swinging room for one yacht or two small boats in the small anchorage which abounds with crawfish under its rocky ledges.

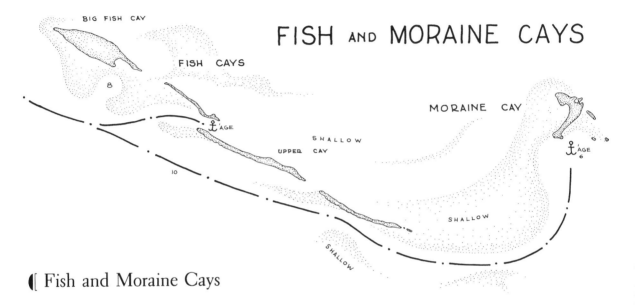

❰ Fish and Moraine Cays

Somewhat off the beaten track, this group of cays is for the small boatman who can get into the narrow anchorage between the Fish Cays and can find his way through the sand bores into Moraine Cay anchorage immediately to the east. A delightful fair weather cruising area.

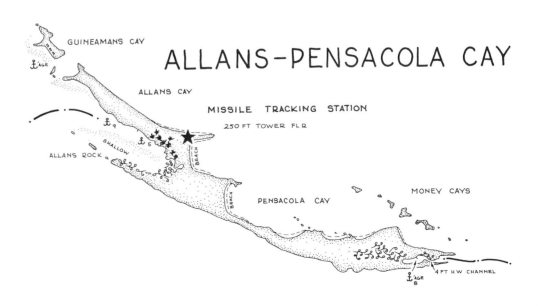

(Allan's-Pensacola Cay

Many years ago these two cays were linked together by a hurricane. They now join at the mangrove swash at the eastern end of the main harbour which is one of the best in the northern Abaco Cays and easy of access. There is a sizable land-locked hurricane hole at the east end of the cay with a narrow channel leading into it through which a yacht could be floated in an emergency. Again, the small crew at the tracking station are most hospitable when they are not busy. Guineaman Cay to the west serves as a crawfish station for the smacks from Great Abaco and always has a goodly supply of conch on its western beach.

(Hog Cay

One of the prettiest of the smaller cays in Abaco, Hog Cay has a tiny, protected inner harbour that is edged on its southern perimeter by a white sand beach. There's a coral head in the center where the colorful sea life of the shallows can be studied in complete protection.

(Great Abaco

Great Abaco is to the rest of the Bahamas as New England is to the United States, displaying a strong superiority towards the rest of the country's easy-going ways, just as New England scorns the Southerner's gentle luxuries. The Abaconians are sturdy individualists, and the austere way of life appeals to them. Their settlements are clean, compact, and well run, in the New England style. The people of Abaco are quite certain that their men are the best sailors, fishermen, spongers, boat builders, and lumberjacks in the Bahamas. I have heard nobody dispute the claim, though it has been suggested that they also were the most successful "wreckers" in their time.

You can spot an Abaco boat anywhere in the Islands by her shapely lines, superior construction, and shipshape condition. We venture that more good

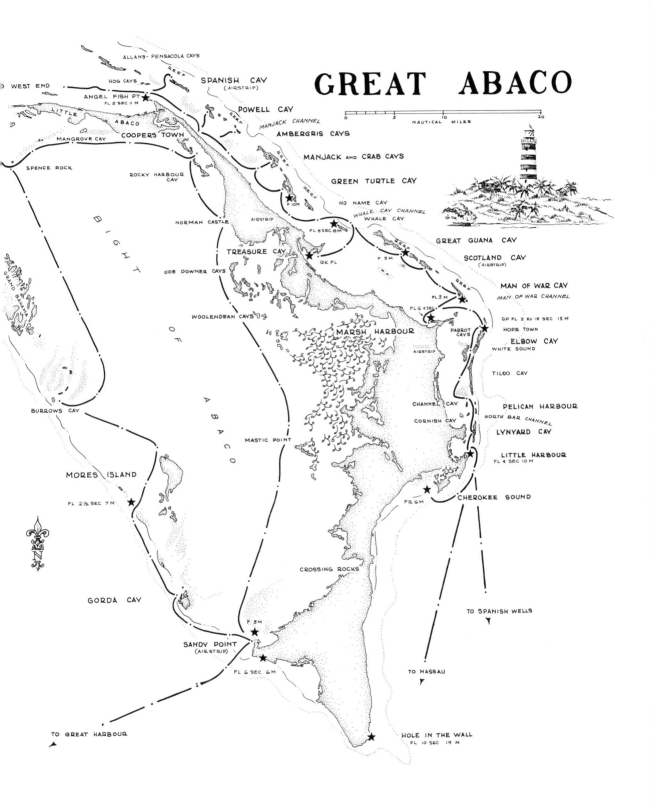

GREAT ABACO

NAUTICAL MILES

0   5   10   20

ALLANS - PENSACOLA CAYS

HOG CAYS

SPANISH CAY
(AIRSTRIP)

WEST END

ANGEL FISH PT
FL 5 SEC 11 M

POWELL CAY

LITTLE ABACO

MANJACK CHANNEL

COOPERS TOWN

AMBERGRIS CAYS

MANGROVE CAY

SPENCE ROCK

ROCKY HARBOUR CAY

MANJACK and CRAB CAYS

GREEN TURTLE CAY

NO NAME CAY

WHALE CAY CHANNEL

F 10M

WHALE CAY

NORMAN CASTLE

AIRSTRIP

FL 5 SEC 8 M

GREAT GUANA CAY

SCOTLAND CAY
(AIRSTRIP)

B I G H T

TREASURE CAY

QK FL

F 5 M

MAN OF WAR CAY

MAN OF WAR CHANNEL

JOE DOWNER CAYS

FL 3 M

GRAND BAHAMA

WOOLENDEAN CAYS

GP FL 5 EV 15 SEC 15 M

HOPE TOWN

ELBOW CAY

WHITE SOUND

O F

MARSH HARBOUR

FL G 43E5

PARROT CAYS

AIRSTRIP

TILOO CAY

A B A C O

CHANNEL CAY

PELICAN HARBOUR

CORNISH CAY

NORTH BAR CHANNEL

BURROWS CAY

MASTIC POINT

LYNYARD CAY

LITTLE HARBOUR
FL 4 SEC 10 M

MORES ISLAND

FL 2½ SEC 7 M

F R G M

CHEROKEE SOUND

CROSSING ROCKS

GORDA CAY

TO SPANISH WELLS

F 5 M

SANDY POINT
(AIRSTRIP)

FL 6 SEC 6 M

TO NASSAU

TO GREAT HARBOUR

HOLE IN THE WALL
FL 10 SEC 19 M

boats have been built at Abaco than in all the rest of the Bahamas combined. At one place alone—Marsh Harbour—they used to build a half dozen large schooners and a score of smaller boats every winter, starting them in the autumn and launching them in the spring. There is no more boat building at Marsh Harbour, however, the trade being carried on almost exclusively at Man of War Cay.

It is, of course, quite natural that the people of Abaco should admire and emulate the traditions of the sturdy New England folk, for the simple reason that they are descended from them. Loyalists came here from the United States after the American Revolution, and a plentiful sprinkling of New York and Boston Irish. It is recorded that 1,450 Northern Irishmen were shipped down from New York in the year 1783 and received a most hostile reception. However, some of them must have stuck it out, for most of the names in Hope Town today have a strong North of Ireland ring to them. Hope Town's Eddie Malone piloted us in to Man of War Cay many years ago, and a good pilot he was!

Boat building at Man of War Cay. *H. Kline*

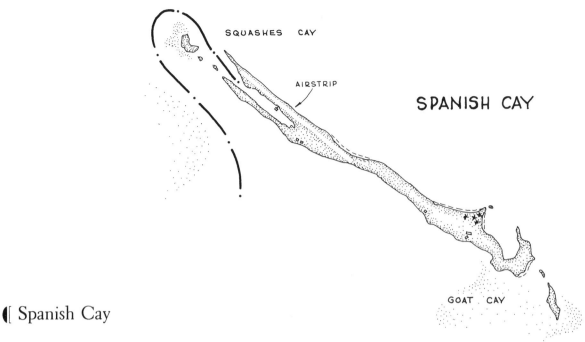

SQUASHES CAY

AIRSTRIP

SPANISH CAY

GOAT CAY

❲ Spanish Cay

Spanish Cay has an excellent harbour which lies adjacent to the private 3,200-foot hard-surfaced airstrip and is accessible via a rather shoal but well-staked channel around Squashes Cay at the west end of the island. However, Texas millionaire Clint Murchison, owner of the cay, entertains many dignitaries there, and has made it known that uninvited guests are not welcome. The main house is snuggled into the wooded hill at the east end of the island and overlooks its own private crescent of ocean beach. Several guest cottages line the driveway which extends east from the airstrip.

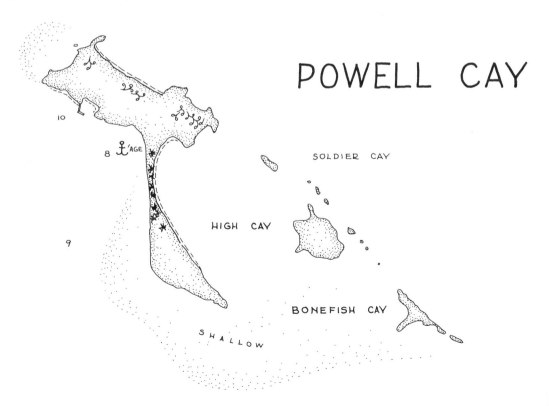

POWELL CAY

10

8 ⚓ 'AGE

SOLDIER CAY

HIGH CAY

9

BONEFISH CAY

SHALLOW

❨ Powell Cay

Powell Cay is high, wooded, has an abundant supply of sweet well water and some of the prettiest beaches in Abaco. There is a sturdy dock adjacent to the anchorage in the western lee of the island which is comfortable, with good holding. The island is being developed by Charles Martin of Stuart, Florida, though nothing much has happened to date. Tie up and go ashore; you will be most welcome and the ocean beach is an ideal place to stretch your legs.

❨ Angel Fish Point

Crab Cay is a long, high, rocky island that extends west from Angel Fish Point and marks the western extremity of Great Abaco Island. It has a light (flashing every 5 seconds, visibility 8 miles) at its western tip. Under prevailing conditions there is a good anchorage under the lee of this island in seven feet of water. From Angel Fish Point there is an average of two fathoms of water all along the shore of Great Abaco, past the friendly little settlement of Cooper's Town where there is a fuel dock, to Coco Plum Cay, and then over to Green Turtle Cay.

❨ Cooper's Town

Near the north end of Great Abaco Island, opposite Powell Cay, is the settlement of Cooper's Town. Here Medius Edgecombe operates a very handy fuel dock for those limited-range vessels that should top off their tanks before beginning the long trek to Florida via West End, Grand Bahama. On the hill overlooking the town and bay is Kenneth Major's Paradise Hill Hotel where a predominantly native menu attracts a local clientele for a night out on the town. Samuel Cooper, a former constable, tends the hurricane lantern at Cooper's Town. "Same one I've lit for the past fourteen years," he says, gesturing toward the rickety ladder and light pole at the water's edge. Mr. Cooper fell off the ladder during a blow two years ago and, considering his age, miraculously escaped injury. Most of the rural settlements in the Islands that have not been converted to electricity as yet still maintain a "hurricane lantern" that is lighted each night to guide the fishermen home. It is a matter of pride to be the lightkeeper even though the job pays very little, as only the most reliable citizens in the community are selected for the responsibility.

AMBERGRIS CAYS

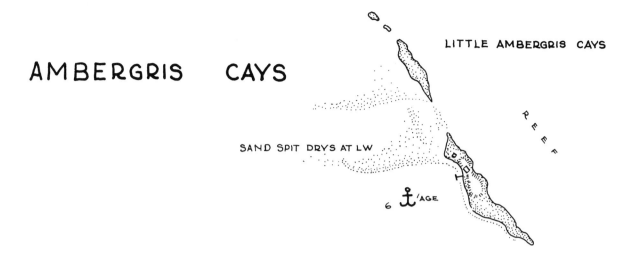

LITTLE AMBERGRIS CAYS

REEF

SAND SPIT DRYS AT LW

6 ⚓ 'AGE

❰ Ambergris Cays

The Ambergris Cays, which lie about three miles SE of Powell Cay, are the private property of John Butler of West Palm Beach, Florida. These cays are joined at low water by a sandy conch shoal which extends almost half a mile to the west, protecting the anchorage in the lee of the southernmost cay from northerly winds. The southern cay is the higher of the two with a prominent headland midway on the cay upon which the Butlers' summer cottage stands.

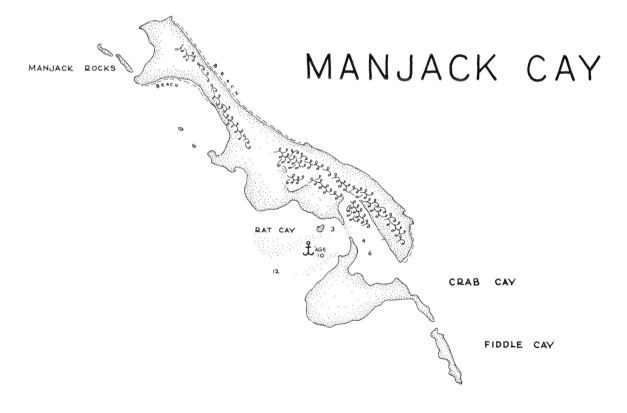

MANJACK CAY

MANJACK ROCKS

BEACH

BEACH

RAT CAY 3

⚓ AGE 10

4

6

12

CRAB CAY

FIDDLE CAY

⟨ Manjack and Crab Cay

Two and a half miles SE of Ambergris Cays lies Manjack Cay which again is joined to Crab Cay at its southern end by a sandy shoal. There is an excellent anchorage that will carry six feet at low water in the bight where the cays meet. Both of these islands are uninhabited, comparatively flat and covered with scrub. There are a number of excellent beaches, both facing the sound, while on the ocean side there are shallow creeks which will supply hours of interesting dinghy exploring. Local interests began developing Manjack Cay several years ago as the presence of several rusty pieces of earthmoving equipment would indicate. For the sake of the cruising yachtsman, however, we're delighted to see that Manjack still affords a comfortably remote, yet tranquil, anchorage. We like it that way.

⟨ Green Turtle Cay

Green Turtle Cay is an intriguing little island with a number of low hills, 40 to 60 feet high, and numerous caves and shallow sounds. There is a good entrance from the sea, four miles south of Green Turtle Cay. This channel, which is a half mile wide, lies just off the northwest end of Whale Cay and is known as Whale Cay Channel. There is a minimum depth of two fathoms over the bar and the best water into Green Turtle Cay lies along the shore of the Abaco mainland.

Lying on the extreme southern end of the Island behind Settlement Point is New Plymouth, one of the most picturesque settlements in the Bahamas. The houses and their inhabitants have a character and individuality that is not found elsewhere in the Islands. Even the narrow paved streets express a community pride that is strictly New England in its tidiness. There is a Church of England, a library, several well-stocked grocery stores, and Commissioner for the District has his headquarters here, which establishes Green Turtle Cay as a Port of Entry for the Bahamas. The comfortably colonial New Plymouth Inn is right in the center of the town. Its main building was erected 130 years ago as the French Exchange, where imports were warehoused and traded. The Inn's cistern served as a storage area for wreckers' loot; a veritable antique collector's dream come true when it was cleaned out and re-established as a cistern a few years ago.

The Inn is now operated by Donna and Bill Rossbach of Baltimore, Maryland, and with its typically "eastern shore" menu, has become a favorite stopover for cruising yachtsmen.

A walk through New Plymouth and up a flight of steps carved out of rock brings you to the schoolhouse, which has a fine view of the country. From here there is a beautiful path to the outer beach, leading through a feathery jumbay copse and palm tree grove. In the jumbay you will find the two hurricane shelters where all the townspeople can be completely protected from winds from every direction.

As you can see by studying the chart, Green Turtle Cay is a maritime community and the best way to visit it is by boat; whereupon you provide your own local transportation. We have cruised and flown to Green Turtle Cay, and found having our own boat there a real convenience. Their airstrip is a combination venture with the other communities on Great Abaco, two miles across the sound, with transportation to and from it by water taxi, a boat meeting all scheduled planes. Floyd Lowe runs a prompt, efficient, personalized service here rivaling only that of the Albury brothers at Man of War Cay, Marsh Harbour, and Hope Town.

Harold Lowe, as one of New Plymouth's leading citizens, and prominent boatman in the area, is the man to know regarding things nautical. It was Harold who rid the Inn's cistern of its worthless "junk" a few years ago. "We just threw out all them ships' binnacles, lanterns and stuff, no need having them clutter up the place," he jibes with a sly wink.

The town dock is on the northwest side of the town, and with the prevailing easterly winds the best place to anchor is off this dock, about 100 yards offshore. If the winds get around to the west, indicating the approach

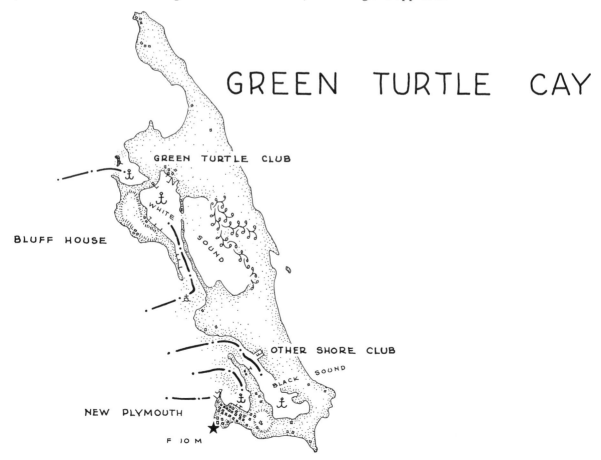

GREEN TURTLE CAY

Green Turtle Cay.
Bahamas Ministry of
Tourism

of a norther, you cannot lie here and should move to the inner harbour
known locally as Settlement Creek, which is in the cove on the north side
of the town. Once inside the harbour and surrounded by the town, you can
lie out anything in safety and comfort in six or eight feet of water. The
entrance channel is marked by stakes which should be left on the starboard
hand when entering.

A short distance to the north of New Plymouth there are two coves
entering deeply into the land, known as Black Sound and White Sound.
Each has a comparatively shallow but well-marked entrance with deep water
inside affording perfect protection in any weather. Vessels drawing up to six
feet should have no difficulty entering either sound at high tide.

On Black Sound, which borders the settlement to the east, Skip Wright
has installed a small lodge and guest house known as the Other Shore Club.
Skip offers housekeeping cottages for sixteen guests and most petroleum
products at his dock, while the town is only a short walk away.

Across Black Sound to the southeast, Doctor Curtis Mendelson of New
York has his winter home. Avid sportsman, yachtsman, and aviator, the
doctor can also testify to the game fishing off Green Turtle's ocean reef. In
1958 while trolling for dinner from his 12-foot Abaco dinghy he hooked into
a blue marlin which he fought and mastered. After towing it back to the
settlement he found it to measure almost six inches longer than his boat. On
another occasion, when fishing from his yacht, one of these monsters
charged the boat and buried its bill in the transom, then broke it off in order
to free itself. Doctor Mendelson treasures this transom plank as first hand
evidence of the fish that did not "quite get away!"

The newest and by far the most complete guest and marine facility at
Green Turtle Cay is the large, 14-room Green Turtle Cay Club, with its
cottages rambling up the hill on the northeast side of White Sound. A young

English couple, Roger and Sue Phillips, have built an attractive port-of-call for the marina hopping cruise buff who prefers to go foreign only so far as the limits of his air-conditioned yacht will permit. There's plenty of everything here to keep his vessel operating properly while the camaraderie of Roger's dockside bar will fill many an evening with cruising tales and Bahamas lore.

Certainly the *pièce de résistance* must be Pearce Coady's Bluff House Club with its spectacular view of the Sound and the islands to the south. It's a long climb up the hill from the dock on White Sound but the view and the food are well worth it. Pearce and Kitty Coady are real Abaco buffs, having sailed here from Rehoboth Beach, Maryland, almost twenty years ago. And being more host than innkeepers, the Club extends a quiet, deep-cushioned atmosphere in which everyone feels completely at ease. Descended from an old yachting family, Pearce has a way with boats, and it is not unusual to find him totally immersed in a visiting yacht's engine room, investigating some mechanical complaint. His current project is converting an ancient Cheasapeake Bay Oysterman into a charter yacht and as adjunct to the Club she will be used to make supply runs to Palm Beach. Below in "Cleopatra's Barge," as she is aptly named, one will find the Bluff House Club's comfortable atmosphere reflected in soft lit cabins hung with Homer prints and filled with classical music. The final touch is her superstructure —painted a bright, happy yellow to match the Club itself—the Coadys are indeed a standout, in more ways than one, at Green Turtle Cay.

Vessels proceeding southeastward from Green Turtle Cay will have to go outside through Whale Cay Channel, unless is it high tide and they do not draw over five feet. The shoals between Whale Cay and Sandbank Point on the Abaco shore have only three feet on them at low tide.

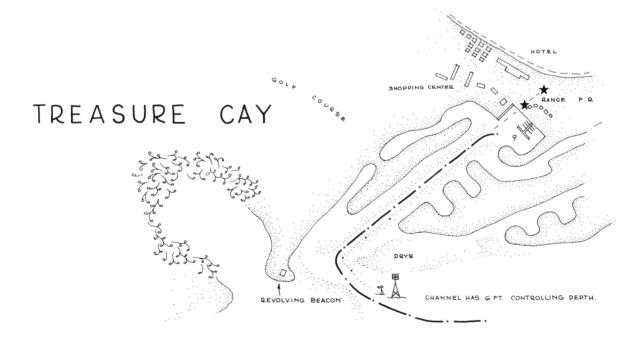

⟪ Treasure Cay

Under Sandbank Cays, Texas automobile dealer Dumas Milner has built a completely Americanized tourist resort, boasting an 18-hole golf course and a 160-room hotel facing a fresh water pool with a protected 40-slip marina containing all marine facilities only a short walk away. Here one will find all the conveniences—grocery store, grog shop, laundry, marine supplies, and the best fresh water in all of Abaco. Naturally a facility of this size makes a major contribution to the economy of the nearby settlements from which its labor force is drawn, but it seems a pity that it cannot at the same time reflect a more genuine feeling of the Islands.

⟪ Great Guana Cay

Though not nearly as large, the settlement at Great Guana Cay will remind you of a rural version of Green Turtle's New Plymouth. The small but industrious populace are mainly farmers and fishermen, so seasonable fruits, vegetables, and seafood can usually be found here. Great Guana Cay is a high, rolling island with elevations to 80 feet and some spectacular ocean beaches along the five mile length of its north shore. The ruins of a once thriving timber industry along with the rusting hulk of a steam engine can still be seen deep in the bush at the northwest end.

The settlement harbour offers good holding over a patchy sand and grass bottom and is comfortable in all but south through west winds. Just west of the town dock lies Great Guana Cay's only visitor facility, the 10-room Guana Harbour Club. Constructed thirteen years ago, the Club has changed hands several times with each new operator intent on giving it a new character. In the mid-sixties Gordon O'Gara established the November Guy Fawkes Day Regatta in which locals, as well as visitors, sailed their boats in a bustling one-day gathering that featured a wild boar barbecue and ended with the traditional fireworks and burning of the "Guy." This event is still carried on annually by the various communities in Abaco, and seems to be gaining more popularity each year.

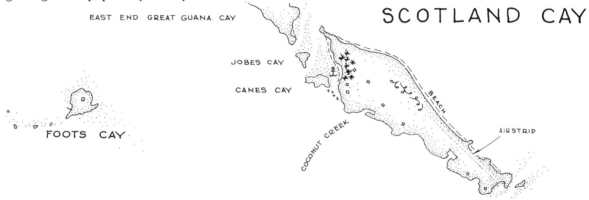

⟪ Scotland Cay

Separated from Great Guana Cay's eastern end by only a few sizable rocks and a treacherous, reef-strewn tidal way, Scotland Cay continues for a mile and a half in a southeasterly direction. Inside the rocks at the west corner of the cay under the protection of a prominent headland is one of the prettiest miniature anchorages in the Abaco Cays. Rimmed on its eastern shore by a steep sand and coconut studded beach, you can anchor in deep water close enough to shore to jump there from your deck without getting your feet wet. The only entrance into this entrancing spot is over a rocky bar which will not carry much over four feet at high water and the tide sluices through, both ebb and flood. The pool inside seems to offer good holding, though we've never really tried it as our various boats draw too near the draft of the tidal cut to venture in.

In recent years a small group of Americans have divided Scotland Cay into building sites and constructed several winter residences. A 2,200-foot, hard-surfaced runway has been cut out of the limestone at the southeast end of the Cay to meet the needs of these winter visitors.

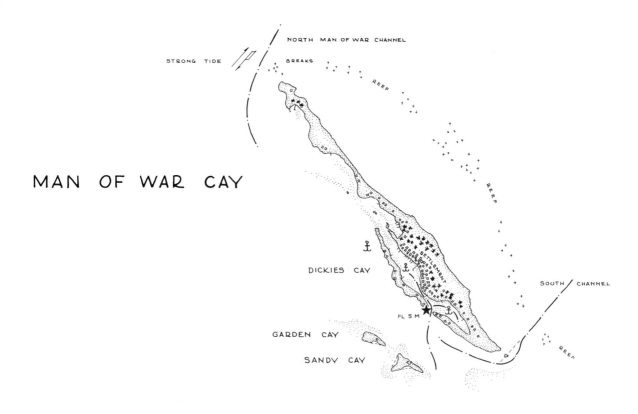

❨ Man of War Cay

As the present center of Abaco's boat building industry Man of War Cay has not only survived its local competition on the mainland, but also exceeded them due to the fact that their craftsmen were able to bend with the times and improve their products to compete on the modern market. Ancestors of these dedicated craftsmen were, again,the Loyalists who fled the Colonies following the American War for Independence and settled here to pursue their trades: fishing, farming, and the construction of sailing vessels of such beauty and precision that the phrase, "She's an Abaco boat," brings a nod of approval for her exceptional qualities from knowledgeable sailors in most Atlantic ports, even to this day. The Alburys and the Sands of Man of War today are the gentle, industrious descendants who continue to live on this tranquil island.

Man of War Cay, which probably derives its name from the ever present man of war or frigate bird, is 2½ miles long. It has two prominent hills at its center and north end with two of the best protected and most comfortable harbours in the Abaco Cays. The straightforward entrance to these harbours, along with the reef entrances at the north and south ends of the island are indicated on the accompanying chart.

Man of War is a model of good judgment as exercised by its town fathers when it first became attractive to winter residents almost a half century ago. It was understood, with considerable foresight at the time, that to survive an onslaught of land sales and to live with and service their "new neighbors," a workable plan must be devised to preserve enough land in the proper areas not to inhibit the future growth of their own community. It was also resolved that no property would be sold to foreigners inside the boundaries of the settlement proper, which comprised the center portion of the Cay. Only land at either end and on Dickie's Cay which borders the Settlement harbour to the west, would be sold to "outsiders." In this way Man of War Cay was able to preserve its own culture and environment, yet add foreign money to their economy. Would that many other settlements throughout the Bahamas had such foresight.

Man of War's settlement borders the north harbour, its palm fringed shoreline and orderly jumble of sun washed docks, neat little houses and building sheds waft the sweetness of fresh cut pine and madeira. There are several stores, a post office, school, two churches, and enough walking traffic along the harbour front to lend the scene an air of unruffled commerce. The town's houses are scattered on up the eastern slope through an assortment of fruit trees and ever-blooming tropical bush.

The cemetery on the ocean side of the island is something that is peculiarly "Abaco." The dead are buried facing the sea and their resting place is a well laid-out field, sloping to the sea, surrounded by a neat white picket fence, and carefully tended. There is another like it at Hope Town.

The south harbour shelters a flotilla of residents' yachts and is bordered by high, wooded ground with boat houses and docks nestled about its perimeter. Beyond these and up wooded paths are the houses, built by the local artisans, aglow with natural wood, and like the boats, boast madeira knees and chamfered beams with scarfed joints.

The late William Albury, known to all as "Uncle Will," was Man of War's leading citizen and principal boat builder. He was the son of Richard Albury who worked on the first boat to be launched on the Cay in 1902, the year "Uncle Will" was born. Uncle Will died in the fall of 1972, having built his first boat in 1915 at age 13 and completing a remarkable 67-year career in the trade. All boatmen familiar with his products mourn his passing.

As in olden times building plans at Man of War were seldom used, the boats being built from a model by hand and eye. Natural curved horseflesh and madeira woods are used for the principal timbers, frames, stem, stern, posts, etc., and unless otherwise specified, Abaco pine is used for the planking. As these woods are practically impervious to dry rot, the boats built here often last 50 years or more. It is not uncommon for one to "wear out" a set of planking and to be re-planked over the old timbers. Many of the tools of the trade are still made by hand, just as in the old days. Uncle Will related several years ago with a twinkle, "When you only made a few shillings a day, store tools were too expensive, so we carved our own to our particular specifications, in the evening when the day's work was done." A friend once told us he saw Uncle Will hammer a socket wrench out of a piece of pipe in the time it would have taken to run next door to borrow one. And it worked just fine. Uncle Will had forgotten how many boats he'd built since his thirteenth birthday, but his renowned handiworks are sailing far and wide today; the 56-foot topsail schooner "Esperanto," the 60-foot motor sailor "Lucayo," "Man-o-War," "Semper Fidelis," and even "Barracuda," a half scale replica of a 17th-century Royal Navy brig, to name just a few.

If it is accepted that Uncle Will was the best boat builder in the Bahamas, it should follow that his cousin, Maurice, holds the reputation for being the best builder of those provocative Abaco Sailing Dinghies whose classic, youthful lines personify the feminine. It follows also that Maurice's appreciation of the feminine should have produced sixteen offspring, three of whom represent the upcoming generation of Man of War boat builders. Willard and Benny build the modern, fast, wood runabouts which have become so popular throughout the Bahamas, while his eldest son, Edwin, operates a topnotch yard where he turns out traditional hulls with a contemporary flair. Edwin inherited his father's eye for the perfect line. Prominent examples of his work are the sleek sailing ketches "Barbara Jean" and "Malolo," both based in Abaco. Edwin and Willard have combined modern techniques with their past heritage to produce some of the best built, prettiest boats sailing southern waters today.

In an effort to make quality work boats available to local fishermen, the Bahamas Government, many years ago, devised a system whereby a person could place one third the cost of a standard size fishing boat with the chief Out Island Commissioner at Nassau, the Commissioner in turn ordering the boat from the Man of War government boat building team, Charles, Basil, and Wilson Sands, who then build it and ship it to Nassau. Upon delivery of the boat in Nassau the customer arranges for a monthly payment schedule, and he pays the remaining two thirds from profits derived from his monthly catch. The Sands build a strong product to aid a remarkably simple plan.

On our first visit to Man of War Cay we were in the process of re-rigging "Spindrift" and had just unstepped the mizzen mast when an erect figure stepped forward and in his characteristic, voluble manner introduced himself as "Uncle Norman." This was Man of War's sailmaker and official town greeter. He agreed to sew a deck awning for us and also offered to store the spar and sail for a possible customer "who might just float by." Two years later on a quick flight to Man of War, Mr. Norman caught my eye as I climbed onto the dock from the ferry. He scanned my face for a moment and then dove into his wallet and presented me with six neatly folded one pound notes; "I know you," he said. "I owe you this for the mizzen mast I sold for you about a year ago." And that's the way it is at Man of War Cay!

"Uncle Norman" and "Miss Lena" have been making sails together for over 50 years and when they retire the closing of the Albury sail loft will, in large measure, mark the end of the colorful era of sail in the Bahamas. Norman is a third-generation sailmaker whose father and grandfather made sails for the old Key Westers, blockade runners and early sponging schooners. Norman's four sons, all successfully occupied in their own particular phase of the Abaco boating and tourist industry, have made no indication that they will carry on their father's work. Eldest son Vernon and youngest son Hilland work at nearby Treasure Cay. Richie and Marcell operate the fuel dock, where all facilities are available, and the daily ferry service for the entire Man of War-Hopetown-Marsh Harbour area. They also manage the island's only tourist facility, the Dock 'N Dine Boatel. The Albury's eldest daughter, Lois, has joined her parents in the sail loft, specializing in a new line of colorful yachting jackets, hats, and ditty bags, all beautifully hand sewn and very durable.

Uncle Norman is the Cay's story teller, a veritable storehouse of accurate information about the old days, which he describes so graphically. He takes a philosophical view of his dying trade, calmly quoting Tennyson: "The old order changeth yielding place to the new." Like his father, Marcell is the accepted authority on all of the Abaco Cays and our invaluable source of maritime information.

When you visit Man of War Cay you feel a world apart, a place where people know how to live, a place to which you will want to return.

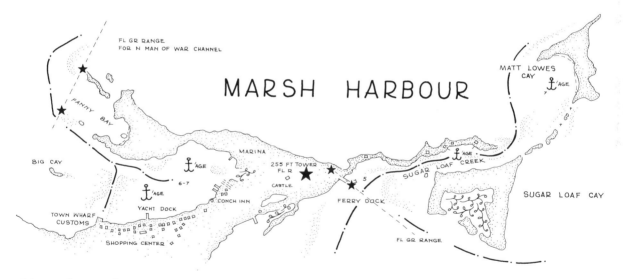

([Marsh Harbour

Southwest of Man of War Cay on the mainland is the settlement of Marsh Harbour. With its government airstrip offering daily flights to Nassau and Florida, its supermarkets, hardware and building supply houses, and its boat yard, capable of hauling ships 150 feet in length, little wonder Marsh Harbour is considered the commercial hub of Abaco. The latest addition to the town's sailing scene is C.S.Y.'s fleet of charter yachts working out of the east end of the harbour. Caribbean Sailing Yachts, with fleets also located in Grenada and the Virgin Islands, is the largest organization of its kind in the world.

Marsh Harbour is not a particularly attractive settlement; spread out and for the most part, flat, it lacks the charm of the cays' settlements. While the streets are paved, they are wide and dusty, like a frontier town. The harbour itself is protected from every quarter with a good holding mud bottom in about seven to eight feet of water. There is a sizable commercial wharf where fresh water and marine fuels can be had.

The Conch Inn, located on the harbour shore a short walk east of the business section, is the bustling center of all social activity in Marsh Harbour. Here adjacent to the town's only full service marina, a Bahamian menu is served, the food rivaling any we've had in the islands, while each noon finds the town fathers gathering for the daily businessman's lunch.

Abaco's Commissioner has his office here, as Marsh Harbour is the seat of government for the entire area. The town is also headquarters for the Abacos' medical profession, all of whom reside in the town and tend their patients in the outlying Cays on a regular schedule. Doctor Ejnar Gottlieb and his statuesque wife, Owanta, serve the area as a team. Doctor Evan Cottman, who lives in the green castle on the highest point in Marsh Harbour, has sailed about the Bahamas for a generation. His book, *Out Island Doctor,* is filled with Island lore.

Neville Roberts, financier, a veritable pyramid of a man, descended from a long line of Abaco shipwrights, has turned his attentions from Nassau to Marsh Harbour in recent years, and with visible results. At this writing, thanks largely to Neville, Marsh Harbour is a boom town. Neville's father, the late Jenkins Roberts, designed and built a number of the freight boats still seen plying the Islands. One of them is the 150-foot "Abaco Bahamas." She was launched in 1921. A quiet speaking, conscientious little man, half Neville's size, Norman Albury tells this story: "Jenkins built the "Abaco" for nine shillings a day. He had a crowd of men you didn't have to hunch to work. She was thirteen months abuilding and the morning they launched her there was a heavy nor'easter blowin'. They knocked the kingpins out and away and she fairly smoked down into the harbour. Then for a celebration they had two barrels of sodys. When someone saw Jenkins didn't have a sody and passed him one he said, 'I couldn't drink anything. When you got 13 months work outa' 20 men and you don't know whether it's all gonna go off all right, you're too full for sody.' "

Always one with a sly twinkle, Jenkins caught me huffing down his East Bay Dock in Nassau one day, visibly upset because one of the local skippers had not kept an appointment. "Now slow down," he said dryly, "you Americans came over here to civilize us and you've got to remember, civilization don't come easy!"

Many years ago an energetic New Englander, J.B. Crockett, founded a farming industry at Marsh Harbour that employs many Abaconians, with some 3,000 acres under cultivation, raising pineapple, cucumbers, and tomatoes. The Crockett packing operation lies handily adjacent to the shipyard, right on the harbour.

Owens-Illinois pulpwood division has cleared much of the pine from the Abaco mainland over the past ten years, leaving the land pretty well picked clean, but better ready to produce a second stand. An experimental sugar cane operation was tried by the same firm in the mid-sixties, but failed for lack of initial feasability and government cooperation in issuing work permits for the foreign engineers to come in to construct the necessary processing equipment.

Despite the extensive farming and land clearing operations, the woodlands surrounding Marsh Harbour have remained relatively wild. For example, the herd of wild horses and pigs said to be descendants of those left on the island by a foundering ship many years ago still provide good hunting and fresh pork on the hoof for those hardy enough to brave the bush in search of it.

Extending East between Marsh Harbour's eastern shore and Sugarloaf Cay is a narrow neck of water known as Sugarloaf Creek where there is six to seven feet in the anchorage pools. The hills on either side offer ample protection from the wind and we have always favored it as one of the prettiest anchorages in Abaco.

([Parrot Cays

Lying immediately west of the north end of Elbow Cay are the Parrot Cays. The second cay from the south, the largest, is the private property of David and Phoebe Gale, residents of Abaco for over eighteen years. Son of a New York artist and sculptress, Dave reflects much of his artistic heritage in his own development of the Cay. The main house commands a panoramic view of the Sea of Abaco to the south, while the guest house seems like a fairy cottage; both are a tribute to this unique couple's imagination and perseverance. On no other spot in the Islands have we seen a small cay so well planned, or so lovingly cared for, as here on this six-acre wonderland set in a turquoise sea. Dave is the Evinrude dealer for the area and maintains a very neat, small boat marine and repair shop on the Cay, as well as a fuel dock in Hope Town Harbour. Phoebe founded the first private school in Abaco and now, with two young sons of her own, is sharing the teaching responsibilities with other dedicated hands. Abaco is lucky indeed to have this enthusiastic and creative young couple as one of its staunchest supporters.

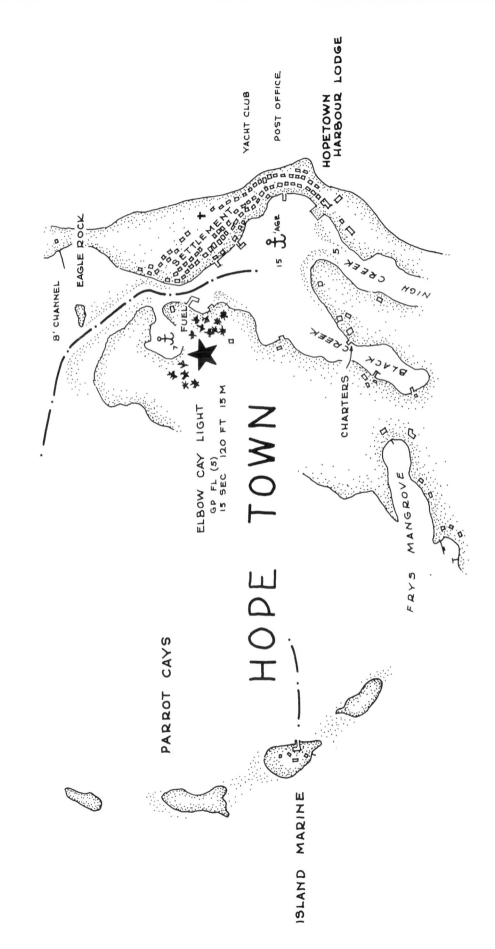

HOPE TOWN

PARROT CAYS

ISLAND MARINE

ELBOW CAY LIGHT
GP FL (5)
15 SEC 120 FT 15 M

FRYS MANGROVE

CHARTERS

BLACK CREEK

NIGH CREEK

8' CHANNEL

EAGLE ROCK

SETTLEMENT

FUEL

15

'AGE

5

YACHT CLUB

POST OFFICE

HOPETOWN
HARBOUR LODGE

([Hope Town

This is the largest settlement of Abaco, a seafaring community not unlike Provincetown, Massachusets, even down to its artists. The village is quaintly beautiful and right in the middle of it is a perfect landlocked harbour, one of the best in the Bahamas. The approach from the outside is obvious and straightforward. Just before entering the harbour, on your starboard hand you will pass the entrance to a deep cove; this is one of the best hurricane holes in the Islands since, because it has a relieving creek on the west side, it does not become over-flooded with the tidal waves that usually accompany a severe hurricane. Passing this, keep straight on into the main harbour and anchor anywhere. There is plenty of water, at least two fathoms with a rise and fall of three feet of tide, four feet at springs. The holding ground is good and as the harbour is landlocked you are secure in winds from any quarter.

Here, for the first time in the Islands, you will probably experience the feeling that you are in a South Sea island harbour. The sleepy little town tumbling along the shore around you, the tall waving coconut palms, the sound of the surf on the seaward side of the island, the rugged looking fishermen and their pretty little workboats—all contribute to the feeling that the outside world is 1,000 miles away.

Anchored here on a brilliantly hot summer day it's great fun to loll on deck under an awning and watch the maneuvering of the town around you: long-skirted ladies strolling to the store, an occasional bicycle flickering silently through the shadows of the palms, and the intermittent hammering of a fisherman at the water's edge affecting repairs to his craft. His arm seems to connect with the sound only on the back swing and you lie fascinated at this visual proof of the speed of sound as you watch it happen across this expanse of the placid anchorage. Then there, on the bench under the big tree, are the village elders who surveyed your every movement as you anchored in their harbour. Ancient mariners in their own right, you can bet your little ship has been thoroughly discussed and re-rigged a dozen times over since your arrival.

Dominating Hope Town Harbour is the most photographed structure in all the Islands, the red-banded Elbow Cay Lighthouse situated on the northwest side of the harbour. The erection of this light in 1862 was the Crown's stern method of bringing to an end the long-established wrecking industry in the Abacos. This settlement's geographical location, bordering the main shipping lanes, made it a natural headquarters for the activity. In fact, wrecking as a legalized occupation in the early to mid-1800's was so lucrative that it supplied as much as two-thirds of the country's total imports for that period. The records at that time indicate there were over 300 licensed wreckers employing over 2,000 men and their technique was to move the navigation lights on which the ships depended—luring them onto the reefs. This new lighthouse was obviously much too large to be moved, so the community did not take too kindly to the Crown's high-handed hold on their major source of income. They fought back in every way they knew, refusing to sell provisions to the lighthouse construction workers, contaminating their water, and drilling holes in the bottoms of the boats that supplied the lime and mortar. Even after the light was finally erected and operating there were a number of ships wrecked. The oldsters like to tell of one particular Sunday morning when a certain minister happened to glance out of the church window in the midst of his sermon. He saw a large ship approaching the reef and with his wits securely about him he immediately called for ten minutes of silent prayer. When all heads were reverently bowed the minister crept out of the church and dashed for his salvage craft, certain of being the first man on the wreck. The story continues that his congregation was so upset over his behavior that they moved the pulpit to the other end of the church so that he couldn't watch the reef on future Sundays; but the congregation could.

When in Hope Town a visit to the lighthouse is a *must*, especially near dusk when the lighthouse keeper goes through the formalities of lighting the kerosene lamp and winding up the ancient turning-mechanism that floats in a bath of mercury. We recommend that you take your camera as the view from the top, at the end of a long, hard climb, is spectacular!

Throughout the Abaco Cays the accented speech is unmistakable but nowhere so pronounced as in Hope Town. The dropped H's and the reversal of V's and W's made the 'ope-towner's accent a surprisingly soft Cockney. The reason for this is the blending, over the years, of the soft, southern Carolina accents of their forefathers with those of the cockney crews of the British sailing ships. When they refer to the "h'other day," it could mean just yesterday, or all the way back and beyond their childhood.

Ashore, Hope Town differs little from the coastline New England towns of a century ago. There are several small stores where limited supplies can be purchased, together with a post office, public library, clinic, and telephone station. Elbow Cay is the largest winter resident community in Abaco and during the season when the social schedule turns into high gear, Marcel Maury's comfortable Hopetown Harbour Lodge, perched high on the eastern side of the harbour, is the focal point.

Heir to one of Nassau's liquor fortunes, Marcel's tales of his family's supply operation at West End, Grand Bahama, back during prohibition days, will entertain you for hours. An avid flyer himself, Marcel's recollections tend toward the use of aircraft in the endeavor and he enjoys telling of the ingenious pilot who, when confronted with a case load weight problem, just offered free rides to as many passengers as he could crowd into his old biplane. When the plane could safely make it off the water the pilot quickly circled back, replaced the passengers with their weight in "spirits" and winged his way toward the U.S. coast and a rich reward.

Comparatively new on the scene, the ubiquitous young Hopetown Sailing Club sports a fleet of nearly a dozen Man-of-War-Bird Class sailing dinghies. All built by Maurice Albury and raced by locals and winter residents over a short harbour course each Sunday, these lively little sailors give constant evidence of Hope Town's standing as Abaco's yachting center. The club house stands near the government dock and displays an extensive array of trophies with mostly local names inscribed thereon.

Many of the vistors keep their boats moored in the harbour year 'round, sailing them only when they are in residence. Lighthouse Marina, the harbour's only fueling facility, has a handy "boat-sitting" service that caters to both residents and visitors, supplying moorings, daily attention to open-stored boats, and repair services in the event of an emergency.

Burton Russell (U.S. Navy, ret.) and his vivacious wife, Doris, sailed to Hope Town aboard their ketch, "Uruguay," in the early fifties, liked it so much that they built a cottage overlooking Fry's Mangrove on the backside of the island. Along with chartering "Uruguay," they built what was for many years to be the only bare-boat charter business in the Bahamas. Now retired for the second (and he hopes the last) time, Russ has turned the business over to Otis Zumwalt and Evans Wilhoyt. Abaco Bahamas Charters, Ltd., maintains a spotlessly efficient fleet of yachts on the western creek of Hope Town Harbour.

Certainly Hope Town is for the sailor; there is no other harbour in the Islands that imparts such a strong feeling of security. The reassuring, rhythmic flash of the lighthouse on your cabin bulkhead lulls you to sleep, and perchance if it suddenly should stop, as it has been known to do, its absence jolts you out on deck to await the lighthouse keeper's steady hand to start it up again. Then as you're finally drifting off to sleep there's a moment of conjecture—have we actually seen the last of Hope Town's wrecking industry?

Important Note

When proceeding South from Man of War Cay, at sea east of Elbow Cay, a vessel should lay her course at least two miles east of Elbow Cay Light to avoid the outer reef there.

From Hope Town South to Little Harbour bar there is good water inside the cays and using the channel around Witch Point a draft of six feet can be taken through on any tide. The more intricate Lubber's Quarters Channel can be negotiated on a rising tide in any boat drawing no more than five feet.

WHITE SOUND

SHALLOW

5' CHANNEL

FUEL

6

FIN AND TONIC CLUB

GREEN LIGHTED RANGE 123°

⟨[White Sound

There is a residential community at White Sound that is connected to Hope Town by road. It is comprised mainly of beach houses that are owned by winter residents. The entrance channel into the community dock will carry 4 ½ feet at low water and vessels of six feet draft can lie at the fuel dock in ample protection.

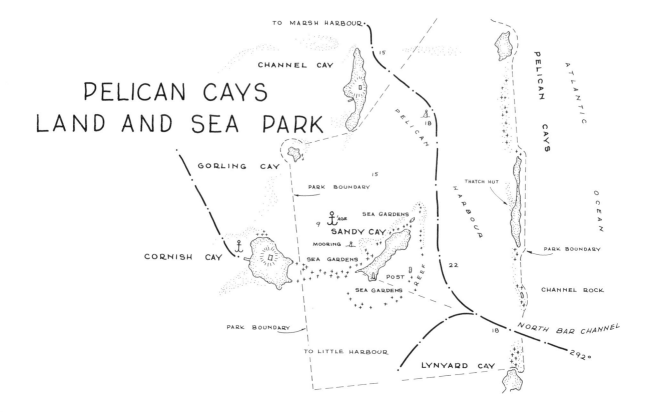

PELICAN CAYS
LAND AND SEA PARK

TO MARSH HARBOUR

CHANNEL CAY

15

PELICAN

18

PELICAN CAYS

ATLANTIC

GORLING CAY

15

PARK BOUNDARY

THATCH HUT

OCEAN

SANDY CAY

9 AGE

SEA GARDENS

MOORING

SEA GARDENS

CORNISH CAY

HARBOUR

PARK BOUNDARY

POST

REEF

22

CHANNEL ROCK

SEA GARDENS

PARK BOUNDARY

18

NORTH BAR CHANNEL

TO LITTLE HARBOUR

292°

LYNYARD CAY

([Pelican Harbour

The entrance known as North Bar Channel lies between the north end of Lynyard Cay and Channel Rock. The Channel is a quarter of a mile wide, with the deepest water on the South side. The bar has a minimum depth of sixteen feet and the seas will sometimes break over it in strong easterly winds, or when there is a rage on. A boat drawing ten feet or less will have no difficulty sailing in on a course due west, staying midway in the channel. There is plenty of water inside and this is a good place to lie out a norther.

This is the area of the Pelican Cays Land and Sea Park founded by the Bahamas National Trust to preserve the natural beauty of the Cays and existing sea life. Here the camera is the only shooting device welcome and the flora and fauna of the beaches and reefs are protected by law. No littering, molesting or removing of birds, fish, shells, coral, or sea life of any description is allowed. A thatch shelter on Sandy Cay has been provided for the visitor's use and it is requested that he tie to the available moorings lest his anchors foul the lovely coral formations below. Cornish Cay, which borders the park to the west, is the private property of an ecology-minded Pennsylvanian, Dixon Downey, who keeps a sharp lookout for anyone violating the Park's best interests and is a most constructive critic of these writers' efforts.

Channel Cay, which borders the park on the northwest side, was developed as a private island by the late Nassau realtor, Bert Roberts, who is buried there in a palm grove that he personally transplanted many years ago.

There are several comfortable anchorages farther south under Lynyard Cay that provide good holding and ample protection in any weather. The beaches on the ocean side of the Cay are easily available and provide excellent combing.

([Little Harbour

There is a good entrance over Little Harbour Bar and a snug harbour inside, one of the most picturesque in the Bahamas. The light at Little Harbour is well inland, on top of a square, white, stone house about one-quarter of a mile SSW of the point. There is a minimum depth of 11 feet on the bar, so that a draft of seven feet can be taken in if there is not much sea. This bar breaks badly in heavy easterly winds.

As soon as you pass the point coming in you will see a cove inside the point on the port hand. This is *not* the place to lie. Stand on around the

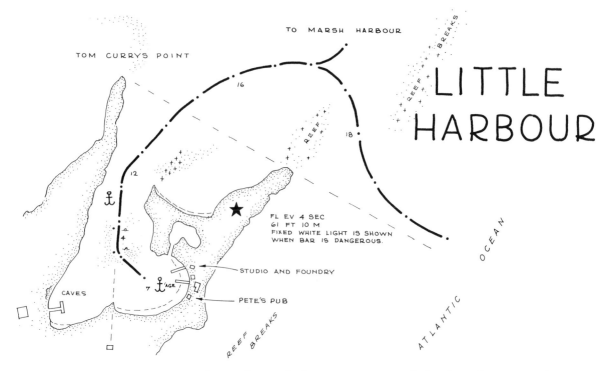

next point on the south shore, giving it a wide berth as there are rocky shoals extending 100 yards out from it. Rounding this you will then see an exquisite little harbour on the port hand, and beyond, the inner harbour or hurricane hole. The best anchorage is in the patch of light green water, over a sandy bottom, abreast of the hanging rock which is on the west side of the harbour. Here you can lie safely, in six feet of water at low tide, though a mild surge usually persists. There are very interesting caves on shore and several beautiful sandy beaches.

The four-foot, low-water channel into the inner harbour is marked by several stakes. Leave them close to starboard, staying over the light sand when entering. Inside you will have seven to ten feet of water over a sandy grass bottom that is good holding. This is a beautiful anchorage but during the summer months the flies will try to drive you right out again.

Little Harbour is the home of Professor Randolph Johnston and his talented family. Artist, sculptor, lecturer, Johnston sailed here in 1951 while on sabbatical from Smith College and stayed on in a near-spartan existence while he lived in the cave and thatch hut on the harbour's western shore, carving coconut novelties, raising a few crops, and chartering out his 53-foot schooner "Langosta." Schooled in Ontario and London, Mr. Johnston is one of the few remaining world sculptors who still employs the ancient "lost wax" technique in bronze casting. Now this is done as a family project in his combination studio/foundry right on the harbour shore. Mr. Johnston's works exemplify sculpture's romantic school and are exhibited in ten countries.

Margo, his petite wife, is an accomplished ceramicist specializing in enamel on silver and copper, delicate work indeed. She met "Ran" while attending one of his classes in Cummington, Massachusetts. Son Peter has his father's powerful frame and stance and is following his bent toward serious works. How fortunate he is to have this fund of design, philosophy, and technological know-how so close at hand. The Johnstons' eldest son, Bill, is an electrical contractor in nearby Marsh Harbour, while middle son, Denny, a writer since the age of sixteen, edits the *Kingston Times* in Kingston-on-the-Thames, England. Their only daughter, Marian, teaches history at Girls' Latin School in Boston. (Quite an impressive record, for raising your children on an "isolated island.")

The Johnstons maintain an interesting little studio at the head of their dock where their works are on display and some genuine treasures are to be found. "Pete's Pub," built from the wheel house of the "Langosta" along with other beachcombing paraphernalia, lies a few steps to the South. Here the main topics, ranging from art to sailing the Abaco Cays, usually commence when the sun is over the yardarm.

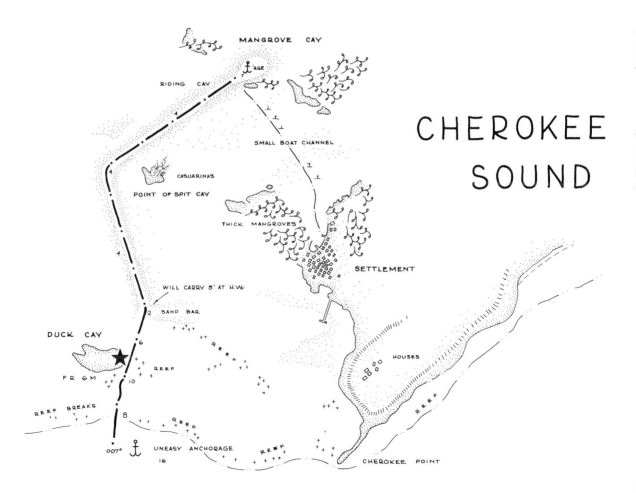

CHEROKEE
SOUND

([Cherokee Sound

There is only one harbour South of Little Harbour on Great Abaco. This is in Cherokee Sound and it is also a fine place in which to lie out a norther.

There is good water on the west side of Cherokee Point, but it ends before you get into the protected anchorage. The best channel lies close to the shore of Duck Cay. There is a fixed red light on Duck Cay, 29 feet high, visible six miles. Steer N x W for this light until it is close aboard, then leave it on the port hand entering. The light is about 30 feet from the edge of the rocks and the channel, so close to the rocks that you can almost jump ashore at this point. There is seven feet in the channel at low water and this draft can be carried in until half a mile inside Duck Cay. The reef, which runs off to the eastward from Duck Cay, forms a breakwater for this anchorage. You can lie here well protected in winds from west to east through north, but it is no good in winds from the southeast or south, as a nasty surge comes in from the sea under those conditions.

The settlement of Cherokee Village lies one mile north of Cherokee Point, and there is a very pretty inner harbour with nine feet of water in it, but the approaches to it are both shallow and intricate. A draft of five feet can be carried in at mean high tide. A local pilot should certainly be engaged for this part of your Abaco cruise.

Cherokee Village is a pretty little settlement, again with quite a New England air about it—clean, tidy, and well kept. Benny Sawyer is the principal boat builder here, his workmanship familiar to boating people throughout the Bahamas. The 60-foot, diesel fishing smack "Blue Water" that works out of Spanish Wells was launched by Benny in the mid-sixties and has proved so successful that he has since launched her sister ship, "Carolpan."

Cherokee has a post office, telephone station, Methodist chapel, and a sizable store where groceries and some marine hardware can be had. The village is linked to the main Abaco highway that runs the length of the island so that you can visit this charming settlement by land if you so desire.

([Sandy Point

The southern part of Great Abaco Island, beyond Cherokee South, has nothing to offer the yachtsman except an inhospitable coastline and strong currents, both best avoided. However, on the western side, at approximately 20 miles northwest of Hole In The Wall, there is a most interesting settlement called Sandy Point.

SANDY POINT

Sandy Point is built on the northern end of a peninsula which is heavily wooded, the village being almost hidden by the dense grove of palm trees and casuarinas. The energetic townspeople are very pleasant and anxious to oblige their visitors. There is a telephone station, a fuel dock and a post office at Sandy Point—also scheduled flight service from Nassau.

The anchorage is about 200 yards off the fixed white light on the tower. It is safe in the prevailing winds from the east, but not in anything from the west or northwest. Fishing boats use the creek on the east side of the village. This is a safe harbour in any weather, but the entrance to it is intricate. It is best to hire a pilot to take you in. Inside the creek you will find a number of Bahamian vessels in various stages of repair, a most picturesque sight, so don't be without a camera.

Gorda Cay

Following the ten-fathom line on a northwesterly bearing from Sandy Point will bring you to Gorda Cay, a privately owned island developed by a Trinidadian, Ivan Tucker, who lives most of the year in Freeport and vacations here on Gorda Cay. It was on the very edge of the escarpment, just a short distance offshore, that Nassauvians Roscoe Thompson and Howard Lightbourne discovered the remains of what they hoped might be the Spanish Galleon "San Pedro" and its silver pound bar that is now on display in Nassau. The 72-lb. pure silver bar represents $20,000 in purchasing power today but as a historical piece it is priceless. Other sunken wealth at the site of the find has remained elusive. Since the escarpment drops off sharply, the discoverers maintain it will hold the secret until such time as more sophisicated, deep-water salvage equipment is developed.

GORDA CAY

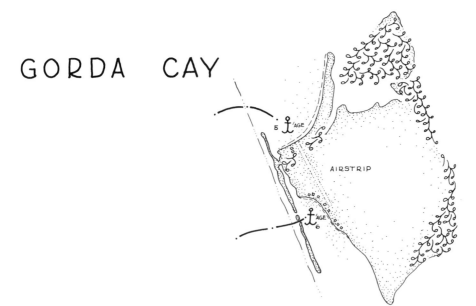

There is a pleasant lee over a deep, sandy bottom off the house and beach at the northwest corner of the island, but a mild surge usually persists. Far better and more protected is the natural harbour ringed by a line of rocks on the west side of the island. Here, entering though the southernmost cut, one can anchor midway in the basin in five to six feet at low water over a good holding sandy bottom.

A splendidly maintained cay; Mr. Tucker has built a 2,400-foot paved airstrip on Gorda Cay, one of the best in the Bahamas. The colors hereabouts are brilliant and the fishing along the edge of deep water superb.

$25,000 silver bar taken from 17th century Spanish galleon off Gorda Cay. *Bahamas Ministry of Tourism*

❨ Mores Island

The entrance to the anchorage at Mores Island lies immediatley south of Channel Cay on which stands the light, flashing every 2½ seconds, visibility seven miles. Channel Cay lies 10½ miles NW along a string of reef-strewn rocks which mark the edge of the escarpment from Gorda Cay. The best anchorage, 7 to 8 feet over conch grass, lies 150 yards off the village of Hard Bargain, a short distance south of the north point of the island. The village of the Bight, further south, offers lee protection for small boats only, there being less than three feet of water for two miles offshore.

The major occupations for the 400-odd citizens of Mores Island are fishing and farming, the seasonable products of which are most times plentiful. There are few other supplies or services except for direct telephone service to Nassau and the mailboat which calls twice weekly. The settlements are quaintly charming and their residents, who see so few yachts cruising this remote area, will be cordially helpful for your entire visit.

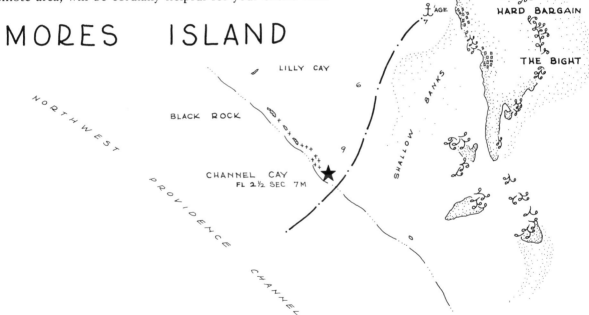

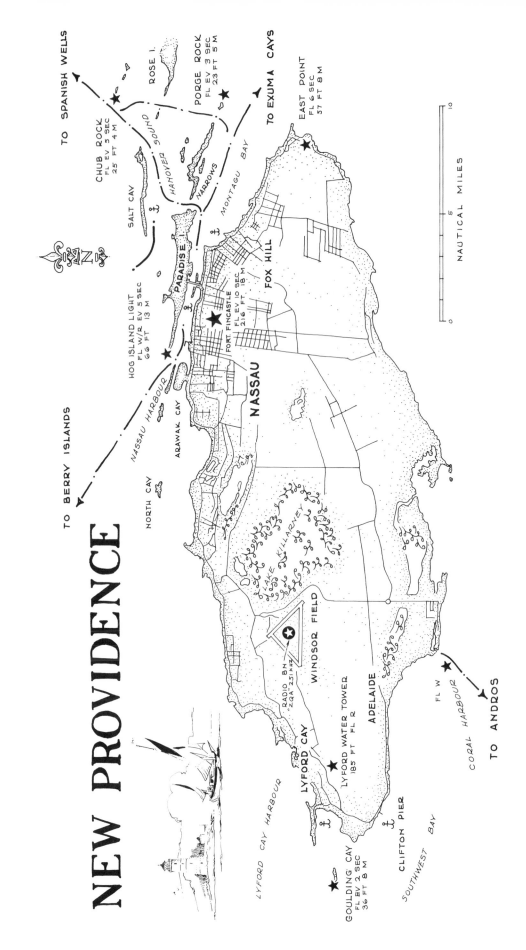

NEW PROVIDENCE

TO SPANISH WELLS

ROSE I.

PORGE ROCK
FL EV 3 SEC
23 FT 5 M

TO EXUMA CAYS

EAST POINT
FL 6 SEC
57 FT 8 M

CHUB ROCK
FL EV 5 SEC
25 FT 4 M

SALT CAY

HANOVER SOUND

NARROWS

MONTAGU BAY

TO BERRY ISLANDS

HOG ISLAND LIGHT
FL W/R EV 5 SEC
66 FT 13 M

NASSAU HARBOUR

ARAWAK CAY

PARADISE I.

FORT FINCASTLE
FL EV 10 SEC
216 FT 18 M

FOX HILL

NASSAU

NORTH CAY

NAUTICAL MILES

10

5

0

LAKE KILLARNEY

RADIO BN
"ZQA" 251 HZ

WINDSOR FIELD

LYFORD CAY

LYFORD WATER TOWER
185 FT FL R

ADELAIDE

FL W

CORAL HARBOUR

TO ANDROS

LYFORD CAY HARBOUR

CLIFTON PIER

SOUTHWEST BAY

GOULDING CAY
FL EV 2 SEC
36 FT 8 M

Nassau, New Providence, and Adjacent Cays

7

Everybody sing when the boat come in
Everybody shout when the boat go out
In Nassau—in Nassau.

Nassau is a sailors' town and all the Sybarites ashore cannot change that fact. It has been a sailors' town for more than 250 years and has a history as exciting and violent as can be found anywhere, a history of naval warfare, piracy and pillaging, buccaneering, slave running, blockade running, wrecking, and bootlegging. Captured first from the Spanish, it was recaptured and sacked by them in 1684, and rebuilt by the British in 1695. It was seized and later evacuated by the Americans in 1776 and again captured by the Spanish in 1782. Recaptured by the British in 1783, it has been in their hands until July 10, 1973 when the country gained full independence.

During the American Civil War, Nassau was one of the chief bases for Confederate blockade runners and large fortunes were made here. An even greater boom was experienced in the days of U.S. prohibition, everybody and his brother taking some part in supplying bootleggers with the wherewithal for their business. Much of modern Nassau was built from the proceeds. One of the island's most extraordinary laws also stemmed from that era; the Executive Council had the authority to deport any alien summarily, without charges, trial, or right of appeal.

Nassau today is certainly not the sleepy little town of the Fifties, but a lively Island metropolis that commerce and tourism forced to grow up "too soon." You can get just about anything you want here, but you'll have to work for it, it will not be volunteered. Service, by foreign standards, has always been inefficient and still is, but pleasant nonetheless. Clerks, waitresses, and the telephone system will wear down your patience if you try to buck them, high blood pressure being your only reward. However, relaxed pleasantries will invariably bring smiles in return, so while here, slow down and enjoy yourself and let Nassau grow on you.

Nassau Harbour has two entrances, one from the north and the other from the east. The north, or main entrance, lies just to the west of Hog Island (now known as Paradise Island) and is well marked, with flashing red buoys to be kept on the starboard hand all the way in, and flashing white lights on black buoys to port. There is also a range of two fixed red lights on shore, on a bearing of 151° (true), but they are hard to distinguish among all the hundreds of other lights there. The channel is dredged to a depth of 36 feet at low tide. Approaching New Providence Island from the sea, the first thing which appears over the horizon is a gray concrete water tower which is on the ridge in the middle of the city of Nassau. Its elevation is 216 feet above sea level. On it is a beacon, flashing white every five seconds.

The Nassau lighthouse, a conical white tower 66 feet high, stands on the western end of Hog (Paradise) Island. It has a white light which flashes every five seconds and is visible for thirteen miles. When there is a "rage" on, the five-second flash is then changed to red. At these times, a red flag is flown from this lighthouse in the daytime, indicating that the bar is too dangerous to cross. A "rage," in Bahama parlance, is a heavy sea breaking

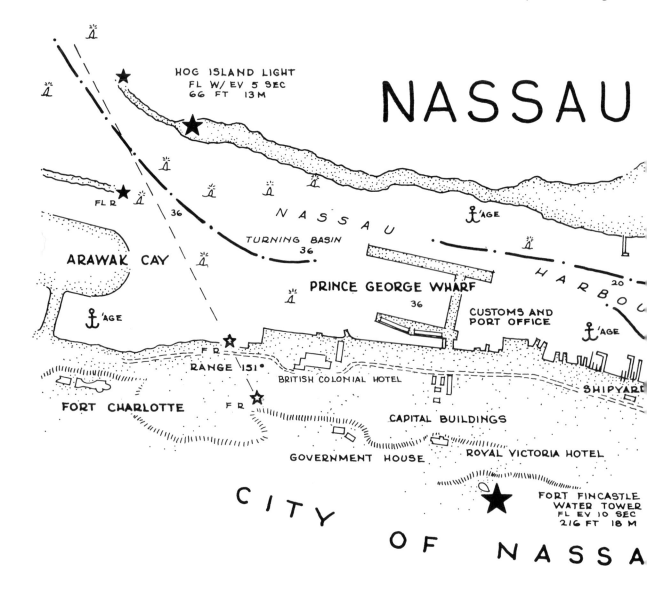

on the bar making it extremely dangerous, if not impassable. While usually accompanied by high winds, a rage is not immediatley caused by them, but by sea conditions which may originate hundreds of miles away. We have seen a heavy rage on the bar with only a very light breeze prevailing locally, but tremendous ocean swells heaving in from the open sea. If, on your arrival, the bar seems too dangerous for you to negotiate, a sensible plan is to run east for three miles into the lee of Salt Cay, where a good anchorage will be found. This was the favorite anchorage for the bootleggers who did not find it convenient or wise to be caught in Nassau Harbour. You can also come into Nassau Harbour by the back way, or eastern entrance, which is through Hanover Sound, if your vessel is of light draft, or through Chub or Porgee Rocks Channel or Douglas Passage if you are drawing more than six and not over ten feet.

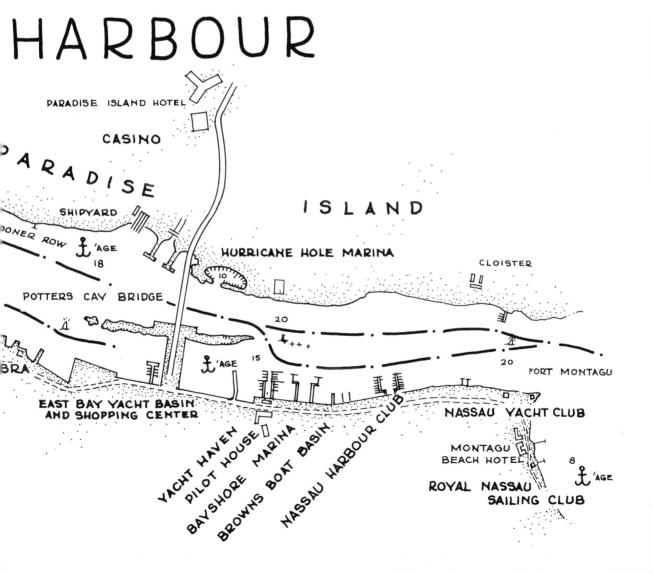

All this sounds very fearful, but the fact is that you will very seldom find the bar in a rage, and usually only in the winter months. At all other times you can sail in with perfect safety, carrying in any draft which will move in 36 feet of water. If you are entering from a foreign country you should fly your yellow quarantine flag and no one should leave or be allowed to join the ship until you have been boarded and cleared by the customs officials. This is of course not necessary if you have already entered at another Bahamian Port of Entry, and been given a transire permitting you to cruise Bahamian waters.

In a mid-sixties bid to attract the larger cruise ships, the Bahamian Government had the harbour extrance channel and turning basin dredged to a uniform 36 feet. The entire project took the better part of three years to complete and resulted in the building of a new, 18-acre island at the extreme western end of the harbour, named Arawak Cay. The land area is almost double the size of downtown Nassau and we understand that there are plans to develop it into a modern tourist extravaganza. When we recall the colorful history of Nassau, it is hard to conceive of the amount of artifacts and treasure the giant teeth of the dredge consumed in skimming the top ten feet of silt from the harbour floor. Whatever there might have been is now spread thinly over what might be considered the "gold paved" streets of Arawak Cay.

Eastward in the harbour beyond the Paradise Island bridge and lining both shores, are Nassau's many facilities for the yachtsman. Remember, if yours is a sailboat whose mast exceeds 70 feet in height, you will have to enter the harbour by the back way, previously outlined. If your draft exceeds ten feet, you should remain anchored west of the bridge in what has always been known as "schooner row," and to eliminate the roll from the bustling harbour traffic we suggest you anchor as close to shore as practicable. It is wise to put down two anchors to avoid fouling, but be sure that you don't put them down where there are signs that say, "Cable." There is also a heavy hurricane chain stretched across Nassau Harbour, 1,000 yards east of the Prince George Dock, from the foot of Armstrong Street over to Paradise Island, lying roughly NNE and SSW. This chain is something to hook onto in a hurricane, but not when you wish to get your hook on board short-handed.

Nassau Harbour can sometimes be quite rough and uncomfortable. Being open at both ends a considerable current flows through it, and the current bucking the wind can make a most unpleasant bobble. Your vessel, being tide-bound, will tend to lie broadside to the chop and roll and roll and roll.

Having now secured your ship in one of the most interesting ports of call in the world, look around you and you will see everything to delight the soul of the sailor and artist. Watch the Out Island boats come in laden to the gunwales with handsome Out Islanders, youngsters singing calypso chanties, giggling girls, pigs, goats, sheep, chickens, sometimes a cow, all this on a

**Fishing smacks line
Nassau Harbour.** *Bahamas
Ministry of Tourism*

small sloop only 25 or 30 feet long. Once we saw a Turks Island sloop come sailing into Nassau Harbour with a deck load of sheep. Whenever the skipper yelled "hard-a-lee" the sheep all ducked their heads. A lesson no doubt learned the hard way on their long ocean passage.

Watch a conch fisherman sail his anchor out—a thrilling sight. First he makes full sail, then apparently "throws his cable away," sailing off in fine style as if he had completely forgotten his ground tackle. Then with full way on, a terrific luff, and the anchor cable in as fast as hands can handle it, over the anchor, broken out, up and away, all without a lost motion. These little ships are like the Bedouins who roam the deserts, folding their tents and disappearing into the night. Many of them, coming from nowhere in particular, make sail and disappear over the horizon bound for wherever the fish are, or conch, or turtles. Sometimes they will be headed for a lonely little cove where a thatched hut stands on the shore. Sometimes they never make it. Carrying no more provisions than a yachtsman would stock up for a day's sail, with leaky hulls and patched up sails they sail off on long voyages in weather that would try an ocean racer.

Yachts are here, and the world's largest tourist ships, fishing sloops, Navy vessels, mail packets, almost every type of vessel to be found in the Western Hemisphere today. Island sloops and bum boats (water taxis) are everywhere. We have spent years living in Nassau Harbour and never tired of watching its traffic.

There are five major marinas in the harbour, each with its own special character. The first you will see after you pass under the bridge is on your port hand. Known as Hurricane Hole Marina, this cozy 45-slip facility was dubbed Hurricane Hole by Axel Wenner-Gren (the original developer of Paradise Island) when he closed off the Island's hurricane-proof inner lagoons as private property and designated a more convenient area adjacent to the main harbour as a hurricane hole in which local boats could take refuge. He constructed a breakwater, bordered the hole with a stone wall, and planted the surrounding area with a thick stand of casuarinas to give added protection from the wind.

Following his purchase of Paradise Island, Huntington Hartford saw great possibilities for the Hole and as part of his controversial art colony of the early sixties, had it dredged to a depth of twelve feet, installed concrete piers, and finally landscaped the surrounding casuarina grove with flagstone walks and imported French street lamps—all giving it the continental flavor it somewhat retains today. Since then it has been a marina and our home for the years we lived aboard in Nassau Harbour. Before the Paradise Island bridge was built, living at Hurricane Hole was like living in the Out Islands, with Nassau still handy. Our home slip was on the coconut-rimmed outer breakwater right on the quay itself. Commuting to the office downtown was done by ferry or our own dinghy. Where else could you remain barefoot year 'round until you were within a city block of your office? Then there was little need for an automobile unless you received word of a package awaiting you in the dim recesses of the old Parcel Post Department at Oakes Field; or if you planned a Sunday outing to drive around the Island! But the towering Paradise Island bridge changed all that and now cars, motorcycles, and trucks crunch over Mr. Hartford's imported flagstone as the busy "commuters" come and go from their slips at Hurricane Hole.

Ragged Islander Edwin Monroe is the dockmaster at Hurricane Hole, having been a man about the docks there since Hartford's days. A nicer young Bahamian you will not find anywhere in the Islands.

Just west of the bridge is the Paradise Island Shipyard, the only Nassau facility capable of handling vessels of 100 feet in length (when it is open for business). Maintaining a virtual monopoly on the handling of large yachts in Nassau, the shipyard occasionally has been known to use this to its benefit. So, when dealing on a job, whether it be a periodic hauling or a simple scrub, agree on an estimated price before the work is begun so as to avoid any unpleasantness on completion. This, we might add, should be the rule while making any transaction in the Islands, even if it amounts to no more than hiring a taxi—and be sure *you* have the proper change. As seagoing visitors we are often liable to emulate the affluent yachtsmen and it must certainly tempt the working Bahamian to "take it while he can."

On the mainland, under the western crook of the Potter's Cay Causeway, lies East Bay Yacht Basin, Nassau's oldest marina. It was named for East Bay Street, Nassau's main thoroughfare, that parallels the waterfront for the entire length of the harbour. Neville Roberts built "Easty Bay," as it is known locally, as a marine fueling facility adjacent to his service station and shopping center, across the street. He left his father, Jenkins, in charge and the dock quickly became a favorite with the early charter skippers, many of whom live there still. Since the Roberts' interests back home in Marsh Harbour have been growing, the facility has changed hands and, due largely to the jumble of rotting hulls which line its shore, has deteriorated. However, no matter how unsightly broken boats may be, they are ever a photographer's delight and there is always a group of tourists snapping pictures at East Bay.

Half a mile east of the bridge on the south shore is the 100-slip Nassau Yacht Haven and Pilot House complex, the city's major boating headquarters. Built by international yachtsman R. H. (Bobby) Symonette in 1951, it was under the early guidance of Bahamas fishing editor, Don McCarthy, his pert wife, Mary, and Bahamas Olympic Gold Medalist, Durward Knowles. The dual facility immediately caught on and has for a generation remained Nassau's sportsman's rendezvous.

Nassau Yacht Haven. *Bahamas Ministry of Tourism*

Ocean Race starts off Nassau Harbour. *Bahamas Ministry of Tourism*

Certainly no single person has done more to promote the Bahamas as a year 'round boatman's paradise than the creator of this unique place. As a competition class sailor, especially in the Star and 5.5. classes, Bobby's name is recognized in every yachting center in the world, while his efforts with the Southern Ocean Racing Circuit, with special emphasis on the now 100-boat Miami-Nassau Yacht Race, have made the event the top sailing event in south Atlantic waters. The Miami-Nassau Power Boat Race, the more recent Bahamas 500, the piloted cruises, and even the Flying Treasure Hunt—fashioned in essence after the cruises—are all Bahama sporting events that grew up under Bobby's tutelage.

Pioneer Harbour pilot John Newton Brown had named the original harbourside building the "pilot house" when he purchased it for a residence around the turn of the century. It was then almost 100 years old. In the years that followed the quaint old structure served as a hostel, a private home, and a restaurant where a Bahamian cook named Old Tom made what was considered the best conch chowder in Nassau. Even now when the dining room has gone to a predominantly French menu Old Tom's recipe is still found on the bill of fare, and is a favorite still.

On any one evening during Nassau's yacthting season it would not be surprising, from your place at the old Pilot House bar, to spot veteran ocean racer/author Carleton Mitchell of "Finisterre" engaged in a casual cocktail/conference with National Geographic Society President Mel Grosvenor; or U.S. 5.5 Champion, Gardiner Cox, and the design wizard Britton Chance deeply engrossed in a point of hull design as it might be applied to a phase of sailing strategy; the George Hinmans (post-war America's Cup defender, "American Eagle") dining with world circumnavigator and British cruising author, Eric Hiscock and his wife, Susan, who might have just arrived from Grenada aboard their ketch "Wanderer II."

It has been this way ever since Bobby built the place, and even though year after year the Miami-Nassau Yacht Race falls under the sponsorship of the Miami and Nassau Yacht Clubs, the Pilot House remains unofficial race headquarters because that's where the action is!

Immediately east of Yacht Haven is the newly enlarged Bay Shore Marina specializing in storage for residents' smaller boats, runabouts, outboards, and the like. This installation includes a complete marine repair shop, marine store, and outboard rental facility.

Moving along to the east you come to Brown's Boat Basin, owned by harbour pilot Chris Brown and run by his two sons, Sidney and Donald. They make repairs and excellent quality hull work to boats up to 50 feet in length. We have known Sidney and Donald for many years as it was here that we rebuilt "Spindrift" and hired a local mechanic, Bill Minns, to repower her with a brand new Perkins diesel engine. During this often traumatic experience, we moved into Sidney's second-floor apartment overlooking the boat yard. And there began the "Bill Minns saga" and one of the most frustrating endeavors of all time. To quote from my log. "Gave Bill a check to order the new engine from England, hauled "Spindrift" and proceeded to tear her apart. We salvaged what we could, like selling our old Chrysler engine to a Haitian skipper who burned it out on his first trip home. By the time the new engine arrived from England, Bill had, with much prodding and cajoling, installed the new engine bed and the V-drive; while our master carpenter, Abaconian Weldon Roberts, had the new cabin and bridge well underway. Meanwhile, Sidney, noticing Bill's slackened pace, offered to mount the engine himself, but we foolishly insisted, 'a deal's a deal,' assuring him (and ourselves) that Bill was aware of our deadlines for the *Guide* and we were sure the installation would be completed on time. As it turned out, we were about to learn a lesson in Island 'patience'?? Apparently our mechanic was prone to start jobs and not finish them. It was not that he could not install the engine, or that he was too busy, he just didn't feel like it! All he had really wanted to do was experiment with a V-drive, and that he had done. Eventually however, in true Minns' fashion, the installation was completed and a success; which is proved every time we see "Sprindrift" cruising about Florida's canals today with her 'new' power plant still going strong."

Through this moving testimonial Sidney Brown alone had remained calm, keeping his cool until the very end. After four months on the ways he admitted "Spindrift" was as "dry" a boat as he'd ever launched and loaned us a three-inch pump to keep her from sinking until she swelled up once more. This took two days. The Browns are men of their word, their price is right, and the view from their apartment overlooking the Basin and Nassau Harbour made the whole experience *almost* worth it.

For the yachtsman who prefers his home away from home to be as much like home as possible, the Nassau Harbour Club, just a short walk east of Browns', is the answer. Here, with all the good things a modern marina should have, amid a dockside swimming pool and 50-room motel, are sturdy concrete slips for 65 yachts of any size. Somehow since its completion some ten years ago the Harbour Club has remained typically stateside, never quite melding into the Island atmosphere. We have enjoyed tying up there, especially in the summer when that fresh breeze wafts in from the east.

⟨ Nassau

The flavor of picturesque old Nassau, surrounded by its vivid blue-green waters, will remind you of Winslow Homer at every turn. No wonder he painted his most invigorating water colors here.

Goombay, not calypso, is the music characteristic of the Bahamas and naturally Nassau is the place you will hear it played best. Old timers such as Blind Blake will entertain you with earthy topics to an unusual native beat that reflects the Islanders' work, troubles, loves, and hates in such tunes as: "Conch Ain't Got No Bone," "Sarah Jane," "John B. Sail," Men Smart—Woman Smarter," "Water," "Sail'er Down to George Town," and "Wings of a Dove."

This being a seafaring town there are a number of ship chandleries. John S. George Company in Palmdale carries a large assortment of yachting supplies and its president, Herbert McKinney, who is a yachtsman himself, takes a personal interest in all the sailing people who visit there. Other reliable ship chandleries include the City Lumber Yard, General Hardware Company, Kelly's Hardware, and Maura Hardware Company on Shirley Street.

Nassau Harbour Club.
Bahamas Ministry of Tourism

The charm of Nassau, having being voiced far and wide by the Bahamas Ministry of Tourism, has had a profound effect upon the town. Nassau has doubled its hotel rooms in the last fifteen years, with many of the quaint old hostelries already gone or fast disappearing, making way for the new super-structures of tomorrow.

The enormous British Colonial Hotel is the square, pink building you first notice as you enter the harbour through the main entrance. It has fared well and expanded with the onslaught of increased business. It looks like something from Alantic City and, in fact, it is said that it was originally designed for that city and the plans, in toto, purchased and brought here in a hurry to catch the post-war boom in 1923. Debutantes and secretaries now dance beneath the trees from which convicted pirates dangled in the old days. On the other hand, back from the harbour and half way up the hill toward Government House, where you can watch the brisk changing of the Guard each Saturday morning, is the grand old lady of Nassau, the Royal Victoria Hotel. Here you can still see the loveliest grounds of any hostelry in the Western Hemisphere, looking much as they did during the days of the American Civil War when Union and Confederate spies ate, slept, and conspired under the same roof. The tropical trees, plants, and flowers in these grounds have been attracting visitors for over a century, but now the yellow and white balconied frame structure is closed, awaiting a complete restoration. It will eventually provide office space for any number of Government departments, a truly fitting function for so grand and experienced an "old girl."

The island's tourist and subsequent hotel boom has in recent years seen new twelve-story buildings spring up over its entire length, heralding in a new phase of the country's economy. They've been built with such dispatch that we barely chuckled several years ago when, during the gala opening of the Paradise Island Hotel, my wife looked out over the hotel's glittering main ballroom and stretched out her hands as she asked, "Isn't this just about where we used to picnic with the kiddies last year?" And it certainly was—a year before this spot had been a small clearing in the midst of a tiny casuarina grove next to the lagoon.

Paradise Island was originally known as Hog Island becuase it was separated from Nassau by the harbour and since it also lay in Nassau's lee it was the natural place, in years past, to keep livestock. There are a number of Hog Islands in the Bahamas and they all, for obvious reasons, lie in the lee of the nearest settlements. But now, with the hogs gone and its name changed to suit its image, Paradise Island is connected to Nassau by a 5 million dollar bridge. The span makes for more convenient transportation to its lavish casino and the new government eventually annexed the island to the city.

During the early thirties, Swedish industrialist Axel Wenner-Gren purchased about four-fifths of the Island and built his own Shangri-La in the center of it, a magnificent estate with many landscaped acres, canals, and formal gardens. In 1959 he sold it all to A & P heir Huntington Hartford, the American philanthropist and art patron, who began developing it into a plush vacation resort. Plans called for a large, modern hotel, a theatre, golf course, yacht marina (Hurricane Hole), and even a miniature A & P, but when he voiced a need of a gambling license to pay for it all, the former government's ears closed to him. Then the Mary Carter Paint Company purchased all but 20 per cent of it and by playing their cards properly maneuvered a trade for the once exclusive Bahamian Club's gambling license (the only one permitted in Nassau). This license was carried over to Paradise Island where ground was promptly broken for the casino. Then after it was opened and operating, "Mary," rejoicing over the results, sold all her paint so she could focus her attention on the more lucrative casino business.

Both the Royal Nassau Sailing Club and the Nassau Yacht Club are situated at the east end of the harbour where it opens into Montagu Bay. The Sailing Club, which now lies on the Bay just beyond the Montagu Beach Hotel, was granted a Royal Charter by King George V in 1925 when its original location was in the old barracks which stood where the British Colonial Mall stands today. The Club moved to its present site following World War II, as both real estate and harbour were becoming too "dear" and too congested with commercial traffic to foster good racing. The Club now has an active Snipe fleet that hosted the World Championships in that class in 1967 under SCIRA's Bahamian Commodore, Basil Kelly. The early spring competitions were sailed in the protected waters off Coral Harbour at the southwest corner of the island.

The Nassau Yacht Club, standing next to Fort Montagu on the small point of land that separates Nassau Harbour from the Bay, harbours a crack Star fleet whose Gold Medal sailor, Durward Knowles, brought world fame to the Bahamas during the 1964 Olympic Games in Tokyo. The Club hosted the 5.5 World Championships in 1967, sailing a modified Olympic course on Montagu Bay. It was founded in the mid-thirties by the first Premier of the Bahamas, Sir Roland Symonette, when, together with the Miami Yacht Club, he organized the now 36-year-old ocean sailing classic, the Miami-Nassau Yacht Race, main and concluding event in the Southern Ocean Racing Conference. This event has grown from a dozen entries the first year to recent fleets of around 125 of the top racing craft in North America whose supporting crew spend close to one million dollars during their five-day visit to Nassau each year.

Sir Roland Symonette is responsible in large measure for promoting the Bahamas into the sailors' year 'round cruising mecca that it has become today. A sailor himself, Sir Roland (during prohibition) built a fleet of smacks large enough to warrant his own shipyard to maintain them. There was a fortune to be made in keeping the Bimini supply lanes brimming with booze and he made his, doing just that. A memorable excerpt from Sir Roland's many-faceted success story tells of those early days when he was too busy loading his boats to keep close account of his finances. When he finally got around to it he itemized the six digit figure and exclaimed, no doubt in shock, "My God, I'm hardly through my twenties and I'm a millionaire!"

It was Sir Roland's frugal leadership as the Bahamas' first Premier that established the Islands' "foreign so-near" tropical–tourist–tax–haven atmosphere of the 1950's and 60's. He surrounded himself with a goup of Nassau merchants which the news-media dubbed "the Bay Street Boys" and ran the Colony like a business. Lawyer and financial wizard Sir Stafford Sands was given a free hand in the country's tourist promotion, plowing back as much as one-fifth of the government income into a vast advertising program aimed at all media. (At one time the Bahamas were spending as much as $7.00 per tourist visiting the Islands—the highest advertising program of its kind in the world.) Visitor figures soared, swelling the pockets of the nucleus group running the show, and why not? I have never met a group of harder working and harder playing men in business or government. I can recall being third in line at innumerable breakfast conferences held in their homes *hours* before the offices downtown had opened their doors.

One of the major targets of the growing Black People's Liberal Party (PLP) was the highly publicized conflict of interests of the incumbents who had brought prosperity to their country. In retrospect we feel sure that they would be the first to admit that their "piece off the top" was quite a bit thicker than it should have been, but had they shared it, would their position have been more secure? We doubt it—possibly their power might have lingered for another election, but their team was outnumbered and with the world press against them it was only a matter of time before the issue of racism would take its toll. The results of the '66 election were no great surprise to Sir Roland or his group.

In the other camp, however, the election results were a great surprise. So much so, in fact, that Leader Lyndon Pindling took a week to select his Cabinet, regrouping in his own constituency on Andros Island, before making his triumphant return to Nassau. When he finally did return it was to a tumult of cheers and victory celebrations that lasted well into the night. His opening words to the nation and the international press, leaking through the Cabinet's thin partition into the Ministry of Tourism offices, were: "So here we are!"—and they always will be.

Prime Minister Pindling takes great pride, and rightly so, in the fact that his party moved into political power by peaceable means, a political fight waged without bloodshed, but the going has not all been easy. The growing pains of a neophyte group of politicians plunged, literally overnight, into big business, have been evident indeed. In their effort to better the lot of their people some foreign investors have been discouraged and internal splits have occurred.

The most significant move yet made by the Pindling Government has been that toward independence, initiated in 1972 and granted the following year. As has been the Crown's policy in the flow of similar cases in recent years, while she may not be totally convinced that the country is entirely ready for independence, it is her feeling that to withhold it until the hour of "readiness" would be fruitless, as without the full responsibilty of independence no Government could ever learn to be so. Really, it's not unlike learning to ride a bicycle; there might be a minor upset or two, but they will learn more by doing than by stringing it along for another five years.

In any case, "C'est la vie!" The best way to enjoy these 70,000 square miles of Islands is to live aboard. In this way you can savor all the anchorages, explore the best reefs, and fish the best waters without becoming involved in the Islands' inner workings—in a way you'll "own" them all.

(New Providence Island

The Coral Harbour Club is on the south side of New Providence Island, almost directly opposite the Windsor Field International Airport, and about five miles from the western end of the island. The entrance to the harbour is well marked, the outer beacon being a white light, flashing every five seconds. It should be left on your port hand when turning in for the entrance. This beacon is about one mile offshore. The entrance lights are also five-second flashes, green on the west side, and red on the east side of the entrance jetties. Inside, there is a very well designed yacht basin, perfectly landlocked and safe in any weather. The channel has been dredged to eight feet at low tide. The harbour has a turning diameter of 1,000 feet and 30 acres of maneuvering space. There are two docks, with slips to accommodate up to 75 yachts. Complete fuel supplies are carried here, also plenty of fresh water, ice, and foodstuffs. On shore there are the usual club facilities; golf course, restaurants, shops, beauty salon, barber shop, a bank. The architecture, furnishings, decor, etc., are all freshly Florida rather than Bahamian, and, in fact, this is very much like a little bit of Fort Lauderdale transported to the Bahamas. Until recently it has been the most popular port of call in the Islands for larger visiting yachts and a natural home base for those intending to fish the Tongue of the Ocean and Andros shore, only 25 miles to the west. Currently (1973) the hotel and marinas are shut down pending sale of the entire facility. This we hope will happen soon as Coral Harbour is still one of the nicest places to tie up in the Bahamas.

A few miles west of Coral Harbour, lying inland from the sea, is the settlement of Adelaide, a step into the past. Probably named for the queen mother of King William IV, it is believed that Adelaide served as a liberation point for the African captives found aboard captured Spanish and Portugese slavers of the 1830's, Britain having given up that trade 30 years previously. There were a number of other settlements in the interior of New Providence

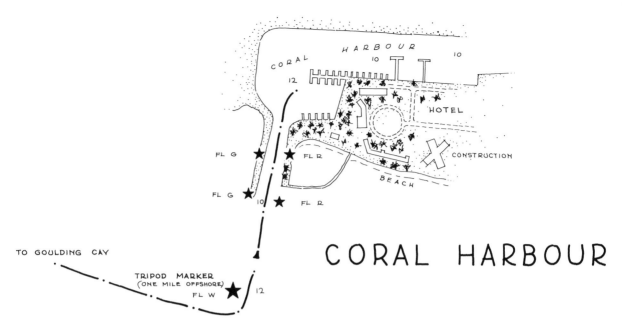

CORAL HARBOUR

where these unfortunates were taken to make it on their own, but Adelaide is the only one remaining that has retained much of its early character. Life here is simple and unsophisticated compared to Nassau and Coral Harbour, both just minutes away by car. Cooking is still done on an open fire and the diet consists of what the season and hands of the men of the settlement can produce day to day.

Over 100 years old, Julita Balfour is the village matriarch. Her keen memory can transport you far into the past if you've the time to listen. She can name her lineage and that of her husband back five generations, and her descriptions, however basic, are authentic. Yes, Adelaide, and especially Mrs. Balfour, should provide an interesting little pocket out of the past for the person interested enough to pay a visit.

The Lyford Cay Club is one of the more fantastic enterprises in the Bahamas. Covering some 4,000 acres at the western end of New Providence Island, where the land is high and pretty, it is just about the last word in elegance. It is the dream come true of E.P. Taylor of Toronto, Canada— a big man, with big ideas and the where-with-all to carry them through. The original membership list read like a page from Debrett's Peerage: The Earl of Feversham, Lord Astor, The Hon. Reginald Winn, The Earl of Dudley, Lord Bruntsfield, Sir John MacTaggart, Sir Victor Sassoon, to mention a few.

This is one club which is not crowded, and consequently everything is on a magnificent scale. There is a well laid out, eighteen-hole golf course, tennis court, swimming pool, stores, service stations, offices, two yacht basins, a yacht club, and many beautiful private residences, all done in the best Bahamian style. Nothing has been spared to make this one of the finest private clubs in the world. A small yacht basin is entered from West Bay, and the entrance, which is alongside and on the north of a long pier, is

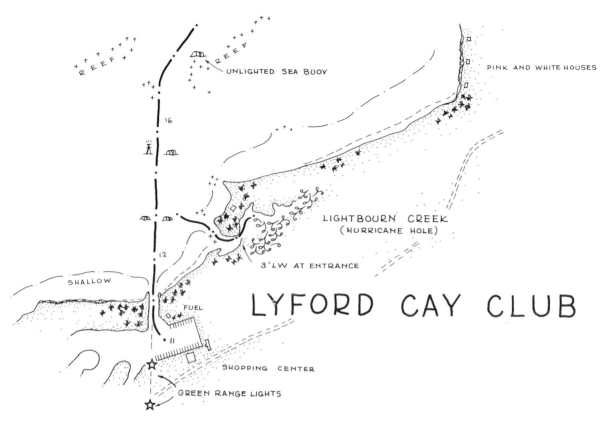

Map labels:
REEF · REEF · REEF · UNLIGHTED SEA BUOY · PINK AND WHITE HOUSES · 16 · 12 · LIGHTBOURN CREEK (HURRICANE HOLE) · 3' LW AT ENTRANCE · SHALLOW · FUEL · LYFORD CAY CLUB · 11 · SHOPPING CENTER · GREEN RANGE LIGHTS

dredged to a depth of 6½ feet at low tide. The basin is over 1,000 feet long, with an average width of about 100 feet, and is dredged to a depth of ten feet throughout. The main yacht basin covers about 30 acres, has a depth of nine feet at low tide in the entrance and eleven feet inside. It opens on the north side of Lyford Cay and is a perfectly landlocked harbour, safe even in a hurricane. The entrance lies five miles from the western tip of New Providence Island and is straightforward, once you take the conspicuous sea buoy to port.

For those people who cannot be too far away from their obligations in the outside world, this is an ideal retreat. Thanks to the Windsor Field International Airport, Miami Florida is only 35 minutes away by air, and New York, 2½ hours. You can have a morning swim here, a round of golf, a leisurely luncheon, even a nap; and still be in New York for dinner the same day.

⟦ Adjacent Cays

Stretching away to the east and northeast from New Providence are numerous small islands and cays which are frequented by small boats day-cruising out of Nassau.

ATHOL ISLAND

This lies just east of Paradise Island and is uninhabited. On it stands the ancient quarantine station, a remnant from the days when Hanover Sound harboured a fleet of coastal schooners clearing for Nova Scotia with their holds bagged with salt. Between Paradise and Athol islands is a passage known locally as "the Narrows." A maximum draft of six feet can be taken through here at low tide. Alongside the cut are the famous sea gardens; on a calm day they are a beautiful sight with the waters over them crystal clear and less than a fathom deep.

SALT CAY

Also known as Treasure Island, this cay is owned by Mrs. John T. McCutcheon, widow of the famous cartoonist of the Chicago *Tribune.* Her residence is at the east end of the island and an entrance cut through the rocky cliff leads to an anchorage in the pond inside. This is a real hurricane harbour and is used as such by many small boats from Nassau in the hurricane season. The entrance, having only about two feet of water at low tide, can only be entered at high tide. The Salt Cay anchorage, on the south side of the west end of the island, was extensively used by the bootleg fleet during prohibition days.

SPRUCE CAY

Lying parallel to and on the north side of Athol Island, this charming little cay has a good anchorage in the cove on its south side—a delightful place for a picnic and swimming , out of sight of the city. We anchored here on the "Liza" one Christmas Eve and trimmed our "conchy joe" tree (casuarina) with sand dollars in hopes that Santa would find us even in this remote spot. He found us alright, but not until after the tide had changed and the high water surge had deposited tree, presents, sand dollars and all at the bottom of the companionway. Obviously, "Santa" kept a constant vigil over "Liza" that night, even moving her into quieter water closer under the Athol shore. Luckily the children, tucked into their bunks, never heard Santa's engines or noticed the broken sand dollars next morning.

ROSE ISLAND

Nine miles long and only about 100 yards average width, this is one of the most popular of all the outlying islands near Nassau, having numerous excellent bathing beaches. There is only one good harbour on Rose Island, called Bottom Harbour, or Lower Harbour, and it is found on the south side of the island, two miles east of the west end of the island, and approximately

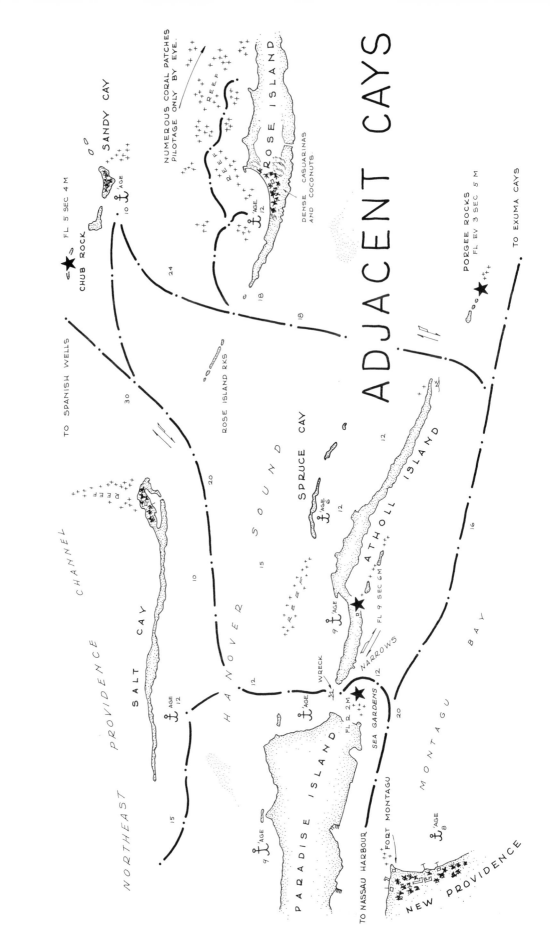

ADJACENT CAYS

the same distance NE x E from Porgee Rock Light. The entrance is from the west, and there is ten feet of water there, shoaling up to six feet inside.

On the north side of the island are many lovely beaches, but to get to them you must pick your way through the reefs, which can only be done by piloting with the eye. Quite a large part of Rose Island is owned by Neil MacTaggart, son of the late Sir John MacTaggart, Bt., a Scottish nobleman who lived in Nassau and at Lyford Cay. The salina at the western end of the island has been opened to the sea for waterfront building lots and a future marina.

SANDY CAY

This cay, which is often misnamed Treasure Island, lies north of Rose Island and is one of the most photographed places on earth—very picturesque with high coconut trees. It has been a very popular background for television commercials. Sandy Cay is the private property of Nassauvian Ozzie Mosley who planted the coconuts there as a child under the watchful eye of his grandfather. During the thirties, when Nassau was first feeling the effects of the tourist boom, Ozzie built thatched cottages on the cay for use by honeymooning couples seeking refuge from the crowds. Today, with the steady influx of weekend "yachtsmen," Mr. Mosley prefers that no one land on his cay without his permission.

CHUB ROCK

Chub Rock, lying half a mile WNW of Sandy Cay, is now marked with a five-second flashing white light. This marks the east side of the entrance into Hanover Sound.

DOUGLAS PASSAGE

Lying between the east end of Rose Island and Booby Island, this is a deep water passage from the banks out to sea. The water is deep blue and the channel easy to distinguish.

THE FLEEMING OR SIX SHILLINGS CHANNEL

Vessels from the west bound to and from Hatchet Bay, Governor's Harbour, Rock Sound, and other ports on Eleuthera Island use this channel because it is comparatively easy in any weather, and well marked. There is a white light flashing every six seconds on Six Shillings Cay which is on the north side of the channel, and another light, a red flash, on the south side of the channel.

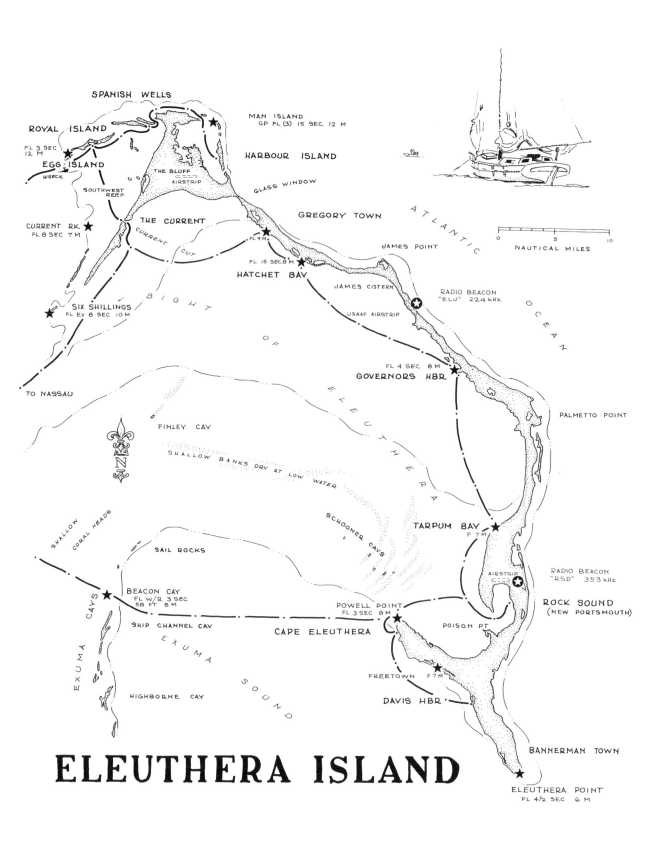

ELEUTHERA ISLAND

SPANISH WELLS

MAN ISLAND
GP FL (3) 15 SEC 12 M

ROYAL ISLAND
FL 3 SEC
12 M

EGG ISLAND
WRECK

HARBOUR ISLAND

THE BLUFF
AIRSTRIP

SOUTHWEST
REEF

GLASS WINDOW

GREGORY TOWN

CURRENT RK.
FL 8 SEC 7 M

THE CURRENT

CURRENT CUT
FL 9 M

JAMES POINT

ATLANTIC

HATCHET BAY
FL 15 SEC 8 M

JAMES CISTERN

RADIO BEACON
"ELU" 224 kHz

OCEAN

USAAF AIRSTRIP

SIX SHILLINGS
FL EV 8 SEC 10 M

BIGHT OF

FL 4 SEC 8 M

GOVERNORS HBR

TO NASSAU

ELEUTHERA

PALMETTO POINT

FINLEY CAY

SHALLOW BANKS DRY AT LOW WATER

TARPUM BAY
F 7 M

SCHOONER CAYS

SHALLOW CORAL HEADS

SAIL ROCKS

AIRSTRIP

RADIO BEACON
"RSD" 353 kHz

EXUMA CAYS

BEACON CAY
FL W/R 3 SEC
58 FT 8 M

SHIP CHANNEL CAY

POWELL POINT
FL 3 SEC 8 M

CAPE ELEUTHERA

POISON PT

ROCK SOUND
(NEW PORTSMOUTH)

EXUMA SOUND

HIGHBORNE CAY

FREETOWN F 7 M

DAVIS HBR

BANNERMAN TOWN

ELEUTHERA POINT
FL 4½ SEC 6 M

0   5   10
NAUTICAL MILES

Eleuthera

Eleuthera is one of the most popular Out Islands in the Bahamas. This is no doubt due to its accessibility from Nassau in almost any kind of weather, and its natural beauty and fertility. There are no less than four important settlements and a score of minor ones here. Its best known settlement, Harbour Island, has been a popular spot for winter residents for the past 40 years.

From New Providence Island, on which stands the capital city of Nassau, to northern Eleuthera there stretches the chain of islands, small cays, and rocks previously described. If the stormy winds do blow from the northwest and north, all you have to do is run up under the lee of these cays. When the prevailing trades set in, use the other side of them. In either case you have a good lee and pleasant sailing.

If you go up on the east side of these islands you will head for Current Cut, which is the passage between Current Island and northern Eleuthera. Current Cut is well named, the water rushing through this very narrow passage at about four knots, sometimes more than that. Its direction depends on the tide and winds. There is a small, picturesque settlement on the north side of the Cut behind a tall stand of casuarina trees known, surprisingly, as The Current. This tiny town is the birthplace of the Bahamas' first Premier, Sir Roland Symonette.

At the northern end of the three-foot low-water channel which works up the settlement's eastern shore past the government dock is the Current Club, a visitor facility comprised of efficiency cottages catering to family groups. Here fuels and fresh water are usually available at the dock which will accommodate two or three boats, while the Club restaurant and lounge offer cool relaxation to tourists and Eleutherians alike.

Should the wind and weather warrant a pleasant passage outside, it is only 34 sea miles NEE from the Nassau Harbour Bar to Little Egg Island where the rusting hulk of a stranded freighter a mile and half south marks the edge of the reef unmistakably.

Royal Island Harbour is undoubtedly one of the best harbours in the whole of the Bahamas. Royal Island itself is something of a gem of an island, 4¼ miles long and well covered with vegetation. The only light is on the neighboring Great Egg Island.

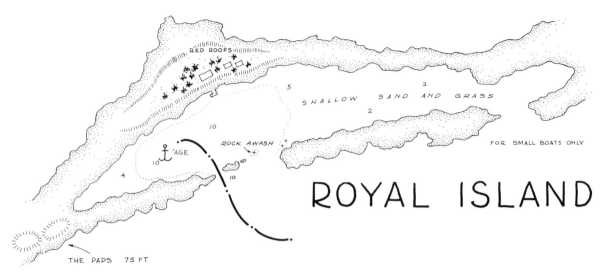

ROYAL ISLAND

Royal Island Harbour lies right smack in the center of the island on its southeast side. There are two entrances, but the one directly opposite the stone house is the best. This entrance is about 200 yards wide with a prominent rock in the middle. A draft of nine feet can be taken in safely. The harbour is about one mile long and perfectly protected from every quarter. Here you can lie on your smallest anchor and sleep soundly.

Royal Island is owned by Mrs. G. T. Stewart of New York. The caretaker and his family are most hospitable and obliging, although the watch dogs are not.

From Royal Island a draft of six feet at low tide can be carried to Spanish Wells, which lies on the east end of Saint George's Cay.

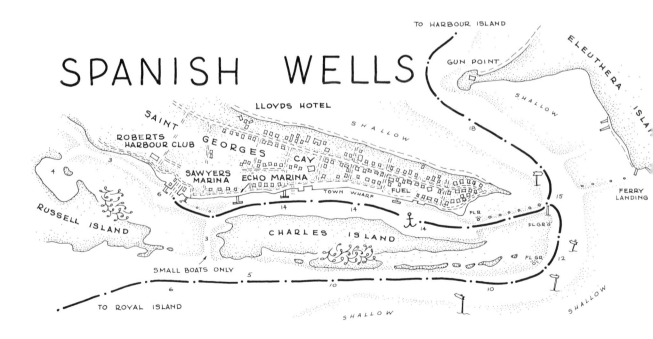

SPANISH WELLS

([Spanish Wells

Ranking as the second oldest settlement in the Bahamas (Governor's Harbour was the first), Spanish Wells is one of the prettiest—a clean, compact little seafaring village of about 850 people, perched on the edge of the sea. The people are largely descendants of William Sayle's group who split away from his original Eleutherian Adventurers in 1648 and were wrecked on the nearby reefs. Their ranks were swelled in 1783 by Loyalists who migrated to Spanish Wells rather than live under the new "rebel government of the United States." Even during the War of 1812 when British renegades sought safety here from their forays on America's shipping, they were protected—for which an American vessel later sacked and burned the town.

Seen from the water, Spanish Wells is a striking panorama of white and yellow houses with red roofs and a luxuriant growth of tall coconut palms. The harbour entrance is off the eastern end of Saint George's Cay. It is well marked and a draft of ten feet can be carried into the harbour basin. A long concrete wharf borders the center of the harbour with the town proper, but this is an all commercial area where the trim-rigged fishing craft and mail boats tie up. It is no place for yachts with delicate topsides. Pleasure craft may berth further west at Echo Marina and Sawyer's Marina which cater exclusively to the cruising visitors.

Spanish Wells has a supermarket, a ship's chandlery, several well-stocked stores, four churches, a telephone system, a power plant, and several hotels. The marinas and town dock offer all marine services including two marine railways which can perform hullwork to top standards.

The main occupations of the lean, bronzed Spanish Wellsmen have been fishing and farming, sailing their products into Nassau every week for almost two centuries. Of course, there has been enough wrecking, blockade- and rum-running to add vitality to this seemingly tranquil existence; consequently their wits, like their sailing ability, have been sharpened. Industrious, frugal, God-fearing people, they are good businessmen too; their fishing schooners have all been equipped with diesel engines, which may seem a pity, but their community has prospered as a result. On our first cruise to Spanish Wells in 1960 we witnessed the first motor scooter to infiltrate the peaceful village streets. It was shipped in by mail boat and the whole town turned out to take a ride. Now (1972) there is a shining new English sedan in practically every garage.

Almost to a man, Spanish Wellsmen are boatmen, often sought out by Atlantic Coast yachtsmen as private captains; it is not too unusual to share a finger pier here with the same Trumpy or Huckins crew you met in Annapolis or Palm Beach six months before. It is not until you chat again with the skipper that you learn this is home port for him and his ship, no matter what the transom hailing port might read. The Spanish Wellsman is a perfect skipper and due to his reliability many East Coast yachtsmen keep their yachts in Spanish Wells year 'round.

The first of these expert boatmen whom you will probably meet will be Aziel Pinder, the town's chief pilot. Having spotted you rounding over the horizon, he will come pounding out over the chop, standing in his skiff to guide you in. We've never called on his services for entering Spanish Wells from the west as our draft never approached the low water depth of the channel, but when entering or departing from the north, or taking the junket around Eleuthera's north end along the Devil's Backbone to Harbour Island, we wouldn't be without his services or those of one of his fellow pilots.

Besides his piloting, which keeps him fairly busy, Aziel tends his farm on nearby Russel Island, serves as a clergyman, and is a good friend. We've always enjoyed being awakened on a sparkling Spanish Wells morning by his cheery greeting as he flashes by in his skiff, sometimes stopping with a gift of fresh fruit just picked from his farm.

One of the few landlubbers in this seafaring community is Lem Sawyer, who has made a success with his clothing store chain in Nassau and the Out Islands. He is neither a yachtsman nor a boatman, but he has built one of the most attractive and completely modern marinas in all the Bahamas. Sawyer's Marina is located at the west end of the harbour where the creek meanders down to the local hurricane shelter known as Muddy Hole. Here Lem has installed an immaculate facility that will accommodate about 20 yachts of moderate size, complete with marine railway, hotel rooms, laun-

Spanish Wells Harbour.
Bahamas Ministry of Tourism

dramat, restaurant, and pool. All marine services are offered along with complimentary bicycles for sightseeing guests.

Halfway down the harbour you will find the smaller Echo Marina which offers space for six boats with all dockside services plus spacious shoreside accommodations on the second floor of the main building across the street, with a splendid view of the entire harbour.

Ashore Spanish Wells resembles a diminutive downeast fishing village of yesteryear. Everywhere you look, net racks are piled high with their bleached loads strung neatly along the water's edge. Sun-seasoned crewmen confer quietly under broadrimmed hats, a Spanish Wells trademark, mend their nets, and affect constant repairs to their vessels. Many of the freshly painted cottages along the narrow streets are over 100 years old and with the madiera knees fit snugly under the eaves, remind us once more of the sailors and shipwrights who built them. The village is only three blocks wide so the sea is always near; a mere turn of the head will bring it once more into view.

The people of Spanish Wells are deeply religious and, much like the Abaconians, do not take kindly to "foreigners" meddling with their social establishment. Several years ago a wealthy American couple breezed into town, bought some prime land along the north beach, and proceeded to build a sports-oriented hotel and tourist complex. For the town's youth they donated a lighted baseball diamond and introduced weekly movies. A great deal of money was invested in the venture and the townspeople were the principal recipients. However, when it was noted that the resultant influx of holiday merrymakers could have a questionable effect on their children's very strict upbringing, the entire community expressed their displeasure by resorting to rather basic "discouragement" tactics. As a result the entire facility underwent some very difficult "growing pains" from which it is only now emerging. For the natives of Spanish Wells, this has been their town for over 300 years; we feel they should be allowed to run it their own way.

Roberts Harbour Club is a spacious, airy, tourist resort which lies just up the curving channel west of Sawyer's Marina. Here, undoubtedly because it was built by local people, the Club has not evidenced problems, even though it has an open bar. Happy hour occurs whenever there is a congenial group as the sun drops over the yardarm, with vivacious Gena Roberts presiding over guitar-strumming, harmonizing visitors and home folk. Roberts Harbour Club offers comfortable rooms and mouth-watering grouper, just one of many tasty dinners available. This is far different from our first visit to Spanish Wells many years ago when we arrived in town at noon, docked, and dashed to the only restaurant to find a note wedged into the locked front door which read: "Out to lunch!"

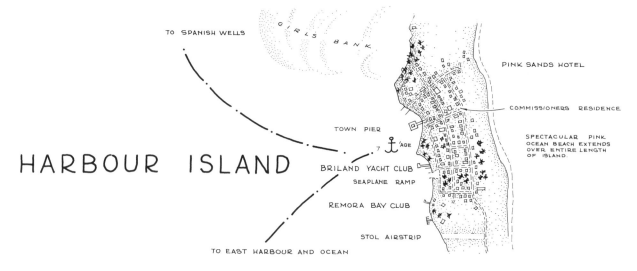

HARBOUR ISLAND

Map labels:
TO SPANISH WELLS
GIRLS BANK
PINK SANDS HOTEL
COMMISSIONERS RESIDENCE
TOWN PIER
7 'AGE
SPECTACULAR PINK OCEAN BEACH EXTENDS OVER ENTIRE LENGTH OF ISLAND.
BRILAND YACHT CLUB
SEAPLANE RAMP
REMORA BAY CLUB
STOL AIRSTRIP
TO EAST HARBOUR AND OCEAN

⟨ Harbour Island

There are only two ways to get to Harbour Island by boat, one inside the "Devil's Backbone" from Spanish Wells, the other clean around by sea outside all the reefs and in between South Bar and East Harbour. The first is only about nine miles, most of it in protected water. The second about sixteen miles and most of it pretty rugged going, for the whole Atlantic Ocean sweeps in on Northeast Bank without a break. However, do not attempt the passage inside the Devil's Backbone without a local pilot from Spanish Wells. You will appreciate this piece of advice better when you are only 50 yards from seas breaking on the beach to leeward of you. A draft

Dunmore Town, Harbour Island. *Bahamas Ministry of Tourism*

of seven feet can be taken through without difficulty by a local pilot.

The harbour, described by some as one of the best in the Bahamas, is in our opinion one of the worst. It is simply the open sound on the west side of the island. You have to lie a half mile offshore if you draw more than six feet and it can be very mean in a norther. The charm of Harbour Island lies ashore, not afloat. The town itself is quaint, its architecture not unlike that along the Carolina shores. There are some good grocery stores, a number of excellent hotels, rooming houses, and cottages, a ship chandlery, Resident Commissioner, doctor, a small shipyard, and, during the season, daily air service to Nassau. The beach on its eastern shore is one of the most spectacular in the Bahamas. It reflects a definite pink cast which some would have us believe is from surf-ground conch shells. We rather believe it stems instead from a subterranean mineral deposit. No matter what their origin, the pink sand beaches of Harbour Island are truly lovely!

Dunmore Town was named for the Earl of Dunmore, Governor of the Bahamas from 1786–1797, who maintained a summer residence here. The Commissioner's residence now stands on the site. The inhabitants of Dunmore Town are sailors, fishermen, and farmers. The farmers cultivate the lands on the opposite shore, which is North Eleuthera, on a community basis called "commonage." This land, about 6,000 acres, was granted to the loyal Harbour Islanders who assisted Colonel Deveaux in recapturing Nassau from the Spaniards in 1783. Regulated by a committee of townspeople, the rights of commonage are jealously guarded and passed down in the family whenever possible. One of the memorable sights of Harbour Island past was the fleet of small boats, all under sail, taking the farmers to work across the bay in the early morning and bringing them back again at night. There is very good fishing off the reefs outside the harbour mouth at the south end of the island.

Harbour Islanders are known throughout the rest of the Bahamas as "Brilanders," a name derived when residents of this community dropped the first syllable of "Harbour Island" and then slurred the remainder together, forming "Briland."

Briland Yacht Club, aptly named, looks for all the world as if it had been transported here from New York's Thousand Islands, with its decorative filigree and covered boat hoists. Yachting facilities are limited to a few boats and fuel must be purchased at the town pier, but the very charm of the club itself makes it an important port of call. Cool, comfortable rooms beckon the yachtsman across the tiny street where delicious meals are served.

Yachts tying up at the town pier should bumper properly and be prepared to anchor off in the event of a squall. As we cautioned earlier, the Bay makes up into a nasty chop in anything but prevailing weather.

The Remora Bay Club is the large, well landscaped edifice just south of town. Here, under the able direction of owner/manager Roy Schmidt, the specialty is skin diving with all of the latest equipment available to the visitor.

Like Spanish Wells and Governor's Harbour, this island was originally settled by a branch of the Eleutherian Adventurers around the year 1648 and due largely to their isolation their settlement strengthened and prospered.

Harbour Island's lofty reputation as an exclusive winter resort began when a few of Nassau's leading families rented their summer cottages here to wealthy foreign friends for the season. Having frequented Nassau, watching its "season" grow, they were discouraged by the tourist numbers and sought out their own special haven further from the crowd. Still quiet, almost pastoral, its architecture is a comfortable combination—a New England seaside town with a southern accent. Harbour Island gives a taste of what Nassau "used to be."

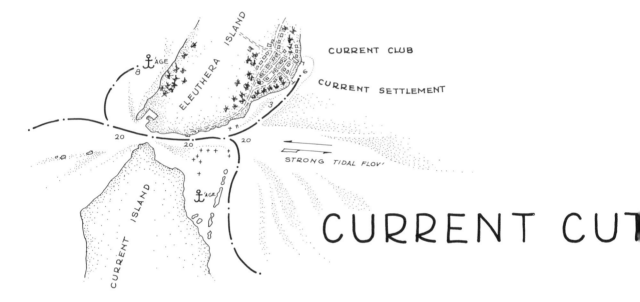

⟨⟨ Current Cut

If you would now visit the rest of Eleuthera by boat you must retrace your course back past Spanish Wells and Royal Island or around Great Egg Island to Current Cut, and so through to the great bight which lies on the southwest side of the island. If the wind should be in the north or northwest, and the current is running from the southeast through the Cut you will get a breaking sea which might startle you, but do proceed, there is plenty of water in the Cut itself and you can take a draft of seven feet through without difficulty. Emerging on the other side be sure to turn south, keeping the rocks to starboard and the east coast of Current Island close aboard until you are well past the silted bars. Then take up East by South for Hatchet Bay, sixteen miles away.

The Island of Eleuthera is about 70 miles long and lies in a NW-SE direction. As the prevailing winds are from the east, from northeast to southeast, it is obvious that the whole southwest side of the island is perfectly protected for small vessels, and therefore an ideal cruising ground. Along the shores of this bight there are five important settlements: Gregory Town, Hatchet Bay, Governor's Harbour, Tarpum Bay and Rock Sound.

If the wind is in the east, as it usually is, you will find smooth water all along the lee of Eleuthera Island, and many attractive little places to see and explore if you are so inclined. In the days of slavery many large plantations were owned and operated by Englishmen on Eleuthera where the ruins of the large stone plantation houses can still be seen.

One of the interesting spots along here is the Glass Window, a narrow isthmus which until the 1926 hurricane was spanned by a natural bridge. It is now bridged by Eleuthera's main highway. Here the island, although 70 miles long, is only about 100 yards wide, and is low enough so that a vessel lying in the bight on the west side in smooth water has a ringside view of the stormy Atlantic breaking on the rocky coast only a few hundred feet to windward.

Between the Current and Hatchet Bay you will pass the settlement of Gregory Town, named after John Gregory, Governor of the Bahamas in the 1850's. It is quite picturesque, looking not unlike a Cornish village, with boats hauled up on the beach in the cove. The anchorage here is uncomfortable, there being a persistent surge rolling in from the bight at all times.

Gregory Town's leading family is that of the Thompson brothers who operate a tomato and pineapple plantation along with the cannery and distillery for their processing. "Bahamian Brand" tomatoes have long been a favorite shelf item in Nassau grocery stores as have been the Thompson's delicious Pineapple Rum found in the usual spirits shops next door.

Gregory Town offers a sprawling water sports-oriented tourist resort known as the Arawak Cove Club that has a short pier with less than a fathom of water, so we do not recommend tying up here. There is an interesting little inn, The Talking Dolphin, restored from one of the oldest buildings in the town, a charming place for a respite when it is open for business.

(Hatchet Bay

The settlement of Hatchet Bay has a splendid landlocked harbour and, in fact, it is used as a hurricane refuge by boats in this vicinity. The first objects which you will recognize when approaching will be several pairs of white silos in the fields stretching away from the shore. These are about one mile west of the settlement. The entrance is through an artificial cut in a gray limestone hill and is quite difficult to pick out as it is very narrow. There is good water right up to the shore, however, and a light high up on the rock on the west side of the entrance. There are three fathoms of water in the

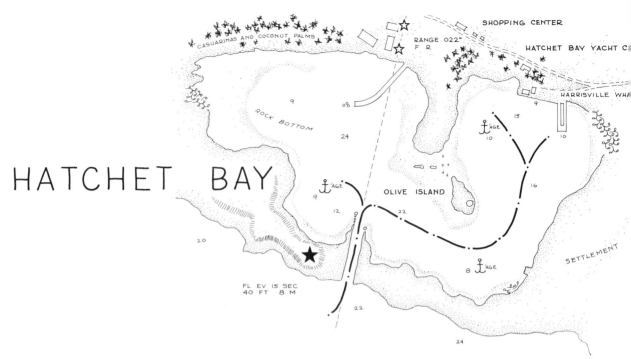

HATCHET BAY

cut, and the pond or harbour inside is practically landlocked, so perfectly safe in all weather. After clearing the jetties, which are inside, head southeast until you pick up the dock, then head for it, in case you wish to get water or supplies.

The best reason we can think of for tying up at Hatchet Bay's sturdy new dock is to meet dockmaster Harold Albury, one of the nicest people in all the Bahamas. With his lovely family, he has been a mainstay at Hatchet Bay since its very inception. Thanks to Harold's particular efforts during Hurricane Betsy in September 1965 there was no loss of life when heavy tides flooded the harbour and stranded a large portion of the Nassau charter fleet that had sought refuge there. A peculiar phenomenon accompanying the storm occurred when thousand of leaves were blown into the harbour from the surrounding trees and covered the water's surface, clogging the intakes of the boats riding it out at anchor, causing their engines to overheat and fail. With their engines out of commission, the larger vessels were blown ashore, one on top of the other, much like matchsticks. But thanks to Harold's herculean efforts, coupled with those of the skippers, there were no serious injuries.

Not that it takes a hurricane to appreciate Harold Albury—he is definitely a "man for all seasons," an able seaman who can always locate the largest grouper or the deepest channel.

If you prefer to anchor you can do so almost anywhere inside the harbour. However, the water shoals from three fathoms to one fathom off Alice Town. This harbour was formerly a landlocked pond, fed by subterranean, salt-water streams. It was used as a turtle crawl, or corral, for large sea turtles which were caught all over the West Indies, kept here, and taken out as needed.

Hatchet Bay Plantation was founded by New England textile manufacturer, the late Austin T. Levy, in the mid-thirties. It is a very successful poultry and dairy farm that has supplied most of Nassau's needs in recent years. Mrs. Levy, now in her eighties, is still active as president of the plantation's interests, with retired Bostonian banker Phil Potter managing the operation. Mr. Potter, an avid sailor, established the popular Hatchet Bay Yacht Club which serves as the main meeting place for this section of Eleuthera. Overlooking the harbour, the club's kitchen turns out one of the best chicken dinners in the Islands, and Saturday night's patio movies, while not "current box office hits," are the best of their particular vintage. Watch out for the Westerns though, because when they're shown the whole audience gets into the act!

A stroll ashore is a must, particularly if you are interested in farming, or replenishing your fresh stores. Milk, butter, eggs, poultry, and vegetables produced by the plantation are available at the "Company" store, just a pleasant stroll up from the dock.

Old "East Bay" friends Ed and Clarissy Lathrop manage the plantation store and always have a hearty welcome for visiting yachtsmen. They sailed here from New England following Ed's retirement from the Marine Corps in 1960 aboard their sturdy Abaco ketch "Ask No Quarter." The Lathrops' son, Lester, and his wife, Gloria, now charter the boat out of the marine sports operation at Governor's Harbour. A former Marine flyer, Ed keeps his own plane at the nearby airstrip and remains on constant standby as BASRA's one-man, air "search and rescue" team for the Eleuthera area.

There are several caves west of Hatchet Bay that are well worth a visit. One is so extensive that the local people claim it has never been completely explored. Any one of the local youth would be glad to guide you there if you supply the flashlights and a reasonable fee.

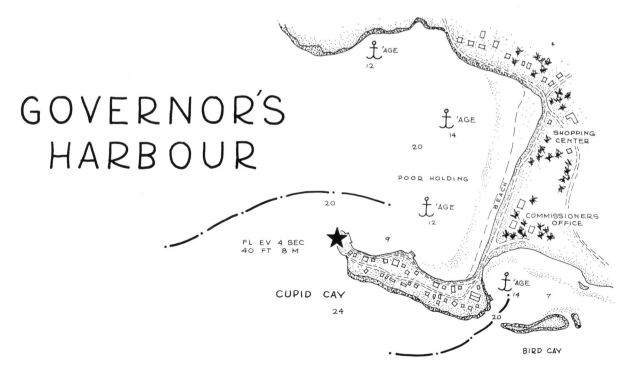

GOVERNOR'S HARBOUR

(Governor's Harbour

Certainly the most interesting settlement on Eleuthera, and generally considered to be the capital of the island, is Governor's Harbour. It was the principal settlement of the Eleutherian Adventurers and it lies fifteen miles SE 3/4 E from Hatchet Bay. The houses high on a hill north of the harbour will be your landfall. As you get closer you will pick up the houses and light on Cupid's Cay, all very picturesque. Cupid Cay was a small island, but is now a peninsula connected to the mainland by a substantial causeway over which a paved road runs. There are two harbours, one on each side of the causeway. The harbour on the north side is a deep cove, almost a semicircle, opening to the northwest. The harbour to the south of the causeway is also a deep cove and has the additional protection of an outlying cay, named Bird Cay. It is therefore possible to lie on either side of the causeway well protected in any weather, choosing whichever side gives you the best lee; however, a mild surge exists in both. Vessels drawing as much as two fathoms can be taken into either harbour. There is a reliable light on the end of Cupid Cay, flashing every four seconds, 40 feet high, visible eight miles.

On Cupid Cay will also be found the post office, library, most of the old business houses and residences, and a rambling settlement that undoubtedly inspired some of Winslow Homer's paintings. The settlement on the mainland, or north, side of the harbour is of comparatively recent growth, very

Cupid's Cay, foreground, was the original settling place of the Eleutheran adventurers in 1647.
Bahamas Ministry of Tourism

pretty and with a wonderful view of the sea. This is a most romantic place with many fascinating connections to the Colonial history of America. Here, in Colonial days, the three-masted schooners from New England and the Baltimore clippers from Chesapeake Bay came sailing in with cargoes of goods from the north, returning with cargoes of pineapple and other fruits obtained from the large plantations which once existed on the Island. Each captain brought with him a bag of gold and everything was paid for by gold on the barrelhead. The best of British goods were shipped out from England to Governor's Harbour, and so found their way to America. Life here was prosperous, elegant, and to some extent cosmopolitan. Many of the early settlers were Royalists from America who, although loyal to the British Crown, still had sentimental and sometimes family attachments to the United States. It is recorded that a gift of £200 was sent by the people of Eleuthera to buy lumber to help build Harvard University in Boston. Even today traces of such attachments can be found. Miss Enid Bethel is a descendant of one of the signers of the Declaration of Independence. George Bethel, with the same lineage, is now in his seventies and has lived in Governor's Harbour all his life. From his rocking chair he still operates the small grocery store his father started three generations ago and he likes to recall the days of his youth when he sailed pineapples to the Nassau market, long before Florida or Hawaii ventured into the business.

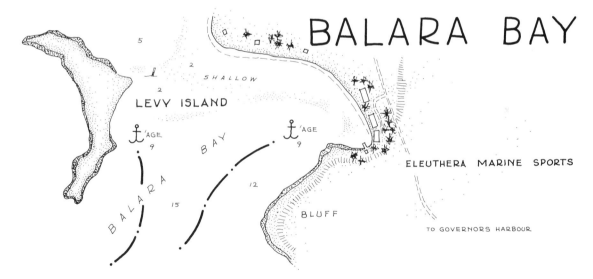

There are no docking facilities for yachtsmen in Governor's Harbour except the rough mailboat pier on Cupid Cay which always gets a dangerous surge. However, around the bluff in Balara Bay there is an extensive marine-sports operation that could refuel a yacht of moderate draft in an emergency. The docks, which supply fresh water and fuel, can accommodate several small cruisers up to 30 feet in length.

⟨ Governor's Harbour to Tarpum Bay

Between Governor's Harbour and Tarpum Bay, a distance of fourteen miles, there are upwards of three fathoms close into the rocky shore all the way. Along here you will pass Ten Bay, previously known as "Tent Bay" for the pineapple traders who erected temporary camps here during Eleuthera's productive pineapple period. Ten Bay is marked by two long rock promontories which might offer a little protection from northerly winds. A little further south the Pineapple Cays offer a lee in west through northerly weather, but it would be advisable to make for Rock Sound or Hatchet Bay if conditions appeared strong. The bottom here is poor holding and with the bight's ever-present surge a strong wind could make for an uncomfortable night.

⟨ Tarpum Bay

Charming is the word to describe this settlement, one of the oldest on Eleuthera, and still with much of the original flavor. There are no docks or shoreside facilties for yachts, so anchor about 200 yards off the government concrete pier in two fathoms over a deep sandy bottom. Here you will ride comfortably under normal conditions and you can visit the town by dinghy. Surrounded by fertile soil, Tarpum Bay flourished during the nineties when pineapple was king, as evidenced by the town's architecture which reflects that period. It is rumored that at the same time a considerable amount of rum was distilled here. There are a number of tidy little guest houses and two restaurants, any one of which could arrange dinner for you and your crew on reasonable notice. Tarpum Bay's seemingly endless crescent beach extends both north and south from "Patriarch's rest" under the big tree at the head of the pier. This is the focal point of the town and if you happened to foul your anchor on arrival it was noted and discussed, in great detail, right here. The usual host of casuarinas, fishing boats, and nets bask in charming disarray under a relentless summer sun the entire length of the settlement.

A particularly interesting stop ashore is schoolmaster McMillan-Hughs' art gallery where both his paintings and sculpture are on display.

A few miles north of Tarpum Bay on the ocean side of the island is the Eleuthera Beach Inn, a 100-room, Americanized vacation complex where, in the event you've become "too Island oriented," you can shake the sand out of your shoes and play it straight for a few days. Here, with the overseas telephone, the modern, air-conditioned rooms and excellent American cuisine you can relax, and in hours you'll feel like you've never been away.

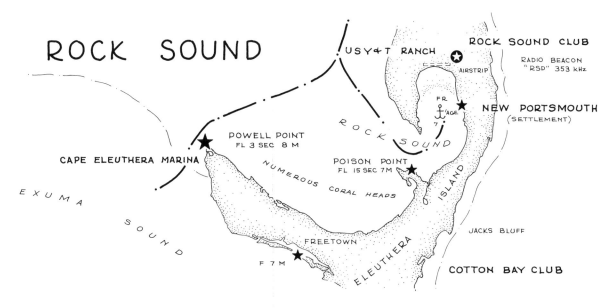

ROCK SOUND

USY&T RANCH

ROCK SOUND CLUB
RADIO BEACON
"RSD" 353 kHz

AIRSTRIP

FR
AGE
7

NEW PORTSMOUTH
(SETTLEMENT)

POWELL POINT
FL 3 SEC 8 M

R
O
C
K

S
O
U
N
D

CAPE ELEUTHERA MARINA

POISON POINT
FL 15 SEC 7M

NUMEROUS
CORAL HEADS

E
X
U
M
A

S
O
U
N
D

E
L
E
U
T
H
E
R
A

I
S
L
A
N
D

JACKS BLUFF

FREETOWN

F 7 M

COTTON BAY CLUB

❪ Rock Sound

From Tarpum Bay the sailing distance to Rock Sound is almost thirteen miles with deep water all the way. Care should be taken, however, from Kemp's Point (the point of land to port that extends farther west) to Poison Point, as there are several coral heads in this area that carry little more than four feet at low water.

It is generally accepted by local people that Rock Sound is the inner, smaller sound rather than the large bight which lies between Poison and Powell points. Further, it was indicated on earlier charts as Wreck Sound, as many of the inhabitants were in that trade. We would guess then that Rock Sound is merely a derivation of the latter. Also, the town ashore, New Portsmouth, is generally known as Rock Sound.

Again, there are but limited facilities for the cruising visitor, the bulk of yachting activity being concentrated at Davis Harbour, some 20 sailing miles further on. Several grocery stores and a supermarket, a ships' chandlery along with a superb machine shop, are to be found ashore, while fuel can be

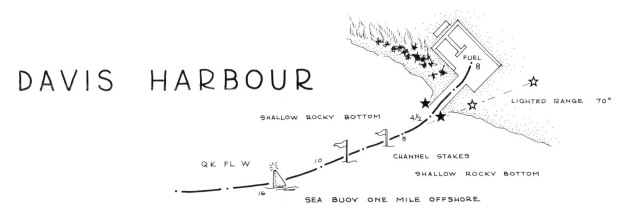

DAVIS HARBOUR

FUEL
8

LIGHTED RANGE 70°

SHALLOW ROCKY BOTTOM

4½

5

QK FL W

10

CHANNEL STAKES

SHALLOW ROCKY BOTTOM

16

SEA BUOY ONE MILE OFFSHORE

delivered by truck at the government's long wooden pier. Rather than lay alongside other than to refuel or discharge your crew, we recommend anchoring 100 yards off in a fathom of good holding mud bottom and visiting the town by dinghy.

The neat little village has been one of the most prosperous settlements on Eleuthera ever since the late Arthur Vining Davis, Chairman of the Board of the Aluminum Company of America, purchased a large tract of land and built a winter home here. Since then his Three Bays Company has developed the land and community into a thriving settlement.

Rock Sound has a hospital with the resident physician for all of Eleuthera. Just east of town is Ocean Hole Park where there is a most remarkable "blue hole" right in the center of the Island. It is 40 fathoms deep and filled with fish of all kinds.

Mrs. Grace Kemp runs the town's only guest house right along with her sundries store, next door. Mrs. Kemp's guest house is a godsend to the sea weary sailor who would like to leave his boat at anchor and rid himself of his sea legs for a spell. Nellie Lowe operates the only bakery in the village where meals can be arranged on short notice. If you prefer a tot of rum with your supper try Mr. and Mrs. Bethel's snack bar-restaurant where fresh seafood or chicken with the best peas and rice we've tasted can be had.

Juan Trippe, former Chairman of the Board of Pan American Airways, is the current prime mover of Rock Sound, with considerable interests in the Eleuthera Beach Hotel, South Eleuthera Properties, and G.A.C. at Cape Eleuthera. Due to the personal efforts of Mr. Trippe there is jet service twice daily to Nassau and Miami; not bad for a community of little over 2,000 people, and surprisingly enough, the jets seem to be carrying their full complement of passengers for most of their trips.

The Rock Sound Club, a very fashionable resort with accommodations for 100 guests, is not on the waterfront but in the country, about one mile from the village. About seven miles south of the village there is one of the finest golf courses in the Bahamas, known as the Cotton Bay Club. It was designed by the well-known golf course architect, Robert Trent Jones. This is an exclusive club patronized chiefly by influential businessmen seeking escape. It is part of Mr. Trippe's vast interests here and money has been spent freely to make it the best of its kind.

A frequent visitor to Cotton Bay is Edgar Kaiser, son of the famous industrialist, Henry Kaiser who some 60 years ago began polishing silver for a West Coast hardware store and parlayed his profits into the World War II victory ships and finally the post-war Kaiser automobile. Mr. Edgar Kaiser maintains a vacation home at Cotton Bay.

The yachtsman's portion of the Cotton Bay Club is Davis Harbour, which lies four miles further south but on the west side of the island. Here in a small, dredged, inner harbour the club maintains its fishing fleet and provides dockage for its seagoing members. All services are available to the visitor, along with the best drinking water on all of Eleuthera. Davis Harbour's location provides easy access to the good fishing of Exuma Sound along the Schooner Cays and the superb deep sea game fishing off Eleuthera Point.

Located in some of the prettiest pastureland on the island is U S Y & T Industries. Founded originally by Armour and Company, it comprises a select breeding herd of 60-odd Charolais cattle. In 1969 the herd produced a U.S. Grand Champion, "Eleuthera," whose worth is estimated at $400,000. Doctor Larry Delva of Saskatchewan, Canada, is ranch manager.

One of the most ambitious projects since Freeport or Great Harbour Cay is the huge G.A.C. land development scheme—Cape Eleuthera, occupying some 5,800 acres south of Powell Point. The overall picture contains the usual landlocked marina, a Von Hagge designed golf course, and a promise that 2,000 of the acres will remain as parks, recreation, historical, and wilderness areas.

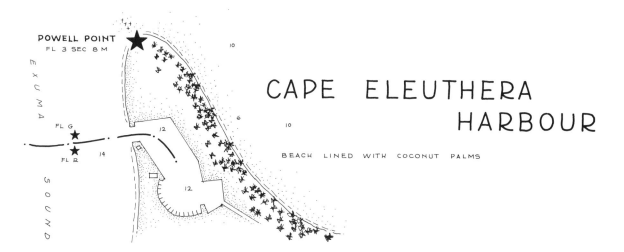

⟨ Cape Eleuthera

Ragged Islander Captain Stan Lockhart was dockmaster at Hurricane Hole for some twelve years before he made the move to Eleuthera to take the helm of the new marina there. He is a professional yacht skipper and has delivered boats to ports on the mainland as far north as the Canadian border. Some of the most able seamen come from Ragged Island and Captain Stan is an outstanding example. He can be a most handy source of information for the Islands, one of the few Bahamian skippers who knows all the Islands well. We're delighted that our two children could enjoy a few years of his tutelage in Island lore.

The historian for Eleuthera lives at Bannerman Town, close to the south tip of the island. He is Captain Henry Finley, descended from a slave family brought here from Florida in the early 1800's. Wise and chipper at ninety, Captain Finley serves the Bannerman Town population of twelve as Justice of the Peace, Postmaster, Church Catechist, telephone operator, tour conductor, and local historian. In his own words, he pretty much "takes care of the whole place." Strange as it may seem, however, the good Captain is not a seafaring man, never having gone to sea at all. He was named "Captain" at his birth in 1882 on the advice of an uncle, himself a seafarer, who knew well the respect this name would bring his nephew.

The Captain's photographic memory can bring back, vividly, descriptions of the days of slavery as told by his parents and grandparents when he was a youngster. How they lived, their work, the overall organization of the plantations, and their relationships with their owners, are all recorded on his indelible memory. His grandparents worked on the cotton plantations of the Gibson and Miller families, which occupied the entire south end of Eleuthera. Now, with his third wife and a granddaughter, the Captain lives in a four-room stucco house which he built in his youth on a portion of the 1,000 acres Robert Miller left to his slaves. Miller also donated the land on which stands St. Matthew's, the oldest church in Nassau, and is buried in its churchyard.

In 1961 Captain Finley was awarded the Queen's Badge of Honour for meritorious service. During World War II he organized a search which saved the lives of a Royal Air Force crew, guiding them to safety across the island in darkness.

Andros

Andros, the largest of the Bahama Islands, remains a mysterious and romantic isle, mainly due to its many years of comparative inaccessibility. Rumor has it that this island is the home of the Chick Charney—Andros' legendary leprechauns. A small being in the form of a bird with large eyes, it is said to build its nest on the tops of three neighboring pine trees which it draws together, tripod fashion. Legend has it that it was the Chick Charneys who trained Billy Bowleg, the famous Seminole medicine man who could cure all ailments. They say, "You can tell a Chick Charney 'cause he don't cast no shadow. If you're nice to 'em they can be mighty nice back, but if you're mean they can be your death." Neville Chamberlain, former Prime Minister of England, learned about Chick Charneys the hard way. As a lad he lived on Andros, managing his father's sisal plantation. Disregarding the advice of his men he cut down one of the Chick Charneys' favorite nesting trees and they "put the sign on him"—even up to Munich, which probably changed the whole course of modern history.

Andros abounds in good shooting and fishing. The shooting consists principally of duck shooting, although there are also some pigeon and dove. The fishing is superlative with all kinds of reef fish, tarpon in the inlets, and some of the best bonefishing in the world. Conch and crawfish are plentiful everywhere.

All of Andros' settlements, with the exception of Red Bay, are on the east side of the island. Red Bay was settled by runaway Carolina and Georgia slaves who had been offered refuge by the Seminole Indians in Spanish-owned Florida in the early 1800's. They sailed their families here in large dugout canoes from the mainland to escape recapture when the state was being annexed in 1821. Having mingled for several generations with the Seminoles, their descendants reflect the handsome Indian feature to this day. To meet these people it is not necessary to take the long trip across the island. They are the Newtons, Lewises, Colebrooks, Bowlegs, and Rileys of North Andros' eastern settlements.

Although the nearest point of Andros Island lies only a little over 20 miles from New Providence Island, it is considered a difficult place to visit, as it lies "down to leeward." Easy to get to, but hard to get back from, in case the wind comes in fresh from the northeast. Between the two islands

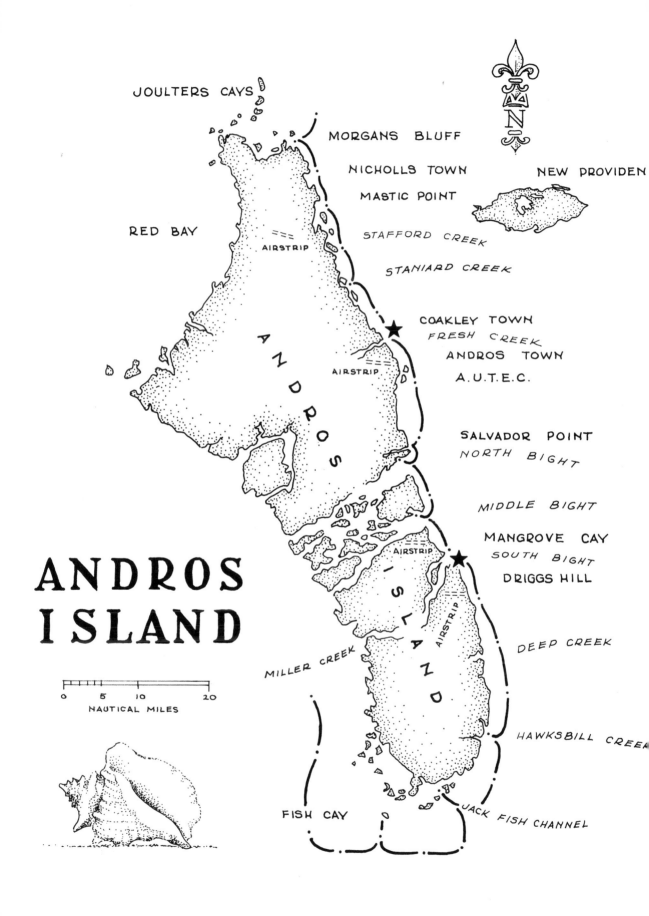

JOULTERS CAYS

MORGANS BLUFF

NICHOLLS TOWN

MASTIC POINT

NEW PROVIDEN

RED BAY

STAFFORD CREEK

AIRSTRIP

STANIARD CREEK

ANDROS

COAKLEY TOWN

FRESH CREEK

ANDROS TOWN

AIRSTRIP

A.U.T.E.C.

SALVADOR POINT

NORTH BIGHT

MIDDLE BIGHT

MANGROVE CAY

SOUTH BIGHT

DRIGGS HILL

ISLAND

AIRSTRIP

ANDROS
ISLAND

DEEP CREEK

MILLER CREEK

HAWKSBILL CREE

0   5   10   20
NAUTICAL MILES

FISH CAY

JACK FISH CHANNEL

lies the "Tongue of the Ocean," a deep ocean trench with soundings up to 1,000 fathoms, a mighty rough place when it blows. Then on the Andros side is a great barrier reef, one of the longest in the world, with very few breaks in it and all of them rough in a rage. It almost seems as if nature had deliberately put up as many barriers as she could think of to keep the crowd away from this sleeping island paradise.

It is possible to visit Andros in a deep draft boat, but you will be confined to only one entrance and harbour, which is that of Middle Bight. William L. Mellon of Pittsburgh, Pennsylvania, an enthusiastic bonefisherman, used to take "Vagabondia" in there. She was 222 feet in length overall, and drew twelve feet of water. Mr. Mellon even had a mooring put down for her in Middle Bight. Bill Labrot took his 82-foot schooner "Seaweed" into Morgans Bluff and she drew eight feet. In both cases we would say that these are the extreme drafts which can be taken in those two entrances, and then only if there is no considerable sea running. A draft of seven feet can be taken through the reefs at Nicholls Town (the Bethell entrance), at the Staniard Creek Channel, at Fresh Creek, also just north of High Cay, at North Bight and at South Bight. In any case passage through the reefs should not be attempted at night, when a high sea is running, or when visibility is poor.

Passage north and south, inside the reefs, should not be attempted by a boat drawing more than five feet, and then only when the visibility is good. If it is not good, anchor and stay there until you can see where you are going. We have been run aground, and hard too, by so-called expert local pilots who couldn't see a rocky patch any better than we could with the sun in their eyes.

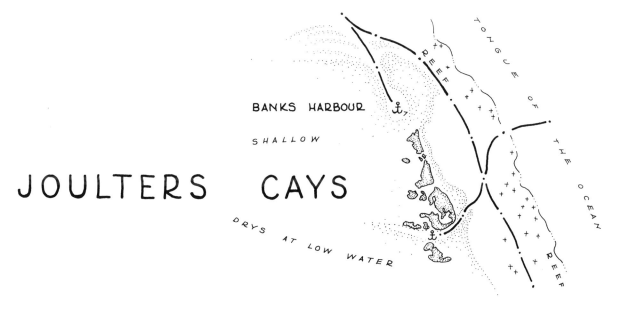

You must remember that the native Bahamian sailors expect to run their boats aground frequently, and that their boats are built to stand it, while a light yacht is not. It is a common sight to see a native boat go charging in to a sand bank under full sail, stop with a crunch, lower the sails, furl them and hoist them to the mast head, run an anchor out ahead, put the crew out on the main boom, heel her over and kedge her ahead at the same time, until they have bumped and scraped over the bar into deep water; then up sails and away with a grin, as if nothing unusual had happened. It is one of the reasons why no Bahama boat is built with a centerboard.

The last time we observed this "maneuver" we were dashing for the cover of Banks Harbour off Andros' north end with a black squall line closing fast on our heels. The local crawfishing fleet had "upped" anchor and were racing us in. Every vessel including our "Spindrift" had everything up and we were scurrying before it as fast as we could go. Probably the only yacht in the fleet, we even had our engine going. As we neared Banks Harbour we could see the slanted masts of the crawfishermen taking the short cut across the sand bars, fairly manhandling their boats into the safer water inside.

We had been pleased with our progress until a giant Andros sloop off our stern began to gain on us. She sat low in the water, raising a bow wave like a New York Harbour tug and as she crept abeam we counted eleven men on deck plus three heavy fishing dinghies in tow. The boat couldn't have been over 35 feet long but she had a good knot and a half on us with no engine at all. We shouted across to inquire if the captain could sell us a few crawfish and he allowed he could "spare some" as he had about 500 below. However it wasn't until we were anchored and rowed over to pick them up, that we discovered he was running with a wet well which made the big sloop half full of water. Yes, those Andros sailors can sure sail their boats!

(Morgans Bluff

This bold, rocky headland forms the northern extremity of Andros Island. It lies only 25½ miles W x N ¾ N from Goulding Cay Light, which is on the western end of New Providence Island. As you approach the Andros shore probably the first object which will catch your eye is the wreck of a large steamer in two parts which lies on the reef about four miles below Nicholls Town. She was driven ashore there during the hurricane of 1928 and will be there for eternity.

Soon after that you will pick up Morgans Bluff, which at first looks like three small hills rising above the flat land. When you get closer you will see they have houses on them. Morgans Bluff is headquarters for Owens Illinois Pulpwood Division and this modern community perched on the bluff itself houses its employees. Extending northwest from the tip of the bluff is an

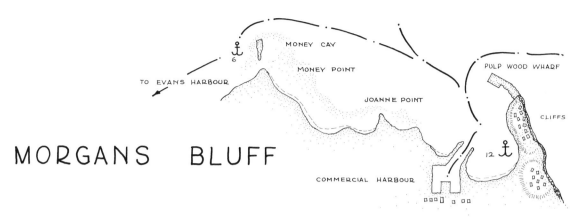

MORGANS BLUFF

immense wharf piled high with racks for loading pulpwood on barges for their trip to Jacksonville, Florida. The small, inner harbour to the west is commercial where fuel can be supplied by truck in an emergency.

When making for the anchorage, round Morgans Bluff in a westerly direction about 200 yards off. Sound your way to the best anchorage for your draft. There is six feet of water at low tide in the pretty cove inside, well protected from easterly winds. However, this is no place to be in a norther so keep a weather eye when anchored here.

The caves along the shore are very interesting and are said to be the pirate Morgan's safety deposit vault. Many people have searched for treasure here but nobody, to our knowledge, has ever found a thing. Richard LeGallienne's book *Pieces of Eight* might explain why.

About a mile west from Morgans Bluff and just inside Money Point, there is a very picturesque little harbour called Evans Harbour, the entrance being 50 yards off the pole marker. This is a good harbour for small boats in a norther; three feet at low tide.

North of Morgans Bluff there is a good anchorage in the lee of Hog Cay, with six feet of water at low tide. There is very good bonefishing and some tarpon around Joulters Cays, and a good anchorage on the south side of lower Joulters Cay for a boat drawing not over four feet. Plenty of conch and crawfish all around here.

If you are cruising in a shallow draft boat, as recommended, you can now enjoy a very plesant cruise down the coast of Andros inside the barrier reef, in protected waters, with a good, though sometimes rough, anchorage almost anywhere. Boats drawing over five feet should not attempt it. The dangerous shoals are black patches, usually composed of black rocks and white coral, with green ferns and grass growing between them. They are easily seen in the very clear water unless the sun is ahead of you. As noted before, if light conditions are such that you cannot distinguish these dark patches easily 100 yards away, then anchor and wait until you can.

Proceeding south from Morgans Bluff follow the shoreline about 100 yards off the beach. The first thing you will come to is the Andros Beach Hotel where a pleasant tourist atmosphere prevails. The hotel is part of the huge 8,500-acre Parker Pen complex that has been developing truck farming techniques on the island over the last 20 years. You will see a long towering dock amid a jumble of pilings. Here fuels are available, but unless it's dead calm, it is best to anchor off and go ashore in your dinghy.

⟨ Nicholls Town

A little further south along the highest elevation on Andros is the picturesque settlement of Nicholls Town, where the Commissioner for North Andros resides. There is a good general store where some provisions may be had, but the anchorage is an uneasy one, rocky and poor holding. A nasty reef called the Devil's Backbone parallels the shore for four miles south of Nicholls Town. There's a deep break in it immediately south of the town known as the Bethell Channel. Here a reliable lighted range will lead you through in eight feet of water.

Again, proceeding south, stay inside the reef, keeping about 50 yards off the shore. There's good water all along here, about eight to nine feet.

There are good anchorages just south of Coconut Point and in Conch Sound a quarter mile off New Town. The normal rise and fall of the tide is about three feet and the anchorage offers six feet at mean low. New Town has nearly 500 inhabitants and is the site of the old Chamberlain sisal plantation which belongs in most part to Parker now.

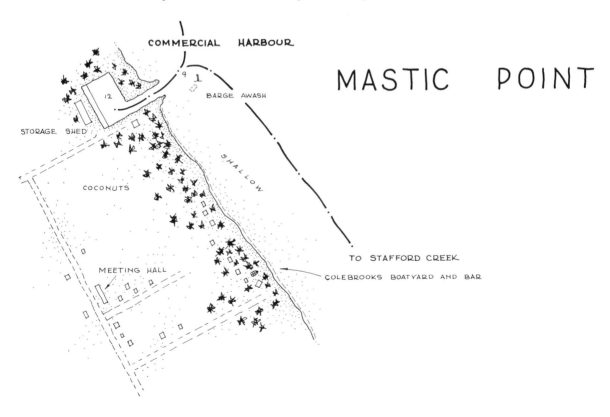

❲ Mastic Point

The Parker Company has cut a small inner harbour into the land north of Mastic Point, which offers ample protection in a confined, casuarina-shrouded hurricane hole. Here excellent potable water can be piped to your boat and the same fuel truck that serves Morgans Bluff calls here. A short walk up the road is the plantation house in which Neville Chamberlain lived while he managed the sisal interests. It's an old, graceful, gabled and porch-rimmed frame structure that typified Island architecture after the turn of the century.

Clarence Colebrook, descendant of the Red Bay Colebrooks, is Mastic Point's foremost boat builder and barman. His boats, like all Andros craft, are crude by yacht standards, but deep footed, sturdy, and fast. Clarence's little bar stands just in from the beach in a conconut grove and is well worth a visit as his humor, like his boats, is "Robust" and "Quick."

Passing south from Mastic Point there is good water around Rat Cay to Saddleback Cay. Rat Cay is easily recognized, having a prominent lump on its East End.

STAFFORD CREEK

Stafford Creek lies inside Calabash Cay, a high, wooded island. There is only three feet of water on the bar at low tide, so it is necessary to wait for the tide to get in and out, but very pretty and worth the trouble.

Pigeon Cay is a charming little island with a nice sandy beach and a large pond in the middle. A very bad rocky patch lies N x W three-quarters of a mile from the north end of Pigeon Cay. Pass to the east of it.

A reef extends about 300 yards north from Staniard Rock, which has a light on it, and just north of this reef there is a good channel, about 100 yards wide, coming in from the sea. This channel should not be attempted at night as the light there is not reliable.

STANIARD CREEK

⟨ Staniard Creek

Staniard Creek is one of the most attractive of all the settlements on Andros Island, a clean and well laid out little village with about 300 inhabitants. It is beautifully situated on the banks of two creeks, with a lovely sandy bathing beach on the ocean side. Unfortunately the entrance to Staniard Creek is obstructed by a shallow sand bar with only three feet of water on it at low tide. There is a very snug anchorage, in six feet of water at low tide, just inside the north end of South Cay. A good road now connects all of the settlements of North Andros with swing bridges crossing all the navigable creeks.

A mile north of Fresh Creek, snuggled behind an endless rough-hewn dock is the comfortably rustic Small Hope Bay Lodge where Canadian diving enthusiast, Dick Birch, has developed a cottage facility naturally slanted toward divers. The dock has too little water for yachts of any size, but again anchor off and visit the Lodge by dinghy as Small Hope Bay is a fun place.

⟨ Fresh Creek and Andros Town

Due to the developments which have taken place on shore here in recent years, this is the most important harbour on the north coast of Andros Island. A white flashing, five second light on a steel column ten feet high marks the entrance through the reef. Leave it on your starboard hand when entering, about 100 feet away. The course from here to the creek entrance is SW x W ¼ W. The channel is marked by one barrel buoy. The bar is two-thirds of the way between the light and the shore, and the maximum draft which can be taken over this bar at low tide is six feet. There are considerable currents around the entrance, which must be taken into account as the flood tide sets from SE to NW. In entering the mouth of the creek keep to the north side. After passing the entrance move over to the south side along the yacht club piers, where the deepest water will be found. After passing the yacht club piers swing back to the north side of the creek where there is a wide basin and anchorage. Large yachts should proceed to this basin before turning, as the current is strong, up to four knots at times, and the channel opposite the yacht club pier is too narrow for safe maneuvering. On the north side of the creek, abreast of the church, you will notice a pier built very high out of the water. That pier is only one foot above the level reached by the water in the creek in the 1929 hurricane.

Fresh Creek derives its name from this tidal creek which runs back in to the wilderness of Andros for some 40 miles, there joining up with some small fresh water lakes. There is good bonefishing in the creek, and some duck shooting in its uppper reaches. Andros creeks are not safe in a hurricane, due to the tremendous amount of water which pours through them from the interior.

On the north side of the creek is the village of Coakley Town, a cluttered, sprawling hamlet which has changed little in recent years. Poverty stricken for most of its history, it is just now beginning to achieve some measure of prosperity by its proximity to its neighbors across the way. The Commissioner's office and residence is at Coakley Town, where there is also a very handsome Anglican Church.

Andros has always been considered the Bahamas "seat of black magic," probably because Haitian ties have always been stronger here than anywhere else. Among the countless tales of Haitian voodoo (known here as Obeah) is that of "Uncle Gabe" at Coakley Town who could "fix" a field to keep out the thieves. Upon payment of a few shillings he'd get you a ghost from the local cemetery to put in your field to protect your crops. They say he even had a brisk mail order business with old friends who had moved away to Nassau and Florida.

Andros Town is the name given to the settlement on the south shore of the creek. It is a resort village built around two very elegant club and hotel facilities, the Andros Yacht Club and the Lighthouse Club. The late Axel

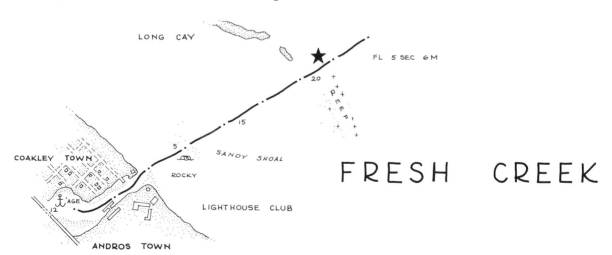

Wenner-Gren, Swedish industrialist who originally developed Nassau's Hog Island, built the club here to attract sport fishermen to the heart of the best bonefishing grounds in the Bahamas. There is also good deep sea fishing in the Tongue of the Ocean and along the reefs within sight of the club, where a number of record catches have been made. Sadly, however, following Wenner-Gren's death the entire project has lost momentum. It seems the various new managements have been unable to sustain the impetus set by Wenner-Gren and his unlimited funds. The empty yacht club and threadbare hotel stand as a decaying monument to better times.

Immediately south of Andros Town lies the Atlantic Undersea Test and Evaluation Center, a multi-million dollar joint British-American project for the testing of scientific defense equipment. AUTEC, as it is known locally, maintains a perfect, manmade harbour which is strictly "off limits" to the casual visitor but will offer refuge in the event of an emergency. Scattered up and down the Andros shore line are several annexes to the AUTEC operation. Fairly bristling with strange antennae, radar grids, and domes, each has a snug little harbour where the same visiting rules apply. Occasionally you might encounter an unlisted buoy in the Tongue of the Ocean as there are a number of these that seem to come and go with the changing experiments. A wise yachtsman will maintain a sharp lookout.

The passage inside the reef from Fresh Creek to North Bight is good for a draft of five feet providing there is good light and an able lookout. Otherwise, it is best to make the passage outside where trolling, just off the reef, will bag anything from barracuda and giant grouper, to dolphin in the spring and summer months. High Cay, being a part of the reef, is high and wooded and there is a narrow passage through the reef off its north end. Green Cay offers a temporary anchorage in six feet of good sandy holding for those braving the passage inside.

The AUTEC auxiliary station marks Salvador Point unmistakably and those cruising down outside the reef may enter the Banks here via the well-marked, nine-foot AUTEC channel.

The most protected anchorage hereabouts is that of Pye's Harbour, 2½ miles into North Bight. Here you will find a cosy anchorage in seven feet over good holding mud. From this point boats drawing no more than four feet can begin exploring North Bight.

The passage inside the reef between North and Middle Bight is treacherous but entirely possible, and with the proper guide six feet can be carried through safely. If you have doubts retrace your steps to the Salvador Point AUTEC Channel and proceed south on the outside, entering again via the new AUTEC sea buoy at Middle Bight. It is also possible to gain Middle Bight by the back way, that is around the lee of Big Wood Cay. But here again, we recommend no more than a 3½-foot draft for this passage, plus a reliable guide.

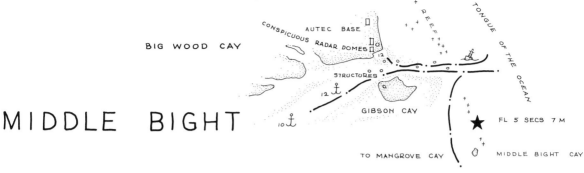

MIDDLE BIGHT

⟪ Middle Bight

The best entrance and anchorage in the whole of Andros. When nearing Middle Bight, evident by the conspicuous AUTEC auxiliary station at the south end of Big Wood Cay, round the sea buoy and proceed in between Gibson Cay and the AUTEC channel markers on a westerly head toward the tripod structures straight ahead. When approaching these, favor the deeper, blue channel which trends away to the southwest, and anchor wherever you wish in ten to twelve feet of perfect protection from any quarter. There are strong currents setting in and out with the tides. The rise and fall of tides here is about 2½ feet. Big Wood Cay has a luxuriant growth of coconut trees. Gibson Cay is flat and rocky. The entrance between cannot be mistaken. There is a remarkable "ocean hole" in the center of Gibson Cay, connected to the sea by subterranean tunnels, and teeming with ocean fish. Well worth a trip ashore.

North Bight, Middle Bight, and South Bight cover an area of about 250 square miles, which might well be called an archipelago within an archipelago. Here are literally hundreds of little islands sprinkled around on a miniature sea so clear and shallow that walking is often easier than sailing through it. The Bights run clear through to the west side of the island, and a draft of four feet can be taken through by working the tides. These are waterways of great natural beauty and an indescribable charm. They lead into vast lagoons, thickly wooded on the banks, where will be found colonies of pink flamingos, pelicans, ducks, black parrots, mocking birds, iguanas, and all sorts of fish—bonefish, tarpon, and others. The interior is quite uninhabited but occasionally you will come across a cay with a tiny house on it, usually the property of a local fisherman who works the area regularly.

Some of these cays, being in protected waters, are unbelievably fertile. One day, while bonefishing, we asked a naturalist friend to list the flora on Herbert McKinney's little Mastic Cay, in Middle Bight, a tiny island not over five acres in area. Here is the list:

Coconut Palm	Mandrake	Poison wood
Lemon	Pigeon plum	Black torch

Grapefruit
Lime
Banana
Sour orange
Sweet orange
Sugar apple
Sapodillo
Guava
Alligator pear
Almond
Rose apple
Rose
Cabbage palm
Aloe
Sisal
Mastic
Seven-years' apple
Bay lavender
Bay parsley
Snake wood
Christmas vine
Wild brier
Mistletoe
Wild cotton

Cocoa plum
Strong back
Locust
Ram horn
White buttonwood
Black buttonwood
Joe bush
Joe Segree bush
Sea grape
Thatch palm
Love vine
Bastard logwood
Strangler fig
Wild sapodillo
Black mangrove
Red mangrove
Poppy
Bastard horseflesh
Wild marigold
Guana bush
Wharf stopper
Sweet Margaret
Moker tea-aromatic
Poor man's strength

Joe wood (not the same
    as Joe bush)
Stopper
Pawpaw
Cassava wood
Ganep
Sugar cane
Salve
Sage
Bird pepper
Pigeon peas
Gale-of-wind bush
Stinking pea
Granny Kinney
Bay cedar
Tear coat
Rabbit grass
Needle grass
Sea parsley
Salt water grass
Pigeon berry
Crab bush
Bed grass
Saw grass

Strangely enough, although Andros Island is low, marshy, and almost tropical, it is very healthful, no doubt due to the complete absence of the malaria mosquito and the beneficial trade winds. The chief ailment seems to be the common toothache and we are told that the Roman Catholic Church has gained many converts by sending down priests who can save souls and pull teeth at the same time.

MANGROVE CAY
LISBON CREEK

❨ Mangrove Cay and Lisbon Creek

Meandering along the coast of Andros for some nine miles, all the way from Middle Bight to South Bight, the settlement known as Mangrove Cay is certainly the largest native settlement in the Out Islands and as the capital of Andros Island it has a population of well over 2,000 people. From offshore the settlement is difficult to see as the houses are nearly all hidden by the towering coconuts which continue down the length of the island. Most of these were planted under the personal supervision of the late Mr. L.E.W. Forsyth who was resident commissioner for Andros for over 50 years. At Mangrove Cay there is a post office, telephone station, several small stores and Prince Jolly's swinging little night club, the Zanzibar.

At its southern end Mangrove Cay settlement joins up with the settlement of Lisbon Creek which is one of the most beautiful of all Out Island villages and is the center of boat building on Andros, some of the fastest fishing smacks and the most able sailors hailing from here. In the many years of their attendance at the Out Island Regatta, held in George Town, Exuma each spring, Lisbon Creek boats have never failed to bring home their share of the prize money. Lisbon Creek has fine people, industrious, independent, and religious. The very names of their vessels reflect their character— "Alert" "Unity B.," "Charity," "Mystery J.," "Sea Cloud" and "Matchless Rose" are some of them. At Lisbon Creek the best known boat builders and sailors are the Longleys, Bains, and Bannisters, all descended from James Carr, an emancipated Long Island slave who came here in the 1800's to ply his boatbuilding trade. It is a memorable sight to see the products of their efforts hauled up on the shore of the creek for cleaning and others being built under the coconut trees just as James Carr had done. In the midst of all this Leroi Bannister and Bernard Longley operate very comfortable guest houses for the casual visitor. They are named Bannister House and Longley House respectively. A prominent member of this community is Livingston Bethel, who is also the catechist of the Anglican Church.

Lisbon Creek itself is a fine all-weather anchorage. It will accomodate vessels of five foot draft, but the approach from the Bight is shoal and you should wait for high tide.

On nearby Victoria Cay the late Nelson Hayes and his wife, Emmy, of Roxbury, Vermont, built a lovely home in the Bermuda style and spent six months of each year there. He was the author of *Dildo Cay,* the book from which the motion picture *Bahama Passage* was taken, and of *Roof of the Wind,* another popular favorite.

Due to the fact that the Andros sailors have spent their lives sailing under the generally difficult conditions presented by the 100-mile-long Andros shore, their sailing instincts have been honed to the sharpest edge and they probably represent, as a body, the best natural sailors the Bahamas have to offer. No doubt their heritage and environment have made them a special breed who, as Wendell Bradley so nicely put it, "truly live by the wind."

(South Bight

Continuing down the on the outside, turn in when about three-quarters of a mile from Golding Cay, passing close to Channel Rock, leaving it on the starboard hand. Steer SW from your position abeam of Channel Rock for half a mile to avoid Channel Shoal, which is plainly visible, then due south into the bight. A good anchorage is off Forsyth Point, or further up if you prefer.

South Bight is the deepest of the Andros bights, where a draft of four to five feet can be carried through to the west side of the island. Remembering that the tide enters the Bight at each end with that on the west coast lagging that on the east by two hours, it is possible, entering at the east, to ride the tide clear through.

There are a number of spectacular blue holes along South Bight, one of which provides a unique geological example for scientific study. The famous grotto, first explored in its entirety by blue-hole authority Dr. George Benjamin and later featured in Jacques Costeau's television series, is 300 feet deep and its various features confirm the theory that during the ice age the earth's sea level was some 600 feet below what it is today. According to the experts the entire Bahama Bank is nothing more than the top plains of a limestone mountain range which, during that era, were eroded and carved by the earth's atmosphere. Now the glaciers have melted away, the earth's tide-line risen, and the once dry caves, with their numerous stalactites and stalagmites are deep underwater. Many of the early drippings formed gigantic pillars in these blue holes, the whole effect attracting both scientists and diving enthusiasts from around the world.

(South Andros

At Driggs Hill on the southern point of South Bight is the government wharf. This wharf will accommodate boats of three foot draft at low water and it should be noted that this is the most southerly fueling station on the island, the fuel being supplied by truck. Hatchet Creek, just to the west, will carry four feet at high tide only.

Las Palmas Hotel lies two miles south, and while it offers no particular services to yachtmen, it is the only resort hotel on South Andros and a welcome sight to the cruising seafarer with a yen to stretch his legs ashore for awhile. Here among the towering coconuts surrounding a beachside pool are 20 attractive, modern rooms, a bar, and a dining room that serves an excellent Bahamian-American menu. If you would prefer to stay ashore it would pose no problem to anchor your boat in either Hatchet Creek or South Bight, where it would be perfectly safe. The hotel would be happy to supply transportation.

For yachts drawing no more than five feet it is possible to continue south inside the reef to Andros' southern tip, then north up the lee of the west side. The best water inside the reef is six to eight feet, favoring the reef side all the way. This will take you inside Tinker Rock, but outside High Point Cay where the southernmost AUTEC auxiliary station now stands. Continuing down around the tip of the island it is best to parallel the coast and its adjacent cays, standing off about two miles.

Good protection can be found up Jack Fish Channel in six to eight feet if the shifting sand bar at the entrance will let you in. The adjoining creeks and cays comprise almost a virgin area, seldom visited by anyone but the occasional smack fisherman. Here conch and crawfish abound and the flats offer bonefish at every turn while the tarpon rolling in the creeks at night will sometimes keep you awake in your bunk.

Continuing on around the southern end it is best to go south from Jack Fish Channel for at least eleven miles before turning west. Then to avoid the extensive sandy shoals lying southwest of the island, continue west 20 miles before turning north up the coast.

If you are an avid bonefisherman and your draft will permit, Fish Cay can provide the highlight of your cruise. Here, anchored between conch-strewn sand bars that dry at low water, you will be surrounded by pools of hungry bonefish that will come to your lure at every cast. Nowhere else in the Islands have we enjoyed such consistent and exciting action.

Andros' west coast has little to recommend it, being for the most part shallow for an average of four miles out from the shore its entire length. However, bonefish and conch should be plentiful if the encroaching foreign fishing boats have not already "conched it out." We have heard reports of an abundance of shrimp along here in the "running months" but have not had occasion to see it first hand.

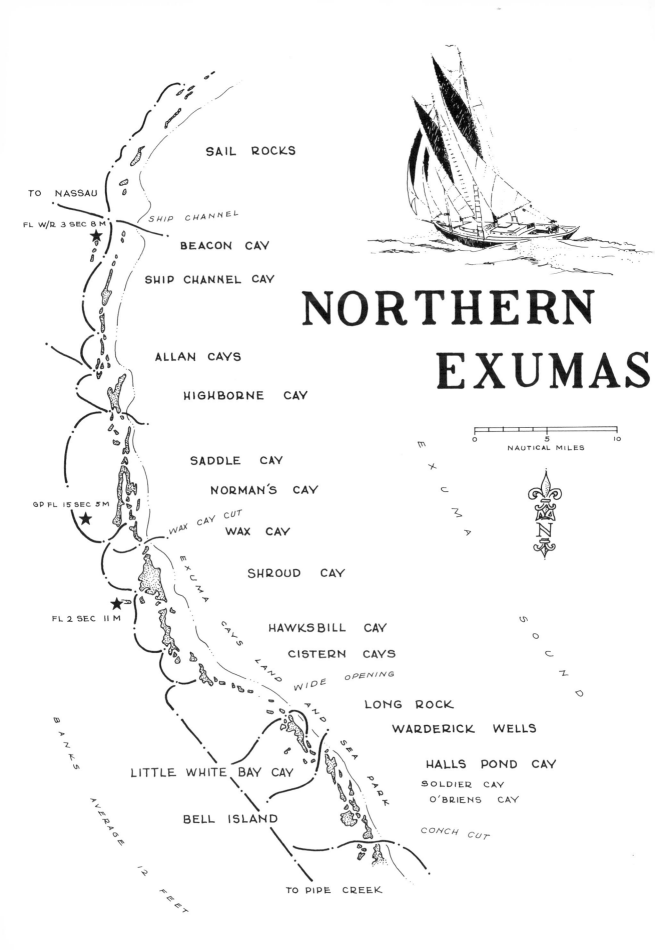

SAIL ROCKS

TO NASSAU

SHIP CHANNEL

FL W/R 3 SEC 8 M

BEACON CAY

SHIP CHANNEL CAY

ALLAN CAYS

HIGHBORNE CAY

SADDLE CAY

NORMAN'S CAY

GP FL 15 SEC 5 M

WAX CAY CUT

WAX CAY

SHROUD CAY

FL 2 SEC 11 M

HAWKSBILL CAY

CISTERN CAYS

WIDE OPENING

EXUMA CAYS LAND AND SEA PARK

LONG ROCK

WARDERICK WELLS

HALLS POND CAY

SOLDIER CAY

O'BRIENS CAY

LITTLE WHITE BAY CAY

BANKS AVERAGE 12 FEET

BELL ISLAND

CONCH CUT

TO PIPE CREEK

NORTHERN
EXUMAS

0   5   10
NAUTICAL MILES

N

EXUMA SOUND

The Exuma Cays: The Pièce de Résistance of West Indies Cruising

The charm of the Exuma Cays is more esthetic than geographic, but isn't charm more a thing of the spirit than the flesh anyway?

Here you will find no mountains, bold headlands, or busy harbours, no rivers, few trees, and only two major towns. Yet it is unquestionably one of the finest and most colorful cruising grounds for small yachts to be found anywhere in the world. From Nassau to George Town, Great Exuma, a distance of about 130 miles, you will find little that the hand of man has spoiled. The few settlements and scattered houses look as if they had been there since time began. The occasional hurricanes which demolish the most substantial buildings seem to have little or no effect on the tiny houses perched on the windiest places.

To get from Nassau to the Exuma Cays by the shortest route you have to cross the fearsome Yellow Bank, which is not nearly as frightening as it looks on the N.O. chart. The flood tide flows east from Nassau to the Yellow Bank, and, a bit beyond it, where it meets the flood tide coming in from Exuma Sound. Local boats bound for the east or south usually plan to leave Nassau on the last half of the flood, so as to carry the current beyond the Yellow Bank, where they will then pick up the first of the ebb tide to take them down the cays.

Most of the available charts, both British and American, scare you to death with indications of nests of coral heads abounding in the area around Porgee Rocks. No need to get excited about them as they were all blasted out by the harbour engineers for the International Star Championships years ago. There are only three shoal spots anywhere near the channel and these are all approximately one mile due West of the Porgee Rocks Light, and they all have at least eight feet of water on them at low tide. If your boat draws more than that, or if you are nervous in the presence of rocky heads, you may avoid the Yellow Bank entirely by standing on past Porgee Rocks Light for two miles, as previously described, then changing course to due south, and holding that for fifteen miles before heading east for the Cays. This course will take you east of the shoals off the east end of New Providence Island, and west of the Yellow Bank and is safe for a draft of ten feet.

It is best to make a start from Nassau late in the morning, or early in the afternoon so that the sun is overhead, or behind you, when the Yellow Bank is underneath you, so as to insure the very best visibility.

On the Yellow Bank you will see plenty of dark rocky shoals. They are very easy to locate, being dark green, purple, or black in color, and as the water is crystal clear you can pick them up when still 50 to 100 yards away. They are usually quite small in area, and easy to go around, which is the safe thing to do. A few of these here have a little less than six feet of water on them and over the white sand bottom between them there is usually from two to three fathoms of water.

The tides appear to divide at or about the Yellow Bank. The flood tide, which flows generally east and southeast in the area between New Providence Island and the Yellow Bank, flows to the west and northwest on the east side of the Yellow Bank. These tidal currents are also considerably deflected by the various openings which carry the water from the banks to the sea and vice versa.

A number of years ago when the *National Geographic* was publishing an article on Bahamas cruising we were queried as to why the Yellow Bank was "yellow," as opposed to brown or white like the majority of other banks in the Bahamas. At the time we could not come up with a satisfactory answer, but it has occurred to us since that because the Yellow Bank marks the points where tides from all directions converge, it is quite possible that minute particles of loose, dead coral, which are predominantly ocre in color, have been washed here for eons from the surrounding patches and deposited at high slack to give the sandy bottom hereabouts a definite yellow cast.

Soon after crossing the Yellow Bank you will pick up either Ship Channel Cay or Highborne Cay. Both are high islands, seen a long way off. You will now be on the threshold of a sailor's paradise. Stretching away to the southeast for some 120 miles is a chain of emerald islands, in a setting of purest turquoise, the clearest, cleanest water you will find anywhere. Some of these little islands are no larger than a small flower garden. One, Great Guana Cay, is eleven miles long. There are big islands, little islands, fat and thin ones, some high, some low, of every shape and character, but all beautiful in their own way. Many of them have the most exquisite pink coral beaches you ever saw, with sand as fine as powder—the Exumas are indeed a sparkling, sun-washed paradise!

Although most of these cays are so close together that they almost touch, there are numerous passages between them leading from the banks out into Exuma Sound. On the windward or northeast side of the Cays the trade winds blow strong, and the seas run high, the 100-fathom curve coming almost up to their shores. On their leeward or southwest side the winds seem to be more moderate, and the water is smooth and clear. A good anchorage can be had in the lee of almost any cay, safe in the prevailing easterly winds. There are several first rate harbours where a boat can lie perfectly protected from wind and sea in any quarter. The following list of the best anchorages and harbours will help a yachtsman plan his precious days.

₵ List of Best Anchorages and Harbours in the Exuma Cays

In every case the draft indicated is the maximum which in our opinion can be safely carried in at dead low tide. All these harbours have considerably more water inside them than there is in the approaches. It is therefore usually quite safe to take deeper draft vessels in at high tide.

SHIP CHANNEL CAY—Good anchorage inside shoal on northwest side, and inside cays lying off south end. Safe for a nine-foot draft.

ALLAN'S CAY—Very good harbour, safe in all winds, ten-foot draft.

HIGHBORNE CAY—Good anchorage in cove at southeast end or harbour inside. Seven-foot draft.

SADDLE CAY—Good harbour, entrance on Exuma Sound side. Ten feet in the channel at low tide. No passage from the west except at high tide.

NORMAN'S CAY—Smooth and safe harbour in cove off dock at the southeast side, good for nine feet at low tide. Landlocked lake in the interior into which a draft of six feet can be taken at high tide.

SHROUD CAY—or Pigeon Cay as it is locally known. Very good anchorage in cove NE from Elbow Cay. Ten feet depth close to beach. Good harbour for small boats, drawing up to six feet, in mouth of creek.

HAWKSBILL CAY—Good harbour in cove on southwest end. Safe for drafts up to seven feet.

CISTERN CAY—Good anchorage on lee side off sandy beach. Not always smooth; however, safe for seven feet.

WEST SHROUD CAY—Good anchorage off northwest end under lee of shore. Safe for a draft of ten feet, though there is as much as 20 feet of water in places. No good in a norther.

WARDERICK WELLS CAY—Two good harbours, one on the northwest side and the other on the southeast side. A draft of ten feet can be taken into either.

BELL ISLAND—Good anchorage on lee side opposite pretty cove.

COMPASS CAY—Good anchorage in Conch Cut on northwest side of cay opposite pretty cove with sand beach.

PIPE CAY—Very pretty cove on southeast end with splendid harbour for boats drawing up to six feet.

SAMPSON CAY—Good harbour in prevailing winds off Club dock. Mild surge at all times.

STANIEL CAY—Off Yacht Club Dock. Good harbour with ten feet of water, limited only by passage in from banks with six feet at low tide.

MAJOR'S SPOT—Landlocked harbour for boats up to ten feet.

GREAT GUANA CAY—Several deep and well sheltered coves where you you can lie safe and smooth in winds from north to northeast.

LITTLE FARMERS CAY—Good harbour with safe anchorages for boats drawing up to twelve feet. Only seven-feet draft can be taken in from the banks at low tide. Deeper draft vessels must enter from Exuma Sound.

GALLIOT CAY—Several good anchorages northwest of the Cut, and in the cove on the southeast end of Big Farmers Cay.

MUSHA CAY—Comfortable lee in prevailing winds. Here you are protected from west and north winds by Lancing Cay and sand banks to the north. Eight feet at low water.

DARBY ISLAND—Tight little anchorage with strong tide north of the shoal marker. Good protection in all weather if your hooks are "dug in." Ten feet low water.

ADDERLEY CUT—Good protection in all weather as close into the north beach of Lee Stocking Island as you can get. Five to ten feet low water. There is also a cove under the hill on the north end of the island where the smacks usually lie. Here there is five and one half feet at low water, good holding sand.

STOCKING ISLAND—A natural hurricane hole with four separate harbours, each of which will carry twelve feet once you get across the entrance bars. These will carry five to six feet at low water. Good holding mud bottom in each basin.

GEORGE TOWN, Exuma—Good all weather protection in six to eight feet (mud bottom) in Kidd Cove midway between Regatta Point and the town shore.

❲ Principal Cays of the Exumas

NOTE OF WARNING

In describing these various anchorages and their approaches, we have endeavored to encourage the cruising man to do a little exploring on his own. No claim is made that such directions as we have given will remain permanently unchanged. This whole area is periodically visited by violent storms which sweep out channels, change sand banks, and blow down landmarks. In these waters even the local pilots navigate by eye. So must you, and the sooner you train yourself to recognize what changes of color indicate, the better cruising you will have.

As outlined in the chapter on pilotage, deep blue indicates deep water, light blue - shallow water, and very *pale* blue - shallow water over white sandy bottom. Rocks are black, grass green or yellow. Coral formations are deep red. The water is so clear that any obstruction can be seen long before you get up to it, if the light is above or behind you. When the sun is in your eyes stay in deep water, or come to anchor until you can see clearly. Going southeast down the Cays, the sun is usually in your eyes all day, so be careful of your courses. Coming back you will have the sun behind you and can relax.

SAIL   ROCKS

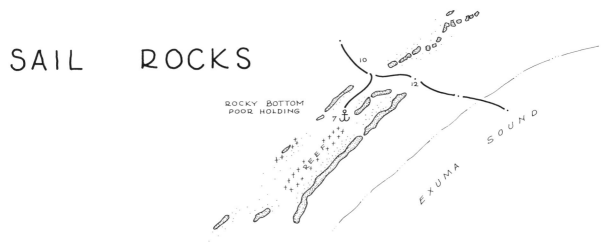

❰ Sail Rocks

A jumble of barren rocks extends north of Ship Channel, an area plagued by strong tides and poor holding ground, the bottom being comprised mostly of hard packed sand.

A few years ago, enroute from the Schooner Cays to Nassau with a load of cleaned conch for our freezer, we sought cover here from what appeared to be a wet, summer squall. Family cruising aboard our "Bertram," we had just kicked the anchor in when we were surrounded by shark. Our sanctuary was a breeding ground and as we surveyed the infested waters around us our feelings were mixed. Should we stay or depart? It was really too late to move on and the approaching squall looked blacker. When it did hit, it hit hard and as lightning struck the waters around us the dark creatures beneath the surface kept milling about, oblivious to the outrage filling the air above.

As the storm passed so did our apprehension, and we all relaxed, peering over the side at the melee below. There were sharks of all sizes, some seven feet long, but mostly young ones of one to two feet, all wagging their way across the bottom in typical shark fashion.

We stayed on, deciding that it was better to spend the night there rather than to cross unknown waters in the dark. Secure aboard, what harm could come from below? So as darkness fell and the neighboring wildlife disappeared from view, we fixed some of the conch for supper and were preparing to turn in when there was a loud splash off the port side. As we dashed for that side of the boat the dripping, frightened face of our six-year-old daughter appeared simultaneously over the stern. Merely slightly damp, she must have indeed walked around the boat to find her way back aboard. Sarah, unbeknownst to us, had gone forward to retrieve her Raggedy Ann and lost her grip coming back along the side. Oddly enough she didn't lose Raggedy Ann during the fall. To this day it is the only time she has ever fallen overboard.

◖ Beacon Cay

This will be your landfall coming from Nassau, if you are bound through Ship Channel. It is a high rocky cay, with several small houses on it, a tank and a light on a steel tower. The light is thirty-eight feet high, a three-second white flash with a red sector. There is no good anchorage here and the lighthouse keepers' houses are abandoned.

◖ Ship Channel

This takes you out into Exuma Sound. It is the best of the channels leading from the banks into Exuma Sound. There are strong tidal currents here, two to three knots, but plenty of water over the bar, a minimum of four fathoms. If proceeding into the sound, pass on the north side of Beacon Cay, about a mile off, and steer SE until you are off soundings.

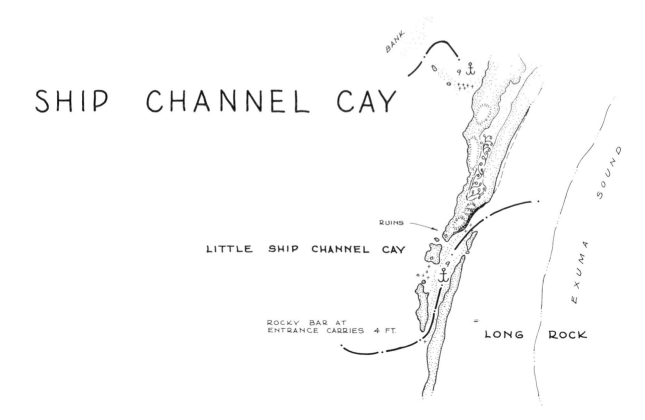

⟪ Ship Channel Cay

This large cay lies on the south side of Ship Channel. It is very conspicu-ous, with the highest ground towards its southern end, where there are white cliffs, 60 feet high. These are striking when seen from the Exuma Sound side. There are two good anchorages at Ship Channel Cay. The best, with the prevailing winds, is on the northwest side of the cay, inside the white sand shoal which extends south from Beacon Cay for about three miles. To get in to the anchorage, round the southern end of this bank, keeping close to the edge of it to avoid the rocky shoal which makes out from the west side of Ship Channel Cay.

The other anchorage is inside the group of small cays which lie off the south end of Ship Channel Cay. A draft of seven feet can be safely carried into either anchorage on the tide.

Back from the white sand beach, on the southwest side of the island, is a small pond, not over seventy-five feet in diameter. Along the north side of the pond a cobble road leads over a rising for three hundred feet to a natural well, twenty feet deep, with twelve feet of water in it. This is good drinking water, and the well has been used by local mariners for generations.

The shack near the wreck of the old boat in South Harbour is the property of old friends Weldon Roberts and Leonard Mather of Nassau, both of whom come here to fish. There is a large bag of feed in the shack with a sign scrawled on the table, which reads, "Please feed the chickens." If they are still there, please do!

⟪ Little Ship Channel Cay

This is the long low cay lying immediately south of Ship Channel Cay. The harbour lies between the two. On the west side the water is ten to twelve feet deep. Near the northeast corner there are a number of small cave holes, each with a few inches of salt water in it. In these at times, turtle fishermen leave turtles in storage.

⟪ Allan Cays

Seven miles south of Beacon Cay, this group of small cays contains several of the nicest and snuggest anchorages in the Exuma Chain. A draft of ten feet at low tide can be taken in at the south end of this group.

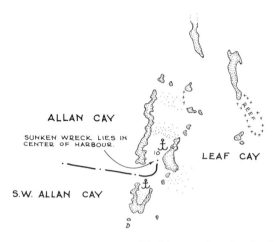

ALLAN CAYS

Highborne Cut leads through to Exuma Sound and there is a strong tidal current in all the channels leading to the cut.

Allan's Harbour is on the eastern side of the longest Allan Cay, about one-quarter mile from its southern end. The entrance is between the south end of the cay and the north end of Southwest Allan Cay. Give the south end of Allan Cay a good clearance, as there is a rocky shoal extending for about 50 feet from it.

Leaf Cay, on the east side of the harbour, is the property of Mrs. Mead Batchelor. It is famous for the iguanas which inhabit it. Periodically local fishermen visit the island and kill off the creatures, but enough of the breed seem to survive to reproduce a new colony in time. There are several ancient wrecks in the vicinity which have yielded known treasure.

HIGHBORNE CAY

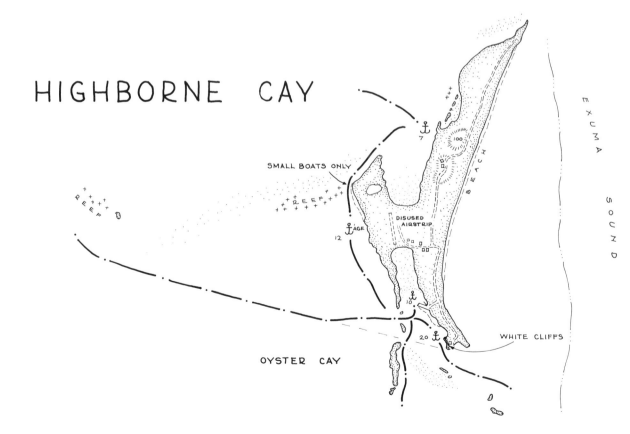

◖ Highborne Cay

This is a large island, three miles long, and is most times the first land you will pick up when coming east from Nassau or west from Powell Point. The entire west and northwest sides are obstructed by a rocky shoal extending for two miles offshore. When south of this shoal a white cliff will be seen marking the southern extremity of the island. Approaching from the west, when this cliff bears E x S, turn in and steer for it, passing north of Oyster Cay. A large and prominent rock will be encountered right in the middle of the channel. Pass on the north side of it. A draft of ten feet can be taken in here, and inside there are three to four fathoms of water, a good safe anchorage, but somewhat choppy when it is blowing hard outside. Anchor one-quarter mile west of the white cliff or sail into the inner harbour and tie up to the concrete wharf there.

The ancient stone fences which crisscross the island indicate that it was once used to raise sheep, goats, and cattle. Now, however, Highborne Cay is the property of William Wykoff Smith of Philadelphia, Pennsylvania, who has developed it into an aloe vera plantation. The aloe vera plant, well known in bush medicine for its healing properties (especially for burns), is raised here for shipment to Florida cosmetic interests.

Bill Smith, a yachtsman himself, has built a breakwater and dredged an inner harbour entered from the south anchorage where he welcomes yachtsmen. He has installed a small store where staples, spirits, frozen meats, and vegetables can be purchased, while fuels can be delivered by truck right on the jetty. Long time favorite of the Nassau charter fleet, Highborne Cay with its spectacular east beach running the length of the island is well worth a visit.

The string of cays south to Highborne Cay, Long and Saddle Cays, are always good for a few giant crawfish under the ledges, while the fishing in the cuts between is excellent.

The small basin under Long Cay is a good all-weather anchorage if you dive up the mooring chain which lies there. Although the swinging room is small you can still lie by yourself and enjoy the sunwashed Exumas at their very best.

◖ Saddle Cay

Locally called Little Norman's Cay, Saddle Cay lies just to the north of Norman's Cay. It derives its proper name from the two high hills with a pronounced dip in between giving the effect of a saddle. There is also a third but somewhat lower hill at the northern end.

Sidney Mitchell of Oyster Bay, New York, owns this cay and has a lovely house with a gorgeous view high up on the hill on the south end. The island is unapproachable from the west side, except at high water, and even then only by very shallow draft boats, as the sand banks extend out from that side for over a mile. However there is a good anchorage on the south side with ten feet of water in it, but to get there you must go outside and come in from the sea. To do so you must use the passage between the north end of Saddle Cay and the south end of Long Cay, steering E x S until outside. Come in close around the south end of Saddle Cay, inside the little cay lying just off the land. The east shore is a series of soft white sandy cliffs twenty-five to thirty feet high. Along the east side of the island there is a buttonwood pond, about six acres in area, and near this pond a number of casuariana trees. There are also some small madeira trees on the cay.

([Norman's Cay

This cay is three and a half miles long, high at its northern end, and low at its southern end. It is easy to distinguish, having a white sand beach on its west side running almost the entire length of the island. In running down Norman's Cay close to the island, care must be exercised to avoid the extensive rocky shoal known as Norman's Spit which extends three miles W by NW from the southern end of the island. It has very little water on it at low tide and is very difficult to see with the sun in your eyes. It has a four-foot low water passage through it, however, about one-quarter mile from the beach. Unless the sun is right it would be best to circumnavigate this area before heading in for the harbour; so after clearing Norman's Spit, head in for the south end of Wax Cay until you see the deep blue water channel which opens up to the northeast. Wax Cay is easy to distinguish, being about one mile in length and its conical hill 93 feet high. Steer NE, between Channel Cay and the south end of Norman's Cay. Anchor 100 yards east of the point on the south end of Norman's Cay. This is a splendid anchorage in which to lie out a norther.

There is a large lake, known locally as Norman's Pond, inside the northern portion of Norman's Cay where boats drawing as much as six feet can get in through a very narrow and intricate passage, with the help of the tide. This entrance is between two small cays about halfway up the island on its east side. It is impossible to give exact directions for using it, because the shoals continually change. There is good bonefishing in the lake which is a perfect anchorage in any weather. The only drawback about lying here is that you can neither get in nor out if there is much sea running on the east side of the island.

At the northwest end of the cay there is a large cave with several rooms

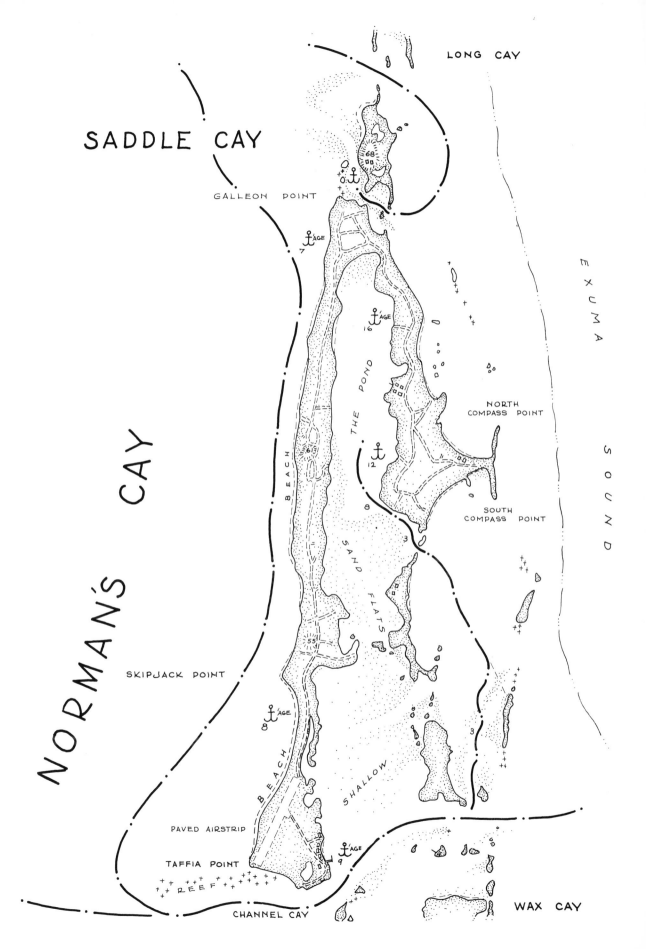

LONG CAY

SADDLE CAY

68

GALLEON POINT

7 AGE

16 AGE

EXUMA SOUND

THE POND

NORTH COMPASS POINT

12

61

8

SOUTH COMPASS POINT

3

SAND FLATS

NORMAN'S CAY

SKIPJACK POINT

55

8 AGE

3

SHALLOW

BEACH

PAVED AIRSTRIP

9 AGE

TAFFIA POINT

REEF

WAX CAY

CHANNEL CAY

in it, and there are several other caves with blocked openings, nice places for some treasure hunting were it not for the fact that Norman's Cay is privately owned and being developed by World Land and Investment Company.

Considered by many to be the jewel of the Exumas, Norman's Cay was first developed in the early sixties by the Bethell Brothers of Nassau as an exclusive retreat for wealthy sunseekers. They began with an overall road system, paved airstrip, reception building, store, club house and marine services dock. William Wykoff-Smith purchased the Cay in the mid sixties for one million dollars, and it is said, he doubled his money a year later when he sold it to Meridian Corporation, a division of World Land and Investment Company. Since Meridian has taken over the Cay, construction has begun on a sizeable hotel and visitor facility, along with expanded docks both at the anchorage and in the pond. Norman's Cay has great potential as the number one yachting base in the Islands. It is centrally located and offers protected and deep water cruising nearby. It would provide an ideal base where yachtsmen flying in for their holidays could permanently moor their vessels.

Marine fuels are available here and your larder can be restocked at the ships store at the head of the dock. Atop the hill the Yacht Club commands a breathtaking view of the harbour and surrounding cays. It's a great place to eat, the food is excellent; so schedule a day off for your galley slave at Norman's Cay.

⟨ Wax Cay

Wax Cay and Little Wax Cay to the south of it are chiefly notable for the fact that between them there is a good deep water passage leading from the banks into Exuma Sound, which is called Wax Cay Cut. The deepest water in this passage lies on the Little Wax Cay or south side. It is dark blue and easy to distinguish. A draft of fifteen feet can be taken through here without difficulty. Both these cays are quite high, the hill in the center of Wax Cay being over 60 feet.

⟨ Exuma Cays Land and Sea Park

The 22-mile string of cays and surrounding sea gardens which extend from Wax Cay Cut to Conch Cut constitute the Exuma Cays Land and Sea Park. Founded by the Bahamas National Trust, this area has been set aside as a natural preserve for the enjoyment of all. Cruising visitors are reminded that sport fishing is permitted with hook and line, while six crawfish (in season) and ten conch can be taken for each person aboard, each day. Spearfishing equipment is restricted to the use of the Hawaiian sling and the removal of any plant, coral, marine or bird life is prohibited. The above is punishable by law with heavy penalties on conviction. The Bahamas National Trust hopes that the rules governing the area will be accepted in a working spirit toward a better ecology.

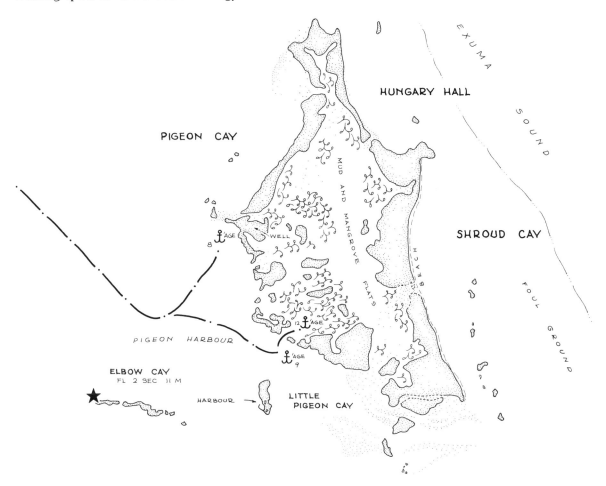

⟨ Shroud Cay—Pigeon Cay

What is shown on the N.O. charts as Shroud Cay is actually a small archipelago containing more than 25 cays and small rocky islands, with numerous creeks winding around between them and an extensive marl and mangrove salina in the middle.

There is some confusion about the identity of Shroud Cay itself. The Bahamians call Hawksbill Cay, Shroud Cay, and the unnamed cay just south of Hawksbill Cay is to them the real Hawksbill, while the Shroud Cay of the charts is their Pigeon Cay. The best authority on the subject, the Crown Lands Office in Nassau, divides the Shroud Cay group as follows: the most northerly cay of the group is Hungry Hall; the largest one of the group facing east on Exuma Sound is Shroud Cay; and the largest one on the west side, facing Elbow Cay, is named Pigeon Cay. The whole group lies north of Hawksbill Cay. From the sailor's point of view, the only one of interest is Pigeon Cay, where the best harbours and anchorages will be found.

Some years ago a Nassau yachtsman, giving us directions for finding the best anchorage, told us to turn in when we got about half a mile from Elbow Cay and stand in until we passed three little rocks on the port hand, and ten feet of water only fifty yards from the beach. What he did not tell us was that there are three little rocks in numerous places, and only about four feet of water inside the majority of them.

To the patient reader we give the following directions with the hope that when his hook is down he will enjoy one of the nicest anchorages to be found anywhere, safe and comfortable in all winds except those which occasionally blow from southwest to northwest. Stand in on a SE course, keeping about half way between Elbow Cay and Pigeon Cay. When the light on Elbow Cay bears SW from you, turn in and run on a NE x E course until you are 50 yards from the beach. You will see the three little rocks to the north of you—two of them connected by a white ribbon of sand. You can then drop your hook in ten feet of water, at low tide, in as lovely a cove as you will find anywhere. All round there are little coves and creeks waiting to be explored and bonefish waiting to be caught. Plenty of whelks, too, for whelk stew. There is a wonderful well ashore with sweet water and plenty of it.

If you are drawing less than six feet we suggest that you stand on down around the southwest point of the cay until the light on Elbow Cay bears WSW. Directly inside of you, to the northeast, you will see an opening in the rocky shore which leads into a lovely little harbour, almost landlocked. You can take six feet in at low tide, and find two fathoms inside. There is a good beach inside and white water for swimming. Barracuda come in to chase the bonefish, but they avoid white water.

❲ Hawksbill Cay

Hawksbill Cay as shown on the charts is the three-mile-long cay lying directly south of the cay shown as Shroud Cay. It is one of the prettiest of the Exuma Cays.

Coming south from Pigeon Cay or Shroud Cay, you can take a draft of ten feet inside Elbow Cay, through it is wise to go around the west side of it. There is an extensive white sand bank which makes out from the northern

HAWKSBILL CAY

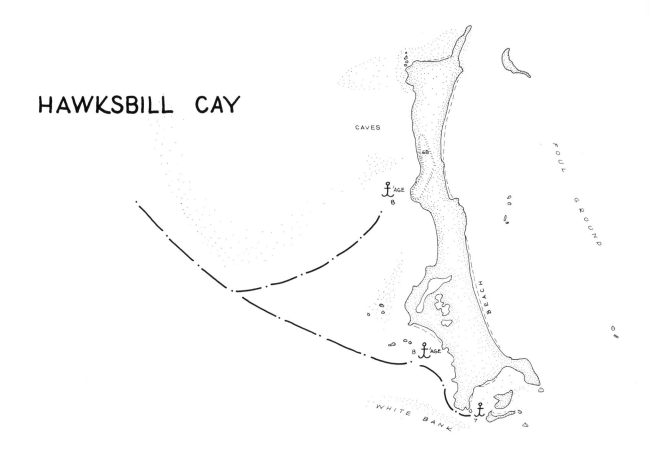

part of Hawksbill Cay, extending in a southwest direction for one mile and a half from the land. You must, therefore, keep on the west side of this bank, standing south until the southern end of Hawksbill Cay bears about SE from you. Haul about half a point to the east, steering SE ½ E to a point about one-quarter mile north of the south end of the cay. This course will take you north of a white sand bank which makes out from the southwest end of the cay. It will also take you south of a group of detached rocks extending out from the west side of the cay. As you approach the beach you will see the deep water stretching away towards the southwest point of the cay. Follow it along the beach, about one hundred yards off, converging with the land until you round the southwest point of the cay about twenty-five yards off. This channel takes you inside the southwest sand bank. It has a minimum depth of ten feet at low tide, with depths of two to four fathoms on the south side of the cay in various places. Anchor just east of the southwest point which you have rounded. The current in the cut is about three knots. The bight on the south side of Hawksbill Cay is in itself a cruising ground for small boats, and here a sailing dinghy would be a delight. There are numerous small islands, coves, inside passages, shallow bays, and at least half a dozen lovely sand beaches, with sand as fine as powder. Several delightful days can be spent here.

CISTERN CAY

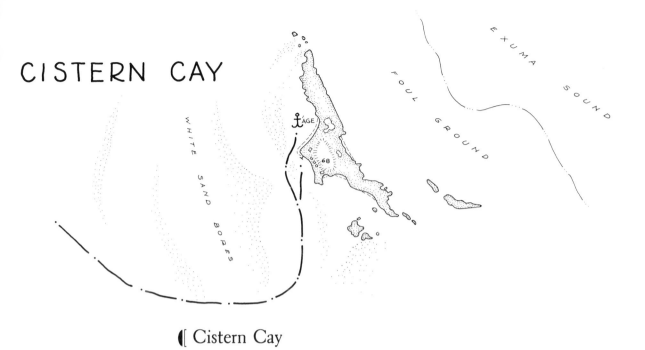

❰ Cistern Cay

Cistern Cay lies two miles southeast of Hawksbill Cut. It can be safely approached from the northwest through a channel which runs out southeast from Hawksbill Cay, passing inside to the west of Little Cistern Cay, which is the small island lying between Hawksbill and Cistern Cays. A draft of five feet can be taken through here at low tide, providing you have a good pilot. If you are on the banks you must stand south until the south end of Cistern Cay bears NE x N and stay at least three miles off the land to avoid the sand banks which extend that distance in a southwest direction. You can then go in on that course, NE x N, steering for the two small cays which lie on the southwest side of Cistern Cay. Being a very light shade of blue, the sand shoals will be plainly visible. When inside the shoals you will find deep water all along the west side of the cay.

The anchorage is off any of the beaches. With the prevailing winds in the east it is safe anchoring here, but not exactly smooth, as the ground swell from Exuma Sound seems to work in at all times. In a norther it is untenable.

The island derives its name from a cistern with good drinking water which lies on the southwest side, on the knoll between the two most southerly sand beaches.

Cistern Cay is owned by W.C. Grant of Winnetka, Illinois, who has built a lovely home on the high part of the island and developed the rest of it in an enviable fashion.

❨ Wide Opening

An extensive area of rocks and reefs with a passage to the sea which is much used by local fisherman. The channel passes close to the north side of Long Rock, which is a long, narrow cay lying northwest of the north end of Warderick Wells Cay. A draft of ten feet can be taken through here at low tide, although there is as much as 25 feet of water in places.

❨ Long Rock

Long Rock is a small island, one-half mile long, lying about half a mile northwest of the north end of Warderick Wells Cay. Its highest land is 42 feet above sea level. Its southwestern shore is very steep, but in a bight near the northwest end there is a nice sand beach about one hundred feet long, and the best anchorage is off this beach. The water is from ten to fifteen feet deep here.

About 300 feet from the northwest end on the northeast side of the island, there is an underground cave measuring about 75 by 40 feet, with a mouth on the seashore about fifteen feet wide. There are several blow holes in this cave, and from one of these, when the waves come in, the current of air is strong enough to knock off a man's hat.

❨ Warderick Wells Cay

This is a wild and rugged cay, about two and one-half miles long, with a most irregular, intriguing shoreline. Within its borders are two of the best harbours in the Exumas, one on the northwest side, and the other on the southeast or ocean side. To find the entrance to the north harbour from the banks steer south until the northern end of Warderick Wells Cay bears NE from you; then go in on that heading, following the dark blue water between the small outlying cays until you are abreast of the sand beach on Warderick Wells Cay; then steer into the harbour, which will then be about southeast of you. There is fifteen feet of water here, well protected from every quarter, but quite narrow and with strong currents, so use the usual two anchors, Bahamian style.

The waters on the west side of Warderick Wells contain a maze of sand banks, most of them with only two to three feet of water on them at low tide. Shallow draft boats weave their way through them, piloting by eye. No specific sailing directions can be given.

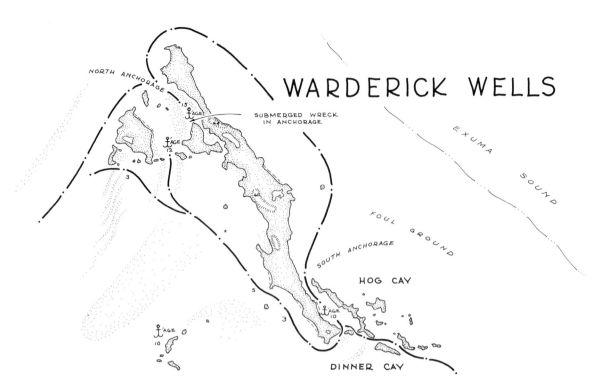

WARDERICK WELLS

NORTH ANCHORAGE

SUBMERGED WRECK
IN ANCHORAGE

EXUMA SOUND

FOUL GROUND

SOUTH ANCHORAGE

HOG CAY

DINNER CAY

On the southeast side of Warderick Wells Cay there is a long thin cay lying about one-quarter mile offshore, and between this cay and the main cay is one of the best harbours we ever saw for the practice of piracy. It can be entered in any weather, from either end, and there is 20 feet of water inside. As a matter of fact, legend has it that a pirate by the name of Warderick once made this his base, taking advantage of the good well water and careening his ships in the north harbour; thus the island's name.

The best way to get into its south harbour is to go outside around the north end of the island, stand south for two miles, and come in at the north end of the long thin cay. There is eighteen feet of water over the bar coming in, but less water than that outside, so the seas, if any, are pretty well broken up before they reach the entrance.

The entrance from the banks is a bit more intricate. Several blue water channels approach from the west, but they all end in shallow sand banks which can not be crossed at high tide. If the tide is well up you can come in on a northeast course headed for the south end of Warderick Wells Cay, keeping close on around it until you fetch up in the harbour. The very best channel, however, lies well to the south of this. Two miles southwest of the south end of Warderick Wells Cay, and approximately three-quarters of a mile west of Halls Pond Cay, there is a small but prominent little island called Little White Bay Cay. It is high and rocky at its east end, flattening out to a long sand spit which extends southwest for half a mile or so. On the south side of Little White Bay Cay there is a deep blue water channel which leads out to sea between Warderick Wells and Hall's Pond Cay. This is the channel to follow. It will take you on the east side of Hog Cay, which is the fairly large cay lying half a mile southeast of the end of Warderick Wells Cay. Then head about NW between the various small cays into the harbour. It is not as difficult as it sounds, as the blue channels are very pronounced and easy to follow. As long as you stay in dark blue water you will be all right with a boat drawing up to ten feet. There is a very small cay lying directly southeast of the main island. You can pass on either side of it in entering this perfect pirate harbour.

Warderick Wells is a beautiful, uninhabited island, fun to visit and explore. The long thin cay which shields Southeast Harbour has several holes clean through it which bark in the high tide swells and might even sing in a norther. There are no signs of any settlements having existed here, possibly due to the fierce legends of pirates and haunts, still rumored by Bahamians and visitors familiar with the place.

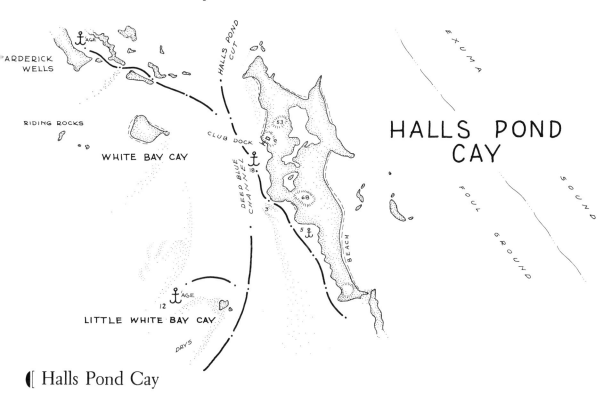

(Halls Pond Cay

A large and picturesque Cay, two miles long and with an average width of about seven hundred feet. Its western shore is a series of high bluffs with deep bights in between, each one with a sand beach at its apex. These bluffs are from thirty to sixty feet high. On the Exuma Sound side there is a marvelous beach extending practically the whole length of the Island. In the interior are several large ponds. Anchorage on the northwest side of the Cay is not very practical or comfortable, owing to the swift tidal currents which run between the Cut and Exuma Sound. Also, there is an uncomfortable surge that works in from the Sound on a flood tide. On the southwest side, where the coves are, there is plenty of water; but you have to get over a sand bank to get to them. The channel runs close enough to the shore so that you can almost touch the rocks, and carries three feet at low tide. Only small boats drawing three feet or less can get down inside the Islands to Conch Cut, unless one goes through on a high tide.

The north end of Halls Pond Cay belongs to Darwin Gardner of Boston, Massachusetts, who has built an attractive little port-of-call there.

⟨ Little White Bay Cay

Across the cut from Halls Pond Cay, Little White Bay Cay glistens as one of those rare jewels of the Bahamas. This diminutive slice of seaside ecology has everything, and more, than most of the larger islands. Perched atop its rocky eastern promontory is a giant osprey's nest on which we've trained our binoculars and cameras for hours on end, watching the handsome masters of their house return again and again, each time in a flurry of winged splendor, gently delivering live dinner to their eager young. Along the precipitous rocky hills below the nest there is a colony of one hundred brown noddys that return each summer to nest and rear their chicks. Beneath subterranean ledges lurk spiny lobster, grouper and yellow tail, even a nurse shark, all in water no deeper than your waist; and further west along the beach, thin-lipped conch by the score.

Along the grassy dunes from the promontory west to the tidal flats we discovered spotted tern eggs incubating in the warm sand as we picked up enough sand dollars, cowry and murex shells to decorate our Christmas tree. It was here that we found one of our first Portuguese glass floats, and here also that we used to turn our toddlers loose for a much needed run. What harm could befall them in such an innocent slice of paradise?

The best anchorage lies in the twelve foot, deep blue channel just to the north of the cay over a sea garden alive with purple, yellow, and coral fans. Best to use the usual two anchors though, as the tide sluices through here at a healthy rate, especially during springs. And if you have a fish trap, bait it with conch, set it amongst the fans, then lean over the side and with your glass bucket watch it snare a grouper or yellow tail just in time for dinner.

For many years we tried to buy Little White Bay Cay through Nassau's Crown Lands Office, but could never determine its availability. In retrospect, however, we would have built a cottage there and unintentionally altered its environment. Now we hope that it reamins forever uninhabited by man; a perfect, sunwashed wilderness for all to share.

❨ Halls Pond To Conch Cut

Continuing down the lee of Halls Pond Cay between Bell Island, Soldier Cay, O'Brien's Cay, and Little Bell Island is a charming short cruise for boats of shoal draft only. Here in the narrow channels between the islands you can find protection from any quarter, while combing the ocean beaches on the weather side of any of them is rewarding indeed.

Once anchored off the western beach of Soldier Cay in the shallow bight between Soldier and Halls ponds, we discovered a crawfish nestled in the sand under the exposed fluke of our Danforth. Naturally when we weighed anchor preparatory to leaving, he darted away. Our young daughter thought my look of sorrow expressed my concern at disturbing the little rascal, when it was really because our visit was made without my Hawaiian sling!

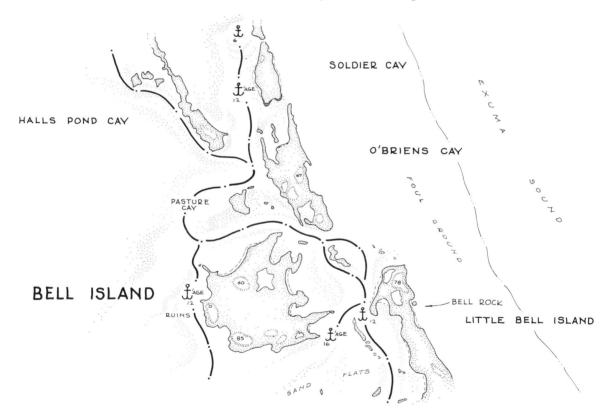

❨ Bell Island

Bell Island is a large, irregular cay about one mile square lying on the northwest side of Conch Cay, facing the banks. It is one of the highest and most interesting cays in all the Exuma chain, being saucer shaped, with high land all around its perimeter and a valley or depression in the middle. In this depression is a fresh water pond, fed by springs from below, and known locally as "The Fountain." This, to the best of our knowledge, is the only fresh pond on any of the Exuma Cays.

On the western side of the island, perched on top of the high cliff, are the remains of an interesting small settlement. The people who lived there were the descendants of a fabulous character named Titus O'Brien. Until recently the island was ruled by three fierce and wizened old women, who settled there in 1862. They considered themselves not only the owners of all the land they could walk over, but also of all the surrounding waters to the limit of their eyesight. They allowed only a few favored people to land on the island, and attempted to collect a toll of fish or conch from any boat stopping to fish in their waters.

There are beautiful long sand beaches on both sides of Bell Island, and deep water on the north side, where a good anchorage will be found with good holding ground.

Little Bell Island forms the northern side of Conch Cut, and faces on Exuma Sound. It derives its name from a remarkable high and bell-shaped rock which projects from its eastern shore line about half a mile north of Conch Cut. Seen from the banks side it is shaped like a pyramid, and serves as a good landmark for identifying Conch Cut.

⟨ Conch Cut

Conch Cut is one of the best cuts of all the passages from the Banks into Exuma Sound. The approach from the west is to some extent obstructed by two long sand banks, but as these run northeast and southwest it is only a matter of finding the deep water between them and following it in to the cut. There are three prominent islands lying on the west side of the cut— the two high bold ones are locally known as Rocky Dundas, and the low one as Fowl Cay. There is deep water on either side of the Rocky Dundas, and a well-protected harbour on the east side of Fowl Cay. The passage from the Rocky Dundas out to sea has only one dangerous obstruction, a rock awash in the exact center of the cut on the ocean side. Pass to the north of it as there is deep water all the way. As you enter Conch Cut from Exuma Sound the white sand beach seen dead ahead is at the head of the harbour on Fowl Cay.

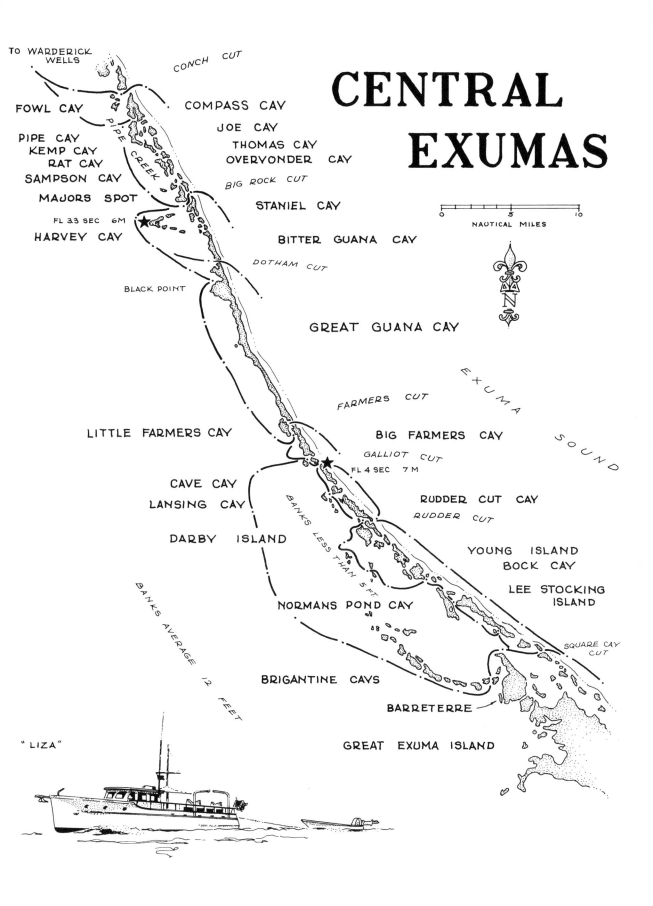

CENTRAL EXUMAS

TO WARDERICK WELLS

CONCH CUT

FOWL CAY

COMPASS CAY

JOE CAY

THOMAS CAY

OVERVONDER CAY

PIPE CAY
KEMP CAY
RAT CAY
SAMPSON CAY
MAJORS SPOT

PIPE CREEK

BIG ROCK CUT

FL 33 SEC 6M

STANIEL CAY

HARVEY CAY

BITTER GUANA CAY

DOTHAM CUT

BLACK POINT

GREAT GUANA CAY

NAUTICAL MILES

0   5   10

N

EXUMA SOUND

FARMERS CUT

LITTLE FARMERS CAY

BIG FARMERS CAY

GALLIOT CUT

FL 4 SEC 7M

CAVE CAY

LANSING CAY

RUDDER CUT CAY

RUDDER CUT

DARBY ISLAND

BANKS LESS THAN 5 FT.

YOUNG ISLAND
BOCK CAY

LEE STOCKING
ISLAND

BANKS AVERAGE 12 FEET

NORMANS POND CAY

SQUARE CAY CUT

BRIGANTINE CAYS

BARRETERRE

"LIZA"

GREAT EXUMA ISLAND

([Fowl Cay

Fowl Cay is surrounded by good anchorages but the natural harbour, which lies between the long, narrow promontories off its northern side, is the best. The holding ground here is good, deep fine sand, but the bottom shoals gradually extend to the beach on the south perimeter of the anchorage. Fowl Cay is the private property of Karlsson Mitchell of Miami, Florida, who, many years ago, built a vacation cottage and 1,300-foot airstrip on the cay to facilitate his frequent visits. As we have stated before, these owners value their privacy, and Mr. Mitchell would prefer that casual callers used his strip for emergency landing only.

Fowl Cay stands out in our memory for its original caretaker, Harcourt Rolle. Harcourt will long be remembered by Bahama cruising skippers as one of the best guides in the Exumas. However, like so many Bahamian sailors, Harcourt could not swim and was drowned several years ago within sight of the cay, while tending traps. We always stopped at Fowl Cay to buy some of Ethel Rolle's fresh bread and usually ended up going back for more after a day's trip with Harcourt as he could devour an entire loaf when covered with stateside peanut butter and my wife's homemade jelly.

Harcourt's educated eye could tell the depth of the water practically to the inch as we learned when we checked his visual soundings with our lead line. As a competitive sailor he was an ardent supporter of the Out Island Regatta, but in his zeal to win he was a perennial problem to the race committee. His boat "Grey Hound" usually captured first prize for the big dinghy class, but on the few occasions when he didn't win, he'd figure out some reason why he should have, and make sure the committee did not sleep until the Regatta was over and everyone had gone home. One year "Grey Hound" arrived at the annual event sporting a six-inch bowsprit and brand new jib. Harcourt claimed she hadn't been designed properly in the first place and this refinement would not only add to the boat's speed but place her in her proper class, Class "B," where, incidentally, the prize monies were considerably greater. It took several members of the race committee a full day of persuasion to convince Harcourt that "Grey Hound" was rated by her length on deck, not overall, and he would have to be content with the prize monies for the big dinghy class, that is, unless he wanted to build a new Class "B" boat. Harcourt was a colorful member of the Exuma cruising fraternity, and we shall always miss him.

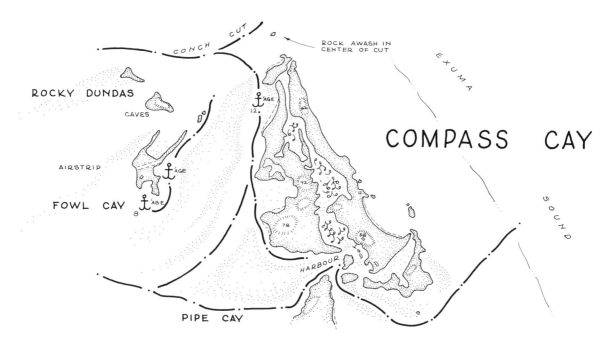

❰ Compass Cay

Compass Cay, on the south side of Conch Cay, is a beautiful island; the northern extremity is a high bold white cliff with two outlying rocks. The main part has the highest hills in this vicinity and is covered with rich vegetation. There is a nice cove on the northwest side of the cay where good anchorage can be had out of the current. An extensive mangrove creek meanders up the center of the island. It has several deep pools surrounded by high land. These would be ideal hurricane holes if you could get your boat into them.

Compass Cay has had a colorful, but stormy history ever since the early sixties when Ned Parmalee of New Jersey began to install a port of call on its south beach. He built a long, rickety, Bahamian-style dock into the deeper water of the anchorage and a club house with a spectacular view of the surrounding cays atop the southernmost hill in the center of the island. To help finance his venture Ned sold shares to a few friends and that's when trouble started. "Too many cooks spoiling the broth" would be understating the situation, especially in light of the fact that none were "cooks" to begin with. As the years passed it was great fun watching bikinied gals and sun-tanned children come and go. Each year we'd stop by to watch the circus, welcoming the new faces and bidding farewell to the old. Exuma cruising habitués aren't likely to forget "Uncle Al" who enlivened many a summer night's sleep with his howls, or the infamous low tide airstrip that took its toll of air traffic to and from the Cay.

Some visitors even came to stay, like Hester Crawford, widow of Jack Crawford (whom I'd known in Alaska during WW II) and author of the famous Air Force song, *Into the Air.* Disregarding the confusion, Hester liked the island so much that she built a charming cliff-top house overlooking the island's eastern shore and settled in for good. Whenever managerial fireworks erupted at the club and the partners again stomped off to Nassau to console themselves at the Pilot House Bar, Hester, with the help of any visitors who might be on hand, would take over and give the place a few days of much needed peace.

Then in 1969 Herm and Helen Wenzel of Saint Louis, Missouri, upped the anchor of their handsome ketch "Tranquilizer II" (long a resident of Staniel Cay) and sailed her here for good, when Herm assumed Compass Cay's crown lease. It is a peaceful spot once again with the Wenzels' conversion of the old club house into an attractive, private residence at the south end.

([Pipe Creek

The eight-mile stretch of cays and intervening creeks between Conch Cut and Staniel Cay is known to all as Pipe Creek. This so-called creek comprises a small archipelago with navigable connecting waters that offer beauty beyond measure and protection from any conceivable wind. Continuing south from Compass Cay, we will endeavor to describe each of the major cays in turn.

([Pipe Cay

Pipe Cay is high and undulating and at one time had a Decca station located on its western shore that worked in close collaboration with the AUTEC stations on Andros. Its small anchorage is a place to dinghy ashore but no place for a yacht.

([Joe Cay

This small island has a mangrove swash in its center and a high rocky promontory at its southeast corner that guards the only navigable channel in from Exuma Sound. The sea gardens in the channel at its southwest corner are well worth exploration.

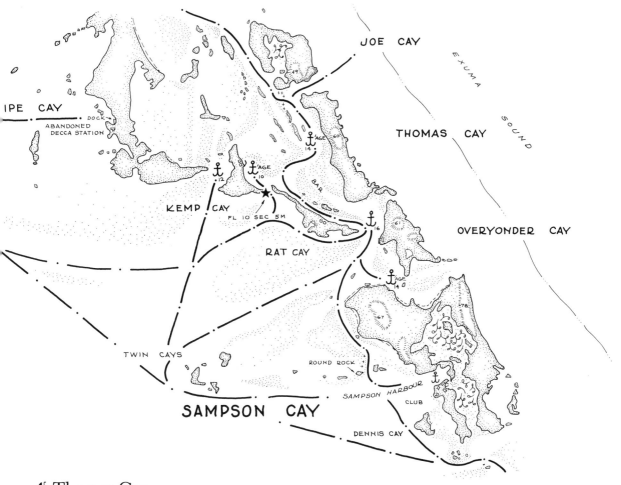

(Thomas Cay

Directly South, narrow Thomas Cay is high and forbidding on the ocean side and low with several beaches and a comfortable anchorage on its lee side. The shoal water channel which rounds its southwest corner is a hard bar and seems to be shoaling even more in recent years.

(Kemp Cay

One of the smallest in Pipe Creek, triangular Kemp Cay has a beautiful anchorage off the sand beach on its western shore and a small private yacht club with one of the best docks in the Exumas on the creek side. Little Pipe Cay Yacht Club was built by Nassau charter skipper Nelville Brown, whose private home on the cay formed the nucleus of the club house. There are a number of attractive bathing beaches here and a thatch overlook at the cay's north point where the water colors across the shallow banks to the north are breathtakingly vivid.

⟦ Rat Cay

Bordering the eastern side of the the entrance channel into Little Pipe Cay Yacht Club is Rat Cay, the private island of James Lewis of upstate New York. The strangely shaped structure on the hill at the south end of the island is actually a pair of inverted wooden vats transported here from his paper mill. Converted into living quarters, these huge pulp mixing tubs nearly gave Mr. Lewis fits their first year on the site. The intense tropical sun dried and shrank the huge wooden staves until the structure demanded a full-time caulking hand to keep it weathertight. Finally, in desperation, he erected a shade roof to protect it from the most powerful of the rays. There is a small harbour midway on the south side of the cay that will accommodate outboards and small craft only.

⟦ Overyonder Cay

The anchorage in the shallow bight at the north end of this cay is deep but care must be taken to dig the anchors in as this is for the most part a rocky bottom. The somewhat shallower anchorage in the channel off the southwest point has closer protection and is more to our liking. Both of these anchorages experience a mild surge during fresh easterly weather. Tying up at the wharf on the westerly point is not recommended without proper bumpering.

⟦ Sampson Cay

A large, irregular cay split down the middle by a vast tidal flat, Sampson Cay is one of the larger islands in Pipe Creek. It is owned by a group of ivy league alumni who are building a private vacation resort on the deep cove under its western shore. The project's manager/builder, Canadian Don Schmidt, has a natural talent for stone masonry and the entire facility blends into the landscape with ease. The cove offers good protection in prevailing winds, but an uncomfortable surge will be felt in westerly conditions. An inner harbour has been dredged from the tidal flat adjacent to the club house affording ample cover to small craft when the winds go into the west. The cay can provide marine fuels and some supplies.

Don's Australian wife, Dusk, is an artist who paints bits of whimsy on stones and ballast rock gleaned from the nearby beaches. A fish, a politician, a sailor or buccanner's head are all creative reflections of the Schmidts' fun outlook on the world from Sampson Cay.

⟮ Major's Spot

Big and Little Major's Spots are divided by Pipe Creek and the anchorages in between are safe in any weather. Both islands are for the most part owned by the people of Staniel Cay and a certain amount of farming is carried on there. Between the north end of Big Major's Spot and Fowl Cay there is a deep narrow cut where the tide sluices through in spectacular fashion. Six feet can be taken through in either direction but make sure your draft will clear the sandy shoal on the creek side, especially if you are bound in that direction. Once you are in the cut there is no turning back. The pretty little beach at the north tip of Big Major's Spot usually has a few conch in the shallows. The two cottages on Fowl Cay belong to American winter residents.

⟮ Big Rock Cut

This is the first good cut south of Conch Cut. It lies between Little Major's Spot and Staniel Cay and carries nine feet at low water. When entering from the Sound favor the Little Major's Spot (north) side of the channel and as soon as you have crossed the bar turn south, taking the western shore of Staniel Cay close aboard all the way into the yacht club dock or anchorage off the town.

⟮ Staniel Cay

Once a quiet and almost unknown beauty spot, Staniel Cay is now the yachting center of the Central Exumas. At a normal cruising speed the voyage from Nassau to George Town takes about two easy days, and as the run from Nassau to Staniel Cay is about half of the distance it is obviously the place to head for the first day out of Nassau (unless you are fortunate enough to be able to leisurely gunk hole down the Cays as previously described). Also, it makes sense to stop here and check over everything: fuel, water, engines, etc., before going outside at Galliot Cut. Boats without a radio telephone can check the latest weather reports, and send or receive messages from the club station here.

Cruising down the banks standing south towards Harvey Cay you notice a prominent white building with a red roof on the port hand in the corner between Harvey Cay and Staniel Cay. This is the church at the settlement on Staniel Cay. When this building is due east turn and head for it. When

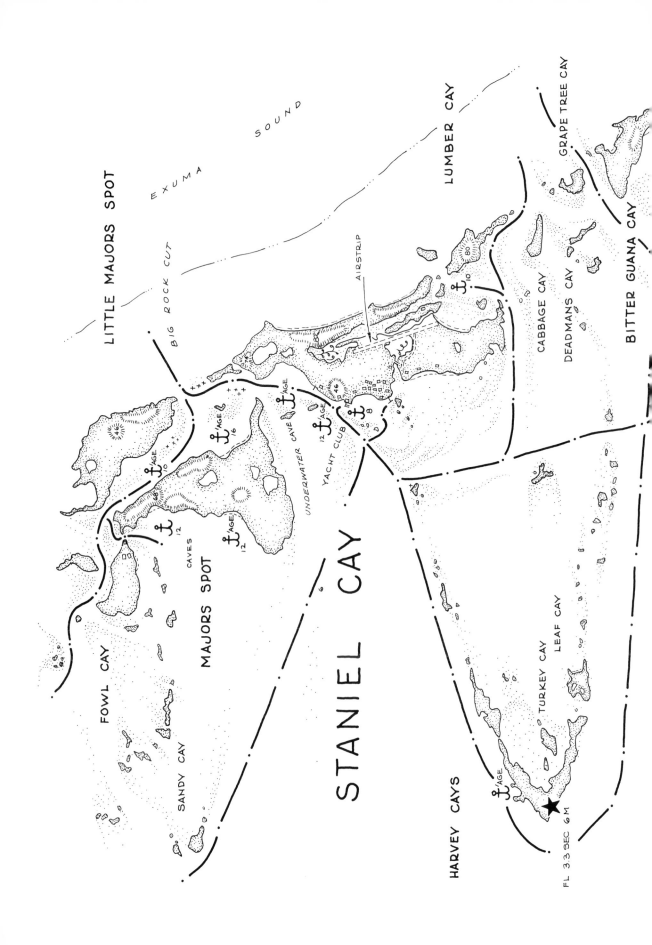

you are about one-quarter mile from it you will see deep blue water on the port hand, or northeast of you. From here a draft of six feet can be taken into the yacht club at low tide. If you prefer to tie up at The Happy People Marina adjacent to the town, continue straight ahead, following the marked channel toward the church. You can carry six feet here also.

Staniel Cay is the cleanest, tidiest and most industrious settlement we have found anywhere in the islands. The land is well cultivated and the people are happy and prosperous. There are several little stores, a clinic and new school, which were built by the people with money raised almost entirely by their own efforts. Cecilia's tiny straw market has some lovely baskets, purses, and the ever-popular straw hats. The church, whose red roof you used for a bearing on your approach, features a picture of Sir Winston Churchill along with the usual ones of Queen Elizabeth and Prince Philip of England. We have attended many Out Island church services but the one that stands out in our memory is Easter service here at Staniel Cay, probably one of the most enthusiastic services we ever encountered.

Behind the little beach, between the settlement and the yacht club, is a graveyard where the original owner of the island is buried, a Mr. Gray, from whom all the present inhabitants appear to be descended. To them Staniel is still "Gray Cay."

Among Out Island sailors Staniel Cay is famous for the fact that it is the home port of the championship smack, "Lady Muriel," and the unbeaten dinghy "Sea Hound," and the home of their equally famous skipper, Captain Rolly Gray. Rolly has probably taken home more champion prize monies from the Out Island Regatta than any other single sailor. One of his protégés, Kendal Miller, is now permanent crew aboard Senator Edward Kennedy's sailing yacht "Curragh."

During the 1959 Regatta Rolly was selected for the honor of taking Prince Philip for a sail on the "Lady Muriel" and the tiller of this smack now hangs in the place of honor behind the bar of Staniel Cay's social spot, aptly named "Royal Entertainer's Lounge." On boarding "Lady Muriel," Prince Philip asked the crew to sing songs for him. The one which he liked best was, "Oh Lord, Give Me One More Year," a sentiment which he expressed as particularly applying to him—for one more year to visit the Islands.

As the settlement's patriarchs have gone to their just reward, one by one, we think it fitting that a seafaring man should emerge as Staniel Cay's town father. Rolly now operates the mail boat "Staniel Cay Express" and is the island's chief spokesman.

Kenneth and Teazel Rolle operate the Royal Entertainer's Lounge and The Happy People Marina which lies adjacent to the town. At the lounge you will find Bahamian dishes available anytime, given reasonable notice; and Saturday nights literally jump with entertainers and guests, all supplying the fun. Most marine services are avilable at the dock, while the most knowledgeable guides in the Exumas claim Staniel Cay as their home port.

Several hundred yards north of the settlement there is a large rock with a cave inside, entered only through an underwater passage at low tide. This cave, about 70 feet in diameter and fifteen feet high, is lit by the sun at high noon through a small opening in the ceiling. The shaft of sunlight resembles that of a kleig light pinpointing the actions of the colorful undersea theatre group moving slowly and silently through their ballet on the golden stage below.

What has made Staniel Cay the cruising headquarters for the Exuma chain is not only the hospitality of its people and the desirability of its surrounding waters, but Bob Chamberlain's Staniel Cay Yacht Club. Downeast salt water sailor and charter boat captain, Bob had been sailing to the Bahamas for many years before settling in the mid-fifties on the Cay. The Club comprises a casual do-it-yourself atmosphere where visitors adhere to the honor system, running their own bar tabs, affecting their own dockside service and, when the master chef himself is in the galley, enjoying the finest cuisine served in the Islands.

The first time we met the club's junior partner, Chicagoan Joe Hocher (a cruising scuba diver at the time) we were sailing aboard Lou Kennedy's charter yacht "Alpha" and had just anchored off Allan's Cay. About sundown there appeared alongside a 20-foot skiff with a 45-gallon drum for an auxiliary tank and an ancient outboard motor that looked like it would empty it in the next twenty miles. "Which way to Staniel Cay?" shouted Joe, looking for all the world as if he were asking directions on the corner of State Street and Madison. We passed him a cold beer and a dog-eared copy of the *Guide* opened to the appropriate page, advising him to head south, staying inside and close along the cays. At the same time we offered him a bunk for the night. "Thanks, anyway, but I'll make it!" he said, turning south as directed and disappearing over the horizon.

Well, "make it" he did. And he's been there ever since expanding the Club's facilities, keeping the machinery running, affecting repairs to visiting yachts, and (in his spare time) escorting diving parties out to the nearby reefs. A recent fun project for Joe was the construction of "Cyclops," the club's airport limousine. Made from a miniature English lorry, this unique vehicle must scale foot high limestone pinnacles to make its tortuous way out to Staniel Cay's airstrip.

Having turned from sail to power, Bob now flies his own Cessna Skywagon, transporting weekly supplies, hotel guests, and Island emergencies when necessary. His wife, Donna, is largely responsible for Staniel Cay's St. Jude's Clinic, having solicited donations and equipment from her more generous friends and guests. Several years ago when her stepsister, Ann, visited the island for a vacation, Joe needed only one look to convince him that this pretty teacher was the only thing lacking in his island paradise and proposed on the spot. Ann fit right into the picture, helping out with the island's educational needs until they gained their own modern school and first resident teacher. In an age when concern for others is fast disappearing, it's refreshing to stop in at Staniel Cay and see how two couples have quietly made their own contribution to the betterment of a village and how, in turn, that village has made them part of its life.

⟨ Bitter Guana Cay

Between Staniel Cay and Bitter Guana Cay there are a number of small cays which have not been given much attention. One of the largest of these —Lumber Cay—lies directly southeast of Staniel Cay, and inside it is a lovely harbour, with ten feet of water at the entrance, shoaling to five feet at its head. Bitter Guana Cay is easily distinguished by the high white cliffs on its west side. Bitter Guana Cut will lead you in from the sea at the northeast end of the island. This is a good passage from the sea and a draft of nine feet can be carried through to Harvey Cay.

Between Bitter Guana Cay and Great Guana Cay there is a fairly large cay named Gaulin Cay. Between Gaulin Cay and Great Guana Cay there is a passage out to sea which is called Dotham Cut. A draft of nine feet can be carried through here at low tide. There is a terrific tidal current.

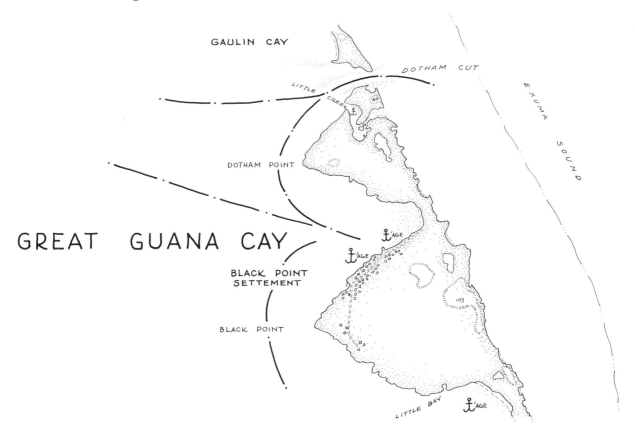

❲ Great Guana Cay

Great Guana Cay is the largest and longest cay in the Exuma Chain, with the exception of Great Exuma Island. It is eleven miles long, and in one place so narrow that during gales the seas sweep right over it. The principal settlement is at Black Point, which is at the northwest tip of the island, facing west. There is a deep cove here where a boat can lie perfectly protected in winds from northeast to south.

Black Point is one of the largest settlements in the Exumas, ranking second only to those on Great Exuma itself. Between three and four hundred people make their living here by farming and fishing, while the ladies supply plait work to the Nassau strawmarket via the weekly mailboat. You will see the curing straw and fibers drying in the sun wherever there is space enough to place them. During the growing season there is an abundance of citrus, bananas, plantains, sapodillas, avacado pear, guavas, bird pepper and pigeon peas being shipped to Nassau.

There is little to interest visitors at Black Point other than a friendly stroll ashore where you will be the focal point of the day, greeted warmly, if not shyly, by the townspeople *en masse.*

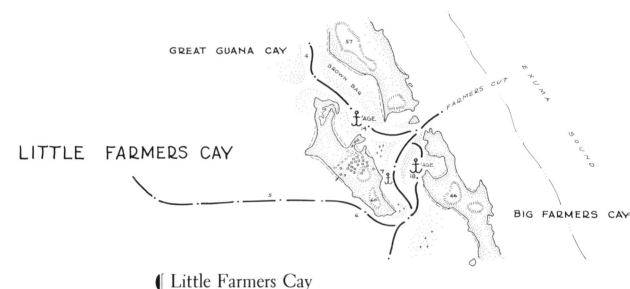

❲ Little Farmers Cay

Referred to everywhere in the Bahamas as simply "Farmers Cay," it is probably the most important settlement in the Exuma Cays outside of those on Great Exuma Island. Its importance is due to no small extent to the fact that it is the home of Henry Moxey, a most remarkable man, who in days gone by was considered to be the best pilot in all the Bahamas. When the British Admiralty, the American Navy, or the oil companies sought any special information about these waters they called on Captain Moxey. Thirty-six years at sea, from cabin boy to cook to mate, then captain and finally pilot, there was no finer seaman anywhere. His limbs were broken in gales at sea and his eyes dimmed by burning tropic suns, but his voice still has the ring of authority in it, a fine fog horn of a voice which can penetrate the deafest ears. Linton Rigg had the privilege of having him as a cook, pilot and companion for many weeks in the original writing of this book. At Farmers Cay he was the preacher, the postmaster, the policeman, the pilot, the house builder, the practical physician, besides being the head of a family of thirteen children, twenty-eight grandchildren and six great-grandchildren. Quite a man!

The harbour lies on the east side of the cay, and can be entered from the north, the south or the east from Exuma Sound. The north entrance is the shallowest and the maximum draft which can be taken in at low tide is four feet. There is a shoal in the middle of this entrance. The best water lies on the west side of this shoal, or along the Little Farmers Cay side.

With the prevailing winds from northeast to southeast, good anchorage may also be had on the west side under the lee of the island. This is where the mail boat lies to discharge and take on her cargo. A road leads from the anchorage here straight to the church in the village.

The south entrance to the harbour is the best one for boats coming in from the bank. A draft of six feet at low tide can be taken in without difficulty. The best course in lies about one-quarter mile off the southern end of the Cay. Steer N by NE for the sand beach and coconut trees on Big Farmers Cay. This course will take you about a 150 yards off the southern tip of Little Farmers Cay. When the harbour opens up, turn in to port and anchor in seven feet of water, at low tide, over the grass, opposite the south end of the village. This anchorage is safe but sometimes choppy when the tide runs against a strong breeze. A smoother anchorage is in the cove on the north side of the village, but as there is only four feet at low tide, it is only available to shallow draft boats.

The eastern entrance to the harbour is through Farmers Cay Cut, which leads out between Great Guana Cay and Big Farmers Cay into Exuma Sound. This is a deeper cut than Galliot, and preferred by many of the local pilots. The shallowest part has twenty feet of water on it at low tide. Coming in from Exuma Sound the north end of Big Farmers Cay appears to be low and rocky, while the south end of Great Guana Cay is comparatively high and covered with vegetation. The current runs about three knots through the Cut.

The Island's school teacher is now L.J. Maycock, who, with his sloop "Mrs. Maycock," is a most enthusiastic supporter of the Out Island Regatta. In the past "L.J." would arrive each year with the entire family, nearly one dozen kids, all signed on as crew in order to collect the crew allowances to help finance the trip. One year, much to the surprise and delight of all the spectators and especially the Maycocks, the two leading boats protested themselves out of the prize money, leaving "Mrs. Maycock" in first place. Suffice to say that "Mrs. Maycock's" homecoming was a memorable one for the days of celebration that must have followed.

The settlement on Little Farmer's Cay is primitive. There are no stores; the only supplies available are fish, crawfish and conch. Both water and firewood have to be brought over daily from the wells on Great Guana Cay, usually by the ladies of the village. Once, many years ago on our first visit to the Cay, we inquired as to why their ancestors might have settled on Little Farmers Cay rather than nearer the source of fresh water on Great Guana, only to be told simply, "Why, they liked it better here, of course."

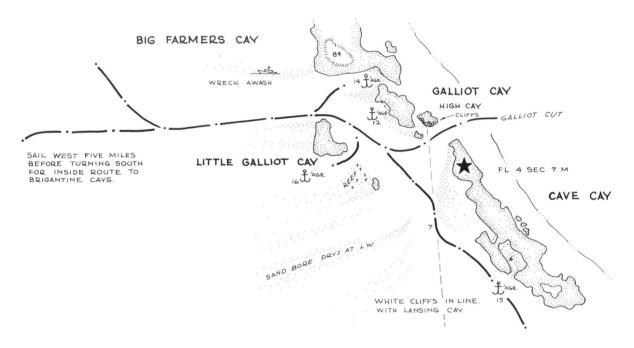

⟨ Galliot Cut

This is the most popular and frequently-used passage from the Banks to Exuma Sound, and has been since the days of the Spaniards. In a report dated August 30th, 1873, Mr. Alexander Forsyth explains that this passage, or cut, was much used by the Spaniards on their voyages from Spain to Cuba in their "Galliots" (Galeotas) of light draft, from whence the name is derived. The hydrographic office's *Sailing Directions for the West Indies* describes it as "narrow and intricate," which by yacht standards it is not.

Galliot Cay and High Cay form the northern side of Galliot Cut. High Cay is easy to distinguish, having a huge, white overhanging cliff 45 feet high, which looks like the bow of a ship, facing the cut. There is also a low-lying cay three hundred feet southwest of High Cay. It is two hundred and fifty feet long and only a foot out of water at high tide.

The northwest end of Cave Cay forms the southeast side of Galliot Cut, and, in extreme contrast to High Cay, this northern end of Cave Cay is low and flat. On the point of Cave Cay is a marker pole with a pointer only about fifty feet from the actual end of the Cay. A little further back there is a light on a pole.

Galliot Cut is the passage between High Cay and the northern end of Cave Cay. It is about one thousand feet wide. The southern part is to some extent blocked by a bar which runs north from Cave Cay. However, the currents which sweep through here are quite strong and the channel is well scoured and easy to see.

Cruising down the banks and entering Galliot Cut Channel from the west you will find that the shoals extend for about two miles on the west side of Big Farmers Cay. You should, therefore, hold off the land that distance until the northwest end of Little Galliot Island bears due east. Then change your course to due east and steer for it, passing about one hundred yards north of the north end of Little Galliot Island. The shallowest part will be found when you are still two miles away on the bank. Here a minimum depth of nine feet at low tide will be had. As you approach Galliot Cut the water deepens until off the north end of Little Galliot Island, you will find three fathoms. Pass on the south side of the low-lying cay, which is southwest of High Cay, and sail out to sea on a NE x E course with plenty of water beneath you. There will also be plenty on deck if the tide happens to be ebbing against a fresh easterly breeze. There is a minimum depth of sixteen feet on the bar at low tide.

In case you wish to anchor and spend the night before going outside, there is a very snug little anchorage alongside the white sand beach on the southwest side of Galliot Island, well protected in all winds except those from the southwest.

¶ Cave Cay

Lying on the southeast side of Galliot Cut, Cave Cay carries the light which guides mariners through this passage. It is an interesting little island, with two good harbours for small boats.

The cay is really divided into two parts, east and west, which are connected through the middle of the island by a low sand isthmus, on each side of which is a good harbour. The north harbour is actually a deep cove, open to the north, with six feet of water in it at low tide. The south harbour is practically landlocked, and is entered through a cleft in the cliffs on the southwest side of the island. This is a beautiful harbour, with a blue water basin at its north end, in which there is six feet of water at low tide. There is a minimum five feet of water at the entrance, and a boat drawing up to that much can lie there safely. Both basins are connected by a dredged channel which will carry five feet at low water. On the inside of the cove in the north harbour of this cay is a remarkable cave, in which many local boats have sought shelter during severe hurricanes.

Cave Cay is the private property of the Oakes family, heirs to the estates of Sir Harry Oakes, the controversial Canadian investor of the thirties and forties. The Oakes maintain a weekend house on the south harbour at Cave Cay.

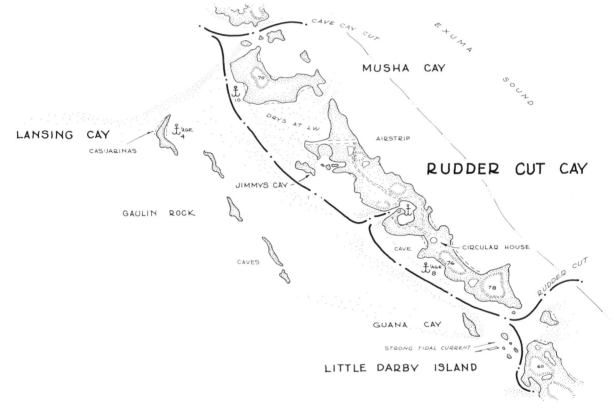

❮ Rudder Cut Cay

Rudder Cut Cay lies on the northwest side of Rudder Cut. Between it and Cave Cay there is another cay called Musha Cay. A draft of six feet can be taken through from Galliot to Darby Island, at low tide. The channel lies close along the western side of these cays, and inside the white sand shoals which lie to the westward. Rudder Cut derives its name from the three remarkable rocks which lie in the cut on its western approach, one of which looks very much like an inverted rudder, and the others like part of the mechanism. A local fable has it that a large margate fish cut off the rudder of a ship passing through here and that it gradually turned to stone.

In the early sixties a British architect, J. Seymour Harris, purchased Rudder Cut Cay for the express purpose of experimenting with some of his architectural ideas there. Apparently building codes in Great Britain are somewhat restrictive and the cay offered him a release for his talents. Mr. Harris built a geodesic circular house supported by flying buttresses, a unique structure which appealed to Californian Mitzi Biggs, who now owns and spends several months a year on the Cay.

There are several good coves along the lee of the island, but the best anchorage is in the lake where there is twelve feet at low water and the dredged channel offers at least six feet coming in. A twenty-seven hundred foot, coral surfaced airstrip has been cleared at the north end of the cay.

⟨ Lansing Cay

A mile west of the north end of Rudder Cut Cay lies Lansing Cay. Surrounded by shallow sand banks this island offers protection on its eastern side to craft drawing no more than four feet. An attractive island with the ruins of several small houses, a citrus and casuarina grove, it was originally developed as a private vacation spot by a Colonel Lansing from New York, whose heirs still own it as far as we know.

There is a long pointed beach on its western side where we've found all manner of shells, while conch are plentiful further offshore. During the summer the banks to the west are alive with sting rays and skates. We prepared a sting ray for eating once, and it is true, they taste very much like deep sea scallops which, we understand, is what deep sea scallops really are.

The Wood Dove Cays which continue south from Lansing Cay are low and flat; under their ledges along the shore there are always enough crawfish to fill your pot.

⟨ Rudder Cut

For those whose draft (five feet) will permit their cruising down the inside from Galliot Cut and will not permit their continuing further south, that is, by way of the Pimblico Cays (four feet), Rudder Cut is where you will enter Exuma Sound for the last thirty-two miles to George Town. As is the case with all of the cuts in the Exuma Cays, a strong tide sluices through here, both ebb and flood; so best to negotiate it in good light.

Entering Exuma Sound pass on the north side of the large rock which lies in the center and seaward of the Cut. Here the channel maintains a constant 20-foot depth clear to the bar.

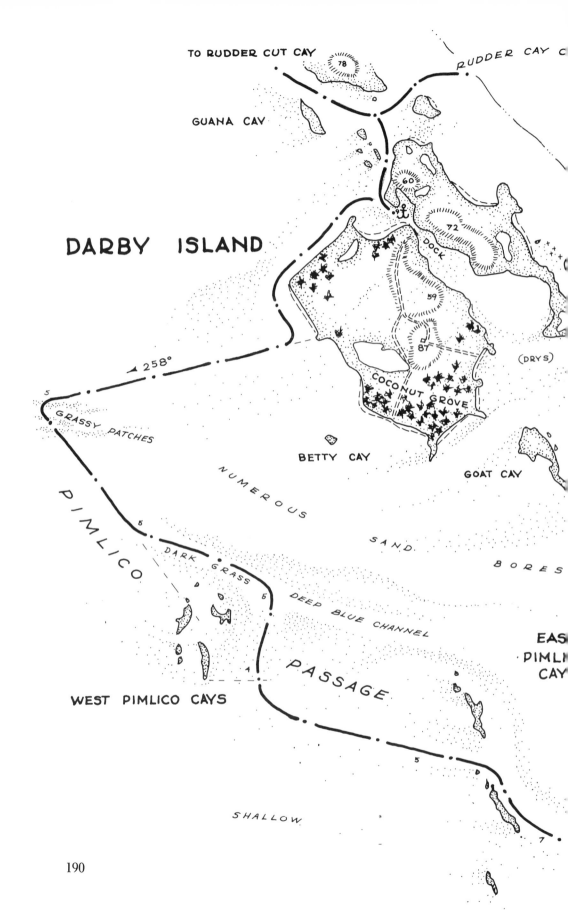

TO RUDDER CUT CAY

RUDDER CAY C

78

GUANA CAY

DARBY ISLAND

60

DOCK

72

59

87

(DRYS)

258°

5

GRASSY PATCHES

COCONUT GROVE

BETTY CAY

GOAT CAY

NUMEROUS

PIMLICO

5

DARK GRASS

5

SAND

BORES

DEEP BLUE CHANNEL

EAS
PIML
CAY

1

PASSAGE

WEST PIMLICO CAYS

5

SHALLOW

7

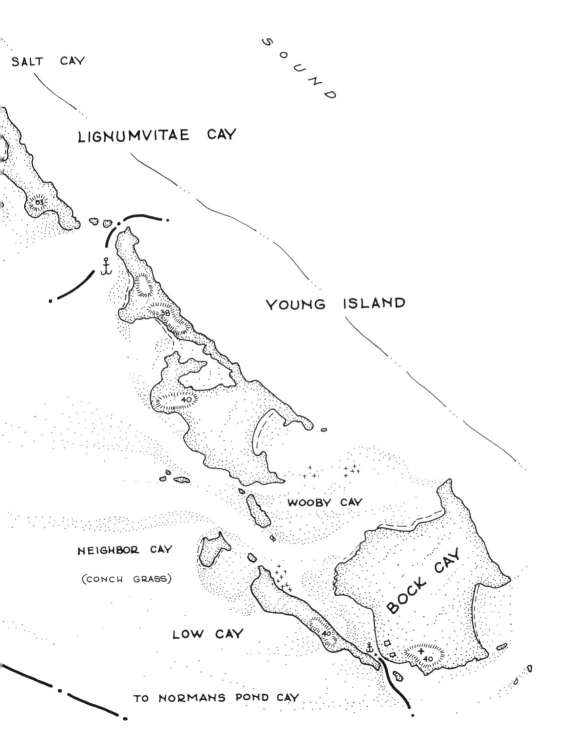

EXUMA

TTLE DARBY ISLAND

SALT CAY

SOUND

LIGNUMVITAE CAY

YOUNG ISLAND

WOOBY CAY

NEIGHBOR CAY

(CONCH GRASS)

BOCK CAY

LOW CAY

TO NORMANS POND CAY

⟨ Darby Island

Darby Island Harbour lies between Darby Island and Little Darby Island and carries twelve to eighteen feet of water. It is easily accessible, the blue water channel in from Rudder Cut offering a least depth of seven feet all the way. Here the flood tide runs north and the ebb south; there is eighteen feet of water in the channel at the concrete pier and seven feet shoaling to three in the pool to the south. We do not advise tying up at the pier as you may be boarded by rats during the night.

Both Darby Islands used to be the private estate of G.R. Baxter of Nassau, an Englishman who was one of the pioneer developers of real estate in the Bahamas. We are told that at one time he owned more than three hundred islands and cays. Darby Island is now owned by Captain V.D. Hewitt, R.N.V.R. It is easy to distinguish, being a high island with a large house on the crest of the highest hill, and a long avenue of coconut trees stretching from the harbour up the hill to the house. When developing this island into a plantation, Mr. Baxter at one time employed more than four hundred Bahamians, planted twenty thousand coconut trees and many acres of corn and other vegetables, besides a large number of fruit trees. The views to east and north from the balcony of the main house are unbelievably beautiful.

The Reverend John Brown of Little Farmers Cay acts as caretaker for Captain Hewitt and is an excellent guide for this area, having spent most of his life here. He raises a few brown hogs on Darby Island; they comb the perimeter of its beaches, counterclockwise, twice daily. You can almost set your clock by their methodical course around the island.

We always look forward to dropping our fish trap in the channel alongside the quay as yellowtail and grouper are always plentiful there. One time the good Reverend came sculling up to "Liza" quite out of breath with word that the trap was full and we'd better empty it before the tide did! When asked if he could use any of the bounty he allowed his congregation could, so together we emptied fifty-three fish into the bottom of his dinghy, then watched as he sailed proudly home down the Cays!

⟨ *Lignum Vitae,* Young Island, and Boch Cay

The four-mile archipelago south to Boch Cay is ideal for outboard skiffs and small cruisers, it being a series of shallow sand bars and intervening channels on the bank side and reef bound cuts separating the islands themselves. There is an abundance of conch on the bars hereabouts and the usual

Exuma fishing smack. *H. Kline*

crawfish along the ledges. Young Island is comparatively high and steep too, while under its lee shore several comfortable coves can be found in which to anchor. Neighbor Cay lies directly south of Young Island and is completely surrounded with a pure sand beach without a single footprint on it. The surrounding water is deep and the tide runs fast. It is a beautiful place for a picnic if your draft will let you get to it.

Boch Cay is the property of Frenchman Paul Louis Weiller, oil and aircraft magnate who built a posh weekend house on the cay. In order to communicate with the outside world he installed his own forward scatter telephone system which connects with George Town and Nassau. The anchorage in the small harbour inside his dock is shallow and riddled with sand bores while the tide runs through at several knots. Mr. Weiller does not welcome casual visitors.

SOUTHERN EXUMAS

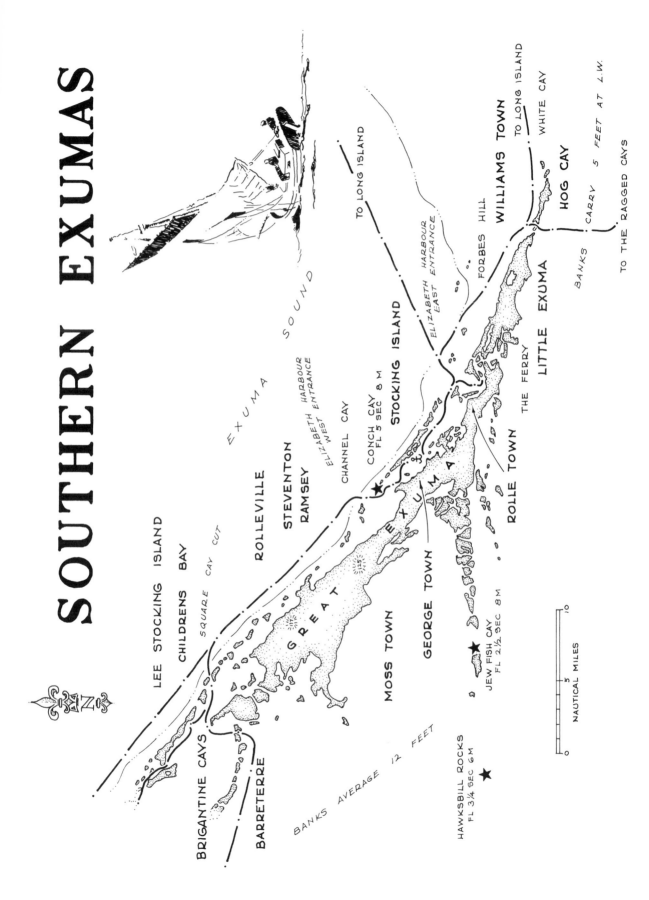

N

LEE STOCKING ISLAND

CHILDRENS BAY

SQUARE CAY CUT

ROLLEVILLE

STEVENTON

RAMSEY

EXUMA SOUND

Elizabeth Harbour WEST ENTRANCE

CHANNEL CAY

CONCH CAY
FL 5 SEC 8 M

STOCKING ISLAND

Elizabeth Harbour EAST ENTRANCE

TO LONG ISLAND

FORBES HILL

WILLIAMS TOWN

TO LONG ISLAND

WHITE CAY

HOG CAY

LITTLE EXUMA

THE FERRY

BANKS CARRY 5 FEET AT L.W.

TO THE RAGGED CAYS

ROLLE TOWN

MOSS TOWN

GREAT EXUMA

GEORGE TOWN

125

JEW FISH CAY
FL 2½ SEC 8 M

BANKS AVERAGE 12 FEET

HAWKSBILL ROCKS
FL 3¼ SEC 6 M

BRIGANTINE CAYS

BARRETERRE

0   5   10
NAUTICAL MILES

Galliott to George Town: Great Exuma Island, George Town, Little Exuma Island

There are many pretty passages in the Bahama Islands, but in our opinion the one from Galliot to Rolleville, at the northwestern end of Great Exuma Island, tops them all. On the outside in Exuma Sound, it is deep water sailing along a rugged and picturesque coast, with the one hundred fathom line within a few hundred yards of the shore. Along this stretch of coast there is some marvelous fishing, especially along the edge of the shelf before it drops off into the deep. Some of the largest wahoo ever hooked in the Bahamas have been found along here. Usually the wind is right on the nose for George Town, and sometimes the sea is a bit on the rough side, but nothing to stop a good sea boat. It is exhilarating sailing!

For those who prefer to keep the pots on the stove there are two incredibly beautiful inside passages, where the water is usually as smooth as a mill pond, though they are considerably longer. Parts are shallow, but local smacks drawing five feet sail through even in the darkest of nights, waiting for the tide where necessary. Power boats drawing four feet can get through like the local smacks, by waiting for the tide, hereinafter described.

The first alternative course is the Pudding Cut Passage. That is using N.O. Charts 26301 and 26303 to make a detour around the shoals which extend west for five or six miles from the cays lying between Galliot and the Pimblico Cays. If this is done you should come in on the south side of the Brigantine Cays, go through Pudding Cut, around the north end of Barreterre Island, and so out into Exuma Sound through Square Rock Cut. A draft of six feet can be carried through here without any difficulty. Through Pudding Cut there is two fathoms of water, which deepen to three fathoms around the north end of Barreterre. From there on the deep water, which is unmistakable, runs east out to the sea. Vessels coming north from Ragged Island and Crooked Island use Pudding Cut frequently.

Proceeding eastward from Darby Island it is best to go outside from Rudder Cay Cut to Adderley Cay if you are drawing more than five feet. This is because the second alternate inside passage lies just west of Darby Island. You can only get through this one by awaiting the tide. We speak of the Pimblico Passage, described below.

The Pimblico Passage south around the Pimblico Cays to Norman's Pond Cay, as illustrated on the Darby Island sketch chart, should not be

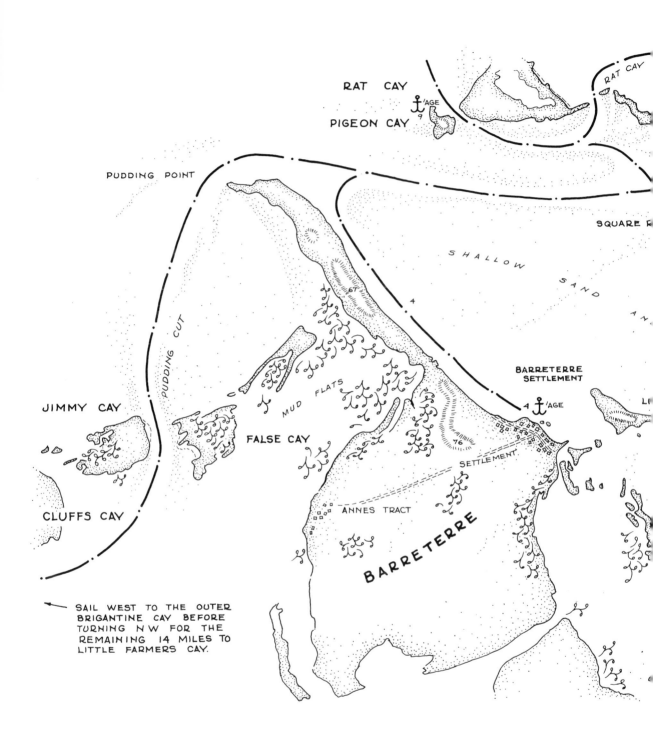

RAT CAY

PIGEON CAY

RAT CAY

'AGE
9

PUDDING POINT

SQUARE R

SHALLOW

SAND

AN

67

4

PUDDING CUT

BARRETERRE
SETTLEMENT

'AGE
4

JIMMY CAY

L

FALSE CAY

16

MUD FLATS

SETTLEMENT

CLUFFS CAY

ANNES TRACT

BARRETERRE

SAIL WEST TO THE OUTER
BRIGANTINE CAY BEFORE
TURNING NW FOR THE
REMAINING 14 MILES TO
LITTLE FARMERS CAY.

196

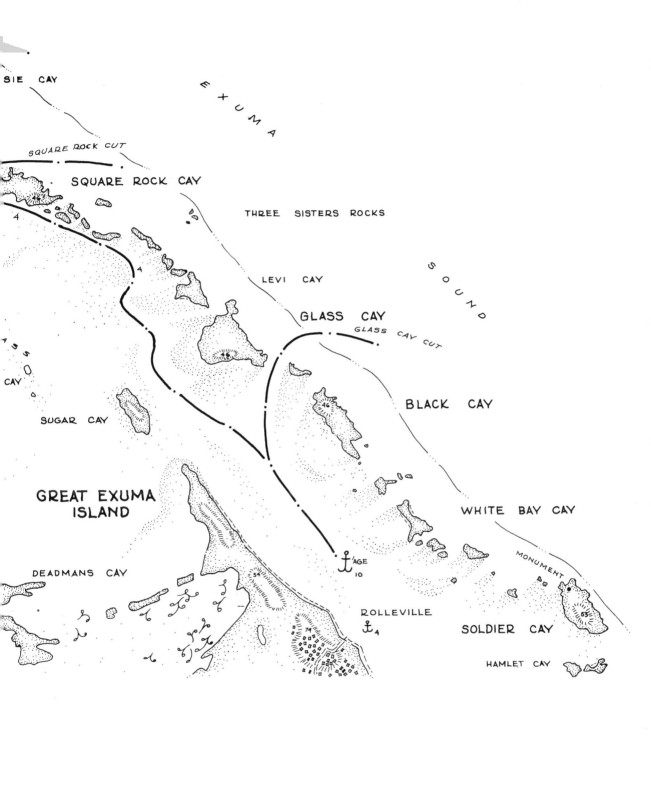

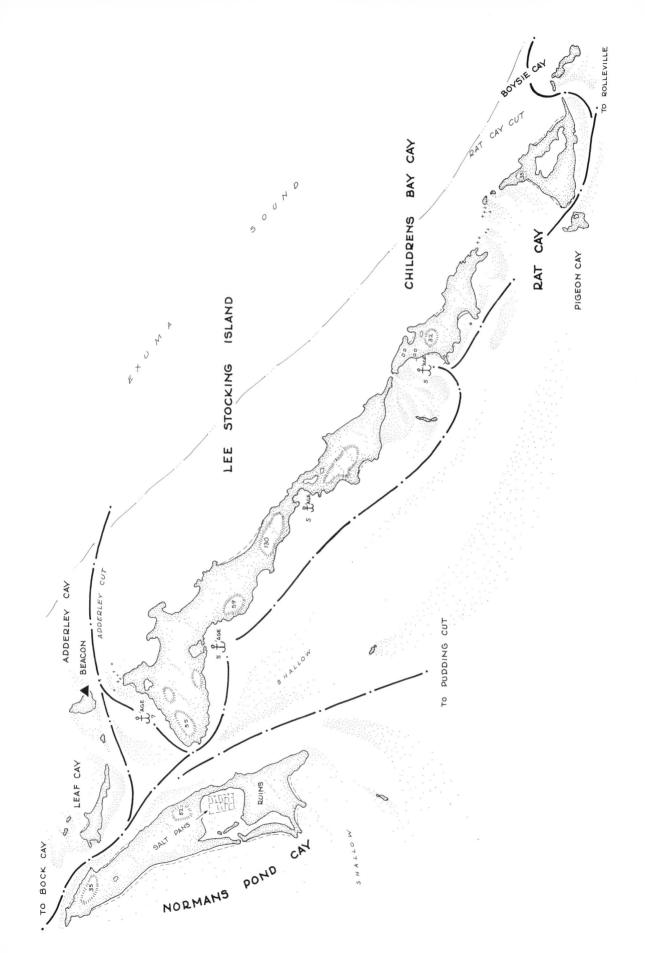

attempted with a draft in excess of four feet. Even that should be carried through on at least half a flood. For the unaccustomed eye the channels are vague and ill defined, so good light hereabouts is a requisite. We have endeavored in the Pimblico Cay sketch chart to point up land marks that will assist you through. Once past the East Pimblico Cays the channel is a well defined, deep blue channel all the way to Norman's Pond Cay.

On Norman's Pond Cay there used to be important salt pans, the outlines of which can still be seen. Large salt schooners came in here to collect their cargoes, and the monument on Adderley Cay was erected to show them the entrance.

From Norman's Pond Cay a draft of six or seven feet can be carried all the way to Square Island. This passage is along the southern side of Lee Stocking Island where a number of coves on the lee side of the island offer good coverage in winds N by SE.

The next island east is Children's Bay Cay, the private estate of John Heinz, the "57 Varieties" person. This island was originally developed by the Hume Cronyns, the famous theatrical couple. A true plantation, the island is complete with a great house, guest house, servants' houses, power house, caretaker's cottage, storehouse, two wharfs, extensive vegetable and truck farming gardens, a number of wells, a seaplane ramp, and a small fleet of pleasure craft. Children's Bay Cay has always been a happy place and we treasure a memorable evening spent listening to Mr. Cronyn reminiscing about his visits to the Bahamas with his grandparents back in the thirties. Here was a man who had always loved the Islands and seemed to have found the peace that so many seek in them!

Going eastward from Children's Bay Cay there is deep water (ten feet) all the way to Square Rock Cay, an umistakable sugar-loaf-shaped, small but high island, rising from the Banks. Here there are two important passages from the Banks into Exuma Sound, Square Rock Cut and Rat Cay Cut. Both have deep and unobstructed water, but Rat Cay Cut is the one most favored by the Bahamians as its opening points more to the north, giving somewhat of a lee with the prevailing winds and sea. This cut is easy to identify from Exuma Sound, as it lies just east of the conical hill on Rat Cay.

The inside passage from Square Island to Rolleville is very shallow and you will have to await the tide.

North of the settlement of Rolleville, which is on the western end of Great Exuma Island, there is another good cut or passage which can be used for shelter if desired. It lies between Glass Cay and Black Cay where the mail boat, drawing ten feet, enters to discharge freight for Rolleville. A monument has been erected on Soldier's Cay, just beyond Rolleville, but the passage way is intricate and we cannot recommend it.

The next settlement which you will see along the north shore of Great Exuma Island is Steventon, another mail boat port of call. But it can be visited only in good weather, as the sea breaks right across the entrance in anything but a calm. There is a beautiful bay here but it should not be attempted without a local pilot. Shortly after passing Steventon the high hill on Stocking Island in Elizabeth Harbour will come popping up over the horizon. Steer straight for it.

❨ Elizabeth Harbour

On approaching Elizabeth Harbour from any angle, the monument on Stocking Island will be seen a long way off. It stands 120 feet above sea level. The entrance between Channel Cay and Conch Cay is a mile wide. A reef extends for one-quarter of a mile southeast from Channel Cay, and another for one-quarter of a mile northwest from Conch Cay. There is a flashing white light on Conch Cay. Vessels drawing up to ten feet can get in safely by following these directions:

Steer SE for the monument on Stocking Island until the white roofs on Simon's Point bear 163°. Simon's Point has an unreliable five-mile light on it. This will lead you in about one-third the distance between Channel Cay and Conch Cay, favoring the latter. Once past the bar off Conch Cay, or when Conch Cay bears due east, alter course to the SE, steering for the Stocking Island Beacon until Simon's Point bears 170°. In this way you will avoid a small but shallow, rocky bar one-quarter mile from Conch Cay light. This bar is marked by a black stake. Rounding the stake steer directly for Simon's Point on the 170° course until over the black patches or within 200 yards of the point; at the same time keep a lookout for rocky patches you will pass on your starboard hand. From this point steer 126° until on a line between the pink houses of Simon's Point and the beacon on Stocking Island. Then alter course to the beacon, thus avoiding the shallow sand bank which extends southwestward from the vicinity of Lily Cay. Then steer toward the beacon until close up under the shore of Stocking Island where there is plenty of water.

As far back as the eighteenth century British Naval Officers and even a Royal Geographer, were advocating the development of George Town and Elizabeth Harbour as the metropolis and principal port of the Bahamas. At that time it was probably true that it compared very favorably with Nassau Harbour, where vessels were frequently storm-bound. Suffice it to say, Elizabeth Harbour today ranks as one of the best in the Bahamas for boats of moderate draft.

Within its reaches are many pretty coves and harbours within harbours, where small boats can lie safely and quietly. The best and most popular one is Stocking Island Harbour, which is also known as "the hurricane hole." This lies directly across the harbour from George Town, and nine out of every ten yachts which come into George Town prefer to anchor there.

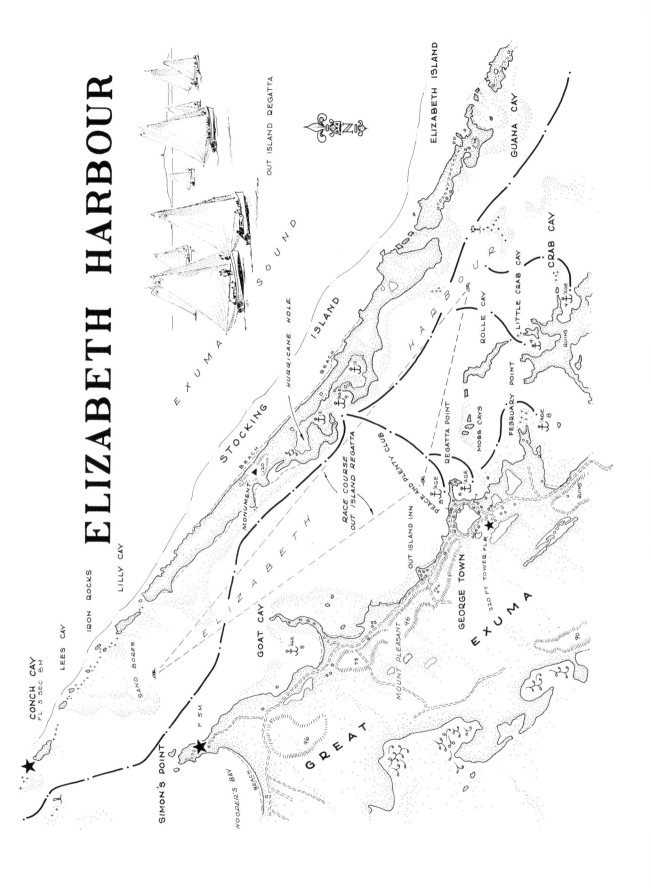

ELIZABETH HARBOUR

OUT ISLAND REGATTA

EXUMA SOUND

STOCKING ISLAND

HURRICANE HOLE

BEACH

BEACH

MONUMENT

ELIZABETH CAY

HARBOUR

RACE COURSE
OUT ISLAND REGATTA

PEACE AND PLENTY CLUB

OUT ISLAND INN

ELIZABETH ISLAND

GUANA CAY

CRAB CAY

LITTLE CRAB CAY

ROLLE CAY

FEBRUARY POINT

MOSS CAYS

REGATTA POINT

RUINS

GEORGE TOWN

220 FT TOWER FL R

EXUMA

RUINS

GOAT CAY

MOUNT PLEASANT

GREAT

EXUMA

HOOPER'S BAY

BEACH

SIMON'S POINT

F 5 M

SAND BORES

IRON ROCKS

LEES CAY

LILLY CAY

CONCH CAY
FL 5 SEC 8 M

There are really three harbours here, one inside the sand spit (where the rotting remains of a large sailboat lies partially sunk just off the inner beach), and two others branching off from it. The first has depths up to three fathoms, and good holding ground. There are no obstructions, either entering or inside. From this harbour there is a channel, with a minimum of six feet at low tide, into the western lagoon, which is generally considered to be one of the best hurricane harbours in the islands. At the head of this lagoon is a large house, built by Mr. Twyman from Michigan, who also keeps his boat there.

On the north side of this western lagoon is the residence of Lawrence Lewis, Jr., of Richmond, Virginia. The views from his house are fabulous. On the ocean side a path leads down to the mile-long Stocking Island Beach, certainly the loveliest in all the Bahamas and a favorite one for shelling. The Spanish villa at the entrance to Stocking Island Harbour was the home of Fritz Ludington, former George Town developer whose interests now lie in the Turks and Caicos Islands. The villa now belongs to Lord John Whittmore of Geneva, Switzerland.

The channel into the eastern lagoon is narrow and intricate, with a depth of four feet more or less, at low tide. The picturesque pink house facing the harbour inside is the residence of Mr. Lewis' sister, Mrs. Molly Wiley, also of Virginia.

Deeper draft vessels use the eastern entrance through Three Fathom Channel into Elizabeth Harbour. Through here naval vessels, some as large as destroyer escorts, sought refuge in the deeper eastern anchorage during WW II. A cut through the reef that extends from Elizabeth Island was dredged and buoyed, but these buoys have since been removed. The cut is now marked by a rotten wooden piling at the south border of the channel, but this will soon entirely disappear.

South of Elizabeth Harbour, on the southwest side of Red Shank Cay, is another snug anchorage called Master Harbour, which is used by local boats in stormy weather. A draft of seven feet can be taken in at low tide. There is nine feet up at the head of it where you can lie perfectly safe in any weather.

East of Man of War Cay, where there are some interesting fortifications, the channel leads into "The Ferry." The passage through is only open at high tide to boats drawing not over four feet. It is much easier, however, to go through Hog Cay Cut at the eastern end of Little Exuma Island.

Behind these islands buccaneers have lain, this being one of their principal lairs. Privateersmen have hidden in the coves waiting for rich Spanish galleons. British men-of-war have come in to rest and refit for sea battles. West Indiamen and Baltimore Clippers have brought in and picked up cargoes. Even vessels of the United States Navy have used this as a center of operations in this area. The stage is still set for great performances, even though the actors have departed.

Opposite, Long Island winner *Tida Wave* races on Elizabeth Harbour. *Bahamas Ministry of Tourism*

❨ Great and Little Exuma

The islands of Great and Little Exuma have been described as "sixty thousand acres of romance." In all the Bahamas—one might well say in all the world—there is nothing quite like them.

Here is bold scenery with rocky headlands, wide bays, deep water, snug coves, safe harbours and harbours within harbours—also some of the best bathing beaches in the world. A boat can cruise around here for weeks without seeing it all. On shore the pages of the book of romance open up for those who are interested in the local history. Here in olden times the art of gracious living reached its zenith in the Bahamas. The large plantation owners were people of consequence, often scions of the noble families in England, and therefore accustomed to the management of extensive properties.

The Emancipation Act of 1834 ended this system as it was obviously impossible to work and maintain large plantations without working labor. The owners sold out, or simply moved away, though it is a historical fact that some of them, being extremely fond of their slaves, deeded their properties to them. The most notable example is that of John Lord Rolle of Stevenstone, England, whose elegant, steel-engraved portrait now hangs in the Hill Top Tavern in Rolleville. This old nobleman is best known for his feat at the Coronation of Queen Victoria. When moving up to make obeisance he stumbled, falling flat on his face, and it is recorded that the Queen got up from her throne and helped him to his feet. Lord Rolle was probably the largest landholder on Great Exuma, and the settlements of Rolle Town, Mount Thompson, Ramsey, Rolleville and Steventon were named after his plantations which occupied those areas. Upon the freeing of the slaves Lord Rolle deeded all of his properties to them, and they promptly adopted his name as well. At any rate, on the Island of Great Exuma where the total population is approximately 5,000 by last count, over 3,000 are named "Rolle," and the right of commonage is available to all bearing that name.

These plantations were large and prosperous. One of them even today, the Forrest plantation near Mosstown, comprises 5,300 acres of land, and more than 50 of the slave houses still stand there. The manor house was deomolished by the 1926 hurricane but the foundations show that it was about 60 feet long and 35 feet wide, and we understand that it had fourteen large rooms. The manor house yard is surrounded by a stone wall seven feet high. Robert Wilder's book, *Wind From The Carolinas*, will give you a taste of what Exuma plantation life must have been like in those early days.

High on the hill at Crab Cay, immediately east of George Town, are the ruins of a plantation house that served as a hospital and rehabilitation center for British soldiers during the American War for Independence.

The 1926 hurricane must have been a terrible disaster for the Exumas, for after it was over there was hardly a public building church, schoolhouse or plantation house left standing. Today there is only one of the old plantation houses left, "Cotton House" at William's Town on Little Exuma.

Great Exuma is 40 miles long and one to seven miles wide. It is separated from Little Exuma Island by a shallow passage called "The Ferry" where the government used to maintain a hand drawn barge for local traffic. A bascule bridge now stands here. The south side of the island is low, flat, and a maze of mud banks, swamps, and shallow creeks, ideally suited for smugglers. All the good harbours are on the north side, which is high, bold, and beautiful. The island itself is rolling land with considerable pasturage for stock. It is well wooded with *lignum vitae*, mastic, horseflesh, dogwood and logwood trees found here in abundance. Today a good deal of truck farming is done and a considerable number of cows, sheep, goats, and swine are raised and shipped to the Nassau market.

The hideous scars of development have left their mark on Great Exuma in recent years as a number of foreign companies have secured sizable tracts of land for lot sales here. A few houses have been built amid the network of cleared swaths, but alas, not enough in relation to the number of lots purchased merely for investment.

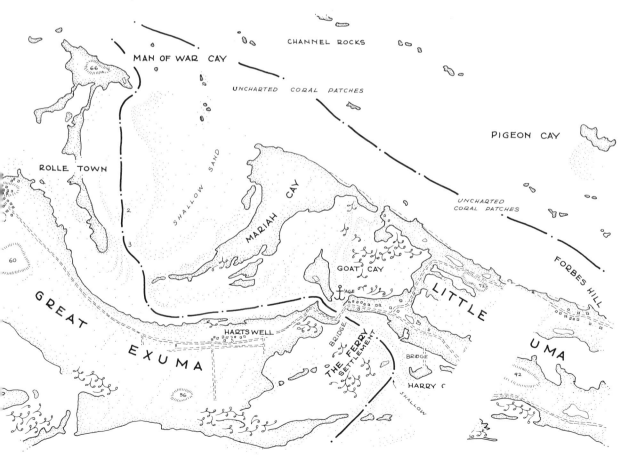

Little Exuma is twelve miles long and one mile wide. It is chiefly notable for its beautiful sand beaches on the north side, some of them over a mile long and open to the sea. There are three settlements: The Ferry, Forbes Hill, and William's Town. The Ferry, as its name indicates, is the village facing the cut which separates Little Exuma from Great Exuma Island. It is a quaint little settlement whose principal residents are the remarkable Irish family of Fitzgeralds with their numerous progeny. One of the interesting sights is the tiny church, in which the whole family assembles on Sundays for divine worship. Clarence Fitzgerald is the leading, if not the only remaining, boat builder in the Exumas today. In his career he has built over forty vessels ranging from dinghys to a recent thirty-one foot Regatta challenger named "Endeavor." "Clarrie," as he is affectionately known to all, is in his seventies and still handles the whole operation single-handed, using mainly an assortment of hand saws, chisels, and an adz in the old style. His only power tool is an electric drill. He works today in his original shop under the same tree that has shielded him from the sun these forty-five years. On a branch over his head hangs a small sign which reads: "Sit, look and ask questions if you must, but please do not make suggestions."

William's Town is at the other end of the island, and Forbe's Hill about half way between. There are large salt pans at William's Town, but they are no longer in operation. Opposite them, on the north shore, is a very interesting monument, a tall Ionic column placed there to direct ships to the salt pans.

The principal industry on the island at present is the canning of delicious guava preserves for the Nassau market, and of course, the ever-present land sales. The town's genial leading citizen, "Squire" J. Vincent Bowe, is a gracious host and lives in "Cotten House," the only livable mansion in the area dating back to Colonial times. These days when sightseeing visitors stream in almost daily from Nassau it's refreshing to know a man who almost invariably invites them in for a visit and a cup of tea. Mr. Bowe seems to fit in Cotten House.

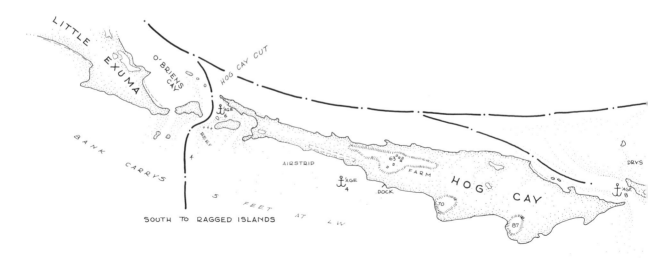

Clarence Fitzgerald of The Ferry, Little Exuma. Bahamas Ministry of Tourism

To the east of Little Exuma lies the island named Hog Cay, which is owned by the Hon. Herbert McKinney of Nassau. It is a very fertile cay, and is reputed to have some of the finest and richest land in the Exumas. Mr. McKinney is raising a variety of crops on it, also sheep and ducks.

Between Little Exuma Island and Hog Cay there is a cut which is somewhat deeper than that of "The Ferry," and consequently this is the best route from the north to the south side of the Exumas. Hog Cay Cut is safely navigable by boats drawing up to six feet, at high tide. The shallowest part is on the south side of the cut, where there is only about four feet of water on the flats at low tide.

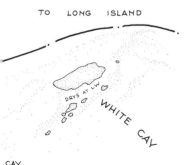

⟨ George Town

The settlement of George Town is the capital of the Exuma group, and
a most interesting village it is. Although demolished in the 1926 hurricane,
it has been completely rebuilt and today is quite a thriving metropolis.

George Town is built around a public square in the middle of which is
a beautiful, large shade tree, an African fig. The principal street of the town
runs along the cliffs out past the U.S. Naval Base, which lies about one mile
from the town. This Naval Base has now been dismantled, although the dock
pilings still stand. The United States holds a ninety-nine year lease on the
property, this having been one of the bases traded for the forty destroyers
during World War II.

There is a substantial pier extending out from the town to deep water
and the mail boat, which draws nearly ten feet of water, lies alongside this
dock on her weekly calls to unload. At dead low tide she has to plow her way
in, however, as there is only eight feet of water right alongside the dock with
ten feet about fifteen feet away from the dock. A yacht may lie alongside

here when the mail boat is not expected, but it's best to put out an anchor to hold her off as there's a healthy surge.

On the south side of the dock, in Kidd Cove, is a good anchorage for small boats, as here will be found six feet of water at low tide. Lying here you are practically inside the town and well protected by all the cays which lie to the east and northeast. Kidd Cove is supposed to have been the favorite anchorage of the pirate, Captain Kdd, who probably careened his boats in the shallows inside the Cay. We have found ballast rock along here, usually pebble size, but granite none the less.

An adventurous, young American, who sailed here to stay many years ago, purchased Kidd Cay and built a causeway over the shallow reef, connecting it with the government dock. Here he built an attractive apartment grouping, landscaped it with flowering vines and trees and, in honor of George Town's major annual event, renamed it "Regatta Point." Howland and Nancy Bottomely met in George Town at Regatta time, she hailing from San Francisco, and he from Island Heights, New Jersey. Together they operate what we consider the finest, small holiday hotel in all the Bahamas. Regatta Point comprises six efficiency apartments, all with their own sparkling sand bathing beach right on the harbour and a superb view of Elizabeth Harbour. For many years Howland has headed the race committee for the Out Island Regatta. He knows each of the contestants personally and has a distinct rapport with men of the sea from everywhere. The Regatta would not have grown into the event it is without his special efforts and unstinting labor of love over the past fifteen years.

Going ashore in George Town one of the first buildings you notice is the large pink store facing the town square. This is Marshall's Store, owned and operated by John Marshall, an enterprising Bahamian who is the leading merchant of the area. A complete stock of food supplies can be had here, including fresh and frozen meats and dairy products. Spirits can be found at his adjacent liquor store. John also has a wing of efficiency apartments over his store for tourists. The town boasts several other food stores, a bakery, several small bars, and a boat rental where amiable Basil Minns is the Evinrude dealer and runs an excellent marine repair service. Basil is an easy-going fellow who will give you all the service he can.

Situated on the village square right next to the "Big Tree" is Two Turtles Inn, where Fritz Ludington built and christened it George Town's after hours fun spot. It remained so for many years with closing hours sometimes extending well into daylight. Today, however, it is just another Island pub.

The commissioner's office, post office, fire and police departments occupy the new, two-story building adjoining the square on the shore.

Just beyond the Commissioner's office and up the hill to the west is Club Peace and Plenty. This famous hostelry was at various times a slave market, sponge market, grocery store, and rum shop. Finally, due to the special talents of Lawrence Lewis, Jr., a very comfortable hotel was built around the original building and cook house, making it one of the most appealing inns in the islands. Prince Philip has dined here, as have all the notables visiting Exuma. Club Peace and Plenty is the gathering place for the winter visitors and tourists alike; its atmosphere is typical of George Town's conviviality.

The Crow's Nest Restaurant on the high bluff west of Club Peace and Plenty commands the best view of Elizabeth Harbour, a perfect place to enjoy the races at the Out Island Regatta, as the entire course is visible from here. Specialty of the house is fish since the proprietors operate the only charter fishing business in town. We recommend the dolphin, usually on the dinner menu. The Crow's Nest is also a popular cocktail spot.

A short distance farther west and down the hill is a government clinic where a resident physician and trained nurse are on duty. George Town's five thousand foot airstrip, two miles south of town, is capable of handling large propeller-driven airplanes and daily service to Nassau and Florida.

The road from George Town rambles along the shore in both directions eastward to The Ferry and westward for some seventeen miles to Rolleville at the northwest end of the Island. The first eight miles of north shoreline are sprinkled liberally with winter residents' homes and cottages while inland you will see the grid scars of the developers.

Racing sloops start from anchor at the Out Island Regatta. *Bahamas Ministry of Tourism*

George Town's Out Island Inn is an attractive group of rambling wood and stone structures which occupy a casuarina grove on the first point west of town. Two miles further west is a long, lovely cay extending out into the harbour named Goat Cay, and now the property of Mrs. "Babbie" Holt of Montreal and Nassau. Here is where Linton Rigg once lived, watching "the day climb out of George Town Bay."

(The Out Island Regatta

Along the wharves in Nassau where the sailing vessels come in from the Out Islands, and at the various marinas where the yachts gather, you will often hear this song:

Sou-Sou-East as fly the crow
To Exuma we will go.
Chorus.
Sail her down, sail down,
    Sail her down to George Town.
Highborne Cay the first we see
Yellow Bank is by the lee.
Chorus.
Harvey Cay is in the moon,
Farmers Cay is coming soon.
Chorus.
Now we come to Galliot,
Out into the ocean we must go.
Chorus.
Children's Bay is passing fast
Stocking Island come at last.
Chorus.
Nassau gal is all behind,
George Town gal is on my mind.
Chorus.
A wiggle, and a giggle and a jamboree,
Great Exuma is the place for me.
Chorus.

This is the theme song of the Out Island Regatta, sometimes pronounced *Regret*ta, a spirited Bahamian sailing event which is held at George Town during April each year. It has been variously described as a fiesta, a jamboree, a riot, and a seagoing carnival but undoubtedly the most apt description of all was made by Carleton Mitchell, writing in the *National Geographic Magazine*, in which he described it as "somewhat like transporting the Milwaukee Braves bleachers to a tennis match at Wimbledon."

It all started in 1953 when yachtsmen Ward Wheelock of Philadelphia and Arthur Herrington of Indianapolis got together with Linton Rigg at

Goat Cay to discuss the possibility of developing a local event that they hoped could improve the understanding between the Bahamian people and their great influx of affluent visitors. It seemed to them that when people of varying backgrounds, race and nationalities got together through a common interest to have fun, the results were almost invariably happy, and it was Mr. Wheelock's conviction that this philosophy, if properly applied, could, like the Olympics, make inroads toward a lasting world peace. Their combined interests centered around Bahamas sailing and the preservation of a fast disappearing workboat fleet which hatched a competition that combined fun with the improvement of the efficiency of the craft involved. An international organization of interested yachtsmen was formed to finance the venture—an annual three-day sailing regatta for Bahamian built and manned working craft. To stimulate national interest on the part of the skippers themselves cash prizes were offered to encourage their attendance. The best scheduled time for the event turned out to be the period following the end of the crawfishing season (April) when the fishermen usually repainted and refurbished their vessels in preparation for the summer fishing season.

The sponsoring organization was named the Out Island Squadron. Its ranks grew to over three hundred members who contributed as much as $9,000 in the event's most shining years. One of the prime purposes of the Squadron was to promote friendship between the working boat crews and the yachtsmen who visit their waters each year; and the burgee of the Out Island Squadron has been cordially welcomed wherever it appeared in the Islands. When the severe winter storm of January 1958 hit the fishing fleet in Nassau, destroying or damaging a large part of it, the Out Island Squadron, within ten days of the disaster, raised over forty thousand dollars to assist in replacing or repairing the damaged vessels. That must have made Ward Wheelock very happy, wherever he is. On the way to the Out Island Regatta in 1956, on his schooner, sailing from Bermuda bound for George Town, he and all hands on board were lost at sea, and never a trace of them ever found.

Those islands which have contributed the most contestants to the Regatta have always been: Andros, Long Island, and the Exumas, the other islands having too few wind-driven boats remaining in their fishing fleets or being too far from George Town to devote the necessary time to attend. In the early years Ragged Islanders were among the most enthusiastic supporters, until they entered a boat named "Ragged Gal" that resembled a six meter racing yacht more than a workboat, and it was barred from competing. Because of this the Ragged Islanders scorned the Regatta for many years, until 1972 when they entered a new Class A sloop, "Jezebel," which placed quite well in the overall standings.

One of the most praiseworthy phases of the competitions are the races held between the individual boats sailing to George Town from their home ports. The settlements of Mangrove Cay and Lisbon Creek lie 150 sea miles to leeward of George Town; and even though they've been plagued with everything from easterly gales to dead calms, these superb sailors of Andros have never missed a Regatta, to say nothing of even being tardy for the Skippers' Meeting.

Since these men sail these distances under any and all conditions without the aid of a compass, the feat is truly commendable. It is said that you can blindfold a Bahamian sailor, sail him miles away from his home port, and when you take off the blindfold he'll look over the side, smell the breeze wafting off a nearby shore, and tell you exactly where he is. We believe it!

There are a number of things which have made the Out Island Regatta unique. To begin with, it has been held in one of the most incredibly beautiful harbours in the world, one of brilliant blue, a mile wide and five miles long, lined with white sand beaches where from any one point an observer can watch almost the entire race. It is an event in which all men compete on an equal footing in a professional activity that has been handed down from their forefathers. Its vehicle is a picturesque sailing fleet, one of the last of its kind, one which will eventually disappear along with all the intuitive artistry it involves, if not given encouragement to continue. The event has sparked worldwide interest in the Bahamas, with sailing yachts arriving from as far away as Honolulu, Canada, and England and the "Regatta" marked bold on their cruising itineraries. In 1959 there were over one hundred visitor yachts in attendance and 85 competitors. That year Prince Philip, Duke of Edinburgh, made the Regatta a part of his world tour. He not only spent a day at George Town watching the races, but sailed one of the large smacks himself, the champion "Lady Muriel" from Staniel Cay. He got soaking wet, but all hands agreed that he handled the vessel like a born seaman.

The actual racing is probably the most unique feature of all. There is nothing quite like it anywhere else. The boats are lined up at anchor with sails furled and when the starting gun fires there is such an explosion of sound and energy that by the time the anchors are tumbled aboard and the sails hoisted, the boats have full way on. Captains and crews shout and jostle each other in a frantic struggle to get clear with collisions being of little consequence, there being only one predominant rule: "when two vessels meet head to head (on opposite tacks) *they both must tack.*" If they don't, both are disqualified. This has only happened once, and since one boat cut the other in half, it was not a very difficult case for the race committee to solve.

All boats, even the small dinghies, are measured on overall deck length, and handicapped ten seconds per foot per mile.

In April the trades blow fresh down the harbour so the starts are usually made toward the east and you can follow the races' progress from any prominent point in town. Twenty billowing sails running down Elizabeth Harbour's sparkling azure blue, with the hills of Stocking Island shining green in the background, is a memorable sight indeed.

Shoreside around the square, thatch huts are set up to serve such native delicacies as conch fritters, crab back and goat stew, all prepared over open fires on the premises and washed down with cold beer.

The Andros and Exuma sloops usually anchor in Kidd Cove for the duration of the Regatta, but the "Long Island boys" anchor in the lee and camp out on the Moss Cays, three hundred yards to the east. "Mrs. Maycock" from Little Farmers Cay always anchors in the center of Kidd Cove, and supplies hot dinners to all boats via her fast-sculling progeny, while the mail boat, "Staniel" Cay Express," leaning on the government pier, supplies the bleachers for a cheering section unknown in the rest of the Islands.

Drawn up along the shore above the high tide mark are the brightly colored, cranky little dinghies with their lilting names; "Sea Wind," "Bitter Lemon," "Morning Dove," "Yellow Tie," "Sarah G.," "Iris" and "Strange Girl." Here you might see a keel being temporarily removed preparatory to entering the sculling race, or a keel fin being added—as we watched Alfred Bain do one year. "So she better go to wind," he explained.

A few years ago one of the leaders in the fleet arrived back across the finish line in incredibly short time. Upon investigation it was found that, having reached the weather mark, she disposed of most of her crew, instructing them to swim to shore, while a skeleton crew completed the lighter part of the course. Since then an amendment was written into the rules which clearly states that a boat must cross the finish line with the same number of crew that it started with. The same applied to "smacks" (a smack is a boat with a live fish well) when it was discovered that to save weight some of the smack boat skippers had plugged and drained their wells. It was decided that to enter as a smack the boat must be sailed as a smack.

Among the $4,000 in prize monies is one prize that pretty much delineates the basic idea of the Regatta. *Yachting Magazine*'s most worthy contribution to the event is the Ward Wheelock Trophy for the "Best Maintained Boat" in the fleet. This trophy carries a cash prize of $70 with it each year and the three administering judges are selected from the Squadron officers present plus visiting yachtsmen.

A cash prize is also awarded by the Prime Minister to the best all round skipper. This prize has been received most often by Staniel Cay's Rolly Gray whose consistent good performance over the years has made him most eligible for it.

Usually hosted by the Resident Commissioner, a "meet the skippers" party is always scheduled so that visiting yachtsmen and racing skippers can get acquainted, swap yarns, and perhaps schedule a match race. We caution visitors not to be too generous with their bets, however, as local knowledge counts for a lot on Elizabeth Harbour.

It was the original hope of the founders that the responsibility and operation of the Regatta would eventually be assumed by the Bahamians themselves. The first step in this transition was begun when the Squadron Chairman, "Bobby" Symonette, then senior representative for Exuma, saw to it that local people were appointed to handle its administration. Clyde Minard, manager of Nassau's Royal Bank of Canada, was named Squadron treasurer; Harry Kline, editor of the *Yachtsman's Guide to the Bahamas*, as secretary, handled the coordination of the event; Howland Bottomely, former Squadron Commodore and George Town resident, with the help of Regatta buff, George Harvey of Chicago (who as of 1972 had never missed a single Regatta) handled the racing. Each alternate year an American or Bahamian Vice Commodore was invited to solicit funds.

A completed transition to an all-Bahamian staff was never necessary because when the present Government came into power it was made known that they wanted to take an active part in the Regatta. Prime Minister Pindling himself said, in his welcoming address at the Snipe World Championships held at Coral Harbour in 1967, that he intended, through the Out Island Regatta, to make sailing the Bahamian national sport. Because of this, and previous political ties, the Squadron officers felt that to again invite their membership to sponsor an event that had become a political convenience would be unjust and they stepped down, turning the entire operation, with the exception of the racing, over to the Bahamas Government for financing and organizing.

In recent years the indecision on setting a date early enough to allow for advance publicity has resulted in attracting few foreign spectators, it being considered even by the Bahamians themselves little more than an excuse for a three-day party. Even the entries have dwindled. None of the local representatives have indicated an interest in the sailing or racing and seem plainly devoid of any knowledge of the original concept of the event. Sadder still is the apparent lack of concern shown by the majority of Exuma businessmen, who would seem to benefit most from the event's continuation.

A number of smaller regattas have since sprung into existence back in the various home ports of the contestants: Mangrove Cay, Salt Pond, Rolleville, San Salvador, Cat Island, Abaco, and even Turks and Caicos. All have their own individual character and premise, but each is still a replica of the original.

So as proof that politics and sporting events do not mix it may very well be that this is the time to retire the George Town affair until it comes to life again on its own, as in its present form it seems to have served its purpose. The Bahamas fishing fleet is certainly better maintained and sailed than it was in 1953, and through the competitions their hull refinements, efficiency and versatility have all improved. What now might appear to the visitor to be dirty, patched sails would at one time have looked like the finest racing gear in comparison. The Regatta as a tourist attraction did much to build George Town to the flourishing hub of activity it has become today. The Bahamian fisherman responds more openly to visitors' pleasure cruising the islands in the vehicles of his trade, and the cammaraderie he came to understand at the Out Island Regatta declares that sailboats are to be raced at the drop of a hat in any language, on any sea. But just in case you get too eager, take a good look at his rig before you drop yours; he just might be a Gray, a Bain, or a Knowles.

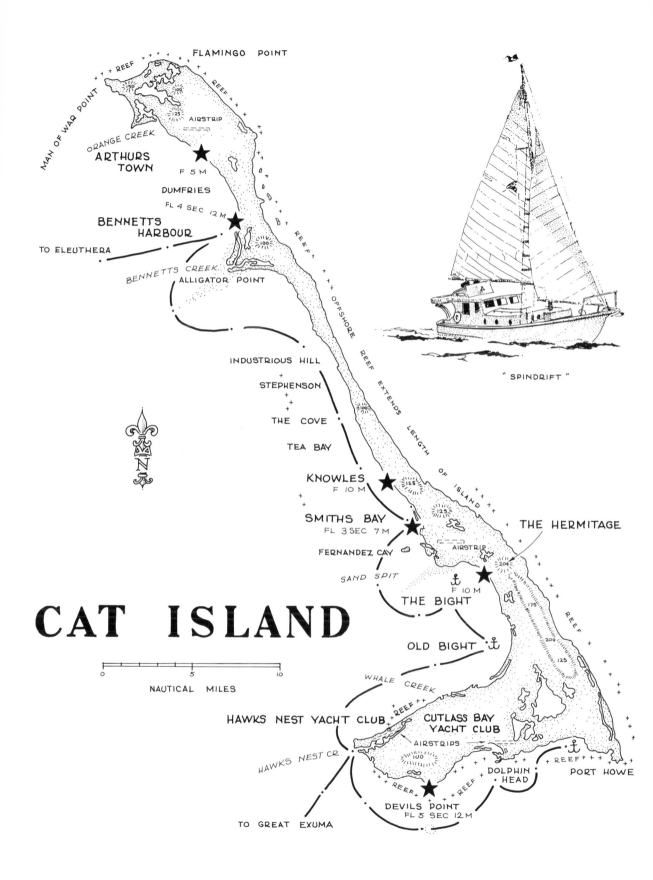

FLAMINGO POINT

REEF

REEF

MAN OF WAR POINT

ORANGE CREEK

ARTHURS TOWN

AIRSTRIP

F 5 M

DUMFRIES

FL 4 SEC 12 M

BENNETTS HARBOUR

TO ELEUTHERA

BENNETTS CREEK

ALLIGATOR POINT

INDUSTRIOUS HILL

STEPHENSON

THE COVE

TEA BAY

KNOWLES
F 10 M

SMITHS BAY
FL 3 SEC 7 M

FERNANDEZ CAY

SAND SPIT

N

OFFSHORE REEF EXTENDS LENGTH OF ISLAND

THE HERMITAGE

AIRSTRIP

THE BIGHT
F 10 M

REEF

OLD BIGHT

"SPINDRIFT"

CAT ISLAND

0   5   10

NAUTICAL MILES

WHALE CREEK

HAWKS NEST YACHT CLUB

REEF

CUTLASS BAY
YACHT CLUB

AIRSTRIPS

HAWKS NEST CR.

REEF

REEF

DOLPHIN HEAD

PORT HOWE

REEF

DEVILS POINT
FL 5 SEC 12 M

TO GREAT EXUMA

Cat Island

CHAPTER

12

Cat Island is the highest of the Bahama Islands, and certainly one of the most interesting. This island is thought to have had the largest population in the days of the Lucayans, and there is some evidence that the Central American Indians were in some way connected with Cat Island's history. Stone hatchets and other implements constructed from a kind of stone (jadeite) peculiar to Yucatan, Central America, have been found, and are still to be found, on Cat Island. It is reasonable to presume that the Indians of Yucatan paddled their canoes across the Yucatan Channel to Cuba, then along the north coast of Cuba up to the Great Bahama Bank, and from there to the Bahamas Islands. Cat Island undoubtedly appealed to them particularly on account of its height and fertility.

In early Colonial days, following the settlement of the Bahamas by the British, it was also a favored spot for the more affluent settlers, and large plantations were numerous. It is recorded in the history of the Bahamas that Colonel Andrew Deveaux, the hero of Colonial days who recaptured Nassau from the Spaniards in 1783, was rewarded by the grant of a large tract of land on Cat Island. Here, as in Eleuthera during the last century, pineapples and tomatoes were grown and shipped north by coastal schooner. Agriculture is still the main source of income.

Between the Exuma Cays and Cat Island there lies a rugged piece of water called Exuma Sound; 50 miles wide and 1,000 fathoms deep, it is like the open sea. The trade winds blow strong and it is often rough. There are numerous passages into it from the Exuma Cays, but when cruising from the west, Ship Channel Passage is the best. Cat Island lies dead to windward from there, about 65 miles away. However, if the wind is east, or anything north of east, you will get a good lee up under the shore of Eleuthera Island, which is only 25 miles away. From there you can coast down, past Eleuthera Point and Little San Salvador Island.

Cat Island can be seen a long way off. The hills at its northern end rise to a height of 150 feet. The island is 43 miles long, with an average width of one to two miles, and is very fertile. It has a population of about 4,000 people. The windward or northeast side is very bold and also steep. But the leeward or southwest side has the usual characteristics of the low lying swampy western shore, two to five fathoms of water over sandy bottom, and a goodly sprinkling of rocky heads. It is *not* a good place to be caught in a norther.

The chief settlement is called "The Bight," and it lies literally within the bight at the southern end of the island, eleven and a half miles northeast of Hawks Nest Point. With the prevailing winds this is all smooth water, and you can anchor close to the shore in two fathoms. The white church about half a mile northwest of the settlement will be your landfall. At the Bight there is a church, a post office, and a store where supplies can be obtained.

Comer hill, behind The Bight, is 204 feet above sea level, the highest in the Bahamas. At its summit is a miniature replica of a twelfth century abbey, the home and final resting place of the late Monsignor John Hawes, a remarkable architect and Anglican missionary who became a Roman Catholic and preferred to be called simply, Father Jerome. Often referred to as "the great heart of the Bahamas," Father Jerome became a legend in his own time when he first came to Nassau in 1908 to help rebuild the Islands' churches after that year's devastating hurricane. Already established as England's leading young prodigy, he had abandoned a promising architectural career in his early twenties to become a clergyman.

Noting that the island's ancient stone forts had withstood the ravages of this sometimes stormy, humid, sub-tropical climate, he simulated their construction in a simple, functional style, using only native rock and mortar. He really re-introduced a medieval method, but one that has proven itself here over all others. Hawe's earliest efforts of that period stand today in his original parish in Clarence Town, Long Island.

A lifelong call to emulate the life of St. Francis of Assisi led to his conversion to Catholicism and his eventual ordaining as a Catholic priest. This led to a 24-year absence from the Bahamas during which time he did some of his most interesting work in the remote reaches of western Australia. In addition to the numerous examples of theological architecture he accomplished there, he is remembered best for his brave work among the camps of the aborigines during the deadly flu epidemics following WW I.

Following a heart attack and back in the Bahamas at the age of sixty-two, Father Jerome began building his rough stone hermitage on commonage land at the top of Comer Hill, which he renamed Mount Alvernia after the hill in Tuscany, Italy, where St. Francis received the wounds of the Cross. Commanding a breathtaking view of both coasts, the hermitage consists of a miniature chapel with a single pew and altar, his own cell which contains a writing desk and straw-matted bed, and a guest cell with plastered walls and a cot. Father Jerome is buried in the crypt beneath the chapel, where he slept amongst his building materials and supplies at the outset of the project. Along the final ascent to the hermitage you will see the stations of the cross which he carved into the limestone hill.

During the last years of his life he spent weekends helping people of the

Father Jerome's Hermitage on Cat Island.
Bahamas Ministry of Tourism

surrounding settlements build their own places of worship. He was on constant call to Nassau where he built a convent and Saint Augustine's Abbey at Fox Hill. The Abbey is executed in California mission style and contains a college, monastery, technical school, guest house, and a church. On the hill opposite his first church at Clarence Town, Long Island, he built St. Peter's Church.

In addition to all of this, the good Father occupied spare moments doing intricate wood carvings and oil paintings for his diocese, also cartoons and essays that sometimes conveyed his sly wit. Of his beard he once remarked, "I regard it not so much as an escape from shaving as I do a penance. How anyone could grow a beard from preference, I cannot imagine."

Father Jerome died in 1959 and there is now a new resident at the Hermitage. Father Lionel Pare of New England, in his mid-thirties, does not always resemble the classic friar, especially when dressed in T-shirt and slacks, driving through The Bight in his Ford pickup. Father Pare says he enjoys visitors who want to see the Hermitage, but cautions them to please ring the bell at the foot of Comer Hill before starting up.

⟪ Harbours and Creeks

Unfortunately there are few harbours in Cat Island, and those are both small and shallow. The first is Orange Creek, at the northwest end of the Island. This is a narrow entrance just above Arthur's Town. A draft of four feet can be taken in at half tide.

ORANGE CREEK

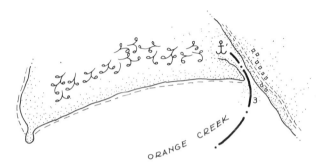

Next is Bennett's Harbour which lies just north of Alligator Point. The entrance is on the north side of the island, leaving the light on the port hand going in. A draft of six feet can be taken in, and there is good protection here in any weather, when once you are inside, but it is small. A number of years ago, waiting for a sick child to rally from a bad case of the flu, we anchored for a week in Bennett's Harbour. Mrs. Roberts, a very kind and accommodating lady who lived just up the road kept us supplied with both fresh bread and clean laundry, plus volunteering her two small boys to help set our fish traps each day in return for a share of the catch. We ate well that entire week, and so did Mrs. Roberts and her boys, with all the fish cleaning being my responsibility. Mrs. Roberts still bakes delicious bread and does laundry for visiting yachts, but I'm sure the boys have long since learned to clean fish, and have gone to sea.

BENNETTS HARBOUR

One placid evening as we glanced out the harbour entrance we spotted what appeared to be a rock. It lay in the center of the channel and we hadn't seen it before. Later when I skiffed out to deep water on the evening's

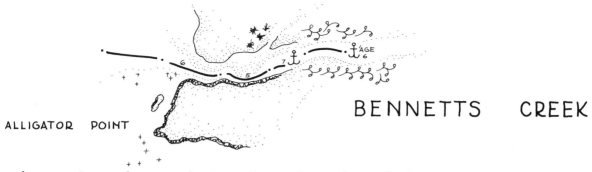

BENNETTS CREEK

ALLIGATOR POINT

garbage run, I swung by to see what it was. It turned out to be our first large, Japanese, netted glass float, a real beachcomber's prize. It now forms the base of the lamp which lights these notes. Most times it really pays to be a tidy camper.

Bennetts Creek will accommodate small boats in a narrow, sandy creek with six- and seven-foot pools with good holding. The commercial wharf at Smith Town affords some protection in prevailing winds and those from the SW if you breast off the bollards there. It would be untenable in a strong northwester.

There is no other harbour until you get down to Hawks Nest Point on the southwest end of the Island. The harbour at Hawks Nest contains the only yachting facility on Cat Island. In the inner harbour off the creek are berths and all marine services for a dozen yachts in complete protection. Seven-foot draft can be taken in at half tide. If you prefer to anchor in the creek itself, there are two pools where yachts drawing no more than five feet can lay to the tide over good holding sand. Best to be screened in securely here, as come nightfall, the sand fleas attack *en masse*.

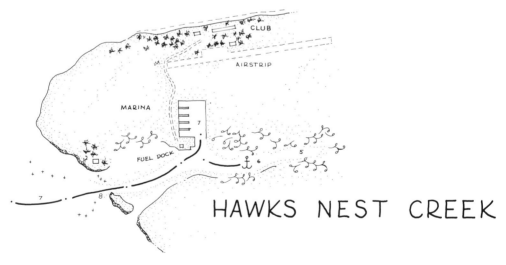

HAWKS NEST CREEK

Ashore, the Hawks Nest Fishing and Yacht Club runs comfortably under the able hand of enthusiastic Out Islander Nan Wright, who migrated here from England in the mid-fifties. It parallels a sloping dune-lined beach just a few yards from the water where shallow, waist-deep reefs offer some of the most colorful reef life imaginable, just offshore. We've caught two pound crawfish here, bare-handed, using only our masks to find them under the coral overhangs. As its name suggests, the club specializes in fishing, bone-fishing in the creek and game fishing offshore. The latter has produced some near record catches in recent years. Just a dozen steps off the front porch is the club's paved, 2,700-foot airstrip where fuel can be supplied in an emergency.

The south coast of Cat Island is steep-to and bound by a treacherous reef which extends its entire length. Be alert when running this coast in calm weather as the coral extends about a mile offshore and just below the surface, and is hard to discern in poor light.

The only harbour of any consequence along here is at Port Howe, which is entered through a wide break in the reef west of the settlement. There appears to be good holding in the sandy holes hereabouts, but with the bottom sloping to the deeps just offshore it would be a difficult place to keep the pots on the stove. Ashore you will find the stout walls of what must have been a manor house. Reminiscent of early plantation days, it is still in excellent repair, and lies just up from the shore at the east end of the settlement.

A port of call midway on this shore is the Cutlass Bay Club, just under Dolphin Head. There is a complicated, unmarked entrance channel which leads in to a small dock and creek that carrys about five feet at low water. Don't try it, however, without an experienced guide or you'll be in trouble. The club belongs to Mike and Melinda Kennedy of Fort Lauderdale, an attractively easy couple who will do their utmost to make your visit a pleasurable one. The club itself offers a barefoot but elegant atmosphere where fresh-caught grouper is served on old pewter and silver, gleaming in the candlelight.

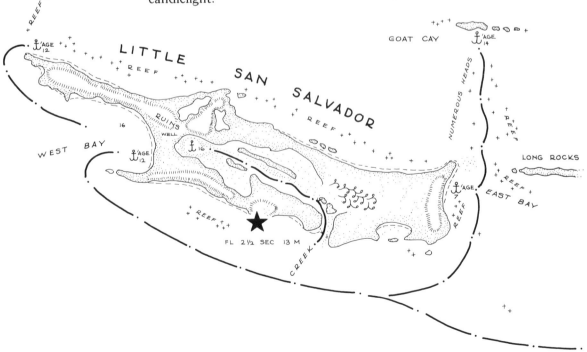

⟨ Little San Salvador

Referred to by local people as Little Cat or Little Island, Little San Salvador is about five miles long with the highest ground at the western end along the north and south coasts. It has been farmed by Cat Islanders for upwards of one hundred years as evidenced by the ruins of their seasonal quarters on the north hill of West Bay. The interior of the island forms a lake and mangrove swash where crawfish, turtles, and bonefish abound. The creek, as it is called, is navigable only by dinghies and skiffs, but the fishing inside is well worth the special effort.

The north shore of the island is reef bound and in calm weather the snorkeling and spear fishing are excellent since the water is clear as crystal. West Bay forms the only anchorage worthy of the name, with good holding sand close in to the beach, in winds from NW through SSW. West Bay provides one of the prettiest crescent beaches in the Island where huge, thin-lipped conch can be picked from the bottom in twelve feet of water. The hill that shelters the anchorage at Eastern Bay will provide you a comfortable lee if you are caught there in fresh westerly winds.

Ashore, amongst the ruins, you will find coconuts, mangoes, and some citrus. We've spent endless days at Little San Salvador and cherished every moment.

⟨ San Salvador

At two o'clock in the morning of October 12th, in the year 1492, an event occurred off the east coast of this island which changed the course of civilization in the world, and made San Salvador forever one of the most historic places on this earth. The lookout on the forecastle head of the "Pinta" sighted the sand cliffs of this island, some six miles away, but plainly visible in the bright moonlight. His cry "Tierra! Tierra!" marked the end of an era, the beginning of a new world. No other landfall in recorded history can compare with it in importance.

Originally named Guanahani, the island was renamed San Salvador by Columbus in 1492. Subsequently the Bahamians named it Watlings Island after a famous buccaneer of that name. The official name, San Salvador, has, however, been confirmed by the British Government, and so it appears on all Admiralty and U.S. Naval charts.

The island is about twelve miles long and half as wide. It is comparatively low lying, the highest hills being only one hundred and forty feet high. There are no less than eight salt water lakes in the interior, the largest, Great Lake,

SAN SALVADOR ISLAND

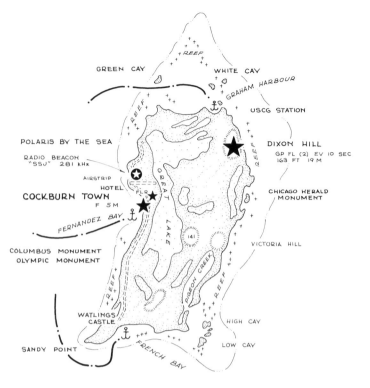

running for three-quarters of the length of the island. The land in between is quite fertile and is extensively cultivated.

Columbus, in his log, speaks of the natives coming out forty to forty-five men in a boat, and describes these boats as canoes hewn out of the trunk of a tree in one piece. Canoes of this size could only be had from an enormous tree, such as the great cotton trees in Jamaica, the lowest limbs of which are often more than one hundred feet from the ground. There is no evidence that such trees ever grew here, and to us it seems very doubtful that the soil which is found here could ever have supported the growth of such tremendous trees.

It has been argued that the soil here, and in many other Bahamian islands, has been gradually depleted over a period of several centuries, first by the cutting down of the virgin forest, then by the planting of such crops as cotton and sisal, without any fertilizing replenishment, and finally by the periodic hurricanes in this area. While this is unquestionably true, we doubt whether any small island so exposed to the full force of the ocean trades, and subject to the occasional violent hurricanes, could have ever maintained a large and luxuriant growth of giant tropical trees.

A much more plausible theory is that the large canoes noted by Columbus were manned by Indians who had paddled them up from South and Central America, where boats of that size and character were, and still are, quite common.

A yacht coming from westward should head for the center of the island and anchor in Fernandez Bay, off Cockburn Town. There is a fixed white light visible five miles, exhibited on a pole sixteen feet high near the small pier. The great light on Dixon Hill is partially obscured by land from this angle. The light on Southwest Point has been discontinued. In daytime the radio towers at Cockburn Town can be seen a long way off.

The anchorage off Cockburn Town is well protected in the prevailing winds, the bulk of the island providing a good lee, and the reefs to the north and south breaking up any sea coming around the island. However, it is no good in a norther, and if the wind starts to work around that way you should move out promptly.

In a norther the best anchorage will be found in Graham's Harbour, on the north side of the island. This is a reef harbour, shelter being provided by the surrounding reefs. A draft of seven feet can be taken in at low tide. The entrance is close along the south end of Green Cay, which is a small island lying one mile north of the north end of San Salvador Island. Columbus explored this harbour in his small boats on the day after his main landing.

If your vessel draws more than seven feet, or if you do not fancy a narrow passage in rough water, you can lie on the south side of the island in French Bay. This is a very snug little bight, with two fathoms of water, just two miles E x N from the tip of Sandy Point.

Father Nicholas, a resident Benedictine monk, maintains the Knights of Columbus Chapel in Cockburn Town. But, until recently, there was nothing more to commemorate the great navigator's first step onto the soil of the new world except a small monument erected at the top of the limestone bluffs overlooking the island's reefbound eastern shore. It carries the following inscription:

On this spot
CHRISTOPHER COLUMBUS
First set foot on the soil of
The New World
Erected by the
Chicago Herald
June 15, 1891

There has been a good deal of controversy over the fact that this monument is placed where it is, and that the inscription indicates that this is where Columbus first landed. We would hazard little doubt that these conspicuous bluffs were the first visual contact, but for a captain the caliber of Columbus to have landed his boats on this lee shore is preposterous. We agree with those who believe the actual landing must have taken place somewhere along the island's western beaches.

In 1956 a more appropriate monument, comprising a simple, white stone cross, was erected just a few steps up from the white sandy beach three miles south of Cockburn Town. Its inscription reads:

On or near this spot
CHRISTOPHER COLUMBUS
landed on the 12th October, 1492 . . . Admiral S. E. Morison, USNR
Dedication ceremony and Christmas services shared by all churches

——25th December, 1956——
Americans and natives worshipped together as symbol of faith, love and unity
between all nations and for peace on earth.

Ruth G. (Durlacher) Wolper

On a sunny day the waters surrounding San Salvador are the most vivid in the Bahamas, the deep blue of the distant ocean graduating to almost a turquoise at the shore. With this for a background, Columbus' twelve foot, white cross is impressive indeed.

For the 1964 Olympic Games, Mexican Olympiad architects built a monument a short distance south of Cross, from which to rekindle the Olympic torch in the New World. Its Tlatelco brazier received its flame from the Olympic torch borne to San Salvador aboard the Spanish warship "Princesa," September 29th, that year.

The Government light at Dixon Hill is one hundred and sixty-three feet high, its group flash two every ten seconds, being visible nineteen miles. It is a very handsome structure and has a kerosene light which has to be pumped every hour by hand.

The island of San Salvador is rather more primitive than those nearer to Nassau, and there is little industry on it; however, a paved road now encircles the island. There are four churches there: Seventh Day Adventist, Roman Catholic, Baptist, and Anglican. At Cockburn Town there is a Commissioner, constable, and telephone station which will enable you to send messages home. There are few supplies, however.

The conspicuous United States guided missile base, north of Cockburn Town, was turned over to the Bahamas Government for use as a teachers' college. It now houses 170 students from all corners of the Bahamas, plus 25 British lecturers who, within a short time, will step down to make the school an all-Bahamian institution. The base's areo radio beacon (281 KHz SSJ) and 4,500-foot paved airstrip are still maintained for civilian use. The beacon is of great assistance to yachtsmen as well as pilots cruising the area.

There is an interesting private museum several miles north of the school known as Polaris By The Sea. It houses a collection of artifacts assembled and displayed by Mrs. Fred Melvin (formerly Wolper), of Stamford, Connecticut. Mrs. Melvin spends little time on San Salvador these days and her most valuable finds she has donated to the Smithsonian Institute in Washington, D.C. However, if you are interested in the contents of Indian burial mounds, you will find a wealth of Lucayan artifacts here if there is someone to let you in.

Watling, a British pirate turned plantation owner, once built an extensive manor house at Sandy Point on the southwest corner of the island. Since this was headquarters for his freebooting operation, all admiralty charts bear his name as the proper one for San Salvador. The ruins of Watling's Castle, as it is called, are well worth a visit and you can drive almost the entire way by car.

Canadians Tony and Barbara Leicester operate the only resort on the island which lies conveniently south of the airstrip, just a short walk from town. Riding Rock Inn offers a comfortable family atmosphere in its combination of rooms and outlying cottages all overlooking San Salvador's matchless western beach. The inn is part of a sizable land development scheme, part of which is to be a marina, now a mangrove swash a short distance south that will eventually be opened to the sea. San Salvador's west coast is much like that of Bimini, a sparkling expanse of loose sand gradually deepening to the escarpment. Without extending the marina's jetties almost to the deeper water, a costly affair, we fear the natural shifting of the sand around an altered shore would eventually discourage the project.

San Salvador is a pretty island with picturesque, tidy settlements. It is a long sail out, but well worth the trip if you take it.

⟪ Long Island

In olden days Long Island was a place of prosperity and consequence. There were large plantations, and some of the wealthiest and most affluent of the Loyalists settled here after the American Revolution. Among the early settlers were the Earl of Dunmore, who subsequently became Governor of the Bahamas, and Major Archibald Taylor, second in command to Colonel Andrew Deveaux, who recaptured Nassau from the Spaniards in 1783. Names of early settlers and planters that still persist on the island to this day are: Cartwright, Simms, Knowles, and Adderley.

A great deal of cotton was grown here and in fact, Sea Island cotton was first introduced to Georgia from the Bahamas. There was also some stock raising and even the diminutive race horses, which are used for racing at Nassau today, were all imported from Long Island. The exhaustion of the soil by burning and single cropping, plus the loss of slave labor, reduced the agriculture of Long Island to an almost primitive state and practically everything grown there now is consumed locally.

From the point of view of the mariner, Long Island is a singularly unattractive place. Its windward or east side is bounded by the Crooked Island Passage, a notoriously boisterous piece of water, and has only two harbours, neither of which are easy to get in or out of in heavy weather. On its leeward or west side the island is beset with shoals; and while there is some very pretty coastline, especially on the northwest end, there are no good

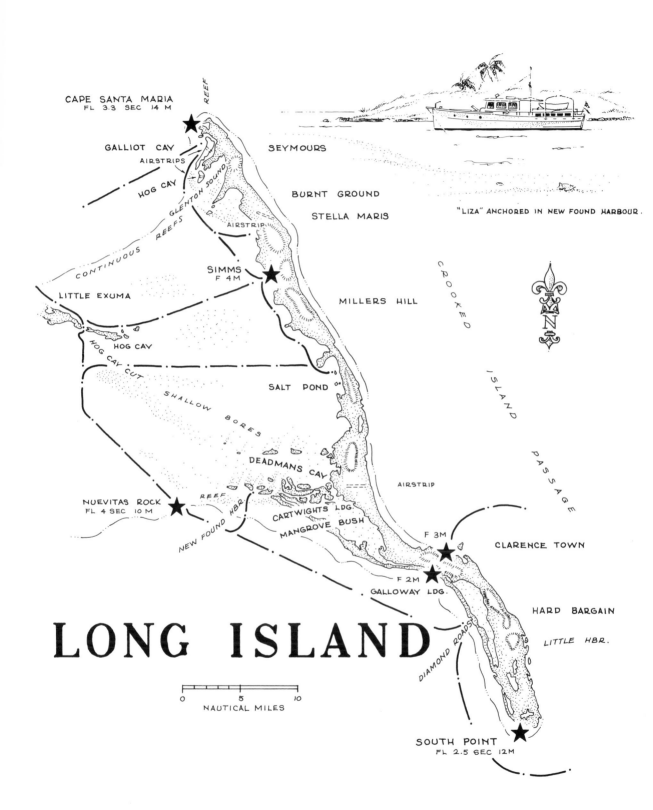

CAPE SANTA MARIA
FL 3.3 SEC 14 M

REEF

GALLIOT CAY

SEYMOURS

AIRSTRIPS

HOG CAY

CONTINUOUS REEFS

GLENTON SOUND

BURNT GROUND

STELLA MARIS

"LIZA" ANCHORED IN NEW FOUND HARBOUR.

AIRSTRIP

SIMMS
F 4M

LITTLE EXUMA

MILLERS HILL

CROOKED

HOG CAY

HOG CAY CUT

SALT POND

SHALLOW BORES

ISLAND

DEADMANS CAY

PASSAGE

AIRSTRIP

NUEVITAS ROCK
FL 4 SEC 10 M

REEF

NEW FOUND HBR.

CARTWIGHTS LDG.

MANGROVE BUSH

F 3M

CLARENCE TOWN

F 2M

GALLOWAY LDG.

HARD BARGAIN

LONG ISLAND

LITTLE HBR.

DIAMOND ROADS

0   5   10
NAUTICAL MILES

SOUTH POINT
FL 2.5 SEC 12M

N

harbours, except for very shallow draft boats. It is a bad place to be caught in a norther. Supplies are pretty much limited to canned and frozen meats, fresh vegetables and, of course, fruit and seafood.

The island is fifty-six miles long, with an average width of about three miles and lies in a N by NW, S by SE direction. Its principal settlement is Deadman's Cay, which is located in the central part of the island, far from the nearest harbour. By water it can be visited only from the Banks by small skiffs on the tide.

The north end of the island forms Cape St. Maria, a headland made famous by the visit to and the naming of it by Columbus on October 16, 1492. For a good many years a considerable controversy raged between the various geographical societies of England and America over the identity and geography of the cape where Columbus said, "I discovered a very wonderful harbour with two mouths, for it has an islet in the middle, and both are very narrow, and within it is wide enough for a hundred ships, if it were deep."

The confusion is understandable for the charts show this headland as a solid piece of high land without any interior waterways or passages leading to it. The fact is that the whole interior part of the cape is a series of interconnected lakes extending from the north coast for several miles southward. These lakes have a narrow outlet to the sea just east of the light on Cape Santa Maria and another and larger outlet on the west side of the cape about one mile south of the light. No one can say what changes have taken place in the intervening 480 years, but if Columbus explored these inland waters in his small boats then, he could still do so now, especially at high tide when there is five feet over the bar of the western entrance.

The land on the northwest side of Long Island from Cape Santa Maria down to Bain's Bluff is a series of bights, coves and bays with many beautiful beaches. For light draft boats, up to five feet, there are good anchorages in Joe's Sound and Glenton Sound, where protection from a norther can be had.

The Cape Santa Maria Club lies at the north end of Galliot Cay, tucked neatly under the rocky headlands of the Cape itself. The narrow, winding creek in between could form a first rate hurricane hole if the need arose to re-open the silted entrance channel there. Interests from Cleveland, Ohio, built the club in the early sixties for a nucleus membership primarily interested in an exclusive island hideaway. They installed a number of beachside cottages, a rustic lodge, and a 2,500-foot airstrip, but have used it sparingly.

Seymours is a picturesque little hilltop village with one of the most beautiful, panoramic views anywhere in the Islands. The entire lake system at the north end is visible from here and on a clear day you can see as far as Conception and Rum Cays to the east and Little Exuma to the southwest.

The topmost house was boarded up when we last visited the village. Robert Smith, our guide, allowed that it had belonged to his grandfather. When we asked if it was ever used, we were invited to live in it anytime,

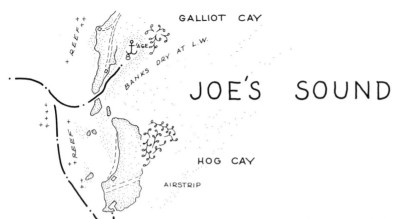

JOE'S SOUND

staying as long as we liked, as it would never be sold (it is on commonage land). That is the way of the Out Island people: though they may have very little by comparison with the materialistic societies, what little they have they will share freely.

For boats drawing no more than six feet there is a good place to sit out the weather at the south end of Galliot Cay. It is known as Joe's Sound and is really a creek and mangrove swash running the entire length of Galliot Cay's east side to the causeway and landing at Seymours, the most northerly settlement on Long Island.

Hog Cay, which lies south of Galliot Cay, is the private property of Peter Graham, M.H.A., of Nassau, representative for the north end of Long Island, San Salvador, and Rum Cay. The Cay is Mr. Graham's vacation home and is a model of simplified efficiency. There's a very attractive, modern house overlooking the western beach, a paved airstrip and a small, dredged harbour cut into the island's southernmost point. Mr. Graham, flying his Cessna Skymaster, is a frequent visitor to the Cay.

Certainly, the most ambitious land development project on Long Island is Stella Maris. Here German interests have built a hotel and villa complex that will accommodate 100 persons, as an adjunct to selling property. Stella Maris' 4,200-foot, paved airstrip with regular air service to Nassau has been a boon to the people of North Long Island. A small marina that can supply most marine services has been dredged into the land at the south end of the property. Four feet is the controlling depth in the vague entrance channel across the banks and into the harbour. So take caution and remember, the tide on Long Island's banks lags that of Exuma by two and one half hours.

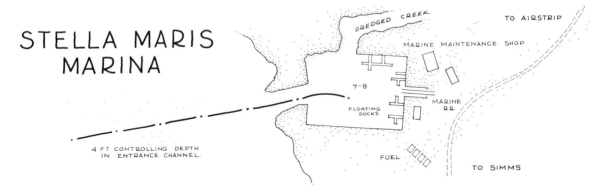

There is an interesting ruin deep in the bush, across the road from Stella Maris. It is the remains of William Adderley's plantation house. He raised cotton here in the 1790's and the story goes that Adderley was a cruel slave master and a drunkard. When his wife fled to Key West with their children he killed himself right here. We once spent a blistering July day hacking our way through the bush in search of the old Adderley ruins, but found nothing but poison wood and a fine rash in the bargain. The next spring, flying over it in a light plane, we discovered that we had been hacking away at the wrong hill. Now that we know where it is we'll try again, next time on a cooler day, and well protected from the bush.

At the rambling settlement of Burnt Ground, a mile or so north of Stella Maris, lives probably the oldest person in the Bahamas, certainly one of the oldest people in the world. Mrs. Ida Lee Adderley thinks she is around 115 years old, but she's not sure. She does remember the period around the Civil War, however, because "that's when everybody growed so much cotton." Mrs. Adderley has lost count of her numerous offspring, but she guesses there have been well over a hundred.

The mail boat from George Town, which draws ten feet loaded, follows the north shores of Little Exuma, Hog and White Cays before taking up E by NE for Simms. There is no harbour at Simms, however, and she has to lie a considerable distance from the shore to unload cargo and passengers into a lighter. She then continues south to Salt Pond.

With its long tilted stands of casuarinas shading the Queen's Highway, Simms is a pretty settlement. The sunbleached frame houses nestled into well-groomed, fenced yards are reminiscent of midsummer country corners of long ago. Even in the tiny country store, where several flies buzz around the inevitable screened cut of store cheese, you have the feeling that you should be seeing this as a child, with your nose barely reaching the worn wooden counter top. Simms is a breath of the past, and welcomes you in to enjoy it.

Leading figure in the village, and the person you will most likely meet first, is the Queen's own Constable Finley. Besides maintaining order in this rare corner of tranquility from his office at the town dock, Constable Finley serves as Justice of the Peace, postmaster, preacher, and official town greeter. He is a veritable one-man tourist board who likes nothing better than to escort you about the village reciting Long Island history enroute. Leaning over the wall at the cemetery adjoining the Episcopal Church, he points to forebearers, long since departed, and recounts their life and times with rare fancy. During the walk your good host will introduce you to passers-by, his people of the village. He took us to an abandoned church to see Ivy Simms, who weaves some of the neatest plait work we've ever seen. Constable Finley has been in the service of "his Queen" for over twenty-five years and does not look forward to retirement. If and when it does come he will probably go right on doing what he's now doing so well!

At Miller's Hill, a short drive south of Simms, are some remarkable caves where Arawak artifacts have been found. One cave in particular, behind Thomas Cartwright's house, has never been fully explored. It is full of gigantic stalactites and stalagmites, similar to those in the surrounding blue holes, proof again that these islands once formed a high, windy, heavily eroded limestone plateau during the ice age when the sea was hundreds of feet below its present level.

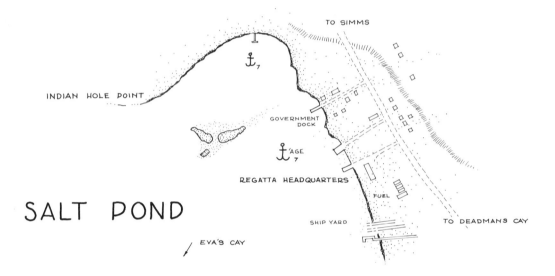

Salt Pond

Salt Pond settlement straggles along a high ridge paralleling the Queen's Highway in the narrowest neck of Long Island. Barely a mile wide at this point, the moderate hills seem even higher, and the rough eastern shore, like that of all the island, is high, rocky, and dangerous to careless seafarers unmindful of keeping a safe offing.

Along here by moonlight, in less violent weather, we have roamed the vast flat expanse of tidal rocks in search of giant crawfish, toting them home through the bush to the sound of night peepers and crickets.

Surrounded by highlands, Salt Pond anchorage provides adequate cover in weather from West through Southeast and in conditions from South through West there is cover for small craft under Salt Pond and Eva's Cay. For the sailor the head man in Salt Pond is Roy Harding, owner/skipper of the island freighter "St. Louis." Largely through Roy's efforts Salt Pond has, in recent years, become the major terminus for the west side of the Island. Through Roy you can get filtered fuel and gasoline pumped directly to your boat or rent a car to tour the rest of the island. He also operates a marine railway that will haul boats up to fifty feet in length and can arrange for repairs. Roy Harding is a stocky man who looks like a sailor, and like many Bahamians, has a sly wit. Climbing aboard "Spindrift" on our first visit many years ago he hastily looked about the boat and, comparing her to his "St. Louis" anchored close by, quipped, "Bet we could get a hundred head of sheep to Nassau in record time aboard this thing!" To which my wife as quickly snapped back, "over my dead body."

It was while anchored at Salt Pond on that first visit that we learned a very basic lesson in seamanship. While lounging in the cockpit one evening, watching the sun disappear behind our cocktail glasses, we decided it would be a good idea to sail our Abaco dinghy over to Eva's Cay and take along the cat so she could stretch her legs. Did you ever hear of a cat who *needed* her legs stretched? Well, I hadn't either, but the cocktails probably told us it was a good idea, so off we went, wife, skipper, and cat into the setting sun, having left the outboard motor hanging in the rigging, 'cause "it would only be excess baggage." The two-mile sail to Eva's Cay was an exhilarating one, a downwind slide freshening all the way. Really enjoying it, we finished the rest of our drinks; the cat, sniffing land, abstained. There must have been a male cat somewhere on the Cay because Sea Ling's station on the foredeck couldn't have been more resolute. Her Siamese eyes were glued to the sliver of land ahead. Nearing the shore, we sailed right in, feeling that to detour around to the lee side would have been a waste of time. When we bumped onto the marle the cat's momentum tumbled her into the receding tidal puddles and by the time we had secured the scuffed dinghy with an anchor off the stern, she was hastily cleaning up for her date under a thicket on the far side of the cay.

We never did see the other cat, but there must have been one as Sea Ling had never dodged us with such determined agility. It wasn't until well after dark, having coaxed her from under every bush on the Cay, that we finally cornered her on a small, rocky peninsula. Stumbling back to the boat was not easy in the dark, and had it not been for the simmering chowder in our galley we probably would have sat out the night on shore, leaving the cat to her own devices. However, not being able to recall whether the galley stove was turned on or off, we were obliged to get the dinghy turned around and be on our way. But checking the tide, the boat was high and dry. Our troubles had just begun!

An Abaco dinghy is heavily built and an old one will soak up a third of its weight in water. In trying to pivet ours around that night we broke out the mast step and I was compelled to lash the mast to the forward thwart, bracing it with my feet while my bride sailed us home. Unfortuntely, our oars awaited us there, on the stern deck, right where I had left them while tidying up the dinghy that afternoon.

By now it was late and in our jury-rigged condition breaking away from that lee shore was not only a feat of superior sailing, it was a small miracle. The lights of the settlement were out, its residents long since retired. The night was overcast and in our pleasure-bound haste to get on with it we had neglected to hang an anchor light on "Spindrift." The only directional reference available was the wind and if it had backed we would have sailed till dawn. Fortunately, in timing our tacks we worked our way into the shelter of the island where we finally caught a whiff of the boiling chowder and a glimpse of the reflected flame from our kerosene refrigerator on "Spindrift's" cabin overhead, and clambered aboard. The chowder had not yet boiled over, but was almost dry.

Suffice to say the following day was spent repairing and re-rigging the dinghy for continued use as a tender, and mulling over these suggestions for those cruising far afield.

1. If you have the choice, never pleasure-sail down wind.
2. Always remember the state of the tide.
3. Never leave the mother ship unattended with a lighted stove.
4. Never leave the mother ship in the evening without rigging an anchor light.
5. Always carry an auxilliary power source aboard your dinghy, even if it's merely a pair of oars or paddle.
6. Every dinghy should carry a survival pack containing: first aid kit, flashlight, tools, outboard spares, compass, fresh water, emergency rations, signaling gear, shoes, and protective clothing. (All of this can be fit into a compact emergency kit and stowed under a thwart or in the peak.)
7. Cocktails, no comment!

We certainly violated all the rules that memorable night, but we like to think the experience paid off in our cautiousness during the ensuing twelve years.

In recent years a number of the regular Long Island supporters of the George Town Regatta, having become disenchanted with the event, began their own sailing competition scheduled for Commonwealth Weekend (late May) each year. Naming it the Long Island Regatta, Roy Harding and American John McKie, whose homes dominate the high ridge immediately north of Salt Pond, are the main promotors of the contest. John is an excellent source of boating information for Long Island, and a one-man welcoming committee for yachts visiting Salt Pond.

Following pretty much the same principles as the George Town Regatta, the sponsoring Long Island Sailing Club raises the equivalent in prize monies, amounting to around $6,000 each year. Recalling George Town's shortage of facilities for visiting crews, the Sailing Club, through the donations, built a one hundred foot long community shed overlooking the shore. Here dinners, storage and sleeping space are available and the building is used as a gathering place during the rest of the year. The races are held around long and short triangular courses on Salt Pond's turquoise bay. Spectators viewing the races from shore from various points along Salt Pond's high ridge can watch each in its entirety.

Deadman's Cay, the largest settlement on the island, lies on the mainland south of Duncanson Point and is not a cay at all. It was probably named for the small cay which lies five miles off the west coast of the island and north of New Found Harbour. The shoal water docks at the settlement cannot be reached by anything but small boats on the tide, there being little to interest visiting yachtsman here. The settlement rambles along the Queen's Highway for several miles. It is hot, dusty, and reminiscent of a frontier town. This being the most densely populated area of Long Island, there is a large store and scheduled air service at the nearby government airstrip.

Between Deadman's Cay and Clarence Town there are a number of small, heavily populated settlements: Buckleys, Cartwright's Landing, and Mangrove Bush, the latter being the home of Long Island's leading shipwright, Rupert Knowles, who builds a fast, distinctive design right in his own yard. Rupert, who always sails his own boats, has contributed more winning sloops to the Out Island Regatta than anyone else. He built sponging schooners in the old days, Long Island lying close to one of the most productive sponging beds in the Islands. Today his talents are concentrated mostly toward pleasure craft with an Island flavor, but always with the idea in mind of that one, unbeatable combination that will dominate the competitions forever. Some of Rupert's recent products that occupy current seats in the winner's circle are: "Tida Wave, "Eastern Wave," "Lady Muriel," and "Rebel."

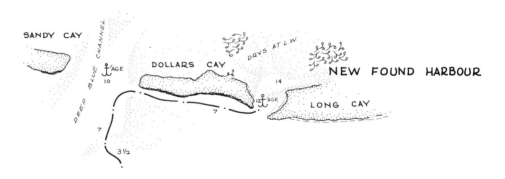

◖ New Found Harbour

Near the western tip of the jumble of cays, salinas and sand bars that make up the western extremity of Long Island are several deep creeks that should be of interest to yachtsmen cruising the area in small boats drawing no more than five feet. To get to New Found Harbour from Exuma you must go through Hog Cay Cut, taking the established route via Nuevitas Rocks. New Found Harbour, is entered from the South over a hard bar that will carry four-foot draft at low water; it lies between Dollars and Long Cays. It carries twelve and fourteen feet in its two protected pools of deep, good holding sand and provides ample swinging room for two 40-foot boats.

Here we have lain for as long as a week in May, watching the endless parade of sharks maneuvering their way through the anchorage onto the banks. The month of May seems to be their family time. One of the more remote corners of the Bahamas, this miniature cruising ground teems with nature's residents above, as well as below, the tide line. Its undulating grassy dunes, topped with waving sea oats, serve as a rookery for bobby and tern, while colonies of brown noddys dwell along the higher rocks. The ubiquitous curly-tailed lizards rattle through the underbrush and the tracked furrows of iguanas can sometimes be seen. In the shallow tidal pools of the creeks spook hundreds of bonefish; no wonder the osprey young are fed so well. And the diligent wandering tracks of the conch across still-wet sand always leads to an easy lunch. Along the chuckling south shore of Dollars Cay turbaned whelks can be picked from under the sculptured overhangs, while crawfish are everywhere.

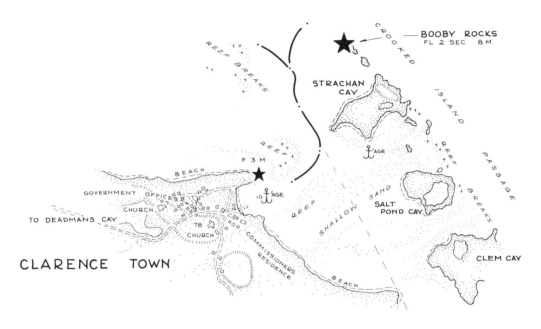

⟪ Clarence Town

Cruising down the east side of Long Island your landfall will be two white churches, each with two spires about one mile west of the entrance. Although not the largest, Clarence Town is by far the most important settlement on Long Island, for here the Commissioner resides in a pretty stone house facing the harbour. Finding your way in is easy in daytime. Simply keep half way between Strachan Cay and Harbour Point, favoring the east side of the channel. The best anchorage is south of Harbour Point in two fathoms—this is safe but rough in a norther. Unless you have to, we do not advise trying it at night. The seas break right across the bar at the entrance to Clarence Town and it is difficult to get out unless you have a surf boat. We came out in a norther once, dead slow, standing on end half the time, and only just made it.

Ashore, Clarence Town presents a unique setting with its casuarina-lined harbour and shaded business corner with Father Jerome's sturdy churches, standing guardian-like over the town.

The Commissioner's house is only a short walk from the dock. The house overlooking the head of the dock belongs to Mr. Saunders, who can supply you with either filtered gasoline or diesel fuel by truck. In an emergency he can even deliver to Diamond Roads across the Island near Hard Bargain. Miss Ena runs the general store at the four corners in the center of town. Her stock is more than adequate. The telephone station and post office are next to the Commissioner's Office on the road to St. Peter's Church, just outside of town.

At Long Island there are a number of interesting ruins which date back to, and before, plantation days. The most imposing one stands high on a hill overlooking the ocean half way between Clarence Town and Little Harbour. It was supposed to have been the summer residence of one of the Bahamas' first Governors.

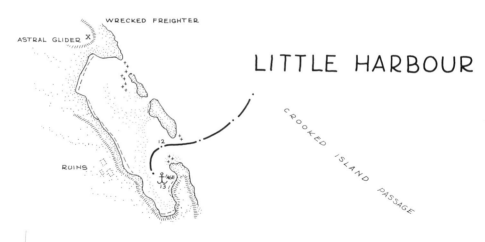

LITTLE HARBOUR

⟨ Little Harbour

A much better harbour than Clarence Harbour, in our opinion, is Little Harbour, which is on the east coast of Long Island, ten miles below Clarence Town. Approximately the same draft can be carried in here as at Clarence Harbour and once inside you are much better protected. There are two cays lying south of a wrecked ship, the first encountered south of Clarence

Harbour. The entrance is just south of the largest and most southerly of these. The best anchorage is in the deep pool close under the headland at the south end of the harbour.

The first time we visited Little Harbour it was on foot. We walked through the bush from Hard Bargain where we were tied up at Diamond Roads Harbour. Dick Moore, of the Diamond Crystal Salt Company, had heard tales of an astral glider, supposedly launched at Cape Kennedy, being seen in the bush near there. Since I wanted to see the harbour, I was tempted into the hike of a lifetime, just so I'd be there to help him find it. Fourteen miles over impossible terrain and "half a cardiac-arrest" later we were back aboard, sharing the trip—the ancient ruins, the high cliffs, the beauty of the harbour, the wrecked WW I freighter, everything but Dick's "pie from the sky." We didn't find the glider, not that trip anyway.

The second time we visited Little Harbour was several weeks later and was, as it should be, by boat (a whaler all the way from George Town). Fascinated by what might be the ultimate in a beachcomber's prize and convinced that another search would reveal it, Fritz Ludington loaded his family into the boat along with his guide and hustled us down the 70 miles of Long Island coast to capture it. After being almost consumed by sand fleas in an attempt that night to sleep on Little Harbour's north beach, and a breakfast the next morning of peanut butter sandwiches chased down with scotch (Fritz hadn't packed anything but cokes for the kids and they had been through them in short order), we found it! The "astral glider" turned out to be a two hundred pound, stainless steel towing vane that had been hurled a considerable distance ashore some years before by an Atlantic storm. We feel *sure* it's there still!

The Diamond Crystal Salt Company had dredged an industrial harbour into the land midway on the south end of the island's western shore. The Company would like it understood that this is a working industrial facility and pleasure boats are welcome here only for cover in adverse weather. We might add that the salt conveyors and the nearby roads raise enough dust to discourage even the most negligent sailors. All of the salinas bordering the western shore of Long Island flow into the harvesting pans at Diamond Crystal.

From Little Harbour to Folly Bay on the south end of Long Island there are numerous reef harbours which were much frequented by pirates as late as the time of the Napoleonic Wars. Being ideally situated for the control of shipping through the Crooked Island Passage, they preyed on the Spanish vessels bound to and from Cuba and points south and west. This business proved to be so profitable that some privateers tuned pirates, and much of the loot—wines, silks, etc.—was sold to the local plantation owners and gentry, with the result that life on Long Island was for a time fairly luxurious. All this has passed away, but the reef harbours are still there, waiting to be explored, and are as good a place as any for a treasure hunt.

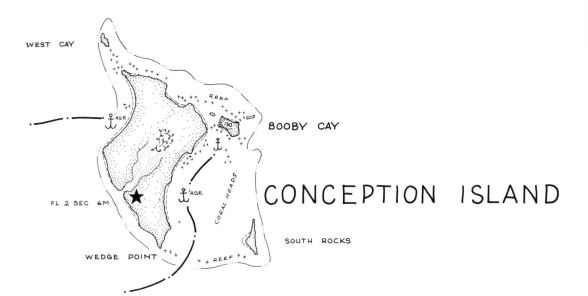

⟪ Conception Island

That first day we stood on Seymour's Hill, Robert Smith gestured towards Conception Island's faint outline on the horizon and called it "the land of plenty." We finally cruised there three years later and found, to our delight, that it still was.

About three miles long from north to south and surrounded by sandy beaches, the high limestone cliffs and headlands of joining Booby Cay at the north end recede gently to the low, grassy hillocks that make up the perimeter of the shallow creeks and swashes of the center of the island. The creek opens to the sea at the Southeast corner and is navigable only by dinghy.

Safe anchorage may be found anywhere along the island's western shore as close to the beach as good holding and draft will allow. When the wind goes into the northwest, the eastern shore provides good protection. In settled weather we like to anchor inside the heads up under Booby Cay and beachcomb the north and east beaches for Portuguese glass floats, bottles, and conch. Crawfish can always be found under the heads and reefs bounding the western shore and in the mouth of the creek. Green turtles can be seen in the upper reaches of the creek itself. The colors surrounding Conception Island are rivaled by those of San Salvador and Bimini. They are unbelievable, even when you are anchored in them.

⟪ Rum Cay

On the afternoon of October 15, 1492, Columbus brought his ships to anchor off the south coast of this island, went ashore to take formal possession, and named the island Santa Maria de la Concepción in honor of the Virgin Mary. Some years later, when a West Indiaman laden with rum

RUM CAY

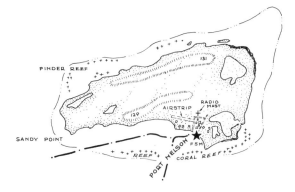

wrecked here, the British, with their characteristic brevity of wit, subsequently renamed it Rum Cay.

Lying just 21 miles east off Cape St. Maria, on the north end of Long Island, and eighteen miles southwest of San Salvador Island, it is a logical stopping place for those bound in either direction, having the only decent harbour hereabouts. This is at St. George's Bay on the south side of the island. The harbour is formed by a long reef paralleling the shore, and is well protected in anything from northwest to southeast through the north. The entrance is one mile wide and its eastern edge seven-eighths of a mile west of Sumner Point. There is a middle ground in this entrance with a minimum depth of nine feet. Vessels drawing up to 25 feet can enter on the west side of the entrance by keeping the houses on Cotton Field Point bearing N by E. Midway along the beach on St. George's Bay you will make out the Rum Cay Club and Villas. The club maintains several moorings toward the west end of the Bay.

Rum Cay is a pretty island, nine miles long, with a ridge of hills bordering the beaches along its northern shore. The island once supported three settlements and a thriving salt industry which ended when the 1908 hurricane demolished the salt pans at each end of the cay. A few cattle still roam through its central valley.

Port Nelson lies at the extreme eastern end of the harbour. There is a fixed white light on a pole just north of the dock. The settlement is small and delightfully primitive. Port Nelson's number one citizen is Constable Ted Bain, whose father was Constable before him. Ted has always lived on Rum Cay, he has a pretty wife, and is raising a small family. He likes it here. The pace is slow. Only a dozen or so families live here compared to the hundreds of people here in his father's youth. But philosophically, in spite of the grand opportunities in Nassau and the other islands, he feels his home and calling is where he believes tourism will eventually reach, and at his pace.

Well, tourism *has* reached Rum Cay, and it is at Ted's pace; but that's its charm. Bud Edgerton of Coral Gables, Florida, has built several guest cottages and a main lodge along with a 2,500-foot, grass airstrip along the center of St. George's Bay, well out of the village. Bud can supply small amounts of fuel, even aviation gasoline in an emergency, and a few supplies. Bloneva Bain, Ted's sister, runs the Club in Bud's absence and is a typically talented Bahamian cook. The Rum Cay Club can rent you outboard whalers for getting around the perimeter of the island and mini-bikes for getting into Port Nelson. In 1861, within sight of the town, "Ocean Conqueror," Britain's first propeller-driven battleship, broke up on the reef here. Its eroded remains are an attraction for sportsmen-divers, but the removal of any part of the wreck is absolutely forbidden.

Port Nelson is a pastoral little village that time has protected with a weathered hand. The easterly trade winds blow constantly here, bending everything before them. The shy, but friendly, people might be considered poor by city standards, but they make a modest living from the soil and the sea. Their homes are neatly fronted with raked-sand lawns edged with huge, pink-tipped conch shells; while backyards reveal a tumble of smiling children and the inevitable dusty chickens followed by one lone turkey. Excellent seafood dinners can be arranged at Deloris Scavella's picturesque little bar and restaurant, right in the center of town.

Flying into Rum Cay on a recent visit we spotted a netted float rolling amongst the breakers on one of the island's eastern beaches. Distances can be deceptive from the air, as proved by the sunburns and aching legs acquired retrieving this prize. The six-mile trek was made across soft sand at the mad dog's time of day.

⟨[Jumentos Cays to Ragged Island

Stretching in a great arc from the western side of Long Island all the way down to Little Ragged Island, a distance of about 95 miles, this range of islands and rocks forms the southeastern barrier of the Great Bahama Bank. The winds blow strong here, especially in the winter time, when a blow lasting ten days from east to northeast is not uncommon. It has been known to blow for 21 days. As the nearest land to windward is over eighty miles away, and the waters between both deep and current-ridden, the whole area may be considered pretty strenuous for a small yacht. Yet, like all such areas, it has its easy weather too, and in such the cruising can be delightful.

Coming down the western side of the Exuma Cays, head for Hawksbill Rock, passing to the west of it. The conch fishermen call this "The Channel," and they can tell exactly where they are, day or night, by looking at the bottom. If they see white sand ridges they are on the west side of The Channel; if grass, they are on the east side. Hawksbill Rock has a flashing 3 1/4 second light that can be seen for six miles.

From here the course to Flamingo Cay, or "fillimingo," as the local sailors call it, is S by SE—35 miles with good water all the way. There is a dependable light flashing every six seconds and visible for eight miles high up on the hill at Flamingo Cay.

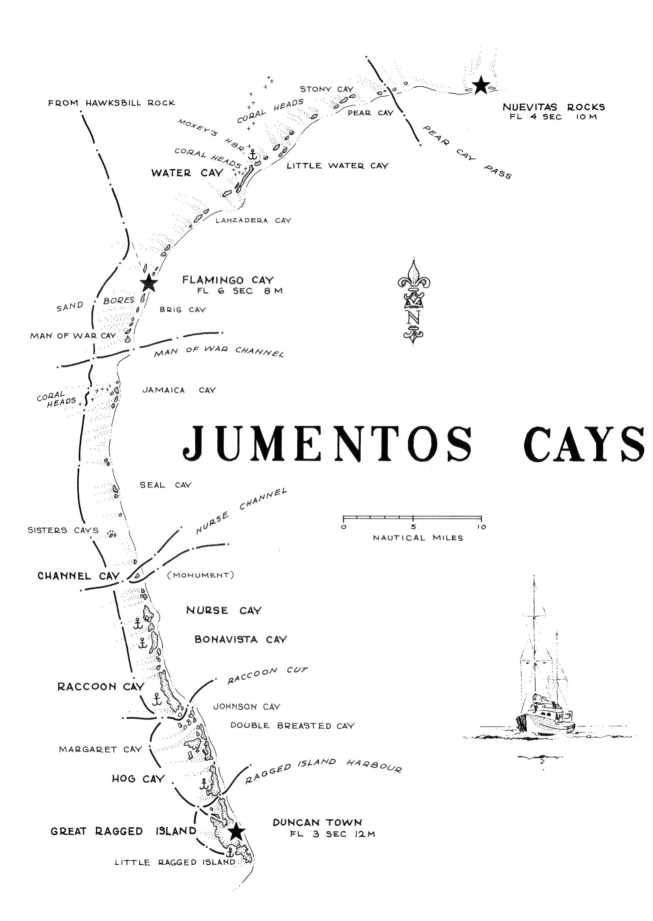

FROM HAWKSBILL ROCK

STONY CAY

CORAL HEADS

MOXEY'S HBR.

PEAR CAY

NUEVITAS ROCKS
FL 4 SEC 10 M

CORAL HEADS

WATER CAY

LITTLE WATER CAY

PEAR CAY PASS

LANZADERA CAY

FLAMINGO CAY
FL 6 SEC 8 M

BRIG CAY

SAND BORES

MAN OF WAR CAY

MAN OF WAR CHANNEL

N

CORAL HEADS

JAMAICA CAY

JUMENTOS CAYS

SEAL CAY

NURSE CHANNEL

SISTERS CAYS

0   5   10

NAUTICAL MILES

CHANNEL CAY

(MONUMENT)

NURSE CAY

BONAVISTA CAY

RACCOON CUT

RACCOON CAY

JOHNSON CAY

DOUBLE BREASTED CAY

MARGARET CAY

RAGGED ISLAND HARBOUR

HOG CAY

GREAT RAGGED ISLAND

DUNCAN TOWN
FL 3 SEC 12 M

LITTLE RAGGED ISLAND

❨ Flamingo Cay

Flamingo Cay itself is a high and well-wooded island with four beautiful sand beaches, each in its own cove, on the west side of the island. Plenty of conch and whelks exist in the coves, and there is good bottom fishing on the bank. We saw a conch smack fill a barrel with fish one evening after supper. There is a good cove with a sand beach on the north side of the cay where you can lie safely in a southwester.

From the west point of Long Island to Flamingo Cay there is no harbour worthy of the name, and practically no safe anchorages, with the exception of that on the west side of little Water Cay, and New Found Harbour.

❨ Water Cay

Eleven miles northeast of Flamingo Cay is a long, pretty and interesting cay which at a distance looks like a group of cays. This is due to the fact that there are several very high white cliffs with extremely low land lying between them. The cliffs which are near the middle of the island are somewhat reminiscent of the white cliffs of Dover, and right alongside them, also in the middle of the island, is low land which is swept clean across by the seas in heavy weather. The best anchorage is off the long white sand beach which lies half a mile north of the high white cliffs. Around the rocky point northwest of this beach is a small but snug harbour marked and surrounded by green mangrove bushes. You can take a draft of four feet in at low tide, and will find six to eight feet inside.

North of Water Cay and separated from it by a narrow cut lies another and smaller cay, locally called Little Water Cay.

❨ Little Water Cay

This little cay has the best harbour between Great Exuma Island and Ragged Island. It is a cove on the west side surrounded by mangrove bushes and practically landlocked at its inner end. You can take in a draft of six feet at low tide and will find ten feet of water inside. It is a perfect harbour for anything except winds from west to northwest, and even then the mouth of it is so small that no heavy seas come inside. Henry Moxey, having been once stormbound in here for fifteen days, has the right to have it named after him —so we call it Moxey's Harbour.

❨ Flamingo Cay to Ragged Island

This is the best cruising ground of this area. The cays are large, interesting, and some of them very beautiful. The fishing is excellent. There are several good harbours. From Flamingo Cay to Man of War Channel the cays are unnamed, but locally the one immediately south of Flamingo Cay is called Brig Cay, and the cleft in it, Brig Cay Cut. It appears that some years ago a brig was caught on a lee shore here in a gale of wind. Unable to claw off, she was faced with disaster on the rocky shore. When the captain spied the cleft in the cliff, he decided that it was a few feet wider than his yards, squared away, and sailed right through to a safe anchorage on the west side.

❨ Man of War Channel

Lying between Man of War Cay and Jamaica Cay, Man of War Channel is three and one half miles wide and six fathoms deep. The tidal currents run swiftly through here and it can be very rough.

❨ Nurse Channel

This is the best entrance from the Great Bahama Bank to the open sea. It is easy to identify Nurse Channel by the beacon which stands in the middle of it, on Channel Cay, or by the Sister Cays (a cluster of five rocks) lying on its north side. The best water lies close along the south side of Channel Cay. A draft of eighteen feet can be taken through to the banks without difficulty. The tidal currents run through here very strongly. With an ebb tide running against a strong breeze from the east the seas are something to behold. The fishing here is tops if you can take it.

❨ Nurse Cay

The first large cay on the south side of Nurse Channel, Nurse Cay derives its name from the nurse shark which frequents the little creek on its south side. The island is well wooded and there are ruins of half a dozen stone houses high on the cliffs. Between Nurse Cay and Little Nurse Cay, which is the next cay to the southward, there is good anchorage in the cove, well protected except for winds from southwest to northwest.

❨ Bonavista Cay

A beautiful cay nearly two miles long, Bonavista Cay has a sand beach over one mile in length on its west side. This is an excellent anchorage with the winds in the east, since the ground swell is broken up by the curving points at each end of the island. In a norther a good anchorage will be found in Low Water Harbour on the southeast side of the cay. A draft of ten feet can be taken in at low tide.

❨ Raccoon Cay

No raccoons here—only goats. All these cays from Flamingo Cay to Ragged Island are uninhabited by human beings and are used principally for pasturage of goats, which have to be caught with dogs, or shot. There are salt ponds on the cay, but they have not been worked for many years.

Raccoon Cay is a little over three miles long, high and wooded. At the north end of the cay there is a deep cove where two fathoms will be found at low tide, and good anchorage in winds from southeast to west. With easterly winds good anchorage may be had anywhere on the west side of the island. In a norther you will find an excellent harbour on the southeast end of the island, between Raccoon Cay and Nairn Cay. A vessel drawing ten feet can be taken in at low tide without difficulty.

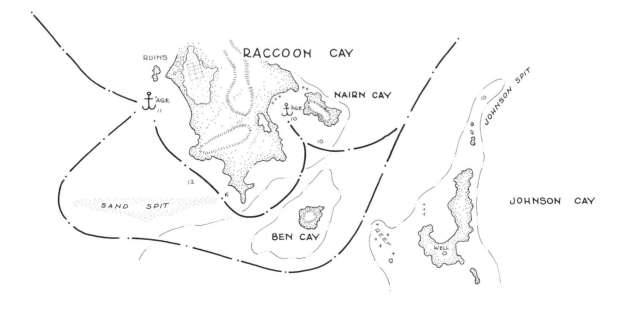

❲ Raccoon Cut to Ragged Island

Vessels drawing up to 25 feet of water, which could not get into Ragged Island, used to come into Raccoon Cut and lie behind Johnson Cay to load salt. There are a number of nice little coves around Johnson Cay and Double Breasted Cay, but the winds and currents here usually put up such a fuss that they are not comfortable to lie in except with certain winds. There is a bad shoal extending to the west for two and one-half miles from Margaret Cay. A course must be laid to clear the shoal before you head for Hog Point and Ragged Island Harbour.

❲ Hog Cay

Lying on the north side of Ragged Island Harbour, Hog Cay is a pretty and well-wooded cay, two miles long. Its southern end extends to the westward in a point, called Hog Point. In the cove on the north side of Hog Point is an anchorage which we consider superior to that in Ragged Island Harbour when it is blowing from the east. It is out of the current and away from any ground swell, even though it is further from the settlement at Duncan Town.

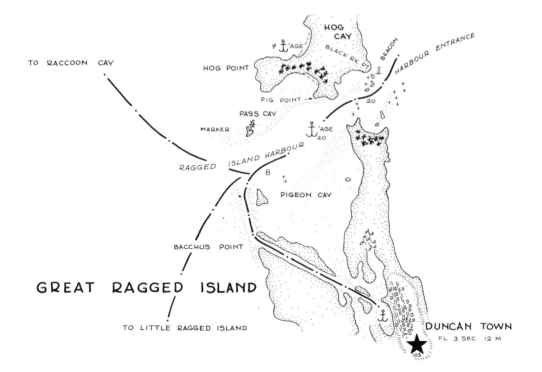

❰ Ragged Island

In the Islands you often hear it said, "Gimme a Ragged Island man and I can do that job." They are a rugged lot and they have to be to live the kind of life they live at Ragged Island.

To begin with, the island itself is bleak and windblown, surrounded by wide and rough reaches of open sea. The main harbour is about three miles from the settlement. In between is what is called the boat channel. This channel was dredged in the sixties so that the mail boat could have closer access to the town. Being narrow, deep displacement boats tend to run through it too fast, eroding the banks and silting it in the narrower places. It is supposed to carry four feet at low water, but we doubt if it will most of the time.

The main harbour lies between the northern end of Great Ragged Island and the south end of Hog Cay. Coming south you can enter from the west. Vessels drawing up to twelve feet once used the east entrance, coming in to load salt. Come in on a SW course, passing on the southeast side of the beacon on the Black Rock Point Reef. The best water will be found about 100 yards off the beacon. This course will take you inside the outer reef, which lies about 200 yards southeast of Black Rock. One-quarter mile southwest of the beacon you will come to the Inner Bar Reef, which is both dangerous and extensive, but easily seen: the seas break over it continually. You can pass on either the northern or the southern side of it but the northern side is best.

Coming in on the west side of the harbour you can carry a draft of six feet at low tide. The best entrance is between Pass Cay and Pigeon Cay, both of which lie directly south of Hog Point. Pass Cay is surmounted by a wooden cross standing on a cairn of rocks, a memorial to a Bishop of the Church of England who was drowned in the harbour. His body was never found, but some of his clothes were washed up onto Pass Cay.

The boat channel to the inner harbour lies north of Bacchus Point, which is the northwest point of Ragged Island. When, as, and if you get in to the settlement, which is named Duncan Town, you will find a community which we can only describe as slightly fey and somewhat reminiscent of an Irish country village. The mood of the place is well illustrated by the following notice, which we saw pasted on a wall near the waterfront:

To all owners of creatures-take heed. The notices and warnings in the past to stop you from letting your creatures run at large have been mocked.

For the last time I am asked you by this notice to keep your creatures in. By this time you ought to realize that the cup is full and running over.

Robert Heplun
Local Constable
Ragged Island

Constable Heplun is surely up against it, for the majority of the creatures in his bailiwick are pretty accomplished mockers. They mock at hurricanes, at revenue laws, even at death itself. When a hurricane blows the roof off a house here, no one would think of putting a new roof on, or rebuilding the old house. They simply let it stand and gradually fall to pieces, meanwhile building a new one right alongside it. Consequently, half the town is in ruins, the other half containing some of the nicest new homes you ever saw.

Adjacent to the cemetery is a tall, white limestone cliff named "Lovers Leap," a very convenient arrangement for impecunious young people, or for those who are delinquent in their dues, to end it all by simply jumping into the sea. The whole place reeks with the romance of the sea, for those who have eyes to see it. High up on the hill to the south of town is a simple masonry mound, designed with thirteen steps all round, on top of which is the mast of a ship with fitted topmast. The inscription on the mound reads:

In memory of ICELY, LLOYD
and one seaman of
H.M.S. THUNDER, who were
drowned near the Brothers Rocks.
23/1/31

On the east side of the town are a number of abandoned salt pans, the export of salt in days past having been the community's principal business. Boats carrying salt sailed out of here to all the seven seas.

Commissioner Ellis Curlin was born on Ragged Island and maintains his office at Duncan Town. Captain Curlin, his brother, skippers the mail boat "Daily Gleaner" on her weekly trips to Nassau where her distinctive blue hull is familiar to the harbour scene around Prince George Wharf.

Just as Ragged Island is noted for its hard workers, it is equally noted for its hardy sailors. Captain Anton Lockhart, who now skippers the Bahamas police boat "San Salvador," had for many years captained the mail boat "Air Pheasant" on her weekly runs between Nassau, Long Island, Crooked Island, and Inagua. On several occasions we have taken advantage of "Air Pheasant's" schedule to visit nearby islands when it was not feasible to cruise there in our own boat. Captain Lockhart has always been a wealth of information on the Islands and sailing in general. On our short passages we usually kept him company on the bridge where he shared many of his adventures with us. In 1931 his eighty-six foot schooner was rammed and cut in half, killing his young wife and child, plus several of his crew. Following WW II, off Cuba's Cape Maisi, he lost LCT 243 with four of its crew. Nineteen hours later, in a swamped life boat, he drifted into the harbour at Bahia de Taco, 35 miles up the Cuban coast. Truly a man of the sea, Captain Lockhart is a most interesting man to know.

Captain Hezron Moxey skippers the police boat "Andros," but has quite another background of sailing experience to account for his seat at the "old salts' table." Hezron learned to sail aboard his father Hezekiah's trading schooners which plied the water of Haiti and Cuba as well as the Bahamas. Later he served as mate and cook aboard Ragged Island's mail packet which many times took as long as a week to make the Nassau passage. In the 50's and 60's Hezron turned to yacht racing when he skippered such SORC favorites as "Tonga," and later, "Big Ty" under New York yachtsman John Heitz. Herzron maintains the roguish look of a Caribbean adventurer and could lead you to treasure if he considered you a serious hunter!

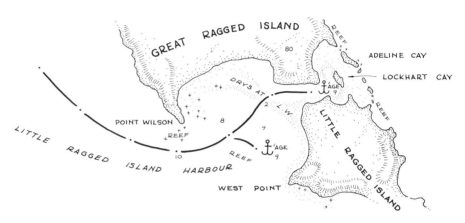

(Little Ragged Island

Lying immediately South of Ragged Island, this island is uninhabited. It was owned by Captain Horace Wilson of Duncan Town, and used only as grazing land for his goats and a few cattle. The nearest part of the coast of Cuba is only 62 miles from here.

In winds from northwest, north, northeast, and east, there is a very good anchorage between the northwest side of Little Ragged Island and the southwest side of Ragged Island. However, this is entirely open to the west and when the wind gets down to southeast a sea begins to run in here. The inner boat harbour can only be reached at high tide by boats drawing not over five feet.

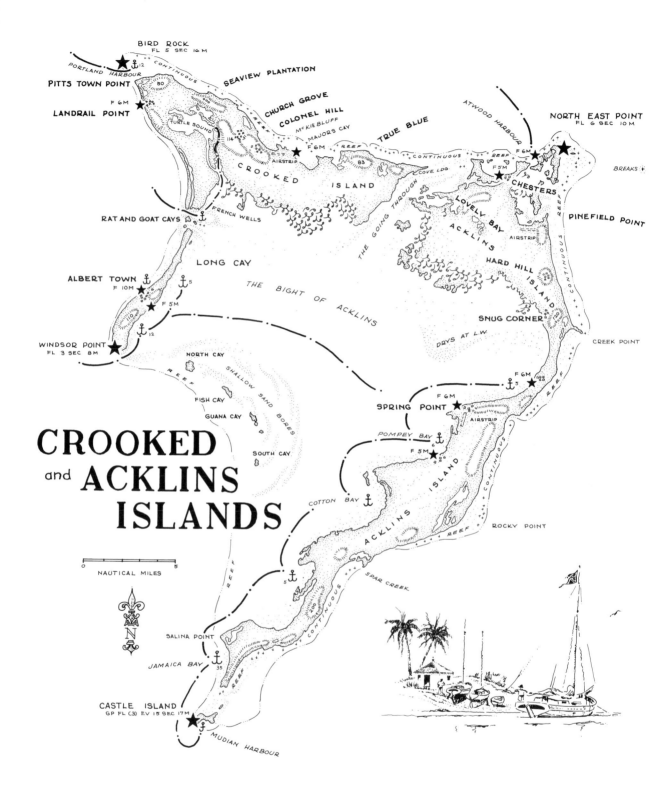

BIRD ROCK
FL 5 SEC 16 M

PITTS TOWN POINT

PORTLAND HARBOUR

LANDRAIL POINT
F 6 M

SEAVIEW PLANTATION

CONTINUOUS

50

TURTLE SOUND

CHURCH GROVE

COLONEL HILL

McKIE BLUFF

MAJORS CAY

114

AIRSTRIP

F 6 M

TRUE BLUE

ATWOOD HARBOUR

NORTH EAST POINT
FL 6 SEC 10 M

REEF

CONTINUOUS

REEF

F 6 M

BREAKS

CHESTERS

F 5 M

CROOKED

ISLAND

83

REEF

COVE LDG.

LOVELY BAY

THE GOING THROUGH

AIRSTRIP

ACKLINS

PINEFIELD POINT

RAT AND GOAT CAYS

FRENCH WELLS

LONG CAY

HARD HILL

ISLAND

ALBERT TOWN
F 10 M

F 5 M

5

THE BIGHT OF ACKLINS

SNUG CORNER

CREEK POINT

WINDSOR POINT
FL 3 SEC 8 M

10

12

DRYS AT L.W.

F 6 M

5

REEF

NORTH CAY

REEF

SHALLOW SAND BORES

FISH CAY

GUANA CAY

SOUTH CAY

SPRING POINT

F 6 M

AIRSTRIP

CROOKED

and ACKLINS

ISLANDS

POMPEY BAY

F 5 M

ACKLINS

ISLAND

COTTON BAY

CONTINUOUS

REEF

ROCKY POINT

ACKLINS

ISLAND

0   5
NAUTICAL MILES

5

REEF

CONTINUOUS

SPAR CREEK

N

SALINA POINT

JAMAICA BAY

35

REEF

CASTLE ISLAND
GP FL (3) EV 15 SEC 17 M

MUDIAN HARBOUR

Crooked Island

13

The group commonly referred to as Crooked Island includes that island, the large island of Acklins, and the smaller one called Long Cay (Fortune Island). They lie around the perimeter of the Bight of Acklins, on the east side of the Crooked Island Passage.

The Crooked Island Passage is to the Bahamas' sailors what the Gulf Stream is to Florida sailors. It separates the sheep from the goats. Considered by many a treacherous stretch of water, it forms one of the busiest shipping lanes bisecting the Bahamas. Small boatmen venturing east of the Crooked Island Passage have reached the far Out Islands where harbours are few and far between, yacht services practically non-existent, and where experience counts in large measure for the pleasure of cruising here.

Many a pale-faced passenger, bound south to the West Indies, has experienced his first whiff of paradise when passing through the Crooked Island Passage on the leeward side of these islands. The fragrance of tropical trees and flowers is often carried for eight or ten miles offshore by a fresh and clean breeze. We once located Bermuda by the smell of oleanders when we were still some fifteen miles away from it. On old maps the Crooked Island Group was called the "Fragrant Islands" and even Columbus when anchored in their lee made mention of their delightful aroma in his log. "There came so fair and sweet a smell of flowers on trees from the land that it was the sweetest thing in the world." One of the fragrances is that of the cascarilla bush, a small tree whose bark is used in the flavoring of medicines and compari bitters. Cascarilla bark is the chief export of the Crooked Island District.

When you are about half way across the Crooked Island Passage the blue hills on the north end of Crooked Island will start coming up over the horizon. They are over 100 feet high. There is a first class Bahamas Govt. Lighthouse on Bird Rock, a small cay lying about one mile northwest of Pitts Town Point. The light is a five-second flash, visible for sixteen miles. The lighthouse is 112 feet high and is surrounded at its base with a building which looks rather like a railroad engine roundhouse. Portland Harbour lies to the east of the lighthouse and north of the Crooked Island shore. It is a reef harbour, safe but not smooth, except when the wind is southeast. The entrance is from the west about one-quarter mile south of Bird Rock Light,

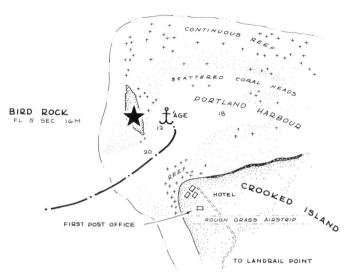

PORTLAND HARBOUR

and there is plenty of water, three and a half to four fathoms all the way in. Having rounded the shoal which extends south from Bird Rock for about one-quarter mile, steer northeast coming in. The best anchorage is just east of the lighthouse.

Columbus' three vessels, "Santa Maria," "Nina," and "Pinta," anchored in this harbour while the explorers visited the natives ashore, looking for gold and making notes of the flora and fauna of the island, which they recorded as being exceedingly interesting and beautiful.

There are some interesting ruins on the northwest corner of Crooked Island just below Bird Rock Light. Here, during the era of the Napoleonic Wars, there was a post office for the distribution of mail for the West India Squadron of the British Fleet, the postmaster being described in *Tom Gringle's Log* as "a stout 'conch' with a square cut goatee and red cape with cuffs." This was the site of the Bahamas' first post office, the well-preserved ruins of which are still visible as part of Marina Inn's main lodge. The United States Privateer "Saucy Jack" raided Marine Farm near here during the War of 1812. Later she tried again but was driven off by guns which had been brought down from Nassau. Apparently, the large plantations here were kept fortified against the raids of privateers and pirates. Our good friend Herbert McKinney of Nassau, who owns over 7,000 acres of land on Crooked Island, tells us that on his properties there are ruins of at least two large plantation houses, and at one of these there are several large guns as big or bigger than those at Fort Charlotte in Nassau.

Marina Inn, the only foreign investment tourist facility on Crooked Island, is the brainchild of ex-Canadian airline pilot Buzz Sawyer, of Vancouver. Here several comfortable seaside cottages are available overlooking Portland Harbour and Bird Rock Lighthouse to the north. Buzz has cleaned a 1,700-foot, grass airstrip adjacent to the hotel, but until he levels it, its hills will keep us away. We landed our "Yankee" there on our last visit and a hairy landing it was. We didn't stick around to watch "Buzz" take off in his ancient Twin Beech, undoubtedly quite a sight to behold.

At Landrail Point there is a government wharf open to the roadstead facing the Crooked Island Passage. In prevailing weather it is usable if you make use of the offlying bollards to breast off the rough concrete wharf. There is a persistent, heavy surge here and in westerly weather the wharf is untenable. It is used by the mail boat on its weekly visits.

Landrail Point is a pretty village shaded by the ever-present towering stands of casuarinas. The people here are Seventh-day Adventists and show great pride in their spotless community. They are mostly farmers, raising a profusion of fruit, citrus and vegetables. Any one of them would be happy to guide you to the ancient British fortifications at Marine Farm or Gun Bluff, on the north side of the island. Fuel and fresh water can be delivered to the government pier.

One of the elders of the town and a former postmaster is Harry H. McKinney, now retired. He is an erect gentleman whose memory is a rich collection of historical notes and anecdotes on Landrail Point and all of Crooked Island. His daughter, Marina Gibson, and her husband, Wilford, who is also the lightkeeper, operate the only restaurant in town. The strictly Bahamian menu is excellent. Mr. McKinney's son, Willis, may be found teaching at any of the schools in the Crooked Island District. Willis is our guide for the entire area and a good friend as well.

"Chippin" cascarilla bark.
Bahamas Ministry of Tourism

Landrail Point is the western terminus of the road which spans the length of the Island, so it is possible to arrange transportation from here to any of the other settlements.

The elaborate ruins of Seaview Plantation lie atop the hill on Crooked Island's north shore, midway along the road from Landrail Point to Colonel Hill. The plantation, established in 1796, was built by Loyalist Tyne of the United States who raised cotton for British export. Susequent operators, the Moodys and the Mosses, marital descendants of Tyne, ran the plantation until the Emancipation Proclamation made it no longer feasible. Two wizened old sisters, presumably in their eighties, Jane and Margaret Moss, are the great grandchildren of a freed slave who took the name of his master at that time. The girls, exercising their right of commonage, have lived amid the ruins of Seaview most of their lives and just recently, being the only surviving heirs to the property, sold it to Colyn Rees of Nassau who has allowed them to stay on here as long as they like.

The remaining stone masonry of the great house and kitchen indicate that the very best effort and materials went into the building of Seaview. There is even an elaborate hurricane shelter referred to by the Moss sisters as "Gale House." From its rusting hinges hang remnants of the trap doors that once sheltered its residents from tropical storms.

Jane, the younger and more communicative of the two, was astonished when we explained that we had flown over Seaview and seen her on the ground the day before. "Could you see my face?" she asked in wonder. We replied that we could. When we departed Colonel Hill Airstrip several hours later we circled Seaview to take a promised picture, but the girls did not reappear. We wonder what they were thinking when they heard our small plane climbing into the blue overhead. Perhaps this new-found knowledge was too much to assimilate so late in their lives.

Colonel Hill is centrally located on the island and with the Commissioner's office and residence, it serves as seat of government for the whole of Crooked, Acklins, and Long Cay. The town crowns one of the highest hills in the district where the view from under the big tree in the village park is one of the loveliest in the Bahamas. From here most of the Island's north shore can be seen, its reefs breaking white to separate the indigo ocean from the pale green shallows at the shore. It is here, in the shade of this great tree, that the town's elders meet to discuss local events, politics, or just to reminisce. Every settlement in the Islands has its meeting tree, like all communities everywhere. Few, however, are fortunate enough to have one with a view as magnificent as this.

John Deleveaux, the town's leading merchant, served also as Constable until he lost both legs several years ago. John and his gracious wife, Unice, operate the Sunny Lea Guest House and Restaurant, adjacent to their store, where we were treated to the best boiled grouper we've ever eaten. Our last visit to Colonel Hill was made during the summer months when the Deleveaux' grandchildren were visiting from Nassau. Like on-the-job training, or a summer apprenticeship, each child exercised his or her own special duties about the house and showed a genuine pride in assisting their grandparents. John's recent handicap has not slowed his pace at all; he spends most of his time driving guests around the Island in his specially-built station wagon, happily greeting each visitor who lands on Colonel Hill's airstrip.

Colonel Hill and its surrounding communities, Cabbage Hill and Church Grove, like Landrail Point, are farming villages and all manner of island fruit and vegetables are available there in season.

Lying west of Church Grove, Turtle Sound is one of the most extensive, deep water creeks in all the Out Islands. Its sprig-marked entrance channel at French Wells lies across mud flats. The channel is hand-dredged annually by the fisherman of Church Grove who depend on this, their only opening to the sea, for their livelihood. We have cruised the Sound in a small boat with Willis McKinney and found in its upper reaches, close under the "Blue Hills" of Crooked Island's north shore, that the water is deep and abounds with the ubiquitous bonefish, some tarpon, and many turtles.

Born in Church Grove, Julius Bonoby lived forty years in the United States before retiring home in the early sixties. Uncle "Ju," as he likes to be called by intimates, has a very American sense of humor. As housemaster for theatrical agent, Otto Hack, of Detroit he is world traveled and has spent most of his life among theatrical people. Now retired, he operates a charming little roadside inn on the Turtle Sound road. It is a natural half-way house for the fishermen of the community. A most entertaining place, Julius' Tiger Bar is a must stop for anyone visiting ashore at Crooked Island.

The vast expanse of flat lands which lie to the west of the channel into Turtle Sound were once earmarked by the district's former representative, Basil Kelly, as a miniature African veldt where the land could be stocked with animals and safaris instituted as a tourist attraction. He even went so far as to invite several experts in to appraise the situation and they agreed after their inspection that the idea was entirely feasible.

Basil Kelly's long political career here is marked by the myriad civic contributions he made to the district. Highways, clinics, and communications were among his principal interests. Even though Basil no longer represents the district he still escapes here often enough to maintain his weekend house which overlooks the rocky headland known as McKi Bluff, east of Colonel Hill.

There is no blue like the view from True Blue, Crooked Island's hillside village to the east. A farm and fishing village that straggles along the bluff overlooking a bight of the purest blue water you've ever seen, True Blue is aptly named.

There are no all-weather harbours on the north shore of Crooked Island, most of the anchorages along here gaining their only protection from E by S Westerly winds. When visiting, the people of Acklins anchor their dinghies at Cove Landing under the eastern tip of Crooked Island.

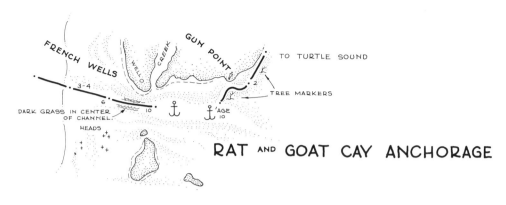

RAT and GOAT CAY ANCHORAGE

❲ Long Cay

At the southern tip of Crooked Island, just north of Rat and Goat Cays, there is a good anchorage for boats drawing up to seven feet. President Franklin Roosevelt used to anchor for the good fishing to the south along the Fish Cays guarding the Bight of Acklins. However, a much better anchorage, especially with the wind in the northwest or north, is the one on the southeast end of Long Cay. The land here is bold and a draft of ten feet can be taken within one hundred yards of the shore until a lee is obtained on the east side of the island. When the wind is in the east, this will be a rough anchorage as the shoals to the eastward do little to break up the sea. Our crew called it, "a perfect ocean locked harbour."

With the prevailing easterly winds you can lie safely in the lee of the island off Albert Town, but watch the surge when you dinghy ashore. This used to be a port of call for the German-American Line, and many a lad has sailed out from here as stevedore or to work on the Panama Canal or to cut mahogany in the forests of Honduras. It was this exodus of labor, following the failure of the salt and sponging industries, which finally killed the place. Today Albert Town is practically a ghost town, with most of its neat, well preserved little houses boarded up for eternity. There is a light here, fixed white, 40 feet high, visible ten miles. Stephen Rose or Sydney Frazier are the men to see at Albert Town.

In the interior of Long Cay, on the east side about two miles from its southern extremity, there is a fresh water pond, one of the few in the Bahamas.

❲ Acklins Island

Acklins Island forms the eastern side of the triangle of islands bordering the Bight of Acklins. Its highest land forms a ridge of spectacular rocky headlands that search the reef-studded eastern shore, and then recede to the low, rolling farm land of its western shore. The only harbour on the entire island worthy of the name is Atwood Harbour, near Chesters, a settlement

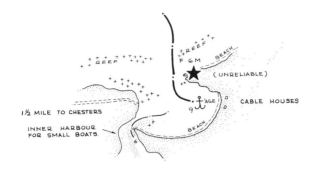

at the north end. Atwood Harbour will carry a draft of nine to ten feet over good holding sand with adequate protection in all but northwesterly winds.

Samana Cay, locally called Atwood Cay, is long, narrow, and lies east and west 20 miles north of Acklins. It is completely surrounded by coral reefs. Farmed by the people of Acklins, it yields ninety percent of the cascarilla bark harvested in the district. We'll bet it would also provide a perfect setting for a beachcombing expedition.

Caution! When rounding the northeast corner of Acklins, or "Hell Gate" as it is called by the locals, give the point a six-mile berth. A mountain of coral surrounded by indigo deeps breaks the surface there. The danger area is about 100 yards in diameter and breaks under all conditions. It bears 100° true from Northeast Point Light.

Frank Moss is the head of the small community at Chesters. He owns the store and fueling depot there, besides making scheduled runs to Nassau for supplies aboard his freight boat, "Bahama Trader." Frank's ninety footer was built with age old hand methods right here at Chesters. She was launched Easter Monday, 1968. If you need fuel and can secure your stern to the road on the west side of Atwood Harbour, he will truck out all you need and pump it aboard. Frank and his wife, Olive, are gracious hosts where a night's lodging is always available and perfectly-prepared seafood is served family-style. Harold and Melinda Black live next door. Harold skippers a second freight boat, "Windward Trader," and is also a fund of knowledge for those sailing about these Islands.

A number of years ago (1965) it was our privilege to accompany the Bahamas' Governor, Sir Ralph Grey, and Basil Kelly to Acklins on the first official visit that district had ever received. During our brief stay at Chesters the schoolteacher, Admiral Ferguson, led his children in song. Gathered on the hill in front of the new clinic, with only the whispering casuarinas for accompaniment, we've never heard "How Great Thou Art" sung with such tenderness.

SAMANA CAY

These Island teachers are an integral part of the life here. Their dedication is deeply involved, and reflected almost at first glance on the face of the community itself. The same was evident again at the sparkling little farm settlement of Lovely Bay, so rightly named, just across the creek.

The first visitor facility of Acklins Island is Newton Williamson's Hilltop View Guest House, which lies adjacent to the highway airstrip at Pinefield. Newton's remote hilltop hideaway commands a 360° panoramic view of the bights, plains, reefs and creeks of Acklins' north end. A more accommodating host you will not find anywhere as Newton can supply a rental car or escort you personally on a beachcombing or bonefishing expedition in his own boat, which is anchored in the bight at the foot of the hill.

Bahamas' eastern beaches seine the north bound currents of the Atlantic of their flotsam and jetsam, ranking them among the most prolific in the world for the inquiring beachcomber. A bottle tossed overboard off the Cape Verde Islands might circumnavigate the North Atlantic several times before it comes to rest at the high tide line on Acklins Island. Or it might have touched a dozen shores, each a thousand miles apart, not being able to decide whether it would prefer to end up a curio on an Irish or a Venezuelan mantelpiece.

Acklins, its great expanse like a net athwart the axis of a stream, is a catch-all for all manner of objects that by virtue of their passage alone make them art objects in the beachcomber's eye. In four hours one blistering July day, walking the five miles of beaches south of Hell Gate, Willis and I collected:

52 Portuguese glass floats
5 aluminum floats
1 large Japanese netted glass float
1 red emergency, or running, light
1 yacht bumper board
1 40-ft. section of yacht main mast which yielded:
    bronze sail track
    spinnaker track
    1 bronze foremast light
    3 bronze halyard winches
    4 stainless steel tangs and bolts
    2 stainless steel turnbuckles
3 thin-lip conch
1 Department of Commerce Coast and Geodetic survey drift study capsule
1 C-119 oil cooler scoop dust excluder
1 ammunition kit cover
1 corked, French champagne bottle with note and address

Having completed our long, hot search, we ate the conch, raw, on the spot. We mailed the form card contained in the drift study capsule to Washington. We received in return a kind note of appreciation and a very informative folder explaining the purpose of the study.

Upon reporting the C-119 part and ammunition case fragment to the Coast Guard we were visited, within the week, by the executive officer of the missing plane's squadron in Minneapolis. He informed us that these parts were the only trace of an airforce cargo aircraft which had disappeared six weeks before enroute to Grand Turk with over a dozen service men aboard. A subsequent search was made by a contingent of marines landed here by the Coast Guard, but their findings amounted to no more than a wooden wheel chock, presumably from the same aircraft.

Our daughter wrote to the Dutch address in the champagne bottle and in a few weeks time received a lengthy note from a 16-year-old Dutch lad who, a year and a half before, had stuffed his address into the bottle following a New Year's Eve party aboard ship. I recall he said the ship was approaching St. Thomas in the Virgin Islands at the time. All of the remaining treasures have found new homes on friends' boats and in our home, emitting that insatiable lure of the virgin beach to those who proudly call themselves beachcombers!

Crooked and Acklins' names are intriguing and, like True Blue, accurately describe their individual settlements: Cripple Hill, Lovely Bay, Hard Hill, Snug Corner, and Delectable Bay.

Barren of all greenery and looking for all the world like a Cornish seaside village of a hundred years ago, Hard Hill justifies its name. Consisting mainly of a steep, rutted, stony road bordered by rough, mortared, limestone and thatched houses and winding stone walls, "to keep the creatures in," Hard Hill appears poverty-stricken, completely out of context with the rest of the island. It was here on the Governor's first visit that we were met with one of the most unusual, but sincerest, welcoming committees of the entire tour. Lean, stately Reverend Samuel Collie, replete in swallowtail coat and derby, met us at the foot of the hill with a huge, bass drum strapped to his chest. He was accompanied by the ladies and children of Hard Hill. Following a brief speech of welcome, the good Reverend, led by an eight-year-old bugler (who had no doubt been taught to "bugle" just for the occasion), marched us to the summit to the tune of, "Never Let The Old Flag Fall." Sir Ralph, a lady on each arm, fell right in step and the rest of the party, following suit, marched up the stony hill to the ruin of a lookout tower where the Reverend recited a very thorough lesson on the history of Acklins Island. Reverend Collie, the residents of Hard Hill, and I will never forget the day he led the Governor of the Bahamas to the top of his hill!

The gentle people of Acklins have an appreciation of wit. They are gifted with that rare quality of being able to laugh at themselves. At Snug Corner, on that same visit, Sir Ralph, having just been introduced by a very dignified and lengthy speech, opened his address with this remark: "The very name Snug Corner must in some way account for the sea of youthful faces before me. . . ." He fairly brought down the house as everyone giggled coyly, realizing that the Queen's representative in their Islands was, indeed, a regular fellow.

Most of the bight communities south from Snug Corner are farming towns. Fishing is not carried on here with the vigor that it once was because of the Cuban boats that have frequented the bight in recent years, overfishing and almost conching it out. Each major settlement maintains its own clinic and resident nurse and the entire island is linked to Nassau by the forward scatter telephone system. Very few food supplies are available, with the exception of seasonable fruits and vegetables. You will find when visiting ashore here you will be compelled to anchor a considerable distance off and your dinghy will get a real workout. Diesel fuel and gasoline can be delivered to almost any settlement along the bight by drum, but it will probably have to be wrestled aboard one of the local craft for delivery to your boat.

A good man to know in these parts is Captain Mervin Ferguson. Now retired from a life at sea, Captain Ferguson lives ashore at Delectable Bay and will regale you with his special impressions of guiding President Roosevelt to the fishing fields of Acklins and Mayaguana; while his memories of fishing with Ernest Hemingway during the rough and tumble days of the thirties at Bimini are strongly reminiscent of *Islands in the Stream.*

Mrs. Ida Williams is tender of the hurricane lantern at Pompy Bay. A warm, friendly lady with a glowing smile, Mrs. Williams has a quick sense of humor. While we were chatting in her living room her cat ambled in. One look at the strangers and it scrambled out the other door. "Guess it never saw any white folks before," explained Mrs. Williams with a grin.

The Bight of Acklins is broad and shallow and therefore a bad place to be caught in a norther. Along the southwest end of Acklins Island a very snug little harbour will be found on the south side of Castle Island. It is called Mudian Harbour and is entered through a break in the reef one-half mile east of the lighthouse. In good light a draft of ten feet can be taken in at low tide.

The light on Castle Island is one of the most important in the West Indies, since there is a tremendous volume of traffic past here. It is a Bahamas Government Light of 400,000 candle power, 130 feet high, and visible for seventeen miles, giving out three flashes every fifteen seconds. During the day it is a beautiful sight from offshore.

CASTLE ISLAND

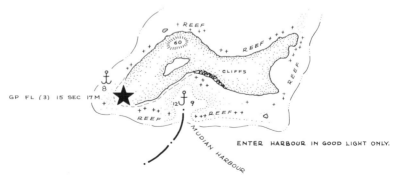

◖ Mira Por Vos Shoals and Hogsty Reef

The 40 square mile area of shoals which lie seven miles west of Castle Island Light is unmarked and has been a danger to shipping in the Crooked Island Passage since the days of the Spanish conquests. Soundings across here seldom exceed ten fathoms and besides the waters surrounding the three small cays where a fairweather lee can be obtained, there are several areas with no more than three fathoms over them. When rounding Castle Island at night favor the Castle Island side of the passage as the Cays are unmarked. The fishing hereabouts is reported to be excellent, but we wouldn't recommend a visit to the Mira Por Vos Shoals in anything but settled weather.

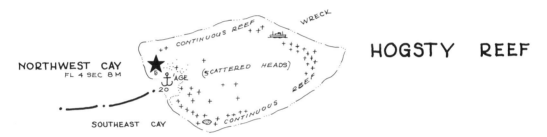

Were it not for the light at its western extremity (Northwest Cay, flashing every four seconds, visible for eight miles), Hogsty Reef, which is an atoll-like, mid-ocean plateau, would be almost as dangerous as the Mira Por Vos Shoals. It lies 37 miles southeast of Castle Island about half way between Acklins and Great Inagua. North and South West Cays, at its western end, border the one fathom entrance onto the bank inside. Here, too, the fishing is supposed to excellent, but like the Mira Por Vos Shoals, should not be visited in anything but settled weather as the anchorage would be an uneasy one indeed. Approaching Hogsty Reef at night from the east, caution should be exercised as a huge stranded freighter, high and dry on the coral at the eastern end of the atoll, will black out the light on North West Cay. This hulk has been rusting away here for some years now and poses a real danger to those who would be inquisitive enough to venture aboard.

◖ Plana Cays

Sometimes referred to as the French Cays, they are farmed in the summer by the people of Pinefield, Acklins, who have actually built a small village there for that purpose. They lie thirteen miles off the northeast coast of Acklins on a line with, and about half-way to, Mayaguana. With the

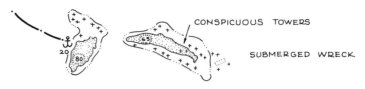

CONSPICUOUS TOWERS

SUBMERGED WRECK

exception of the western shore of the westernmost cay, where there is a good lee anchorage (three to four fathoms sand) off the north end, they are pretty much reef-bound.

A good landmark are the two abandoned coast and geodetic towers at the east end of the easternmost cay. There is a submerged wreck about a half mile off the eastern point of this cay that might bear looking into. It seems to have been a barge load of huge concrete pipe sections. The spear fishing hereabouts should be superb.

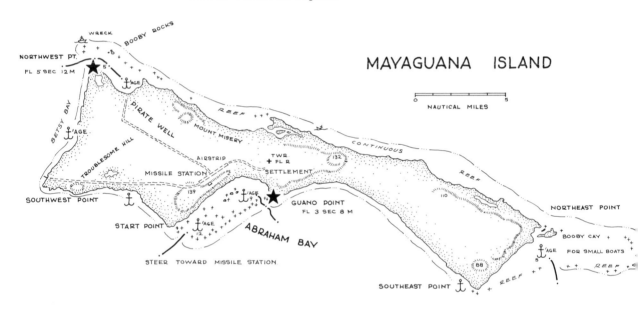

⟨ Mayaguana Island

This island is chiefly notable for the fact that it contains one of the bases leased (during World War II) by the United States Government for ninety-nine years in exchange for the forty old destroyers. This base was never developed, but an Air-Sea Rescue Station of the Caribbean Division of the U.S. Air Force was set up at the settlement of Abraham's Bay. This was later transformed into a missile tracking station which has since become inoperative.

Because it is well off the beaten track, being some seventy miles east of the Crooked Island Passage, Mayaguana is seldom visited, and except for its harbour, has no attractions for yachtsmen. The Island is 25 miles long, from two to six miles wide, and is generally low and heavily wooded. It is very sparsely settled, there being less than 500 inhabitants. Most of these are descended from the Turks Islanders who settled the island many years ago.

Abraham's Bay, on the south side, is an excellent harbour for boats drawing up to twelve feet of water. The entrance is through a wide break in the reef, the center of the channel being three-quarters of a mile southeast from Start Point, and the course in is NE x E. The western end of the harbour is clear, but the central and eastern parts have numerous heads with hardly any water at all on them. The best anchorage will be found under the lee of the reef.

There is another safe entrance to Abraham's Bay, but it is shallower and more intricate than the entrance at the west end. This entrance is through a break in the reef, half a mile west of Guano Point, and close alongside the northeast end of the barrier reef. A draft of seven feet at low tide can be carried in on a course approximately NW. This channel narrows as you go in and a sharp lookout must be kept for heads. The harbour at Abraham's Bay is safe in winds from any quarter, but being five miles long and nearly two miles wide, can be very choppy at times. There is a three-second white flashing light on Guano Point.

At the northwest end of Mayaguana Island there is a very good and safe reef harbour where boats drawing up to seven feet can come in at low tide. The entrance is from the west, and the best water about a quarter of a mile north of the light on Northwest Point. The light on the point is a five-second flash; it is untended, unreliable, and often out. There is a wrecked freighter on the NW corner of reef here, broken in two parts and serving as an excellent landmark.

At the east end of the island, there is a large reef harbour favored by local boats which usually draw up to five feet. The entrance is through a break in the reef four miles E x N from Southeast Point.

Flamingo flight at Great Inagua. *Bahamas Ministry of Tourism*

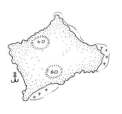

GREAT INAGUA

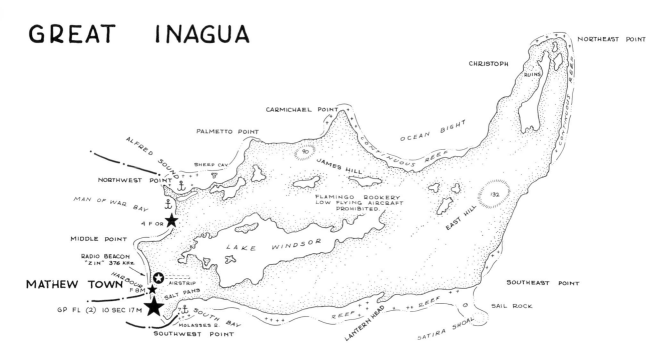

⟪ Great Inagua Island

The most southerly of the Bahama Islands, Great Inagua lies within sight of the mountains of Cuba, and only 60 miles from the north coast of Haiti. The island is 45 miles long and eighteen miles wide, flat, and wooded. The interior has many large salt-water lakes and on the east side there are low hills. The principal settlement is Mathew Town, which lies on the western side of the island, three miles above Southwest Point. Here the Commissioner resides, and there is a post office, customs house, and telephone station. The mail boat comes from Nassau every fortnight. There are about 800 people living in Great Inagua.

Not much is known of the early history of the island. In 1803 there was a flourishing salt industry and there is every evidence that prosperity was general. At Mathew Town the width and construction of the streets and roads would indicate a "carriage trade," and ruins of large houses can be seen. Henri Christophe, the black Emperor of Haiti, had his summer home here, which is not surprising as Cap Haitien is only 110 miles away. Rumor has it that he used to be "rowed" over. There is still a spot near Northeast Point which is known as Christophe.

One of the principal industries of Great Inagua used to be wrecking, and wrecks were sufficiently frequent so that a person's share in the next wreck was considered good enough security for the making of a fair sized loan, or taken as credit in the local stores.

The salt industry flourished here during the American Civil War and until sometime thereafter. However, mined salt took over the market and Great Inagua's native salt business, without mechanization, declined.

The modern history of Great Inagua is largely the story of the Erickson brothers who by hard work (and much Yankee ingenuity) brought prosperity to that somewhat deserted island. In 1936 the Ericksons moved in, literally against the efforts of the hostile and discontented local populace. They brought with them tractors, trucks, bulldozers, and modern machinery—and determination. In the space of only twelve years the salt works of Inagua became, and are today, one of the most successful solar operations in the world. The Morton Salt Company now owns and operates the salt industry at Great Inagua.

What makes good salt also makes good sailing—plenty of wind, a good warm sun, and little rain. In Inagua, the salt water from the sea is run through canals into acres of shallow fields, each with a marl bottom, and there it evaporates. Each "pan," as the fields are called, will assume a different color, depending upon the progress of the evaporation, and it is a wonderful sight to see great flocks of pink flamingos feeding in pans of wine color, or magenta, or chartreuse. Six inches of salt water will evaporate in three weeks into one inch of salt, which is then raked up and stored in great white pyramids. In this form it is coarse and crystalline. When needed for export it is hauled to the factory in Mathew Town where it is ground up, loaded by chute onto lighters, and towed out to waiting ships. The average year's export from Inagua is 50,000 tons of salt, and they have 100,000 tons in open storage, a pretty sight.

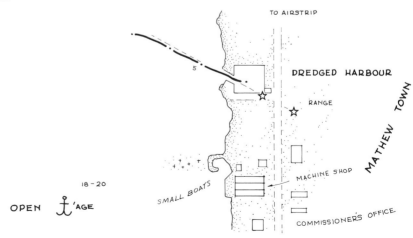

Commissioner's office at Mathew Town, Inagua.
Bahamas Ministry of Tourism

Until recently Great Inagua had no harbours for yachts. In fact it had no harbour at all. Off Mathew Town you could lie in the open roadstead which, with the prevailing Trade Winds, gave you a lee under the island. However, the ocean swells swept around Southwest Point and made it a very uncomfortable anchorage. If the wind went to the west or northwest, you had to get out quickly. The only safe anchorages in a norther were in South Bay, three miles east of Southwest Point, and inside Molasses Reef.

Now there is a 200- by 200-foot dredged harbour located between the town and the airstrip. The five-foot low-water entrance channel will lead you in over a hard bar. Caution should be exercised at night as the leading lights are off the center of the channel; favor the south side. Fuels and water are delivered here by truck. On shore the sportsman will find much to interest him: great colonies of pink flamingos feeding in the salt pans, wild horses and cattle on the prairie, ducks and marsh birds of all kinds, pelicans, parrots, and even mocking birds—all waiting to be "shot" with your telephoto lens. For a closer insight into the ecology of Inagua we refer you to Robert Klinger's *The Ocean Island,* a captivating account of the island and its sea life.

Currently some very interesting experimental "mari-culture" studies are being made here, having to do with raising crawfish in captivity. Diet until now has been the primary stumbling block, but it has been found that marine life attracted to the salt pans might very well augment the diet of this tasty species.

Mathew Town is a Port of Entry for the Bahamas. The light is a Bahamas Government Light, group flashing two every ten seconds.

⟨ Little Inagua

Little Inagua lies five miles off the north point of Great Inagua. It is uninhabited except by goats, donkeys, and an abundance of birds. You may anchor in two to three fathoms off the Southwest corner of the Island, where one can beachcomb the ten miles of eastern shore.

Turks and Caicos Island

14

Over the years there have been many students of Columbus' log who have theorized that Grand Turk was the true "Guanahani," the first landfall on that memorable October 12th, 1492. The more we read on this, the more convincing their arguments appear. However, for the sake of the record, at least for the present, it must be conceded that the great navigator's first landfall was at San Salvador and Ponce de Leon discovered the Turks and Caicos Islands some 20 years later.

Geographically, the Turks and Caicos Islands, lying at the eastern end of the Bahama Group, are almost suburbs of Haiti, only 85 miles from Cape Isabella, which is about in the middle of the north coast of Hispaniola. Politically they are an independent Crown Colony, presided over by a Governor appointed by the Queen. They used to be a dependency of Jamaica, however, and they still use Jamaican currency. Ecclesiastically they are Bahamian, as the parishes of St. George and St. Thomas are in the diocese of Nassau. They comprise an archipelago 80 by 45 miles with only 166 square miles of land area. Their earliest settlers were Bermuda salt rakers who migrated here in the 1670's to ply their trade.

The Turks and Caicos Islands were once the most notorious hiding place for pirates in all the West Indies. Adjacent to the principal sailing ship routes which lead to the Windward Passage, their unknown, uncharted coves and channels were made to order for piratical purposes. Some of the best pirate stories we ever read had this as their locale, and the history of the British Navy in these parts is replete with accounts of the pursuits of pirate craft across these banks by naval vessels, while the reefs of the north shore are dotted with wreck sites dating from that period.

The Caicos Bank is an extensive submarine plateau, about 60 miles wide, not unlike the Great and Little Bahama Banks in character. The average depth of water on it is only about six feet. The edges of the bank are fringed by a chain of narrow, thinly wooded islands, small cays, rocks, reefs, and shoals. The largest islands lie on the north and east side.

An extremely interesting feature of this group is the evidence of progressive shoaling during the past century. A channel across the bank, from Long Cay to French Cay, reported to be fourteen feet deep in 1881, has barely more than six feet in it now. In other places, accounts of naval action against

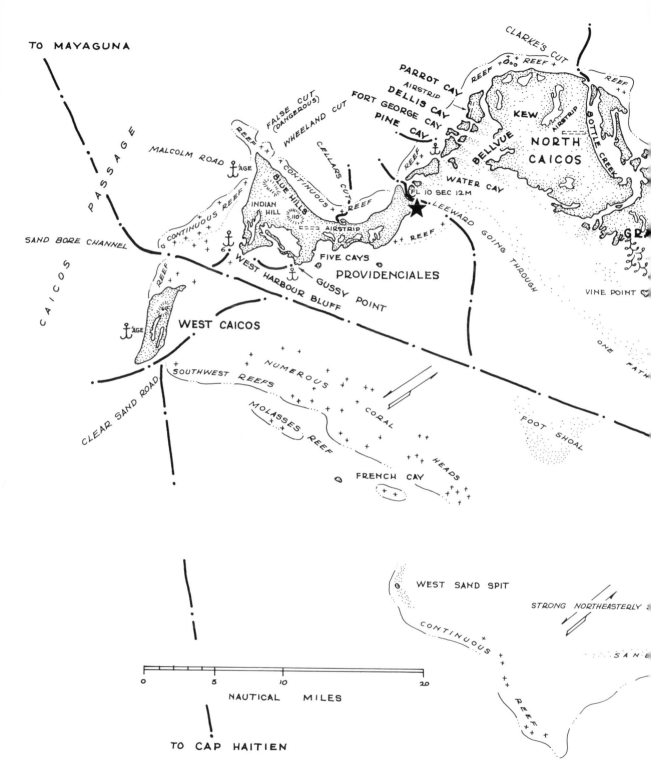

TO MAYAGUNA

CLARKE'S CUT

REEF

PARROT CAY
AIRSTRIP
DELLIS CAY
FORT GEORGE CAY
PINE CAY
FALSE CUT
(DANGEROUS)
WHEELAND CUT
CELLARS CUT
REEF
KEW
NORTH
CAICOS
BELLVUE
AIRSTRIP
BOTTLE CREEK
REEF

MALCOLM ROAD
'AGE

P A S S A G E

BLUE HILLS
INDIAN
HILL
110
AIRSTRIP
CONTINUOUS REEF
CONTINUOUS REEF

WATER CAY
FL 10 SEC 12M
LEEWARD GOING THROUGH
REEF

GRA

SAND BORE CHANNEL

6

REEF
5
WEST HARBOUR BLUFF
FIVE CAYS
GUSSY POINT
PROVIDENCIALES
REEF

VINE POINT

C A I C O S

'AGE
WEST CAICOS

ONE FATH

CLEAR SAND ROAD

SOUTHWEST REEFS
NUMEROUS
CORAL
FOOT SHOAL

MOLASSES REEF
HEADS

FRENCH CAY

WEST SAND SPIT
STRONG NORTHEASTERLY S

CONTINUOUS

SAN

REEF

0   5   10   20

NAUTICAL   MILES

TO CAP HAITIEN

TURKS & CAICOS ISLANDS

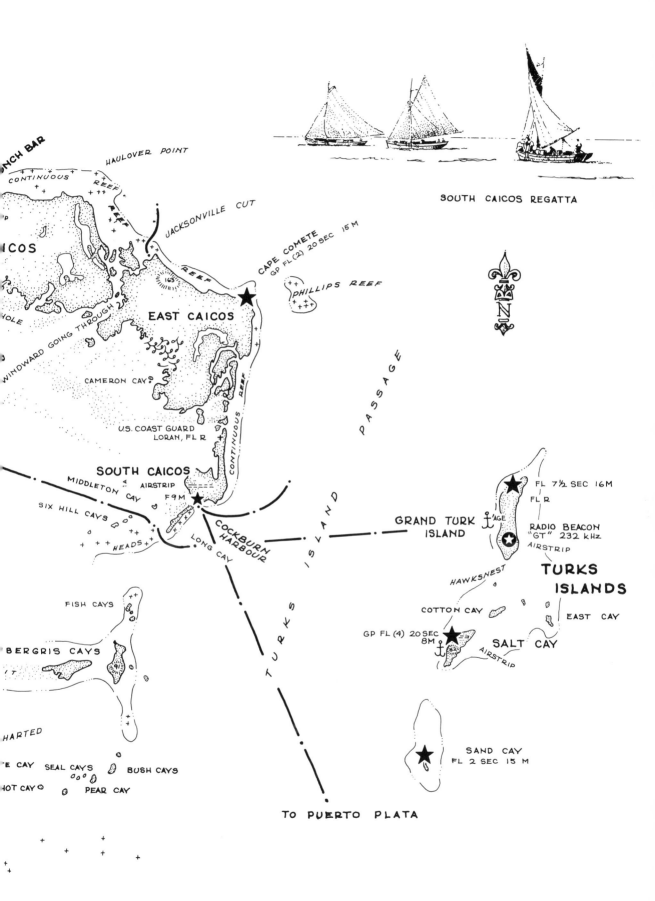

NCH BAR

HAULOVER POINT

CONTINUOUS REEF

JACKSONVILLE CUT

ICOS

REEF

'63

HOLE

WINDWARD GOING THROUGH

EAST CAICOS

CAMERON CAY

CAPE COMETE
GP FL (2) 20 SEC 15 M

PHILLIPS REEF

SOUTH CAICOS REGATTA

N

TURKS ISLAND PASSAGE

U.S. COAST GUARD
LORAN, FL R

CONTINUOUS REEF

SOUTH CAICOS

MIDDLETON CAY

SIX HILL CAYS

HEADS

AIRSTRIP
F 9 M

LONG CAY

COCKBURN HARBOUR

FISH CAYS

BERGRIS CAYS

I T

GRAND TURK
ISLAND

FL 7½ SEC 16 M

FL R

AGE

RADIO BEACON
"GT" 232 kHz

AIRSTRIP

TURKS
ISLANDS

HAWKSNEST

COTTON CAY

EAST CAY

GP FL (4) 20 SEC
8 M

SALT CAY

AIRSTRIP

HARTED

E CAY   SEAL CAYS   BUSH CAYS

HOT CAY   PEAR CAY

TO PUERTO PLATA

SAND CAY
FL 2 SEC 15 M

pirates would indicate that deep water channels must have existed where shoal-draft boats have difficulty getting through today. We have talked to local fishermen who have told about sailing through passages between the islands which are now shoaled up with sand. There seems to be little doubt that eventually this whole group will become one large island. Some of the Caicos Islands are quite high, and all of the larger ones are inhabited. It would take several weeks of cruising to explore them all.

With their meager annual rainfall these islands are a classic example of how an industrious and determined people can wring a living, even some prosperity, from the most barren soil. For, in spite of the unfriendliness of nature, there is considerable industry here. Their salt pans have been known 'round the world for centuries, and more recently the progress in the preparation and shipment of fresh foods has given the crawfishing industry great promise. Three hundred thousand crawfish were exported by air in 1970. Grand Turk, with its U.S. missile tracking station, enjoyed world headlines on early space flights with John Glenn's splashdown and debriefing.

Today the Turks and Caicos Islands are coming to life in quite another way. Emerging finally as the last of the "untrod stepping stones" to the Caribbean, there is a current land rush for space aboard that last island in the sun, and the plots are fast disappearing. The colony has always enjoyed a comfortable, tax-free atmosphere, so that in recent years the Government has been deluged with schemes ranging in promise from the wildest "pie in the sky" to a financial paradise that would make Freeport look like Boys' Town in comparison. All this could easily be at the expense of the Turks Islanders, who in the glamour of the performance might not realize the loss of their heritage until it is too late.

So concerned has been London's Colonial Office that a consultant firm was called in to analyze the needs of the colony and to prescribe a governing plan for development that would lure the prosperity and at the same time give the Turk Islander his rightful chance to be "first at bat." The Turks Islander, like the industrious Abaconian, the hardy Andros sailor, the shy Hope Towner, or the gentle people of Acklins, has a character peculiar to his environment. His reputation as an untiring worker is widespread in the merchant fleets of the world, as well as the work camps of the Bahamas, and we sincerely hope that he gets his just reward on his home island.

We think of the people of Man of War Cay in Abaco, who sold only small pieces of land around the perimeter of their Island so they could service the visitor community from within and at the same time maintain their own individuality. They held control, and with foresight and patient planning, the same principles could apply here.

As a former member of the colony's first Tourist Board, I believe I understood the sensitivity of the decisions on the initial proposal: to preserve the identity of the Turks Islander, and at the same time not inhibit foreign investments—a delicate task indeed.

In any event, the development has already begun here, and is gaining such momentum that it will soon be hard to control. We hope its success will not be at too great a cost to the people of these islands.

⟨ Approach from the Bahamas

On the charts it appears that the Turks and Caicos Islands are part of the Bahama chain, and they are, geographically. They remain, however, a separate country, an independent Crown Colony where all aircraft and private yachts are required to clear customs with the proper authorities at their departure as well as upon arrival. Ports of Entry are: Grand Turk, South Caicos, and Providenciales.

Approaching from the Bahamas by boat, from Mayaguana or the Inaguas, for example, your first landfall will be the high, blue hills of Providenciales. West Caicos is much lower and will be picked up nearer in.

⟨ West Caicos

The notorious pirate, Devlin, used to anchor on West Caicos in the small cove at the north end of the island, where he tied branches in his rigging to foil his pursuers. At present West Caicos might soon become the industrial end of the Turks and Caicos group. Overtures on the part of the Esso Oil Company indicate that a full scale refinery and bunkering operation, even a causeway across West Reef connecting West Caicos to Providenciales where employees would be housed, might be built.

If caught in a norther along here, there is a lee anchorage on the southeast end of the island. It is called Clear Sand Road and is easily entered by holding close to the shore when rounding the south end of the island; there are five fathoms of water inside.

⟨ Providenciales

Providenciales is certainly the prettiest island in the group, with its rolling green hills on the north shore standing out like mountains compared to the surrounding islands. Entering from the west via Sand Bore Channel, which is recommended in strong easterly conditions, you can bring up under West Harbour Bluff in six to eight feet of good holding sand.

Ashore here, under the point, is an interesting cave where we once found some old coins with a metal detector. Too eroded for proper identification, however, they were worthless. A pepper tree grows up from the floor of the cave through a hole in the ceiling. It can be scaled by notches cut in the trunk by local fishermen as the only stairway to the top of the bluff. Carved into the rocky crest above are names and dates, presumably etched there by shipwrecked sailors with nothing but time on their hands. The earliest date we could find read 1784; another tells of a fire at sea in 1842. This, the highest point on the southwest end of the island, must have provided a lone and windy vigil for months, perhaps even years, waiting for their fires to be seen by a passing ship working its way across the Caicos Bank.

Six feet can be carried five miles further east to the pier at Gussy Point, where filtered fuel can sometimes be obtained; six feet can also be taken across the 48 miles of bank to the passage around Long Cay, then into Cockburn Harbour at South Caicos.

A mile and a half around Gussy Point will bring you to the village of Five Cays, named for the five small rocks offshore which form a sort of harbour, and where Providenciales' crawfishing operation, Atlantic Fisheries, is located. Here the community straggles haphazardly along the ridge overlooking the salina and its fishing boats are drawn up onto the shore. There is really nothing here of interest to visitors.

When approaching Providenciales from Mayaguana or the northwest in settled weather, it is best to continue past the north point of the island to the center of the bight outside the reef opposite the cliffside hotel there, and wait for a pilot to show you in. Use your radio phone if you cannot raise Third Turtle Inn on 2738 KHz standby and someone will come out for you, leading you through Cellars Cut and into the Inn's docks at Cellars Pond.

There is a passage through the reef at Wheeland Cut, two miles northeast of Northwest Point. It is plainly visible as the reef on each side always breaks. We do *not* recommend this passage without local knowledge as the winding way through the profusion of coral heads inside could lead you into trouble. Get a local pilot to show it to you while you are here, for it is easy to negotiate once you know how.

The break in the reef directly north of Northwest Point is aptly named "False Cut." A snare and a delusion, it leads nowhere, except onto the dangerous staghorn coral inside. New to the area, we were lured in here several years ago following a most productive day of deep sea fishing, when my wife hooked into the first blue marlin logged for the Inn. There was a moderate Atlantic swell running and in our haste to "get home" we turned into False Cut by mistake. By the time we discovered the error and turned the boat around we found ourselves under the breakers on the east side of the cut with no alternative than to plow through a cresting wave to escape. Fortunately, in the few moments that followed no one was hurt, but for an instant we thought we had lost everything.

Seeing the cresting wave rising over our tuna tower, the skipper fire-walled the engines and we burst through, emerging airborne on the far side.

When the boat crashed to the surface, we figured she must have dropped ten feet. The mate, up in the tower, flew out of his crib and, by holding onto the wheel, as speedily flew back in, this time head first, bruising his shoulder but breaking no bones, I was below and had just closed my camera case when we hit the wave. The windshield shattered, fortunately at my back. My wife had been covering the kids, wet from fishing and spray, with a blanket when she saw the wave coming and threw herself on top of them to protect them from debris. There was glass everywhere, but aside from splinters in our feet for the following week, and bruised egos on the part of the crew and myself, we suffered little damage. And that is our lasting recollection of False Cut, a dangerous place, even with an experienced crew.

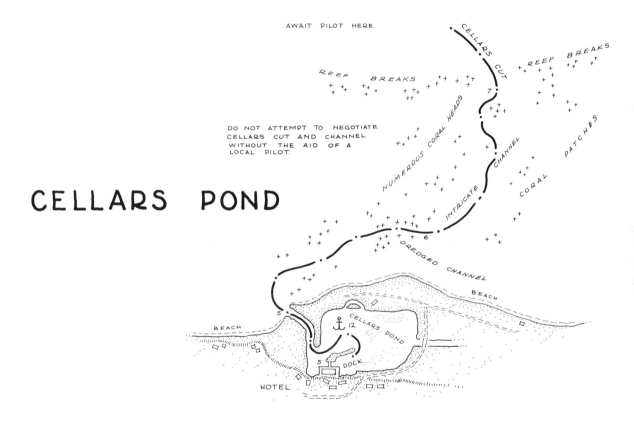

Ashore, Third Turtle Inn is headquarters for the 4,000-acre, sports-oriented, land development scheme known both as Long Bay Hills and Turtle Cove. The Inn, with its casual, clubby atmosphere, overlooks a protected inland pond as well as the island's north shore and is surrounded with docks. Fresh water and electric current is at hand and fuel sometimes can be arranged for; also there is twice weekly air service via the company plane to Palm Beach. The plane is used mainly to augment land sales as the dozen or so American residents all fly their own aircraft down the 535-mile hop from Florida.

Backed mainly by third generation du Ponts and a Roosevelt, George Town's Fritz Ludington has set the Providenciales pace at which the Turks and Caicos Islands will eventually be "cranked up"—as he calls it. Land sales are booming and the American way is getting *its* way here.

The settlement of Blue Hills meanders west along the north shore of the island and supplies much of the work force for the development companies here. Some Lucayan artifacts in the form of jadeite hatchet heads, or "thunderbolts," as they are called locally, have been found here. Finding thunderbolts is quite a common occurrence and the Turks Islander, as well as the Bahamian, believes these to be formed by a clap of thunder, and owning one would be a lasting protection against thunder and lightning. Once we were presented with one to carry aboard our motor sailor "Spindrift," and naturally we have kept it there since.

For interested spelunkers, the caves around Indian Hill at the west end of the island should yield a considerable amount of pre-Columbian material.

There is an entrance onto the Caicos Bank for shoal-draft vessels around the eastern tip of Providenciales. It is known as Leeward Going Through, and while it could at one time accommodate sailing vessels of some size, it will take only a draft of three to four feet on the tide today. We took a houseboat drawing a little over three feet through here last year (1972) and never once riled the bottom, but it was tricky all the way.

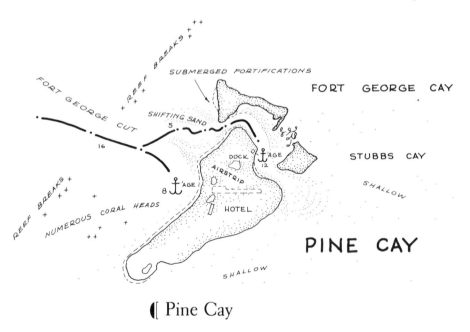

(Pine Cay

The next group of cays to the east includes Pine Cay which has four fresh water lakes in its center. The modern advocates of Columbus' Grand Turk landfall have reasoned that Pine Cay, with its creek harbour along the north shore, is "the harbour with two entrances" where he watered his ships on October 17th. A number of theories have been put forth regarding the ponds. Probably the most plausible is that the existence of a layer of impervious rock or clay lying beneath the limestone surface of this particular Island prevents the rain from being able to penetrate, and it accumulates on the surface here. This amounts to some 600 million gallons, we are told, a most fortunate dividend in an island group that is noted for its scarcity of fresh water.

Pine Cay is presently being developed into a yachtsman's port-of-call, the Meridian Club, by an American group, headed by the South Caicos developer, Liam Maguire. A 4,000-foot airstrip and a hotel with accompanying villas are being built.

Fort George Cut is wide and deep, and yachts of ten-foot draft can anchor in the lee protection of the Bay off the Meridian Club in good holding sand. It is possible to gain the inner harbour but to do so is to negotiate an extensive area of shifting sand ridges with little more than five feet of water on them. There is a stake marking the entrance channel, but we would recommend standing off the entrance or in the Bay anchorage to await a pilot to show you in.

(Fort George Cay

Bordering the north side of Pine Cay Harbour is Fort George Cay, where the cannons, from the small fortifications which once protected the north side of Leeward Going Through, now lie submerged off the island's western beach. Devastating hurricane Donna demolished this landmark in 1960. During the Haitian revolution in the 1790's, Loyalist settlers intercepted several French refugee sloops which were interned in Pine Cay's inner harbour, then open to the south.

(Dellis Cay

Dellis Cay was named for the Greek family who lived here for many years, sponge fishing. Following the blight of the twenties they departed and now little remains of their efforts as the cay is completely overgrown.

(Parrot Cay

Northernmost, largest, and undoubtedly the prettiest of this beach-rimmed group, is Parrot Cay, the home of Countess Helen Czernin of New York City. Extensively planted with citrus onions and Japanese lilies, the island enjoyed a brief export trade with Bermuda in the 1890's. Then in the 1920's much of the cay was planted in cotton which failed for lack of rain.

Probably the longest and most successful tenant of Parrot Cay was the West India Regiment veteran who would walk and paddle here from Kew each week to raise beans, peas, and ochra, only to return to Kew the following weekend so he could regale the inhabitants once again with his harrowing tales of World War I. Most of these crops are still evident about the cay today, while the Countess has cleared a 2,500 foot airstrip for the tourist trade that she feels is on its way.

(North and Grand Caicos

North and Grand Caicos are the largest islands in the entire group with a number of interesting settlements. The only break in the reef along here is Clarke's Cut. It lies at the northeast corner of North Caicos and leads in on a southerly course toward the two cable houses there. Clarke's Cut is narrow and bordered with reef. It should only be entered in good light. The anchorage lies about a mile to the east at the entrance to Bottle Creek. As is the case in most creeks in these waters the entrance is shoal, an area of shifting sand where only the smallest vessels can cross over on a high tide to gain the deeper water of the creek itself.

At the settlements of Bottle Creek, Kew, and Bellvue are extensive ruins from plantation days, but at "Mountain Plantation," near Bellvue, traces of an original Lucayan clearing can still be seen. There are several mounds here, where it is believed the inhabitants built their places of shelter, and digging around the mounds one will unearth animal bones, stone implements, and pottery fragments. There are caves throughout the Islands where wall paintings have been found, but at the Number One and Two caves at Jacksonville, on East Caicos, carved petroglyphs of heads and human figures can be seen.

The peaceful Lucayan Indians reached a high proficiency in the art of ceramics. They also carved dugout canoes that carried scores of people on long ocean voyages. It is believed their decorated caves were originally used as ceremonial halls and hurricane shelters, but after the Spanish persecutions began they lived in them permanently. It is estimated that the Bahamas and Caicos once contained over 40,000 of these gentle souls. Only twenty-five years after they welcomed the first Spaniard ashore, there was not one Lucayan left to tell of the "improvments" their visitors had wrought.

Bottle Creek is a community of about 500 people overlooking the creek itself. The center of the village lies about three miles south of its mouth, and being rather primitive, it offers no supplies, but does have a 3,000-foot airstrip with daily flights to the other islands in the Turks and Caicos Group. The creek is one of the prettier waterways, teeming with tarpon and turtle. It very conveniently connects the north shore with the Banks, but only for small boats.

Another 500 happy people live in the charming settlement of Kew. They attend their six churches which range in denomination from Baptist and Seventh-day Adventist to Quaker, and openly criticize the government. When that doesn't help they even resort to voodoo.

The tallest trees in all of Caicos grow at Kew along with flowering shrubs and flowers. In the past much farming was carried on, but now, with only the young and very old remaining, barely enough is raised for home consumption. Kew lies too far inland for the casual boating visitor, but if you could arrange a ride from Bottle Creek the visit would be well worth it.

⟮ Conch Bar

The windswept settlement of Conch Bar on Grand Caicos's north coast overlooks one of the most dramatic shorelines in the Islands. Here, with an offlying barrier reef, the ocean deeps extend almost in to the shore and the resultant erosion of the lofty limestone cliffs is an exhibition of nature's sculptured artistry at its finest. The rolling, grassy headlands looking out to sea divide the shore into a dozen crescent shaped, practically private beaches, where the water colors are fascinating.

The only way to visit Conch Bar is by airplane, and the hard packed coral airstrip is just a short walk from the village. The open roadstead with the deeps so near at hand would provide an uneasy anchorage at best. Even the reef anchorage, two miles east, presents difficulties. Can you imagine the problems involved in hand-loading cave guano by the bushel into coastal schooners riding in the surf, two miles from the caves?

There is little of interest for the visitor at Conch Bar except perhaps the friendliness of the people, a few barking dogs, chiming roosters, and a bunch of shy little boys you would like to show you "de caves," which are the most accessible of any in the Caicos Islands. A ten minute walk from the airstrip took us down a blistering hot road where we met several strings of ladies walking single file and carrying great bundles of cascarilla bark or firewood on their heads. Each smiled as we passed, but never disturbed an almost perfect carriage. The caves lie under a seemingly endless ridge shelf which parallels the shore and must have been eroded alternately by the sea and the wind during some undetermined prehistoric age. They are entered easily and traversed over gentle, soft hills of cave earth throughout. Most of the guano was harvested here in the mid-1800's. The silence in the caves is most startling, while the tidal pools are mirrors without even the slightest movement to mar their perfect reflections. The children are quick to tell you the caves have not been fully explored and there is probably some treasure still hidden here. The Government used to supply Coleman lanterns to visitors, but on our last trip they were locked in a very strong box at the entrance and no one seemed to know who had the key.

﴾ East Caicos

There is an excellent wide, deep channel through the reef and into the harbour at Jacksonville, at the northwest corner of East Caicos. The harbour was dredged in the 1800's to sixteen feet by Irishman J.N. Reynolds to accommodate his fleet of schooners carrying guano and sisal to New York. At the time a 300-foot long wharf connected to fourteen miles of railroad which crisscrossed the Island's extensive sisal and cotton fields. Mr. Reynolds maintained a herd of 1,500 head of cattle here, supplying Grand Turk and the nearby islands with their only beef. The hides he exported to Haiti. Transportation around the island was mainly by mule-drawn trolleys which carried the sisal and guano to the waiting ships. The only remaining traces of this vast enterprise are the ruins of several houses at harbourside and a small scattering of cattle and donkeys which have managed to propagate here. Local sportsmen from South Caicos hunt them regularly. The large savannahs in the center of the island are sometimes populated by large flocks of flamingos.

Care must be taken in rounding Cape Comete to avoid Phillip's Reef, which lies between three and four miles ENE of the Cape. In daylight hours the reef is always visible, since it is subjected continually to the breaking ocean swells. In settled weather and in favorable light conditions, it is possible for small craft to round inside Phillip's Reef; however, at night or in poor light, it is best to give the light on Drum Point at least a five-mile berth to insure a safe passage. The light, group flashing two every twenty seconds, is visible fifteen miles and is reliable.

The weather shore, extending southward to Cockburn Harbour, like the north shore, is studded with continuous reef close into the land. The beaches along here, like those of Acklins, are a catchall for all manner of debris and the beachcombing, if you can get to them, truly spectacular. Landing on the salina under Drum Point, we have trudged the north beaches of this tortuous shore, gathering glass floats and Haitian trap buoys. We've found parts from ditched aircraft, large sections of guided missiles, charred life-boats, tangled fish nets, expended radio sounders and lengths of nylon hauser line.

⟪ South Caicos

The red-lighted radio towers at the northern tip of South Caicos are those of the U.S. Coast Guard Loran Station (NMA-5). The station is connected to Cockburn Harbour by a road which runs down the lee of the ridge of rocky headlands which guard the entire length of South Caicos' eastern shore.

The only protected harbour of any size in the Turks and Caicos Islands is Cockburn Harbour. It is a safe harbour in winds from any direction, though a mild surge will be felt at most times. Some say it is too exposed to the southeastward; however, the shoals in that direction break up any sea, as do the shoals to the west and northwest. When coming down from the north toward Cockburn Harbour, give the southeast corner of the island a wide berth—a mile—as submerged reefs extend out a considerable distance from shore. The harbour entrance is between the NE end of Long Cay and Dove Cay, which is the small cay lying about a quarter mile SW of the light on Government Hill. There is a snug cove off the fish factory, just around to the west of the Admirals' Arms Inn which overlooks the harbour from its high perch on the shore in the center of the town.

The town of Cockburn Harbour is a clustered settlement of about 800 souls, mostly old people and children; the men have been recruited to the labor forces of the Bahamas. The island's extensive salt pans, the largest in the Turks and Caicos Group, once enjoyed a certain prosperity; however, they now are closed down and with the settlement's natural lack of greenery the community appears poverty-stricken.

A mile north of the town is the 6,000-foot airstrip where a regular air schedule services the island with flights to Florida and a twice daily schedule links the islands themselves.

Some supplies can be purchased at the several small stores, and fueling is affected through a soiled section of PVC hose by gravity. The dock at which this is done has lain unfinished for several years and is difficult to find after entering the harbour as it has no distinguishing feature to set it apart from the jumbled shoreline. (It lies immediately east of the Atlantic Gold Fish Factory.) It is best not to tie alongside here as the dock pilings set in drums can pierce your hull if you are not held off properly. You would be better to drop anchor to windward and tie up stern-to if possible. The last time we fueled here we were on our way to Cape Haitien, and while we did our best to strain the fuel before it entered the tanks, we spent the entire rough, ten-hour passage next day with a wrench in each hand, cleaning fuel filters all the way.

If you intend to clear customs here, the customs office is on the top floor of the two-story frame government building in the center of town. The pleasant young customs officer processes all incoming passengers at the new air terminal also, so you occasionally might have to await your turn.

Second only to the imposing house of the District Commissioner, which stands high on Government Hill, the rambling Admirals' Arms Inn commands a fine view of the harbour. Here, amid somewhat spartan surroundings and a rocky, patio salt water pool, a relaxed atmosphere prevails. The Inn is a favorite stop-over spot for ferry pilots delivering planes to the Lesser Antilles and South America. There is a telephone station at the Inn with good service to Florida, Bermuda, and points south.

Liam Maguire refurbished an old residence in the center of town as an interesting little English pub and restaurant where the manageress, Tina, serves an excellent Island or English meal, whichever you prefer, on reasonable notice.

Cockburn Harbour is the site of the annual South Caicos Regatta scheduled for Commonwealth Day each year. Liam Maguire has run this Regatta, practically single-handed, since its inception in 1967. A derivative of George Town's Out Island Regatta, this event is sponsored by the Turks and Caicos Rescue Squadron. Plaques, trophies and cash prizes are awarded. This is a one-day regatta with the usual shoreside activities, such as a tug of war, childrens' foot and bag races, and a most entertaining donkey race. Owing to the sizable fleet of outboard boats now employed by the fisheries here, the program also includes a small series of power races. All competitions are held within the confines of the harbour, which makes for a big day for the spectator as well as the competitors.

⟨ Grand Turk

Lying 22 miles directly east of South Caicos, Grand Turk is the Government seat of the Turks and Caicos Islands. Because of its comparative inaccessibility to the settlements of the Caicos Group, consideration has been given to moving the complex into new quarters at South Caicos. This undoubtedly would be a wise move due to the excellent harbour and airstrip there.

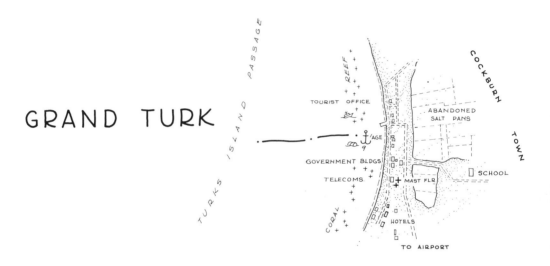

Turks Island boats are seen all over the West Indies, but are very rarely seen at Turks Island itself as the island has no harbour. When a boat comes in she usually goes right out again as soon as she is loaded, or else is hauled out on the beach. The closest thing to a harbour is the break in the reefs, an open roadstead off the town on the west side of the island. On the south side there is a large roadstead called Hawk's Nest Anchorage which is well protected by outlying cays, rocks, and reefs, but it is a most uncomfortable place to lie because there is a constant surge.

Like Salt Cay and South Caicos, Grand Turk had its beginnings in the latter part of the seventeenth century with the Bermuda salt rakers who were sailed here aboard those characteristic Little Bermuda sloops and marooned from spring through summer to produce and pound salt. In that period, providing the weather remained sunny with strong winds, a raking team could produce 200 to 300 bushels per acre of pan. In a seventeenth-century publication the rakers were described: "they live in little huts covered with thatch *leaces*. They have a knife in their pocket and a kittle in their kitchen, their wardrobe consists of nothing but a straw hat, a check shirt and a pair of *Osanburg* trousers."

Today Grand Turk's population numbers a little over two thousand people and its salt pans have not been in operation for many years. They lie idle here, a collection point for every type of refuse, and eminating a most disagreeable odor. Cockburn Town (not to be confused with Cockburn Harbour at South Caicos) has some genuinely interesting architecture which, if landscaped properly, would make the island a most attractive place to visit.

A unique problem of Grand Turk and South Caicos has been the roaming bands of wild donkeys that feed on any greenery they can reach. On first hearing this our initial reaction was, "Well, why don't they get rid of them?" But it isn't all that easy. The donkeys are the basis of strong supersitions. Then again the locals say, "After all, we've worked side by side on the salt pans these many generations, we just can't kill them!" The donkey problem will eventually be resolved and with its success will come a more tourist-oriented community.

Grand Turk can offer some supplies, including frozen meats, dairy products, and fresh vegetables in season. Fueling, however, can be difficult even in the best of circumstances; even at that rare time it must be handled rather gingerly, anchored stern-to at the Government pier in the center of town. There is a telephone station here that, strangely enough, does not connect with the Bahamas. All calls are routed through Bermuda and Jamaica.

One of the nicest couples on Grand Turk are Hubert and Daphne James. Hubert sits on the Tourist Board and operates the Caicos Realty Company. He has a way with visitors and will do his utmost to make your visit a memorable one. Daphne is chief "girl Friday" at the Tourist Board office on Front Street and can supply you with a wealth of information about the Turks and Caicos Islands.

Another interesting person here is H.E. Sadler, the colony's historian. Mr. Sadler can usually be found at his department store a block east of the telecommunications office on Pond Street. He has compiled a voluminous collection of Turks and Caicos history and lore, which includes his very logical reasons why these islands were Columbus' true "Guanahani."

The Victoria Public Library has early papers and relics having to do with the first days of the colony. This library, which is located in the center of town, is a unique, ancient little building well worth a visit.

The Turks Head Inn, formerly the Government guest house, is a charming, century-old building noted more for its congenial bar than for its plumbing. At lunch time, this spot is the meeting place for businessmen, developers, and tourists in Grand Turk as well as for the local populace. It's a pleasant refreshment spot with its fair share of political intrigue!

For a restful night ashore you might try Sunset Manor or Tina Feni-more's brand-new Kittina Hotel, just down the road. Both front on Grand Turk's peaceful south beach, and each establishment offers excellent meals and a comfortably casual atmosphere around their garden patio bars.

At Grand Turk the U.S. Navy occupies the north end of the island next to the lighthouse (Fl.Ev. 7½ secs. 108 ft. vis. 16 mi.), while the U.S. Air Force has its tracking station on the south end. It was at the latter that John Glenn was debriefed following his historic flight in 1962. The 5,000-foot paved Air Force airstrip is open for civilian use, and the local airline serves the nearby islands from there on a daily schedule. Though the prosperity of an eventual tourist economy beckons, Grand Turk is an uncomfortably tight little island at present.

⟨ Salt Cay

Salt Cay lies 5½ miles SSW of Grand Turk. Here is an immaculate, picturesque little community of 450 industrious people. You will find here one of the last salt pans in the world still producing salt by the old methods.

Like Grand Turk, there is no harbour at Salt Cay and the open roadstead boasts only a fair weather anchorage. This is one of the main reasons for the gradual collapse of the salt industry. Skippers could not afford to have their carriers delayed in an open roadstead for a mere 100 tons per day. Deane's Dock, at the north end of the settlement, is an enclosed, miniature, man-made harbour protected by a jetty. A good place to come ashore in your dinghy, but not when a swell is running as the narrow entrance breaks right across.

Ashore, bordering its neat, rectangular salt pans and busy wooden wind-mills with madeira gears and muslin sails, is the most unique settlement in the Turks and Caicos Group. Its houses reflect a pride and community spirit seldom evidenced in the Islands. Each house, nestled within its own stone wall (to keep the *creatures* out), is surrounded by a flower garden that has been nurtured with painstaking care. Magenta and coral bougainvillaea bloom everywhere and the friendly townsfolk answer to your appreciative smile. Along the waterfront are five well-preserved examples of Island and Bermudian architecture, dating back 150 years. White House, the old stone mansion built by the Harriotts, Salt Cay proprietors in better times, is undoubtedly the most outstanding of the five. Its interior, replete with curved staircase, four poster beds, and chests, would startle the most sophis-ticated of collectors. It stands surrounded by salt sheds, shops, and an-tiquated loading paraphernalia—a monument to the golden days of the industry when it was common to see the roadstead here lined with Nova Scotia schooners awaiting their cargos of salt. Now that the Cay is emerging into a tourist age we hope that White House will be preserved and put to use as a symbol of the islands' past history—a potential, small scale Williamsburg. Or perhaps, like Fort Young at Dominica, it would make a beautiful inn, a working display serving the nostalgic, jet-age sunseeker commuting between the Americas.

Kindly James Morgan is the head man at Salt Cay. A good friend, he is quick to let you know that he's not descended from the infamous pirate of the same name. At James' Mount Pleasant Guest House, currently the only visitor facility on the Cay, manager Earle Talbot and his wife will make your night ashore not only comfortable, but interesting as well. It's always fun to end the day here with your feet propped up on the porch rail, waiting for that instant when the world stops and the District Commissioner's residence, high on South Caicos, is silhouetted in the setting sun.

Both dedicated fishermen, James and Earle will regale you with anglers' tales from over the years that are not all as fictional as they might sound at first: about the huge school of mutton snapper that visited Salt Cay for a few months following World War II, that had never been seen before, or since; or how to dig for warm-water clams in muddy South Creek, then prepare them with bird pepper sauce. An antique bottle buff, Earle has several "digs," as he calls them, where he has unearthed hand-blown bottles that date back almost to Revolutionary times.

The Colonial Government is presently considering a plan to resurface the airstrip at Salt Cay. We hope that at the same time they will do something about keeping it clear of grazing donkeys. Obviously it must be one of the most appealing places on the Cay to these ubiquitous animals as we've been compelled to buzz the strip on several occasions to scare them off. In any case, donkeys or no, Salt Cay is a delightful place to visit.

(Sand Cay

Sand Cay lies seven miles SSW of Salt Cay. We feel sure that pirate treasure must still lie undetected in the Turks and Caicos Islands. In 1850 the sloop "Olive Branch" arrived from New Brunswick outfitted for a treasure hunting expedition. It is said that after calling at Grand Turk it called again at Sand Cay, leaving an excavation that had been "brickened and cased with mortar."

⟮ Silver Banks

Considered the Pot of Gold at the end of the West Indian rainbow, the Mouchoir and Silver Banks had $200 million in gold and silver spilled on them by wrecked galleons of the Spanish treasure fleets in the sixteenth and seventeenth centuries. But, owing to the nature of this isolated and treacherous region, little of it has been recovered. In 1686 Sir William Phips, financed by the Duke of Albermarle and using an ingenious diving bell, salvaged the precious cargo of a heavily laden Spanish transport sunk 50 years earlier. For this Phips was knighted and later appointed Governor of Massachusetts.

Yes, the story of the Bahamas is indeed a sea story, where from the Matanilla Shoals to those of the Silver Banks, the most incredible treasure of all is the opportunity to cruise here. This cascade of remote, sun-swept islands and villages forms an archipelago of many moods and faces, and the sweet sincerity of its Out Islanders will leave an indelible mark on your memory. A watery paradise, these islands were carved especially for the sailor, where an eternity could be spent sorting out the interwoven reefs, cays, and channels that go to make the best offshore cruising in the Western Hemisphere.

CHAPTER

15

The Pilot's Pleasures

All the best Bahama pilots are adept at fishing and they love to eat, drink, and sing. It has seemed to me that a few words on some of these pleasures would not be out of place in this book.

◖ Fishing

Your fishing tackle should not necessarily be elaborate, but carefully thought out. Generally speaking, Bahama fishing is divided into three types: deep sea trolling, reef fishing, and flats fishing. If you are a light-tackle enthusiast, there is no greater thrill awaiting you than hooking into your first bonefish or permit. Bonefishing has been referred to as the "champagne of angling" and permit fishing the imported champagne of the sport.

◖ Fishing on the Flats

The best bonefishing is found on the flats that are near deep water. These wary fish come into the shallows to feed on the incoming tide and can frequently be seen finning out. Bait is best presented by drifting it to them, without a sinker, or casting. Silence is essential. The lighter the rod and line the better the sport, but make certain you have a reel capable of holding plenty of line. They make prodigious runs. Permit, tarpon, jack and snapper fishing is best in the cuts or sloughs, adjacent to deep blue water. Check your *Yachtsman's Guide to the Bahamas* for the tides and inquire from the local fisherman about feeding habits; you will save yourself a lot of experimentation. Crabs, crawfish and the inevitable conch are the most productive baits.

Fine sport plug and fly casting can also be had on the flats and in the cuts. But unlike other regions, this form of angling is usually better here at night. We think the reason for this is that the waters are so clear that the fish can detect an artificial lure much quicker in the daytime. To quote our friend Moxey, "Fish walk around like dog with his nose on the ground

286

looking for scraps. He don't see line in night time, he smell conch." Sinking plugs and any streamer fly with dark colors will bring good results.

❨ Trolling

The giant tuna run each spring off Bimini, and the blue marlin and sail fishing in the Stream are, of course, the acme of the sport, if you don't mind having your back broken in small increments. So much information is available on the big tackle fishing off Cat Cay, Bimini Chub Cay, and Walker's Cay, the best known spots, that we shouldn't delve into it here. One word to the wise: if you do land a big one, don't bring him aboard unless you are sure you have a prize winner. Big fish are seldom good to eat, often dangerous, and usually too costly to mount. Always release the game fish as gently as possible.

The best trolling is usually found where the soundings come up almost vertically to a reef or the shore. Shallow water trolling produces mostly barracudas. The most infallible sign of good fishing is furnished by the sea birds. Whenever you see a flock working over a spot you can be sure that there are good fish and plentiful. The one *must* in this type of fishing is a good long wire leader, else you will lose a lot of rigs. Feathers and spoons are equally effective, or if you want to be energetic, use a cut bait. Chumming is practiced here with good results. When trailing a line that is made fast, be sure to put a "tell-tale" knot in it.

❨ Reef Fishing

Like casting, this is generally best at night, unless you fish very deep spots by day. To again quote Moxey, "Fish like a bad man stay in their home in daytime, but at night they walk all over and visit around." Crabs, crawfish and, of course, conch, are the best baits, although sometimes a bare hook will suffice. Don't make the mistake of rigging up too far from the bottom. Many of the best eating fish are bottom feeders. Don't try to eat every variety you catch without first getting local advice. There are some species to be found that are definitely toxic. Crawfish, conch, and small fish may be taken almost everywhere if you have a grane, a water glass, and a good sense of timing. Turtles, of which you may see many, should be left alone. These beasts are difficult to handle, hard to clean, and becoming scarce. The green and hawksbill turtles are the only good ones to eat and it is better to leave them for the Islanders' livelihood.

◖ Bahama Cooking

Time is the cheapest ingredient in good Bahamian cooking, and therefore the most extravagantly used. The secrets of such cooking seem to be: (1) careful preparation of the ingredients, (2) slow cooking, and (3) intelligent seasoning and flavoring. The best dishes take literally hours to cook. Iron pots and open fires are still used in many places, both of which contribute to the principle of good slow cooking. A good Bahamaian cook can make even goat meat taste delicious. When he or she goes to work on the best local food, the results are superb. The best Bahamaian dishes are those made from the sea food indigenous to this area—conch, crawfish, and the varieties of good fish which are legion. These dishes are generally quite hot or spicy in flavor, due largely to the liberal use of a favorite Bahamian seasoning: bird pepper. These resemble chili peppers in size but are bright red in color when ripe. When used fresh they are usually chopped or ground fine, and can also be made into a hot sauce by combining whole bird pepers with salt, pepper, vinegar, and lime juice. This sauce will keep indefinitely in the refrigerator and adds a unique "tang" to your Bahamian dishes. A light hand is best when introducing your guests to bird pepper.

There are numerous cook books published in Nassau, and hundreds of recipes. The following favorites come from no book, but straight from the galleys of our own boats, and those of friends, where many good cooks have puttered away to their hearts' content.

Boiled Fish (fine breakfast dish)

1 two to four pound fish
(red snapper or grouper are best)
lime or sour orange juice
tabasco

2 bird peppers
1 teaspoonful salt
thyme

Soak fish in lime or sour orange juice for one hour. Put in pan and barely cover with fresh water. Place over slow fire on top of stove and boil until fish is tender. Remove fish from water and place on hot platter, retaining the water in which the fish was boiled. To this water now add: butter, one tablespoonful of lime juice, a dash of tobasco, crushed bird peppers, salt, and a pinch of thyme. Simmer this for ten minutes and pour over the boiled fish as a sauce. Serve with hominy or boiled rice.

Old Bahamian Baked Fish

1 large fillet grouper (4–6 lbs.)
limes
stuffing (or dressing)

medium size can tomatoes
bacon

Season fish with lime, pepper, and salt, lay in baking dish and set aside to marinate while making stuffing. (Make same amount as you would for 4–6 lb. turkey.) Then layer in a baking pan: fish, drained tomatoes, and stuffing; alternate several times and then pour tomato juice around, *not over*, the mixture. Cover with strips of bacon and bake at 350° for ¾ to 1 hour. Do not let dry out.

Bahama Fish Chowder

2 lb. grouper fillet	6 potatoes
4 onions	1 green pepper
2 tablespoonsful cooking oil	2 bird peppers
1 small can tomato paste	tabasco (opt.)
small piece salt pork or bacon fat	thyme, bay leaf, paprika

Put salt pork or bacon fat in large cooking pan with oil and diced onion and cook slowly until onion is tender. Add tomato paste, peppers, 2 cups water, potatoes, and seasonings. Cover and simmer until potatoes are soft. Add grouper in small squares, put on top of liquid, cover and cook about ten minutes. Do not overcook fish or it will fall apart. Feeds four.

Poached Fish

2 lbs. fish fillet	2 onions
lime	⅛ lb. butter
bird peppers	whole allspice

Marinate fish in lime, salt, and peppers. Put undrained fish in baking dish with sliced onions, cut up butter, seasonings and pour ¼ cup water around mixture. Cover and bake at 350° for ¾ to one hour.

Bahama Conch Chowder

6 conch	1 teaspoonful salt
2 onions	½teaspoonful black pepper
small piece salt pork or bacon	2 bay leaves
4 cups milk	thyme
2 potatoes	1 teaspoonful Worcestershire
1 sweet pepper	1 tablespoonful sherry
1 tablespoonful butter	

Clean conch, bruise well, and cut into small pieces. Cover with water, add bay leaves, and simmer in large pot until tender. Chop onions and fry with pork until tender but not brown. Dice and parboil potatoes in separate pot. Add all ingredients except sherry to conch and simmer for two hours. Do not let it boil. Before serving add sherry. Serve with pilot biscuit or soda crackers. Feeds six.

Conch Salad

4 conch
2 onions

2 tomatoes (whole, drained
canned tomatoes may be used) diced

Bruise conch, cut into small pieces, and soak in ice water (bowl of ice water with cubes on top) for a few hours to harden. Drain. Add diced onion and tomatoes, season with salt, pepper, tabasco to preference. Bird pepper sauce and sherry may be added for extra zing.

Bahama Conch Fritters

4 conch
2 onions
1 green pepper
2 bird peppers (opt.)
  juice two limes

2 cups flour
2 teaspoonsful baking powder
  water to mix
  salt and pepper

Put white meat of conch through grinder with diced onions and peppers. Add lime juice and seasonings. Add flour, baking powder, and water to make a loose batter. Drop from tablespoon into deep, hot fat (two inches of cooking oil will do). Cook until brown on each side. Makes 15–20 large fritters.

Steamed Conch

This is a very versatile dish, good for breakfast or supper, depending upon your side dishes: grits, toast, noodles, rice, or spaghetti. You can boil the conch ahead (not more than one day) and then steam it just before serving, if you like.

4 conch
1 teaspoonful vinegar
2 onions, diced
4 tablespoonsful cooking oil

4 tablespoonsful butter
  salt, pepper
2 green peppers

Place bruised conch in large pot of boiling water; when foaming, drain and repeat. To a final pot of boiling water add vinegar and boil conch gently for 10–20 minutes depending on tenderness. Drain. (Can be set aside at this point.) Sauté diced conch, onion, and green pepper in combination of oil and butter until onion is soft, not brown. Add small amount of water, cover with lid, and bring to boil. Steam gently for five minutes and serve with any of above side dishes.

Crawfish Chinquapin

1 crawfish tail	1 dash tabasco
1 can cream mushroom soup	1 egg
1 teaspoonful Worcestershire sauce	sherry to taste
1 tablespoon chili sauce or ketsup	

Boil crawfish for 15–20 minutes until pink. Remove from shell, flake, and put in baking dish. Mix in soup, beaten egg, and seasonings. Bake in medium oven for twenty minutes. Add sherry before serving on rice or toast. Feeds four.

❨ Bahamas Nostalgia

(What We Miss Most When We Are Away From The Islands)

Arising to dive overboard into crystal clear water.

Breakfast on red snapper, into the pan only minutes after he took the hook.

The soft musical voices of the Islanders.

Percy Lightbourne sculling up with a dozen conch just because he knows we like them.

Reaching up for a banana from the bunch swinging from the mizzen.

Napping with the trade wind caressing our faces.

The gentle movement of the boat around her anchor.

The view from Comer Hill.

Stopping to chat with old friends while cycling around Spanish Wells.

Uncle Norman's wonderful stories, Richie and Marcell's ready smiles, and Lois' hearty laugh.

Parrot Cay's fairylike spell.

Turtle pie at the sailing club.

Lenny's steamed conch.

Teasel's shy smile and bursting laughter as we catch up on local news at the Royal Entertainer's Lounge.

The windmills at Salt Cay.

The thrill of anchoring in a remote, sunswept harbour and the strange secure feeling that it all belongs to us.

Then—lying on deck that same night watching our topmast search a starry sky.

Looking up from trudging a virgin beach to spot an amber flash of glass ball, half buried in the sand ahead.

Rachel's welcoming smile every time we return to Regatta Point.

Pearce Coady's booming shout as we finally top the hill to his Bluff House.

An osprey protecting its young from our boat anchored off Little White Bay Cay.

Returning to a favorite anchorage after several years' absence to find that the same clump of mangrove still dips into the sea and the setting sun still tints an identical scene—a reassuring timelessness.

Little islands whose only inhabitants, the birds and lizards, the fish in the surrounding waters, are so natural and unspoiled that they gaze at you without darting away.

Bird Rock Lighthouse congratulating us for having made another safe Crooked Island Passage.

The two elderly sisters at Seaview, silhouetted against the ruins, waving goodby long after we've disappeared from sight.

Stocking Island beach, Compass Cay beach, Guana Harbour beach, Man of War beach, and the windswept beaches of Hell Gate.

Finally, the color of Bahamas water—its iridescent changes under sunlight, wind, and tide. We will never tire of it.

CONVERSION TABLE—POINTS TO DEGREES

	Points	Angular measure (° ′ ″)		Points	Angular measure (° ′ ″)
NORTH TO EAST			**SOUTH TO WEST**		
North	0	0 00 00	South	16	180 00 00
N¼E	¼	2 48 45	S¼W	16¼	182 48 45
N½E	½	5 37 30	S½W	16½	185 37 30
N¾E	¾	8 26 15	S¾W	16¾	188 26 15
N by E	1	11 15 00	S by W	17	191 15 00
N by E¼E	1¼	14 03 45	S by W¼W	17¼	194 03 45
N by E½E	1½	16 52 30	S by W½W	17½	196 52 30
N by E¾E	1¾	19 41 15	S by W¾W	17¾	199 41 15
NNE	2	22 30 00	SSW	18	202 30 00
NNE¼E	2¼	25 18 45	SSW¼W	18¼	205 18 45
NNE½E	2½	28 07 30	SSW½W	18½	208 07 30
NNE¾E	2¾	30 56 15	SSW¾W	18¾	210 56 15
NE by N	3	33 45 00	SW by S	19	213 45 00
NE¾N	3¼	36 33 45	SW¾S	19¼	216 33 45
NE½N	3½	39 22 30	SW½S	19½	219 22 30
NE¼N	3¾	42 11 15	SW¼S	19¾	222 11 15
NE	4	45 00 00	SW	20	225 00 00
NE¼E	4¼	47 48 45	SW¼W	20¼	227 48 45
NE½E	4½	50 37 30	SW½W	20½	230 37 30
NE¾E	4¾	53 26 15	SW¾W	20¾	233 26 15
NE by E	5	56 15 00	SW by W	21	236 15 00
NE by E¼E	5¼	59 03 45	SW by W¼W	21¼	239 03 45
NE by E½E	5½	61 52 30	SW by W½W	21½	241 52 30
NE by E¾E	5¾	64 41 15	SW by W¾W	21¾	244 41 15
ENE	6	67 30 00	WSW	22	247 30 00
ENE¼E	6¼	70 18 45	WSW¼W	22¼	250 18 45
ENE½E	6½	73 07 30	WSW½W	22½	253 07 30
ENE¾E	6¾	75 56 15	WSW¾W	22¾	255 56 15
E by N	7	78 45 00	W by S	23	258 45 00
E¾N	7¼	81 33 45	W¾S	23¼	261 33 45
E½N	7½	84 22 30	W½S	23½	264 22 30
E¼N	7¾	87 11 15	W¼S	23¾	267 11 15
EAST TO SOUTH			**WEST TO NORTH**		
East	8	90 00 00	West	24	270 00 00
E¼S	8¼	92 48 45	W¼N	24¼	272 48 45
E½S	8½	95 37 30	W½N	24½	275 37 30
E¾S	8¾	98 26 15	W¾N	24¾	278 26 15
E by S	9	101 15 00	W by N	25	281 15 00
ESE¾E	9¼	104 03 45	WNW¾W	25¼	284 03 45
ESE½E	9½	106 52 30	WNW½W	25½	286 52 30
ESE¼E	9¾	109 41 15	WNW¼W	25¾	289 41 15
ESE	10	112 30 00	WNW	26	292 30 00
SE by E¾E	10¼	115 18 45	NW by W¾W	26¼	295 18 45
SE by E½E	10½	118 07 30	NW by W½W	26½	298 07 30
SE by E¼E	10¾	120 56 15	NW by W¼W	26¾	300 56 15
SE by E	11	123 45 00	NW by W	27	303 45 00
SE¾E	11¼	126 33 45	NW¾W	27¼	306 33 45
SE½E	11½	129 22 30	NW½W	27½	309 22 30
SE¼E	11¾	132 11 15	NW¼W	27¾	312 11 15
SE	12	135 00 00	NW	28	315 00 00
SE¼S	12¼	137 48 45	NW¼N	28¼	317 48 45
SE½S	12½	140 37 30	NW½N	28½	320 37 30
SE¾S	12¾	143 26 15	NW¾N	28¾	323 26 15
SE by S	13	146 15 00	NW by N	29	326 15 00
SSE¾E	13¼	149 03 45	NNW¾W	29¼	329 03 45
SSE½E	13½	151 52 30	NNW½W	29½	331 52 30
SSE¼E	13¾	154 41 15	NNW¼W	29¾	334 41 15
SSE	14	157 30 00	NNW	30	337 30 00
S by E¾E	14¼	160 18 45	N by W¾W	30¼	340 18 45
S by E½E	14½	163 07 30	N by W½W	30½	343 07 30
S by E¼E	14¾	165 56 15	N by W¼W	30¾	345 56 15
S by E	15	168 45 00	N by W	31	348 45 00
S¾E	15¼	171 33 45	N¾W	31¼	351 33 45
S½E	15½	174 22 30	N½W	31½	354 22 30
S¼E	15¾	177 11 15	N¼W	31¾	357 11 15
South	16	180 00 00	North	32	360 00 00